uki presents

HAAH...
HAAH...
HAAH...

THE SEVEN DEADLY SINS 1

Nakaba Suzuki

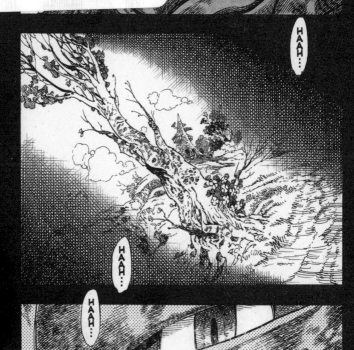

CONTENTS

BOAR HAT

The Seven Deadly Sins

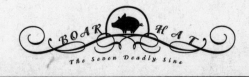

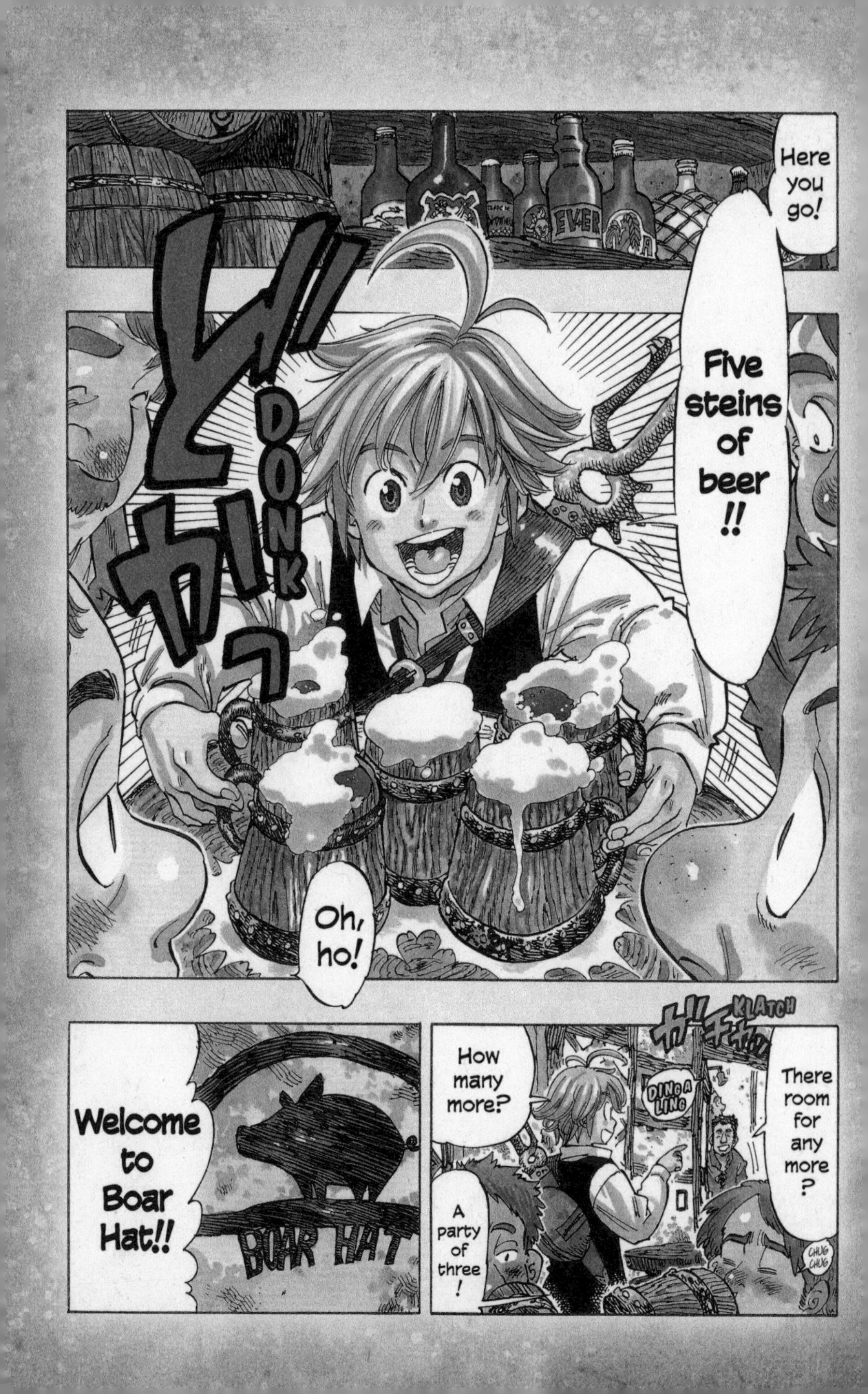
Here you go!
Five steins of beer!!
DONK
Oh, ho!
KLATCH
DING A LING
There room for any more?
How many more?
A party of three!
CHUG CHUG
Welcome to Boar Hat!!
BOAR HAT

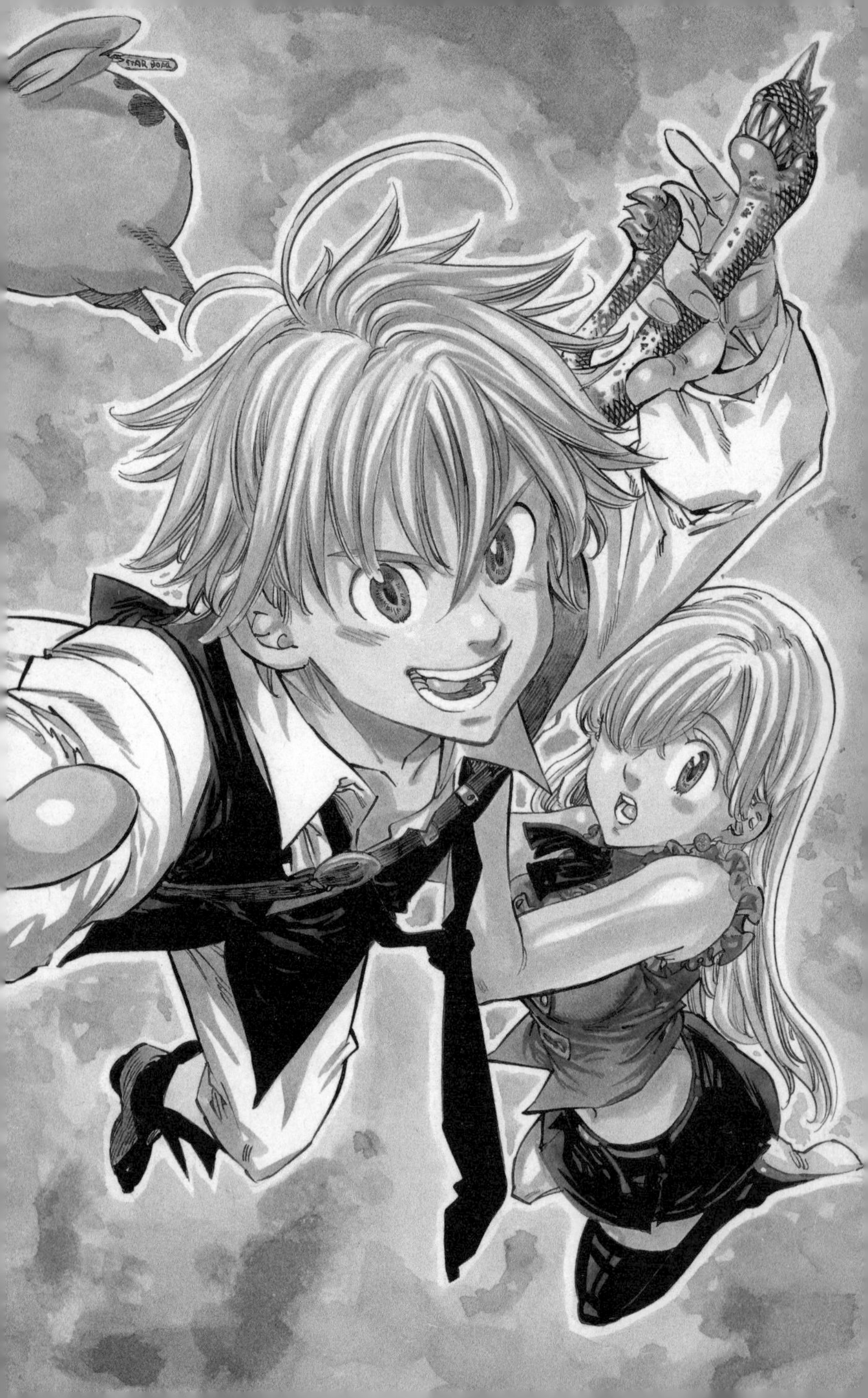
STAR BOAR

Chapter 1 - The Seven Deadly Sins

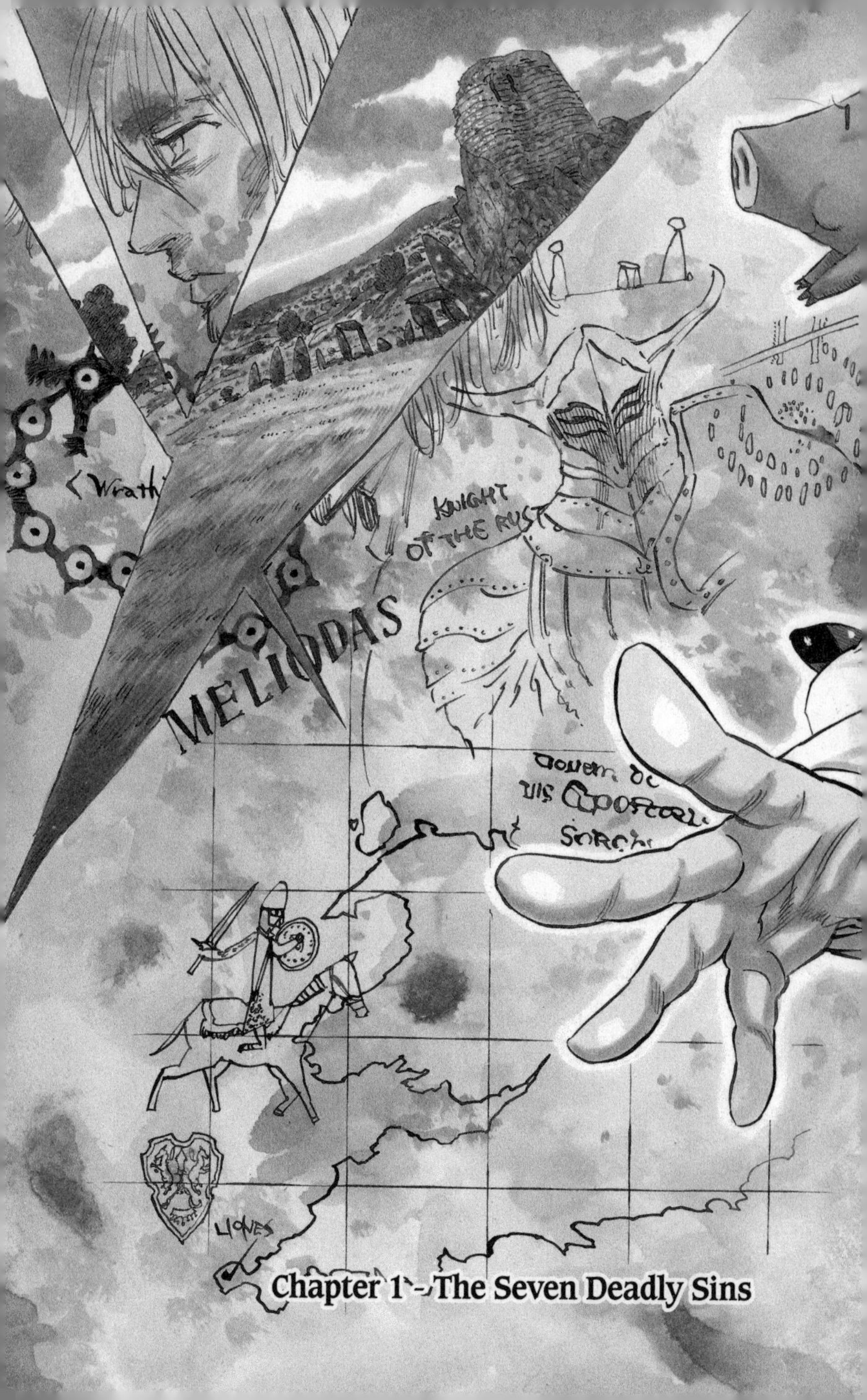
Wrath
KNIGHT OF THE RUST
MELIODAS
LIONES

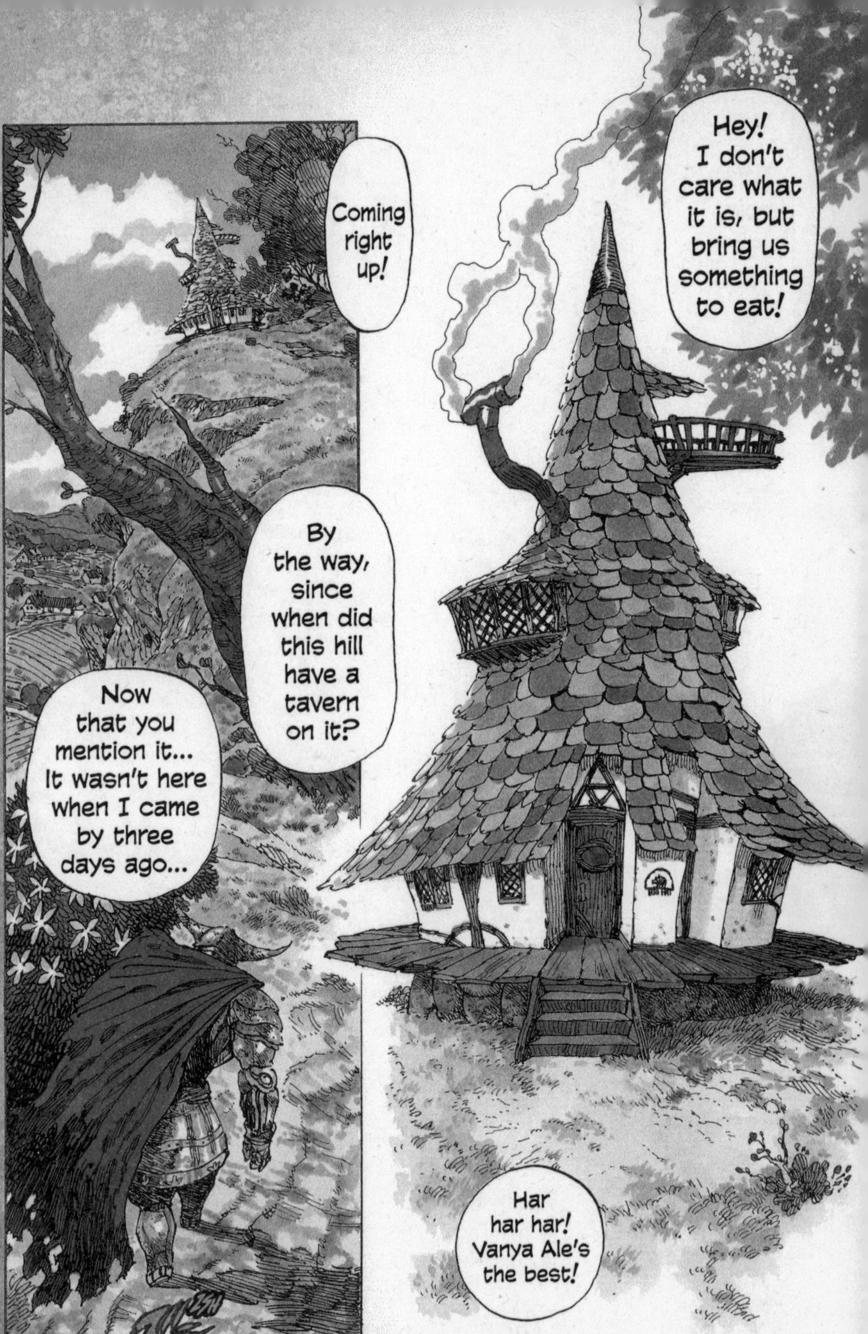
Hey! I don't care what it is, but bring us something to eat!
Coming right up!
Har har har! Vanya Ale's the best!
By the way, since when did this hill have a tavern on it?
Now that you mention it... It wasn't here when I came by three days ago...

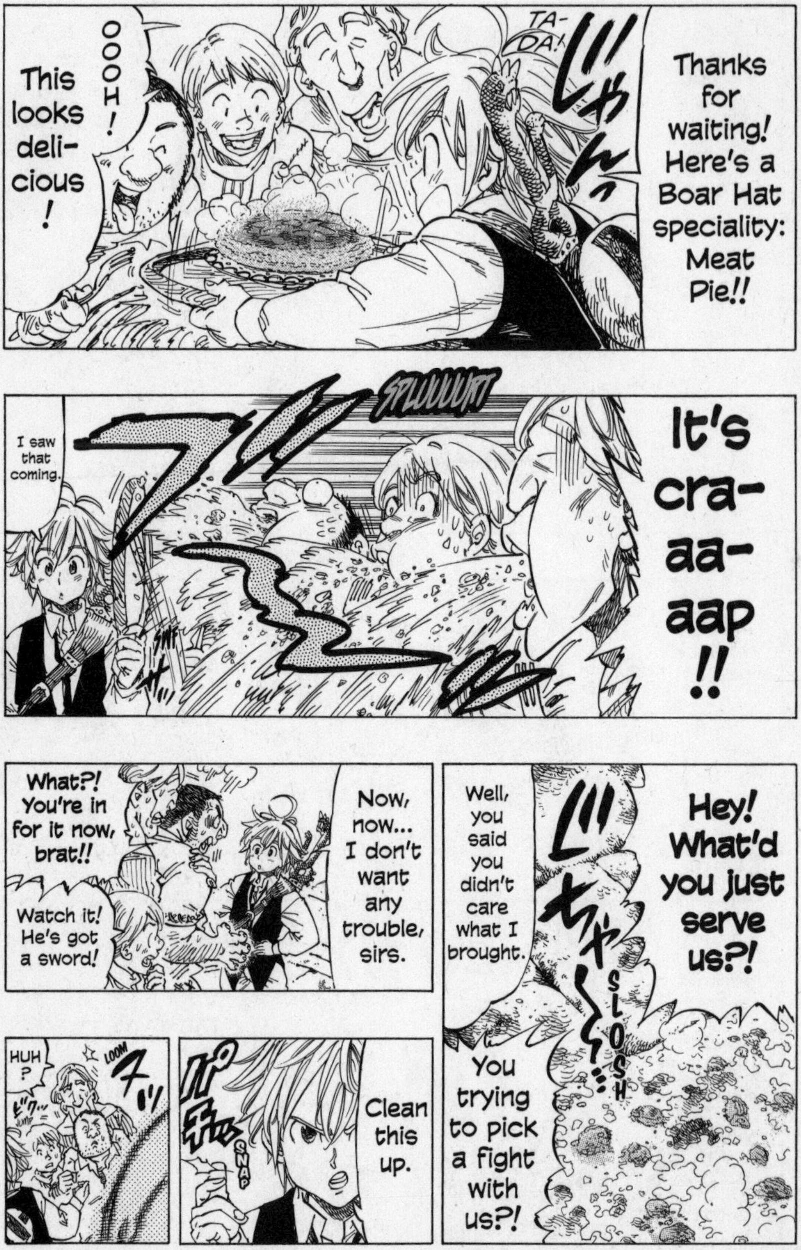
Thanks for waiting! Here's a Boar Hat speciality: Meat Pie!!
TA-DA!
OOOH!
This looks delicious!
It's craaaaap!!
SPLUUUURT
I saw that coming.
Hey! What'd you just serve us?!
Well, you said you didn't care what I brought.
SLOSH
You trying to pick a fight with us?!
Now, now... I don't want any trouble, sirs.
What?! You're in for it now, brat!!
Watch it! He's got a sword!
Clean this up.
SNAP
LOOM
HUH?
JUMP

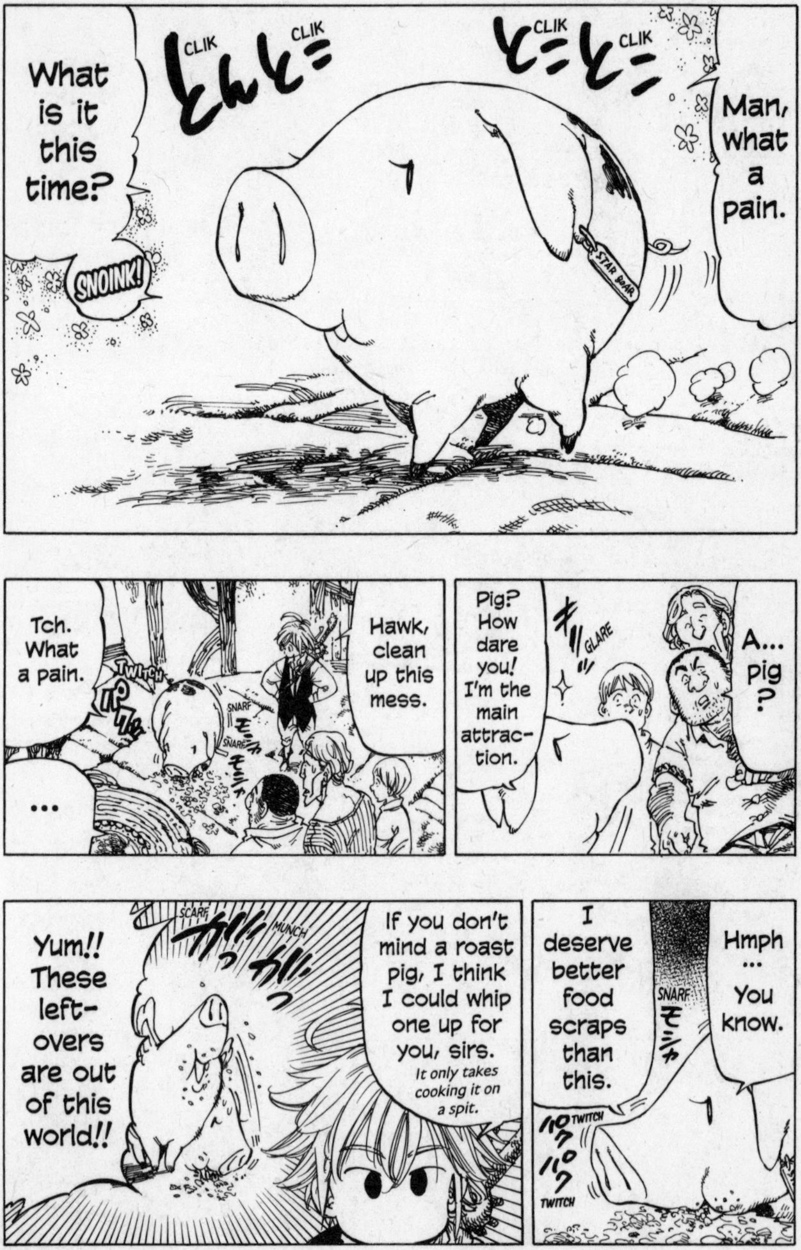
CLIK
CLIK
Man, what a pain.
CLIK
CLIK
What is it this time?
SNOINK!
STAR BOAR
A... Pig?
GLARE
Pig? How dare you! I'm the main attraction.
Hawk, clean up this mess.
SNARF
SNARF
TWITCH
Tch. What a pain.
...
Hmph... You know.
SNARF
I deserve better food scraps than this.
TWITCH
TWITCH
If you don't mind a roast pig, I think I could whip one up for you, sirs.
It only takes cooking it on a spit.
MUNCH
SCARF
Yum!! These left-overs are out of this world!!

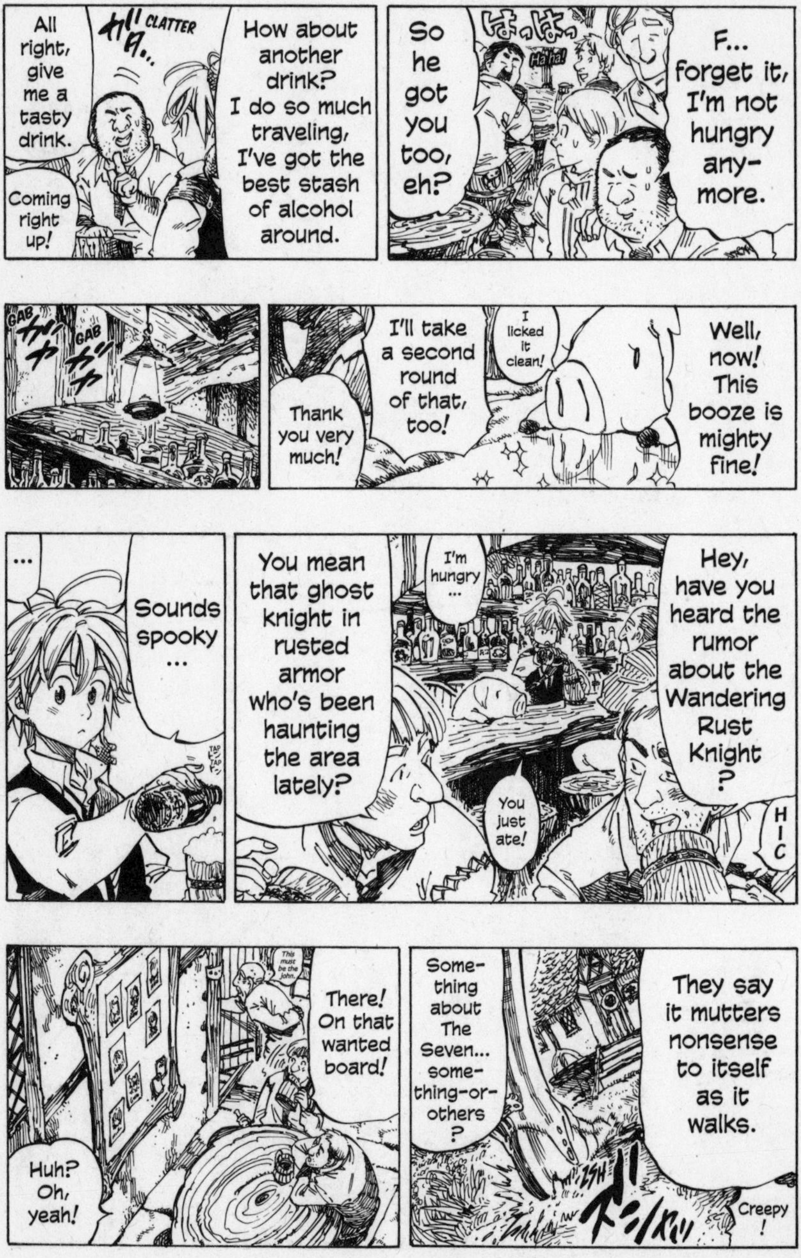

F... forget it, I'm not hungry any-more.
So he got you too, eh?
Ha ha!
How about another drink? I do so much traveling, I've got the best stash of alcohol around.
CLATTER
All right, give me a tasty drink.
Coming right up!
Well, now! This booze is mighty fine!
I licked it clean!
I'll take a second round of that, too!
Thank you very much!
GAB
GAB
Hey, have you heard the rumor about the Wandering Rust Knight?
HIC
I'm hungry...
You just ate!
You mean that ghost knight in rusted armor who's been haunting the area lately?
Sounds spooky...
...
TAP TAP
They say it mutters nonsense to itself as it walks.
Something about The Seven... something-or-others?
Creepy!
ZSH
There! On that wanted board!
This must be the john.
Huh? Oh, yeah!

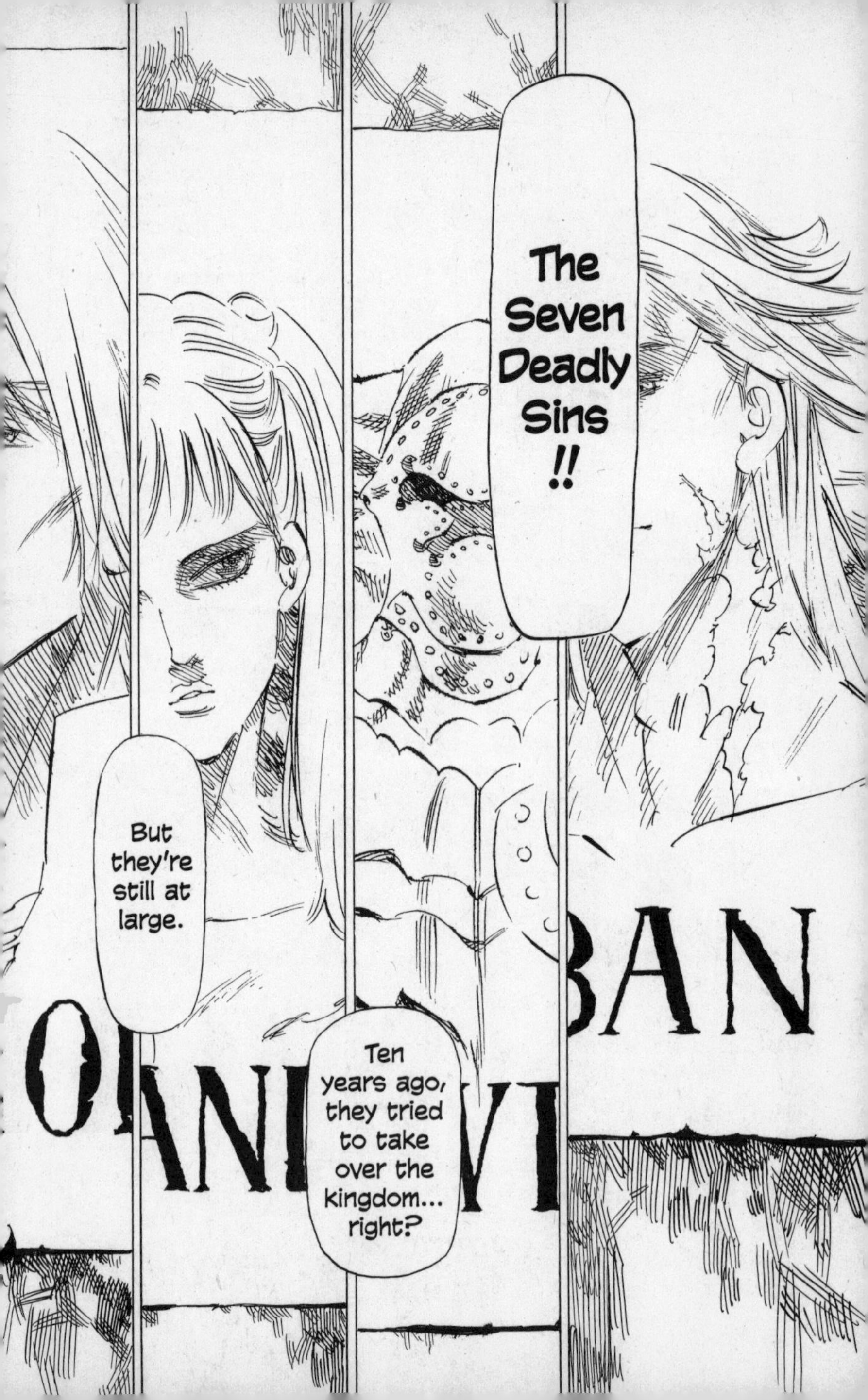

The Seven Deadly Sins!!
BAN
Ten years ago, they tried to take over the kingdom... right?
But they're still at large.

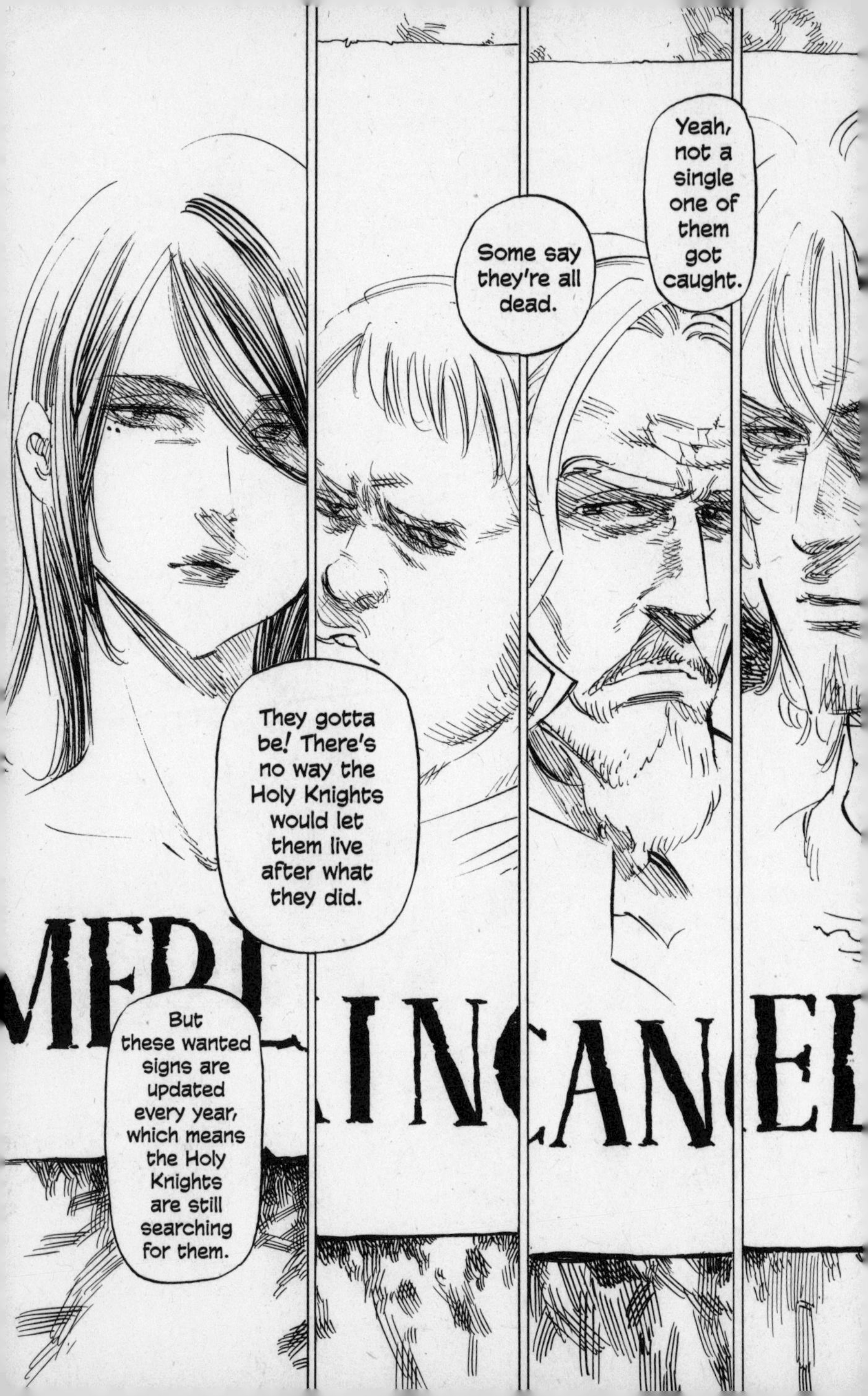
Yeah, not a single one of them got caught.
Some say they're all dead.
They gotta be! There's no way the Holy Knights would let them live after what they did.
But these wanted signs are updated every year, which means the Holy Knights are still searching for them.

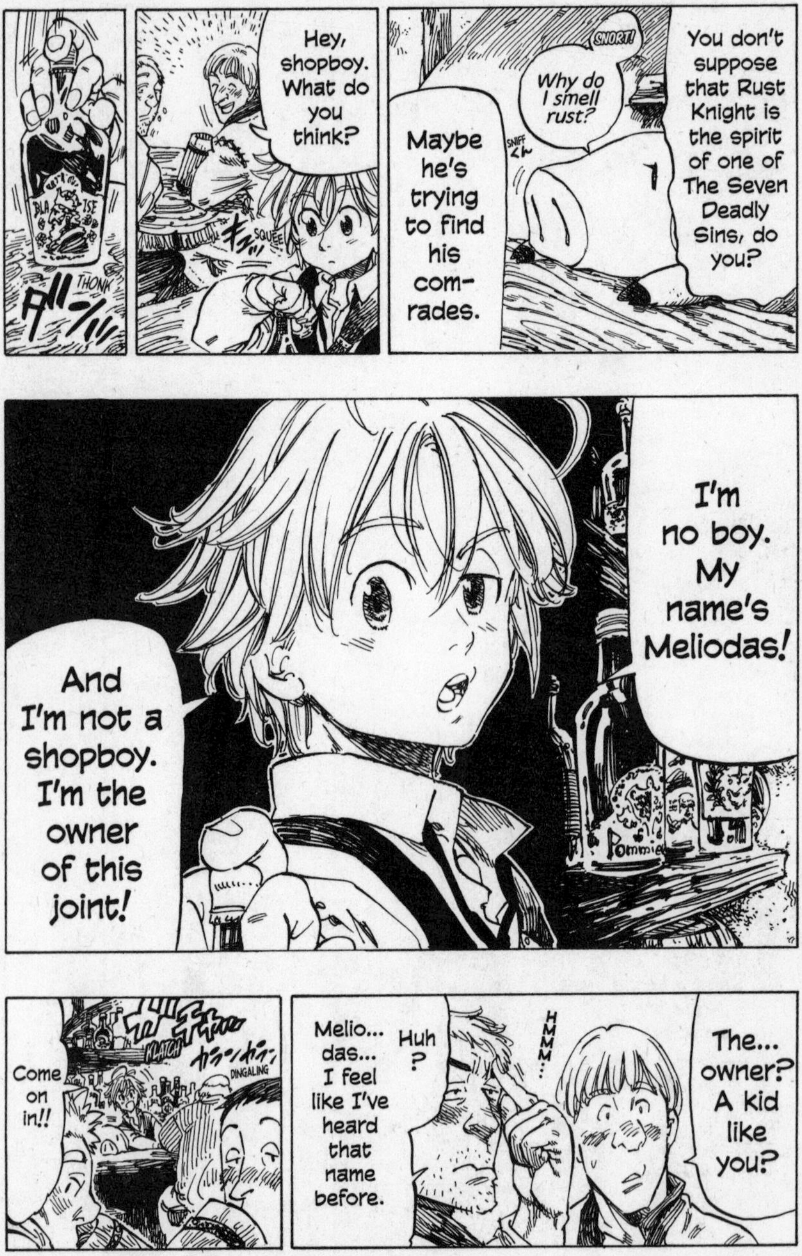
You don't suppose that Rust Knight is the spirit of one of The Seven Deadly Sins, do you?
SNORT!
Why do I smell rust?
SNIFF
Maybe he's trying to find his com-rades.
Hey, shopboy. What do you think?
SQUEE
THONK
I'm no boy. My name's Meliodas!
And I'm not a shopboy. I'm the owner of this joint!
The... owner? A kid like you?
HMMM...
Huh?
Melio... das... I feel like I've heard that name before.
DINGALING
KLATCH
Come on in!!

DING

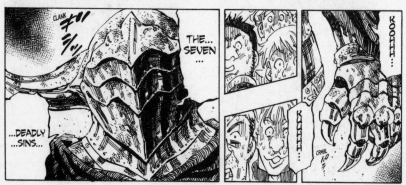

CLANK

THE...
SEVEN
...

...DEADLY
...SINS...

KOOHH...

CRMBL

-13-

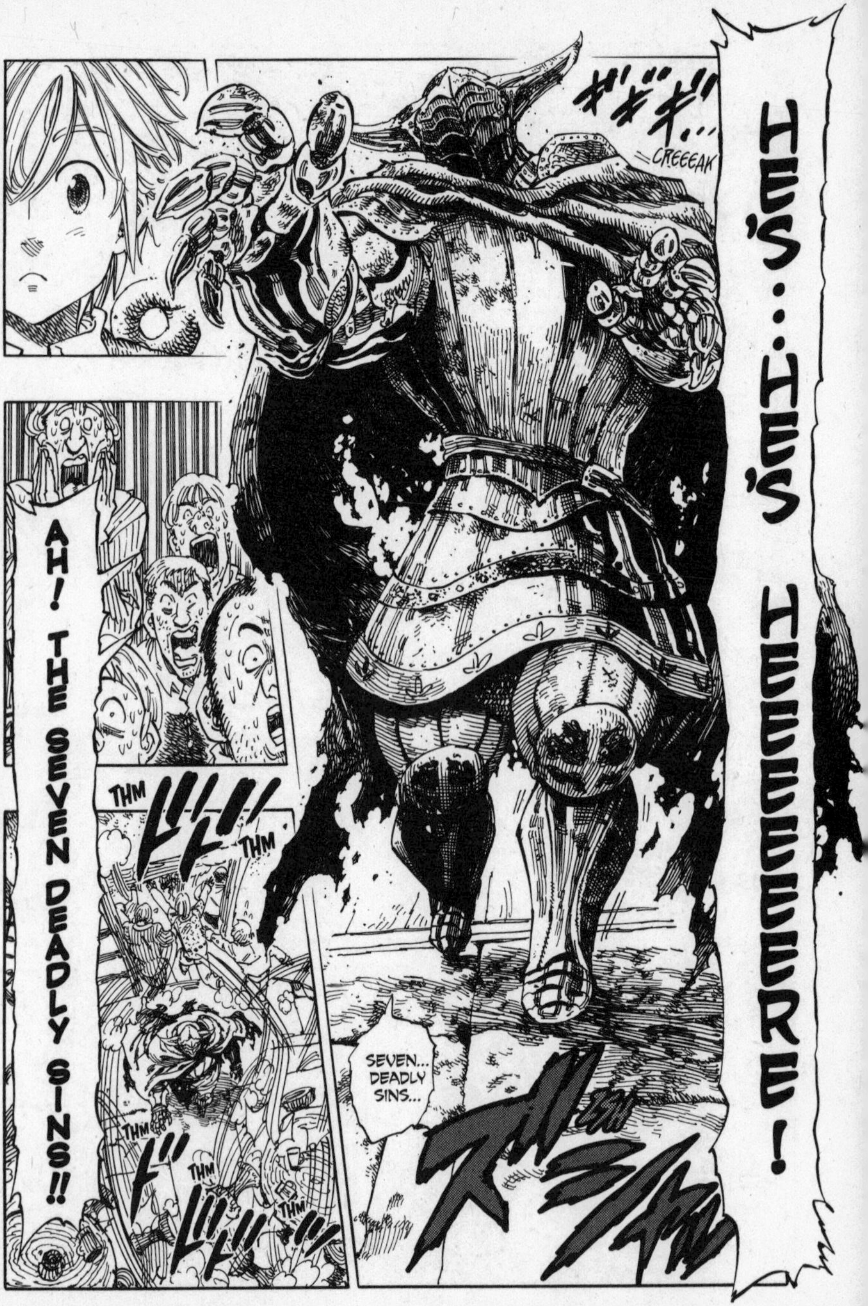
HE'S... HE'S HEEEEEERE!
CREEEAK
SEVEN... DEADLY SINS...
AH! THE SEVEN DEADLY SINS!!
THM
THM
THM
THM
THM

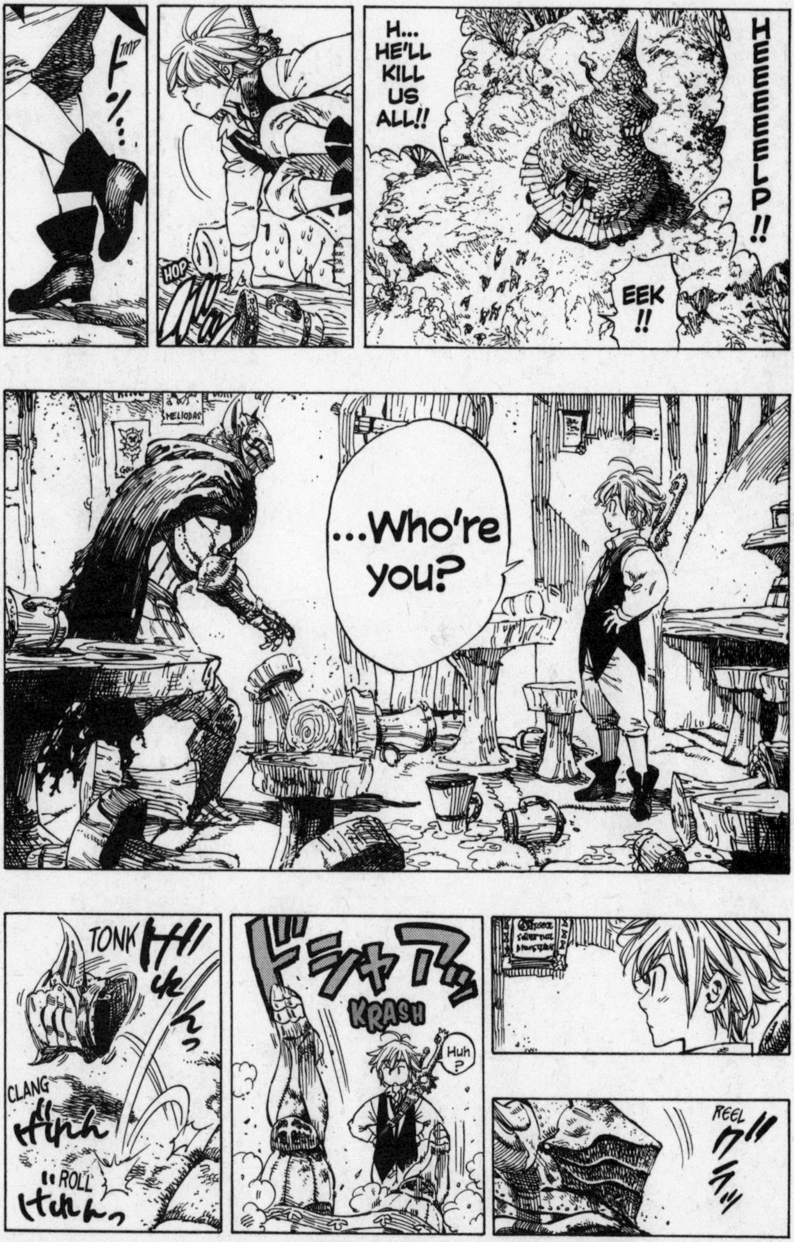
HEEEEELP!!
H... HE'LL KILL US ALL!!
EEK!!
HOP
TMP
...Who're you?
REEL
KRASH
Huh?
TONK
CLANG
ROLL

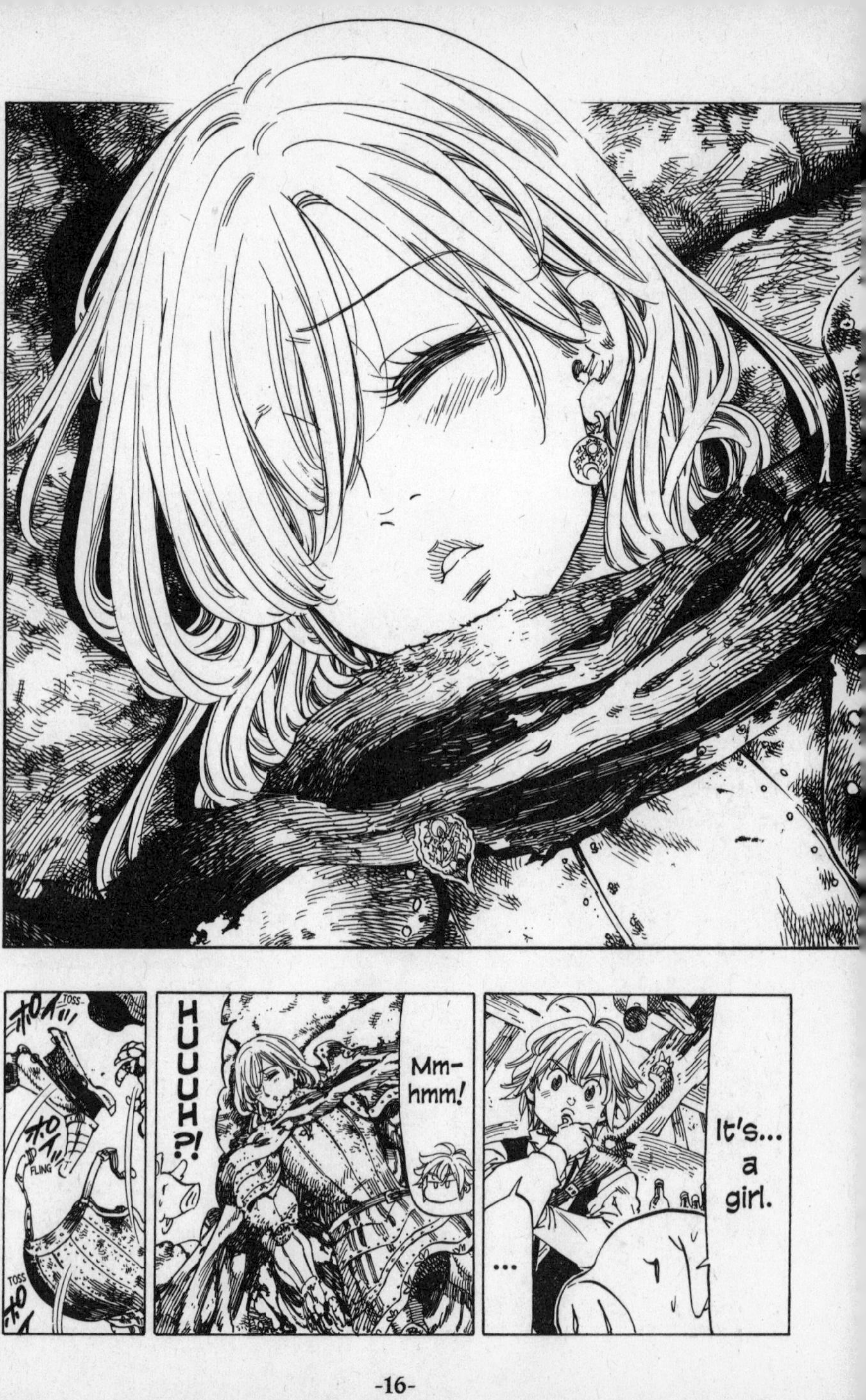
It's... a girl.
...
Mm-hmm!
HUUUH?!
TOSS
FLING
TOSS

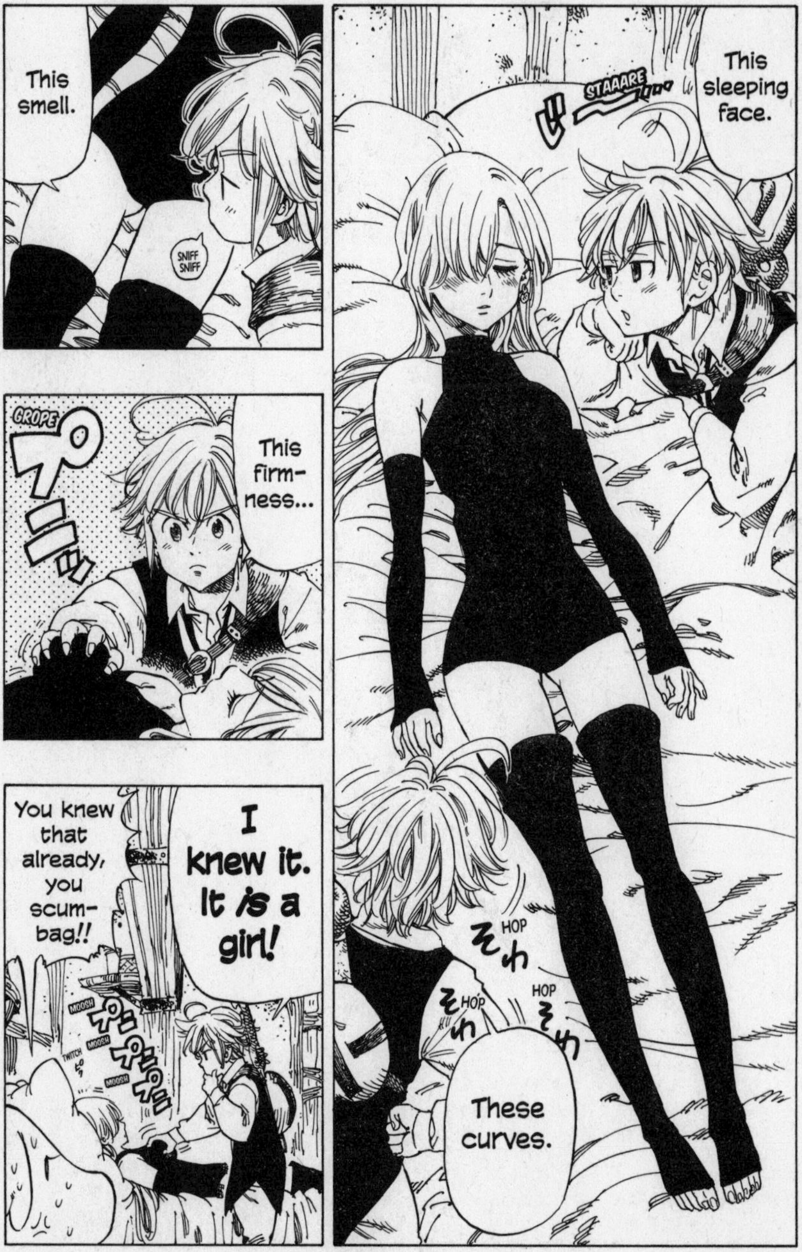

This sleeping face.
STAAARE
HOP
HOP
HOP
These curves.
This smell.
SNIFF SNIFF
This firm-ness...
GROPE
I knew it. It *is* a girl!
You knew that already, you scum-bag!!
MOOSH
MOOSH
TWITCH
MOOSH

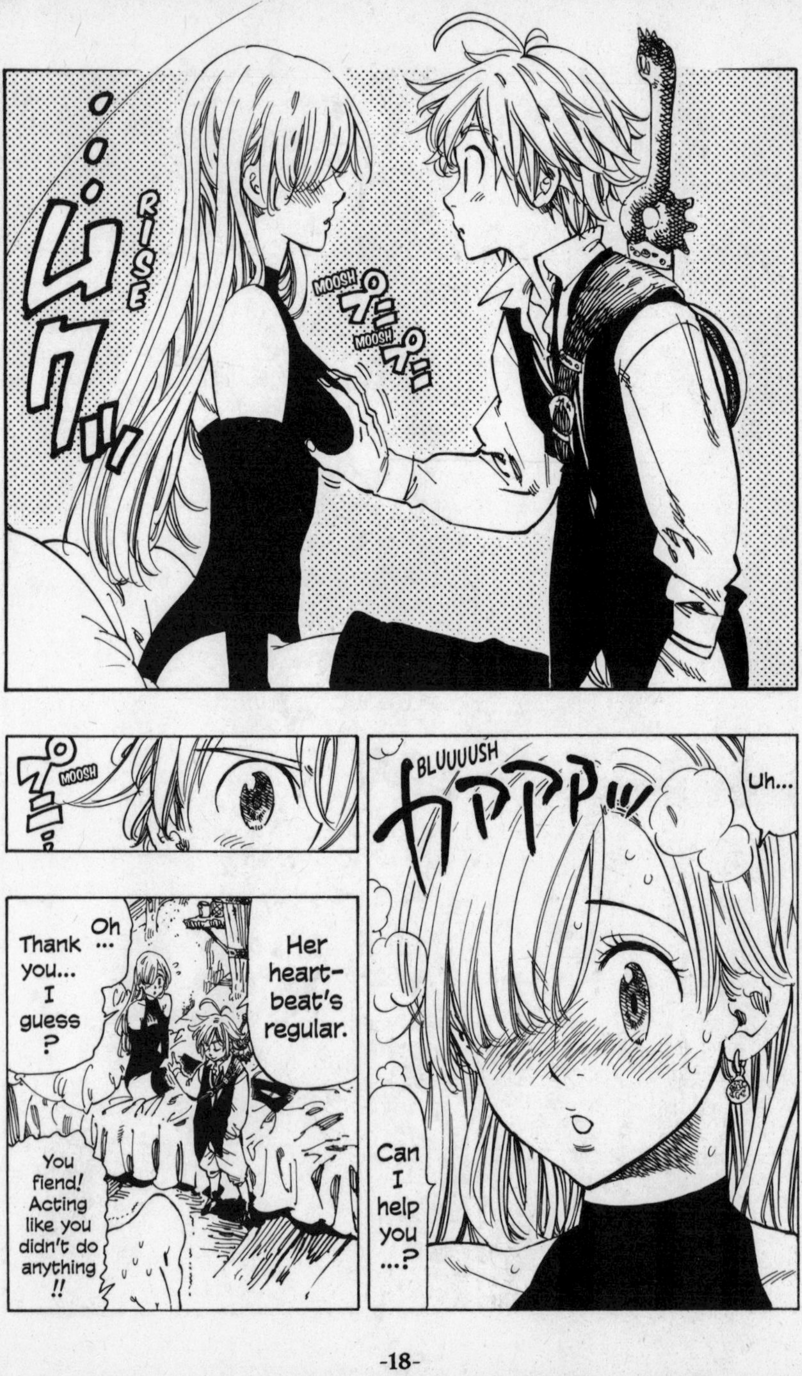
RISE
MOOSH
MOOSH
Uh...
BLUUUSH
Can I help you ...?
MOOSH
Her heart-beat's regular.
Oh ... Thank you... I guess?
You fiend! Acting like you didn't do anything!!

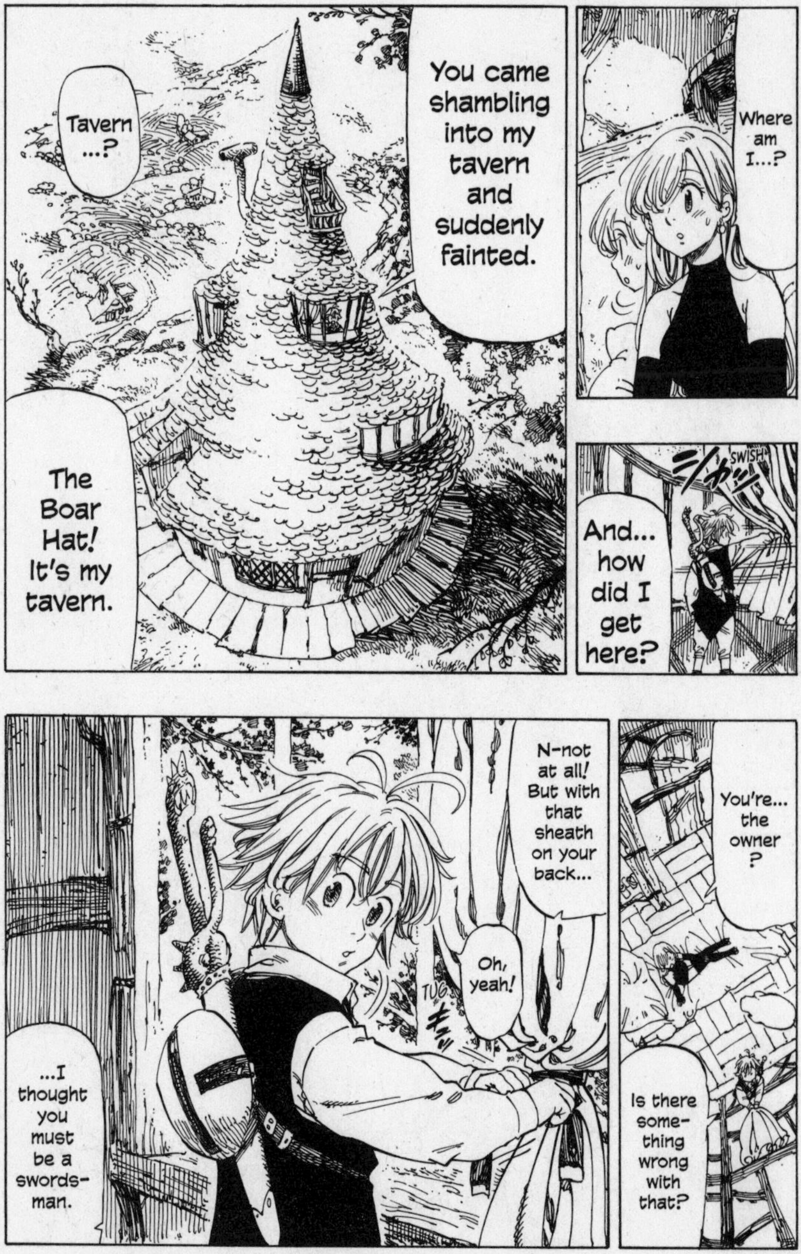
Where am I...?
SWISH
And... how did I get here?
You came shambling into my tavern and suddenly fainted.
Tavern ...?
The Boar Hat! It's my tavern.
You're... the owner?
Is there some-thing wrong with that?
N-not at all! But with that sheath on your back...
Oh, yeah!
TUG
...I thought you must be a swords-man.

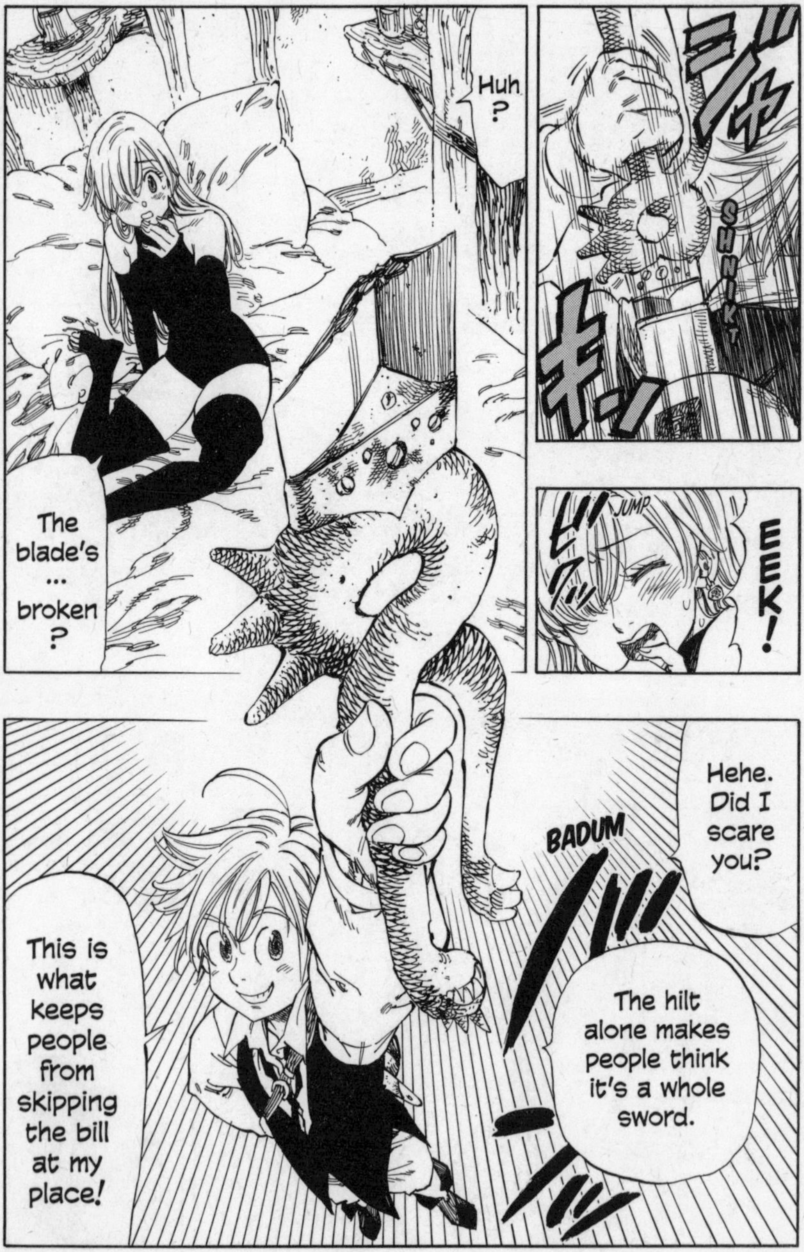
SHNIKT
JUMP
EEK!
Huh?
The blade's ... broken?
Hehe. Did I scare you?
BADUM
The hilt alone makes people think it's a whole sword.
This is what keeps people from skipping the bill at my place!

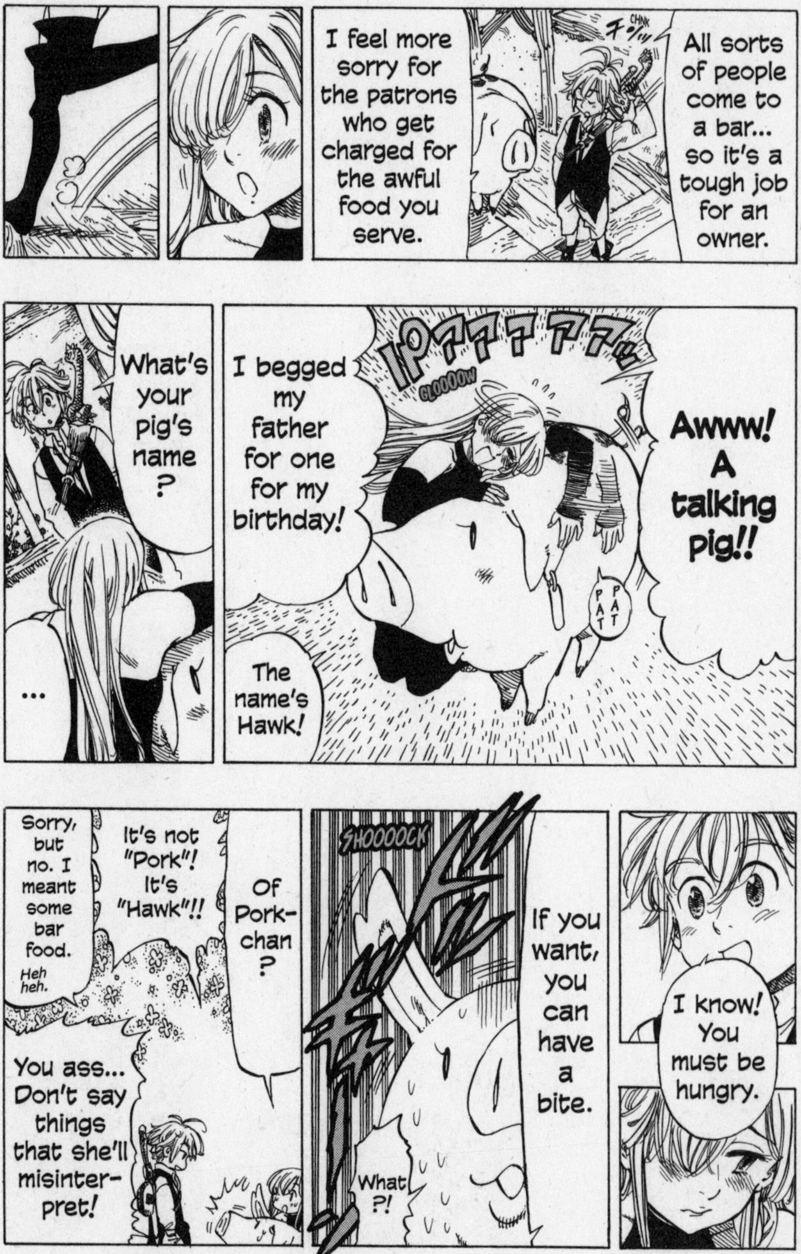
CHINK
All sorts of people come to a bar... so it's a tough job for an owner.
I feel more sorry for the patrons who get charged for the awful food you serve.
Awww! A talking pig!!
PAT PAT
GLOOOOW
I begged my father for one for my birthday!
The name's Hawk!
What's your pig's name?
...
I know! You must be hungry.
If you want, you can have a bite.
SHOOOCK
What?!
Of Pork-chan?
It's not "Pork"! It's "Hawk"!!
Sorry, but no. I meant some bar food.
Heh heh.
You ass... Don't say things that she'll misinterpret!

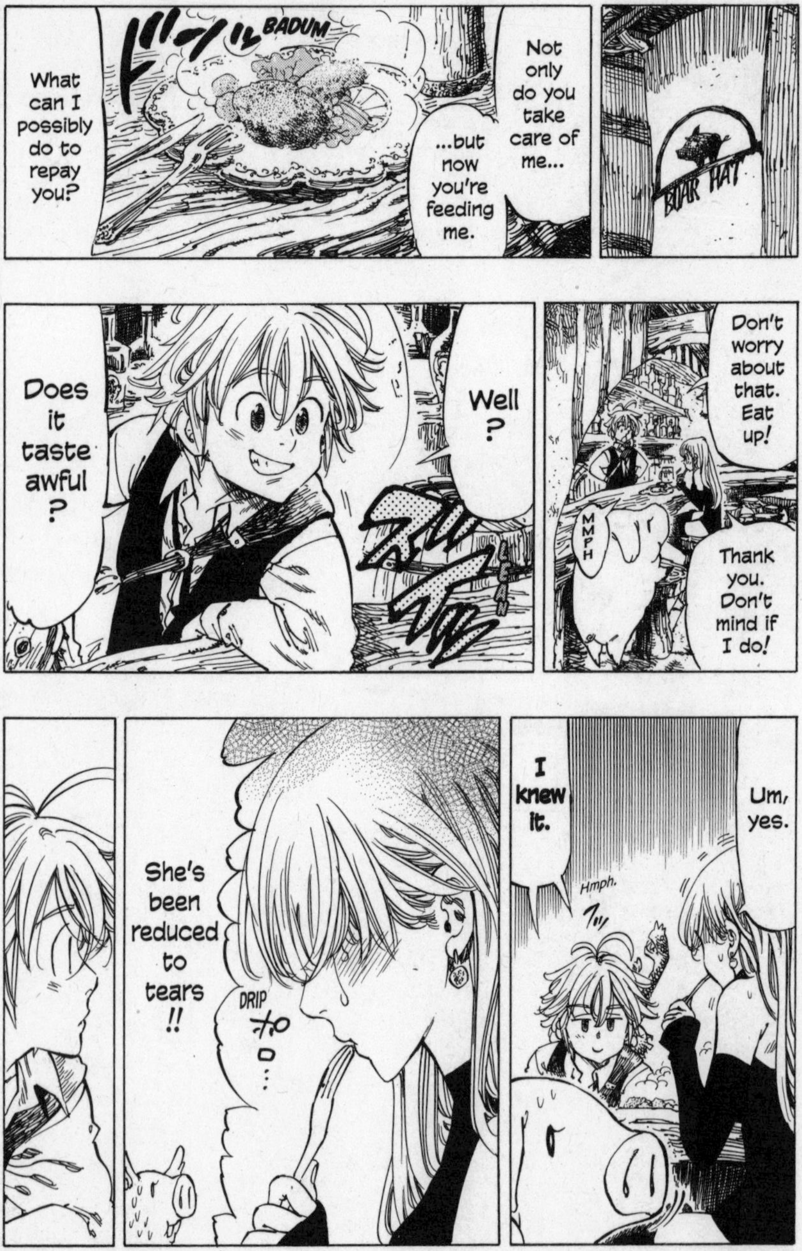
BOAR HAT
Not only do you take care of me...
...but now you're feeding me.
BADUM
What can I possibly do to repay you?
Don't worry about that. Eat up!
MMPH
Thank you. Don't mind if I do!
Well?
LEAN
Does it taste awful?
Um, yes.
I knew it.
Hmph.
She's been reduced to tears!!
DRIP

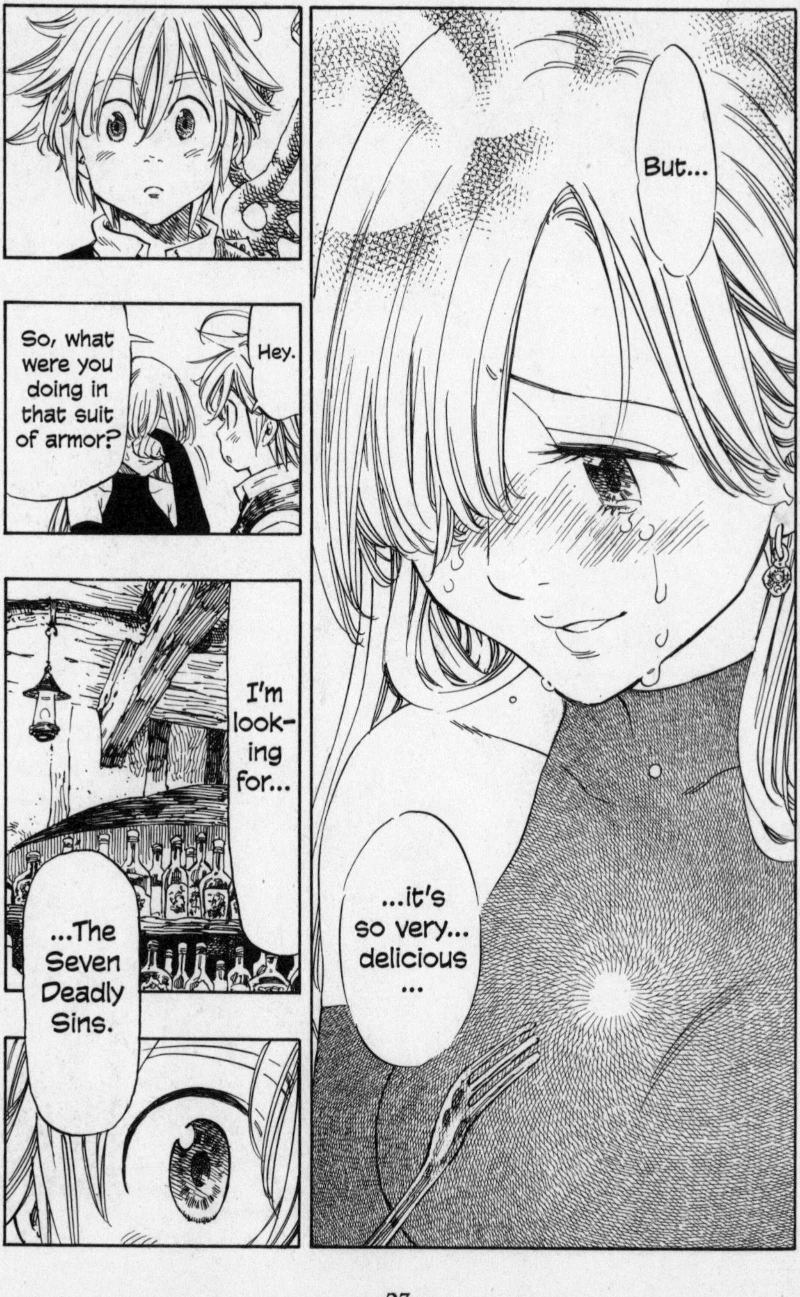
But...
...it's so very... delicious...
Hey.
So, what were you doing in that suit of armor?
I'm looking-ing for...
...The Seven Deadly Sins.

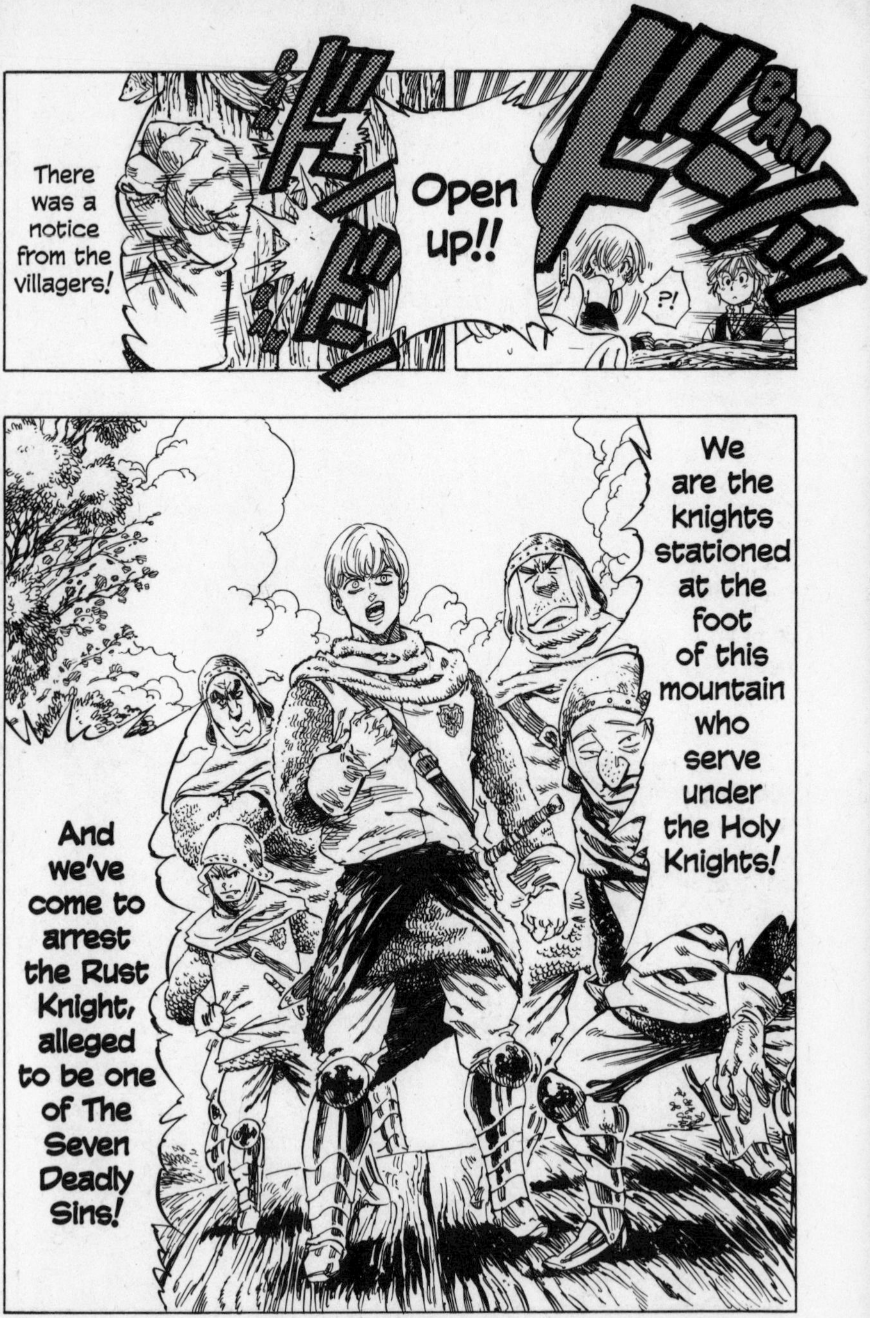
?!
Open up!!
There was a notice from the villagers!
We are the knights stationed at the foot of this mountain who serve under the Holy Knights!
And we've come to arrest the Rust Knight, alleged to be one of The Seven Deadly Sins!

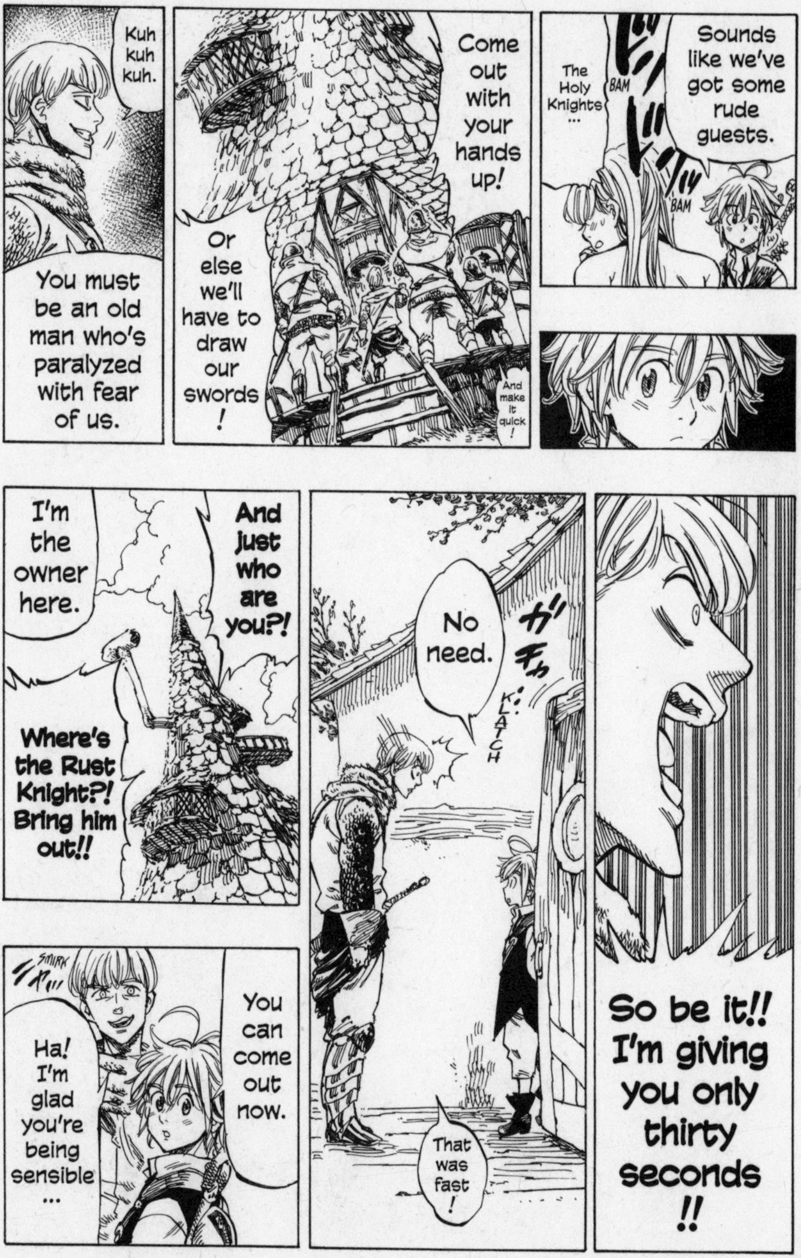
Sounds like we've got some rude guests.
BAM
The Holy Knights ...
BAM
Come out with your hands up!
Or else we'll have to draw our swords!
And make it quick!
Kuh kuh kuh.
You must be an old man who's paralyzed with fear of us.
So be it!! I'm giving you only thirty seconds!!
No need.
KLATCH
That was fast!
And just who are you?!
I'm the owner here.
Where's the Rust Knight?! Bring him out!!
You can come out now.
SMIRK
Ha! I'm glad you're being sensible ...

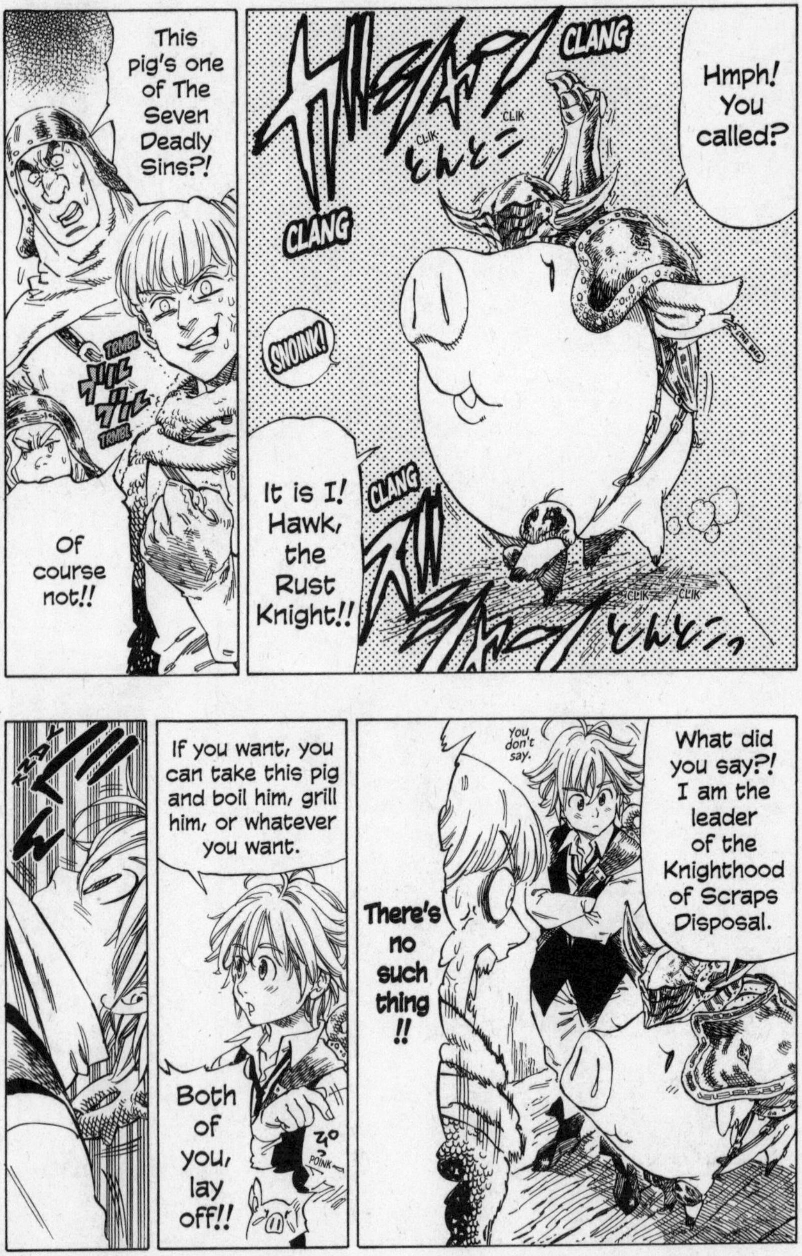
CLANG
Hmph! You called?
CLIK
CLIK
CLANG
SNOINK!
It is I! Hawk, the Rust Knight!!
CLANG
CLIK
CLIK
This pig's one of The Seven Deadly Sins?!
TRMBL
TRMBL
Of course not!!
What did you say?! I am the leader of the Knighthood of Scraps Disposal.
You don't say.
There's no such thing!!
If you want, you can take this pig and boil him, grill him, or whatever you want.
Both of you, lay off!!
POINK
YANK

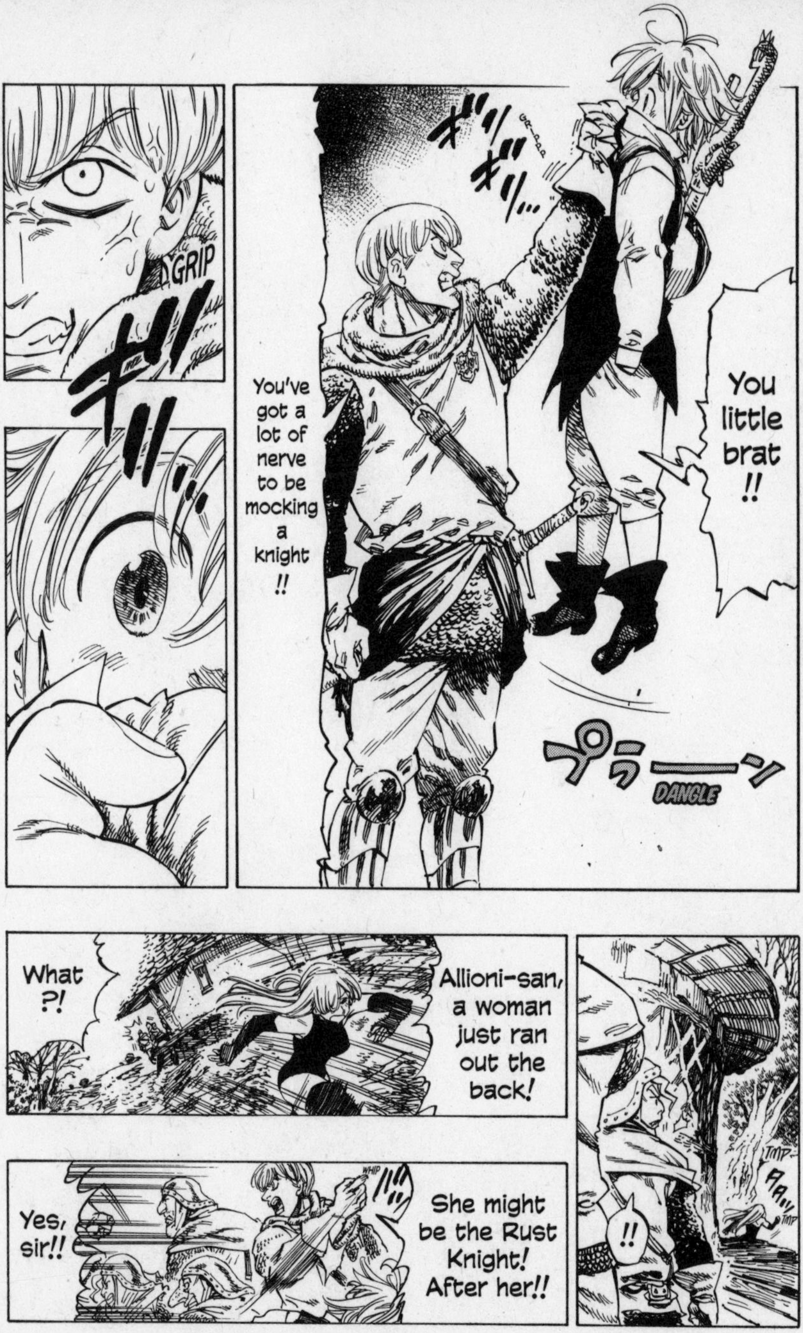
You little brat!!
You've got a lot of nerve to be mocking a knight!!
DANGLE
GRIP
!!
TMP
TMP
Allioni-san, a woman just ran out the back!
What?!
She might be the Rust Knight! After her!!
WHIP
Yes, sir!!

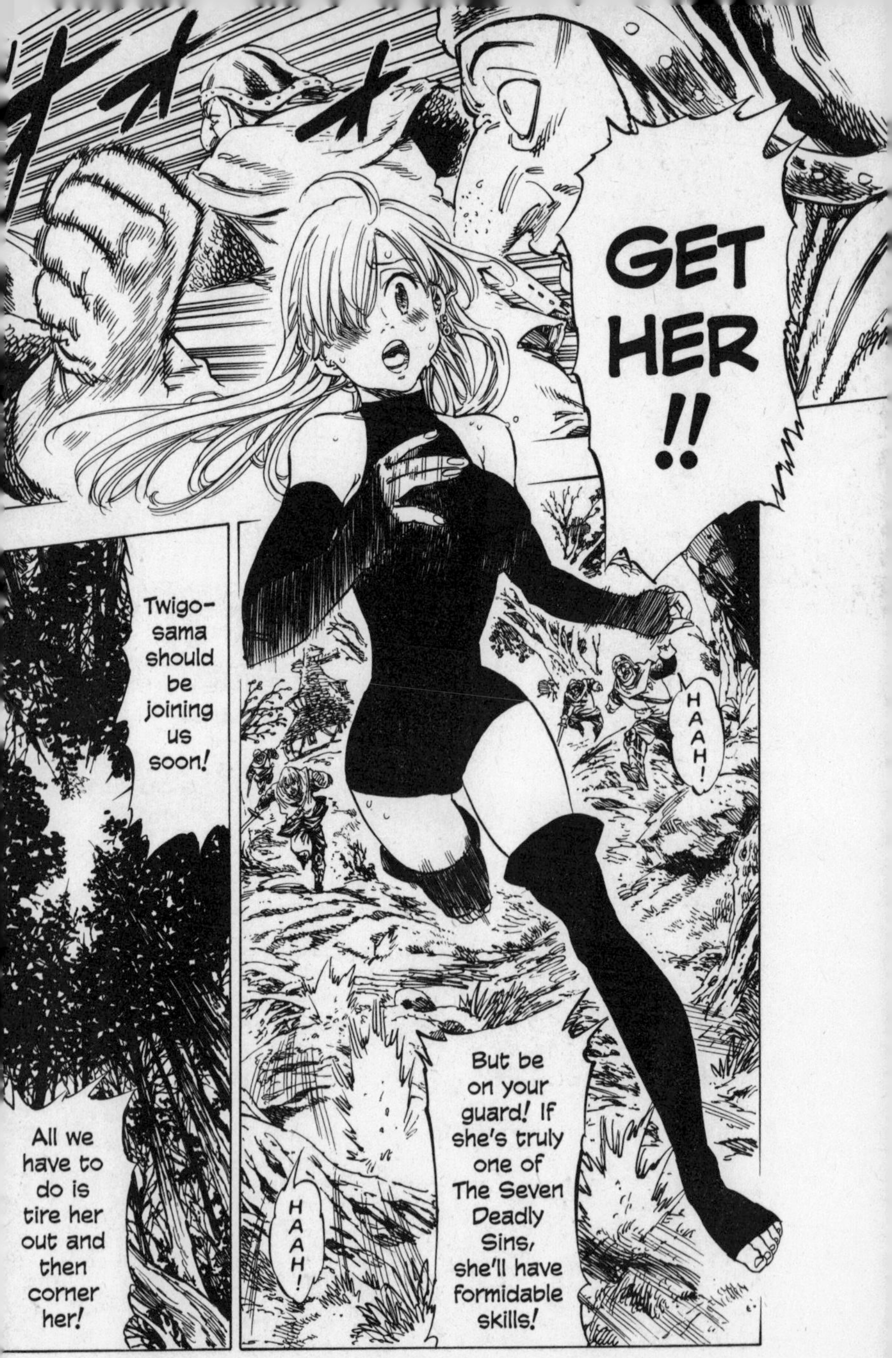
GET HER!!
HAAH!
But be on your guard! If she's truly one of The Seven Deadly Sins, she'll have formidable skills!
HAAH!
Twigo-sama should be joining us soon!
All we have to do is tire her out and then corner her!

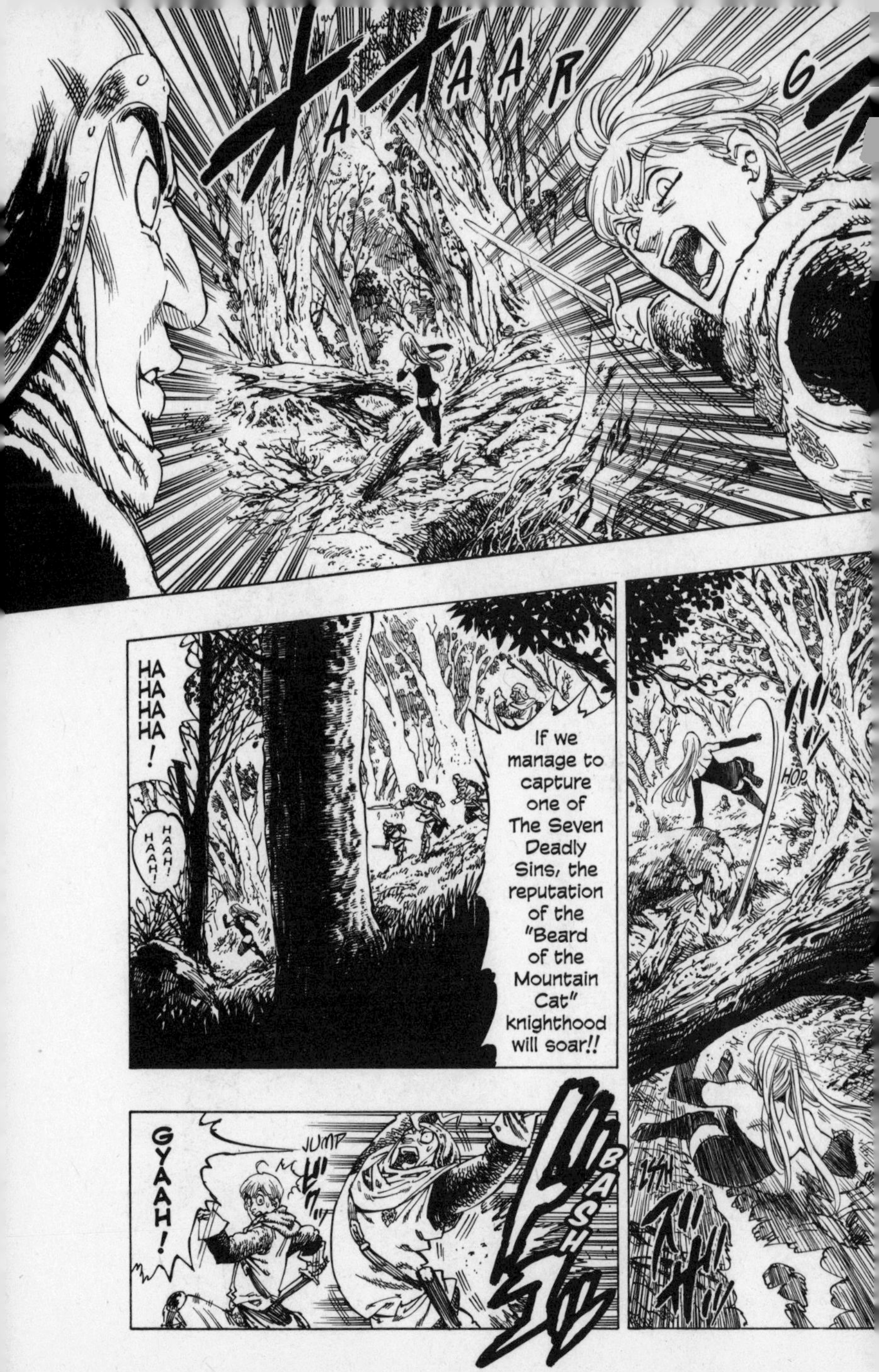

AAARG
HOP
If we manage to capture one of The Seven Deadly Sins, the reputation of the "Beard of the Mountain Cat" knighthood will soar!!
HA HA HA HA!
HAAH! HAAH!
BASH
JUMP
GYAAH!

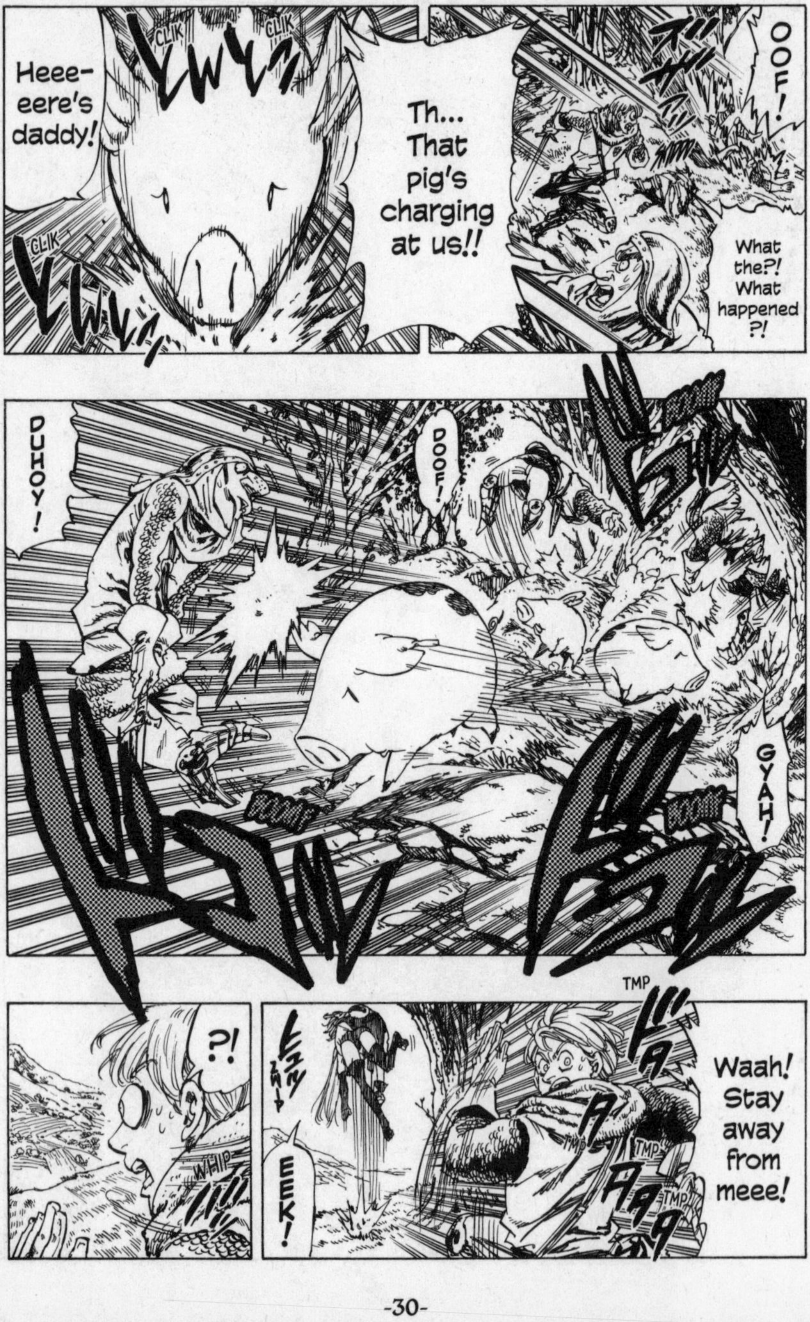
OOF!
What the?! What happened?!
Th... That pig's charging at us!!
CLIK
CLIK
Heeee-eere's daddy!
CLIK
GYAH!
DOOF!
DUHOY!
TMP
Waah! Stay away from meee!
TMP
TMP
TMP
ZWIP
EEK!
?!
WHIP

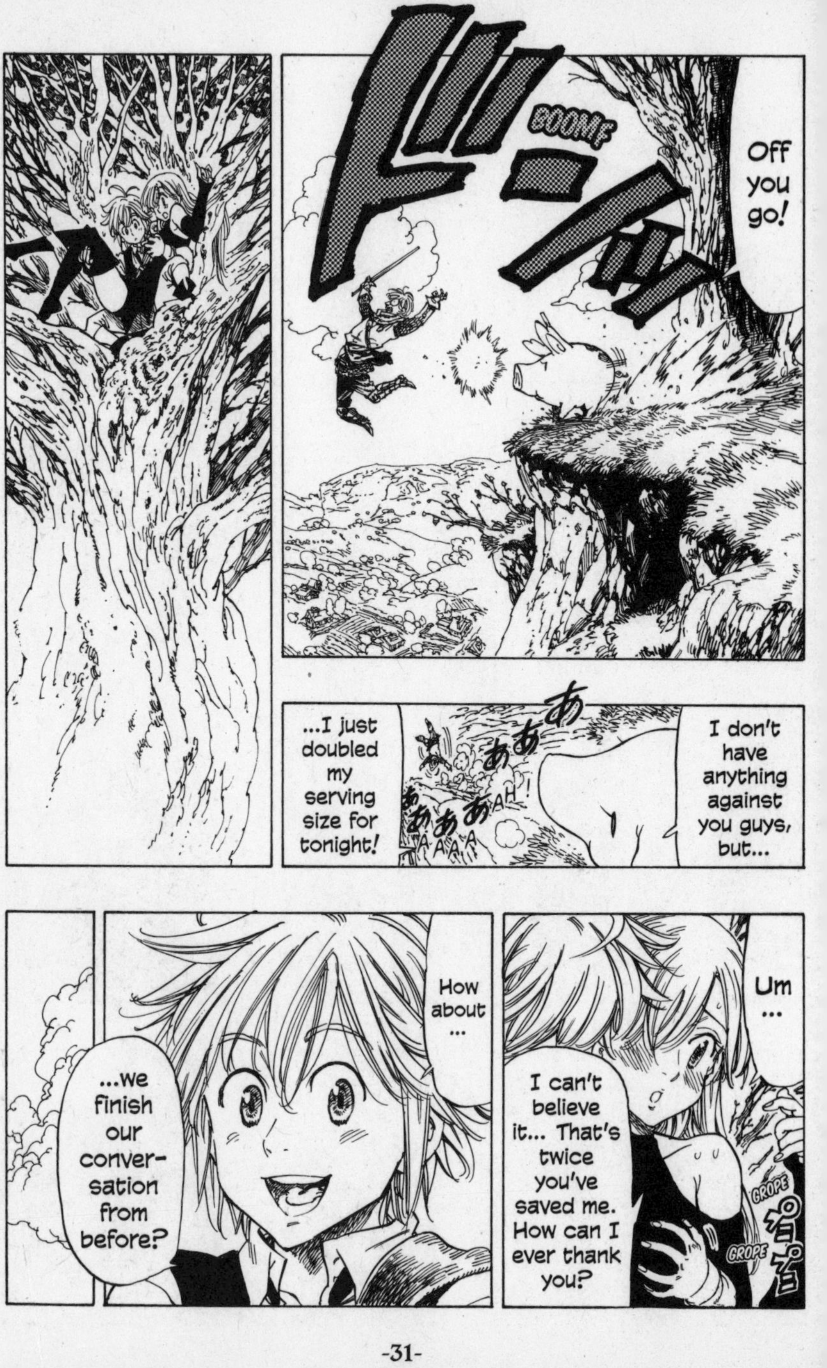
Off you go!
BOOMF
I don't have anything against you guys, but...
AAAAAH!
...I just doubled my serving size for tonight!
Um...
I can't believe it... That's twice you've saved me. How can I ever thank you?
GROPE
GROPE
How about...
...we finish our conversation from before?

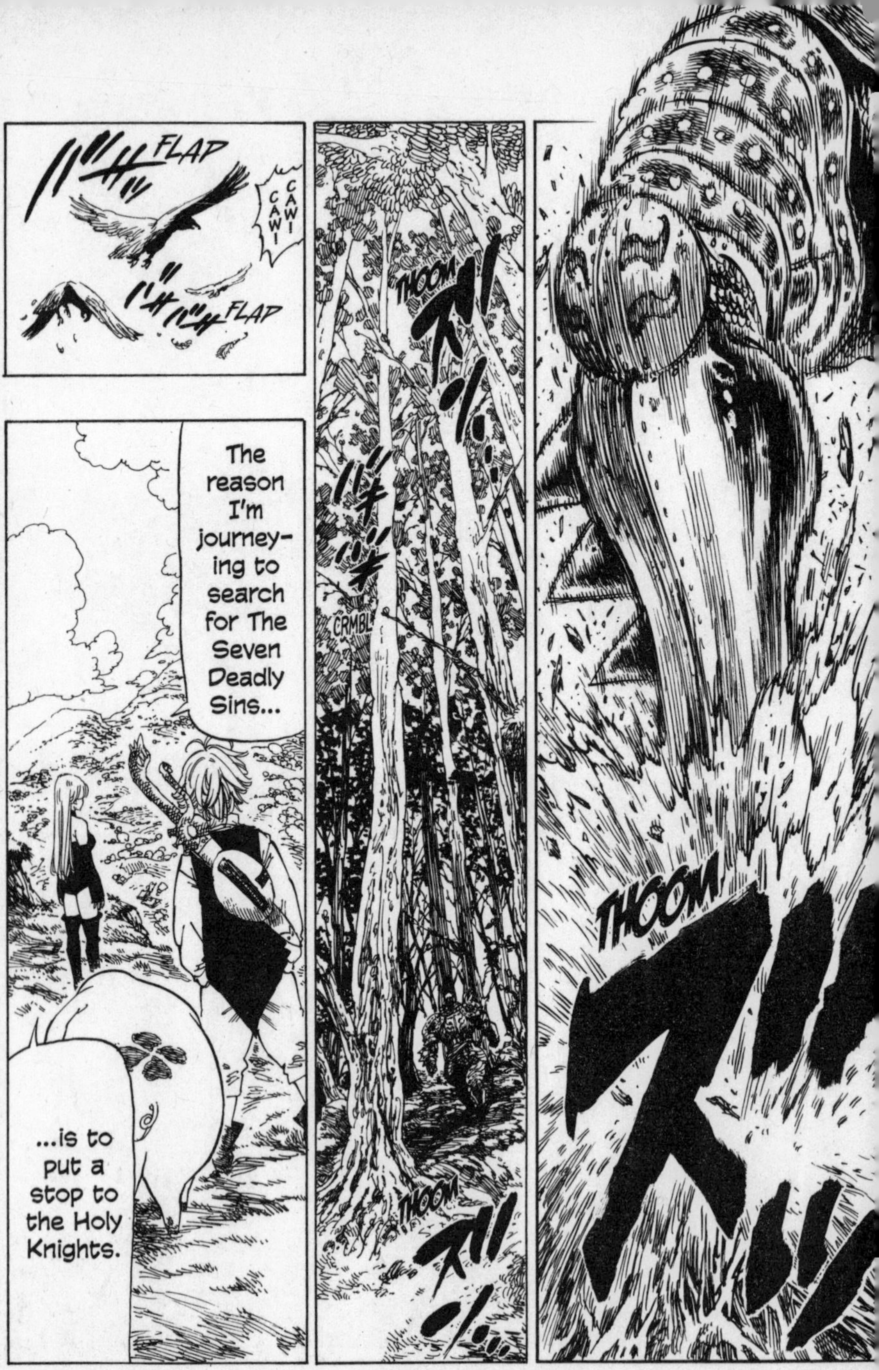
THOOM
THOOM
CRMBL
THOOM
FLAP
CAW! CAW!
FLAP
The reason I'm journeying to search for The Seven Deadly Sins...
...is to put a stop to the Holy Knights.

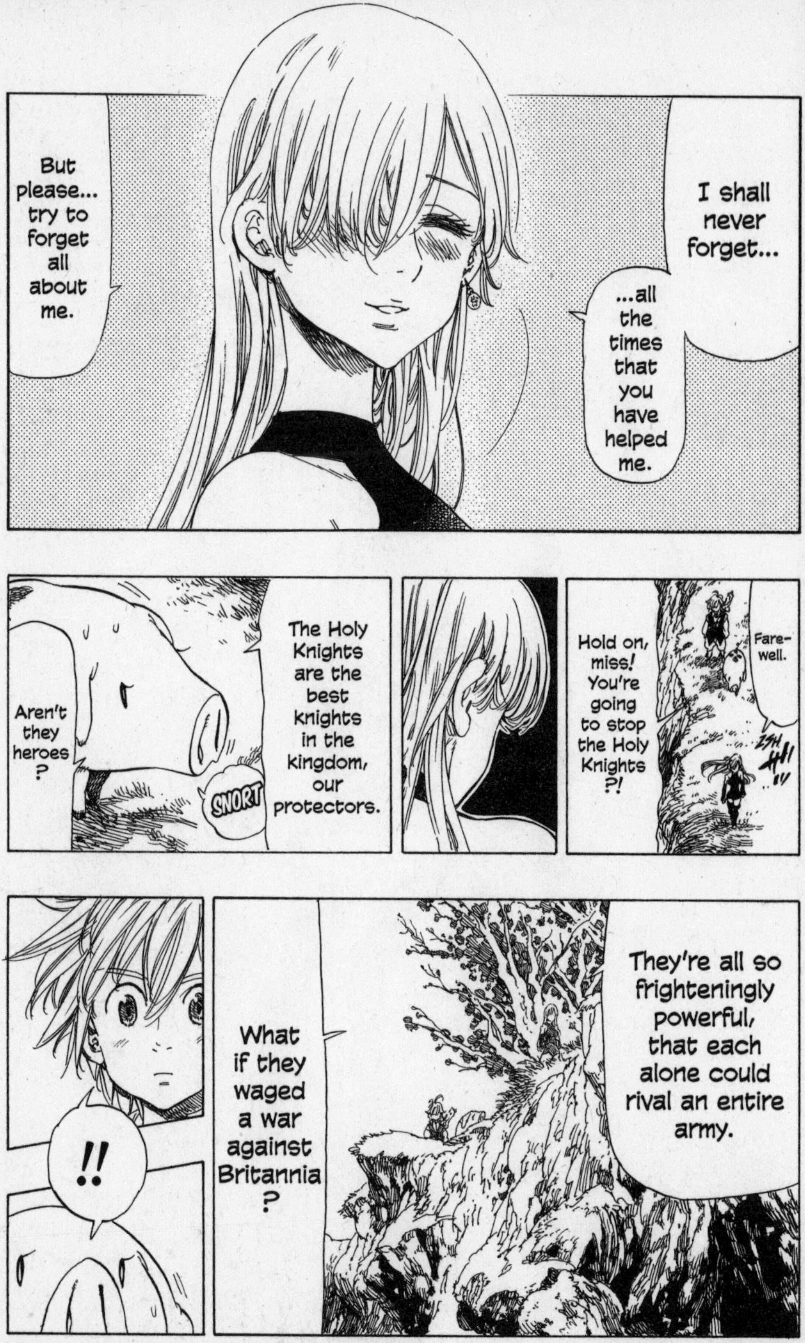
I shall never forget...
...all the times that you have helped me.
But please... try to forget all about me.
Farewell.
Hold on, miss! You're going to stop the Holy Knights?!
The Holy Knights are the best knights in the kingdom, our protectors.
SNORT
Aren't they heroes?
They're all so frighteningly powerful, that each alone could rival an entire army.
What if they waged a war against Britannia?
!!

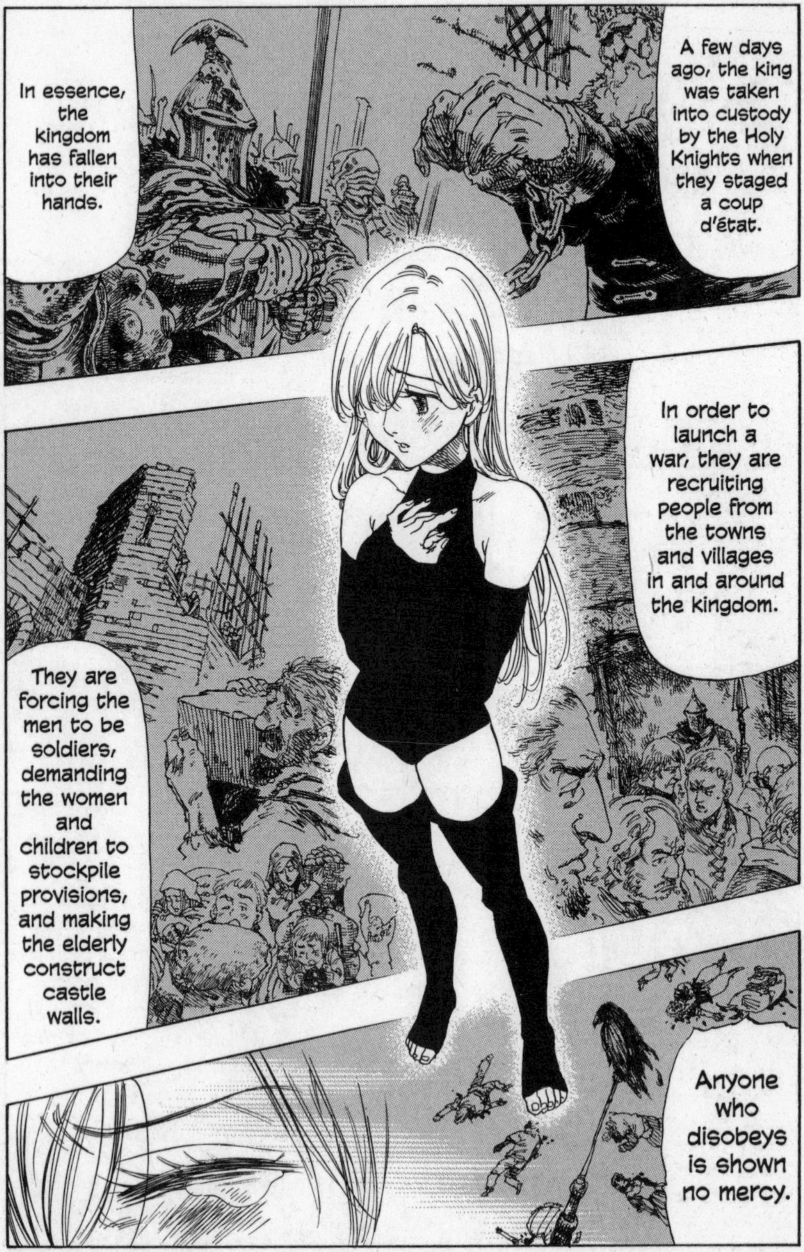
A few days ago, the king was taken into custody by the Holy Knights when they staged a coup d'état.
In essence, the kingdom has fallen into their hands.
In order to launch a war, they are recruiting people from the towns and villages in and around the kingdom.
They are forcing the men to be soldiers, demanding the women and children to stockpile provisions, and making the elderly construct castle walls.
Anyone who disobeys is shown no mercy.

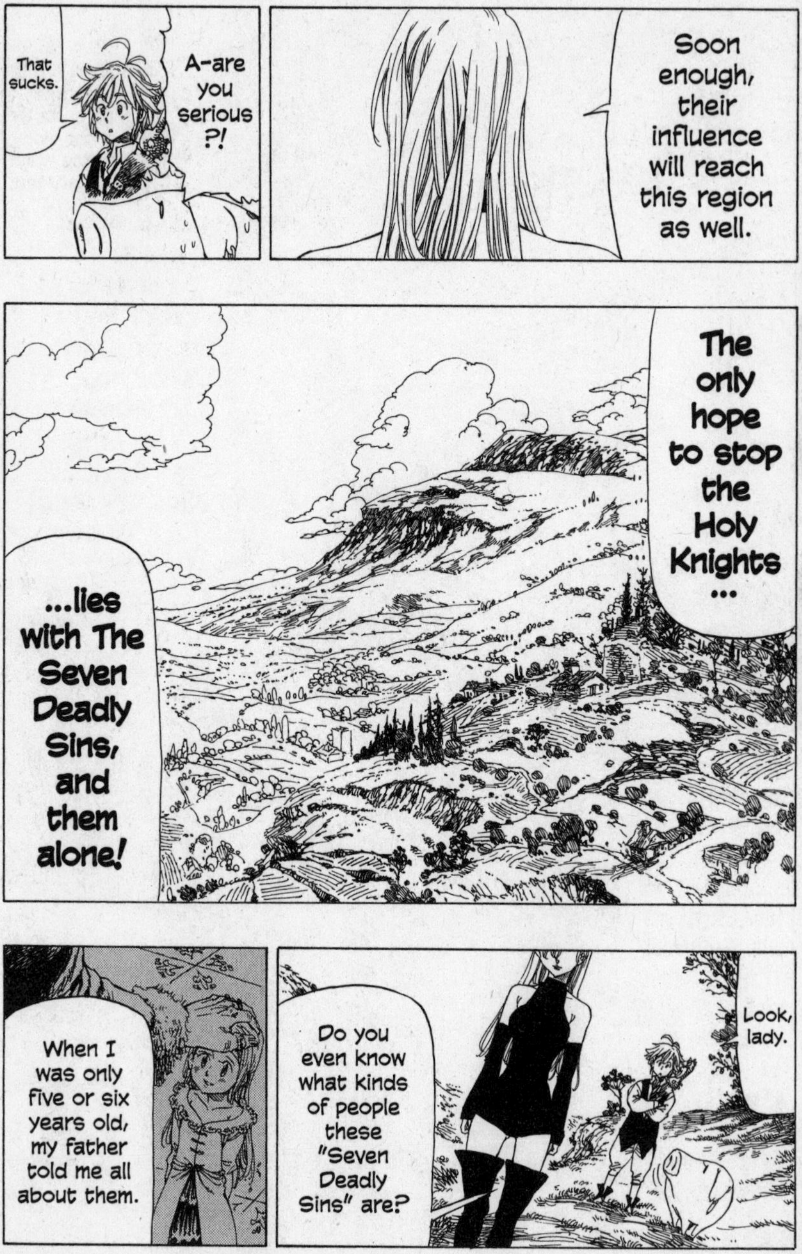
Soon enough, their influence will reach this region as well.
A-are you serious?!
That sucks.
The only hope to stop the Holy Knights...
...lies with The Seven Deadly Sins, and them alone!
Look, lady.
Do you even know what kinds of people these "Seven Deadly Sins" are?
When I was only five or six years old, my father told me all about them.

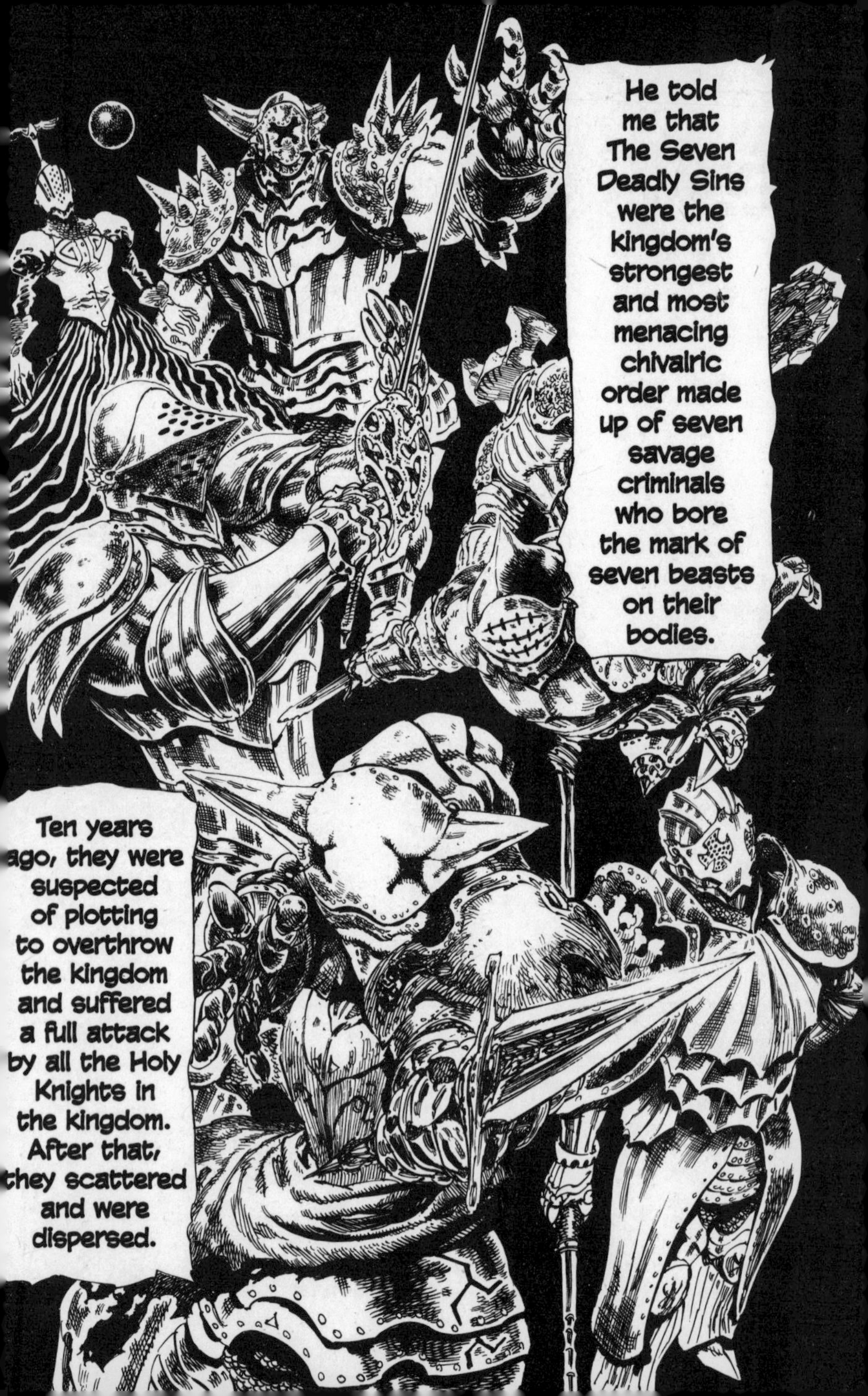
He told me that The Seven Deadly Sins were the kingdom's strongest and most menacing chivalric order made up of seven savage criminals who bore the mark of seven beasts on their bodies.
Ten years ago, they were suspected of plotting to overthrow the kingdom and suffered a full attack by all the Holy Knights in the kingdom. After that, they scattered and were dispersed.

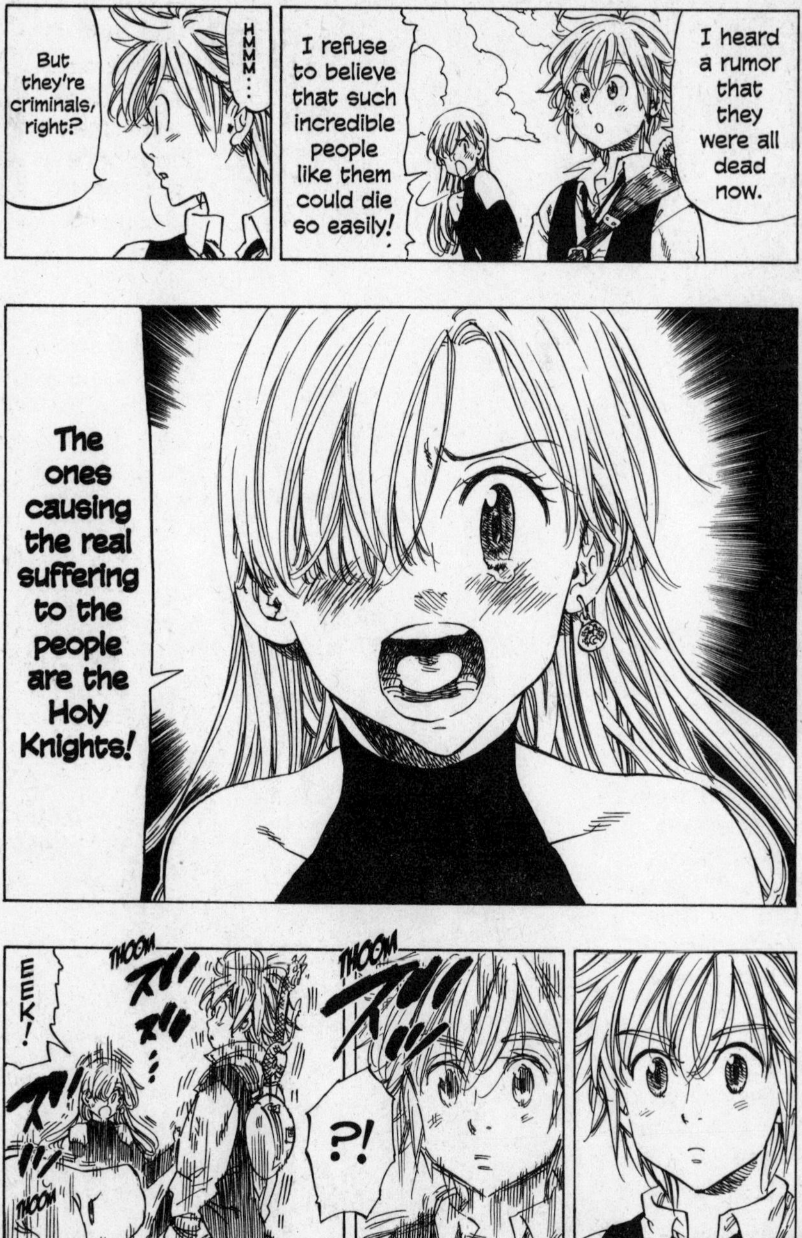

I heard a rumor that they were all dead now.
I refuse to believe that such incredible people like them could die so easily!
HMMM...
But they're criminals, right?
The ones causing the real suffering to the people are the Holy Knights!
THOOM
?!
THOOM
EEK!
THOOM

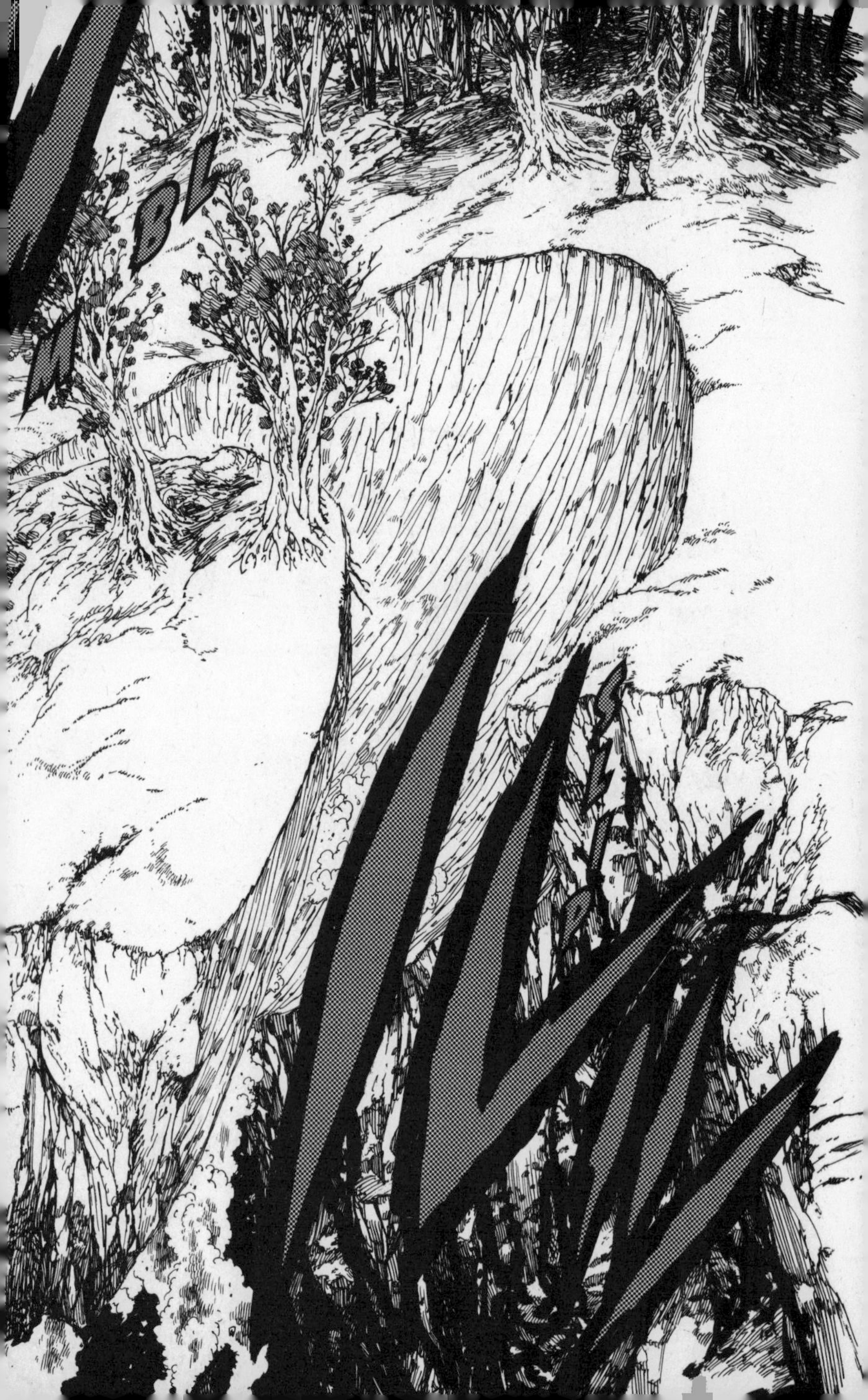

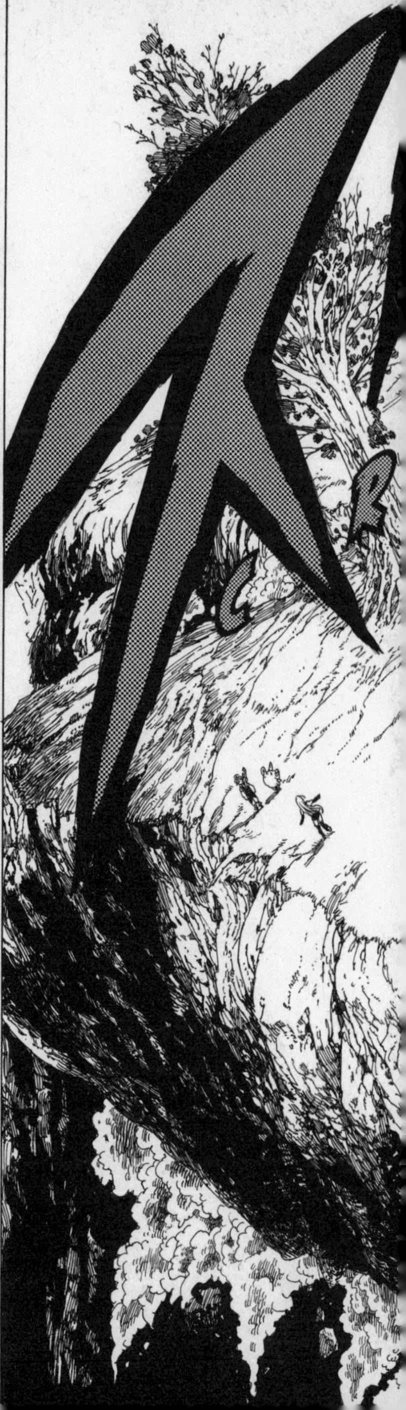

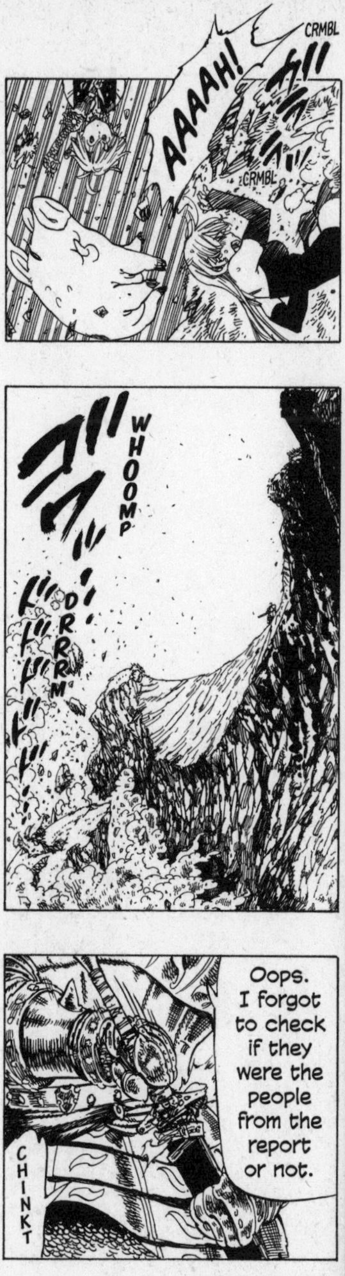
CRMBL
AAAAH!
CRMBL
WHOOMP
DRRRM
Oops. I forgot to check if they were the people from the report or not.
CHINKT

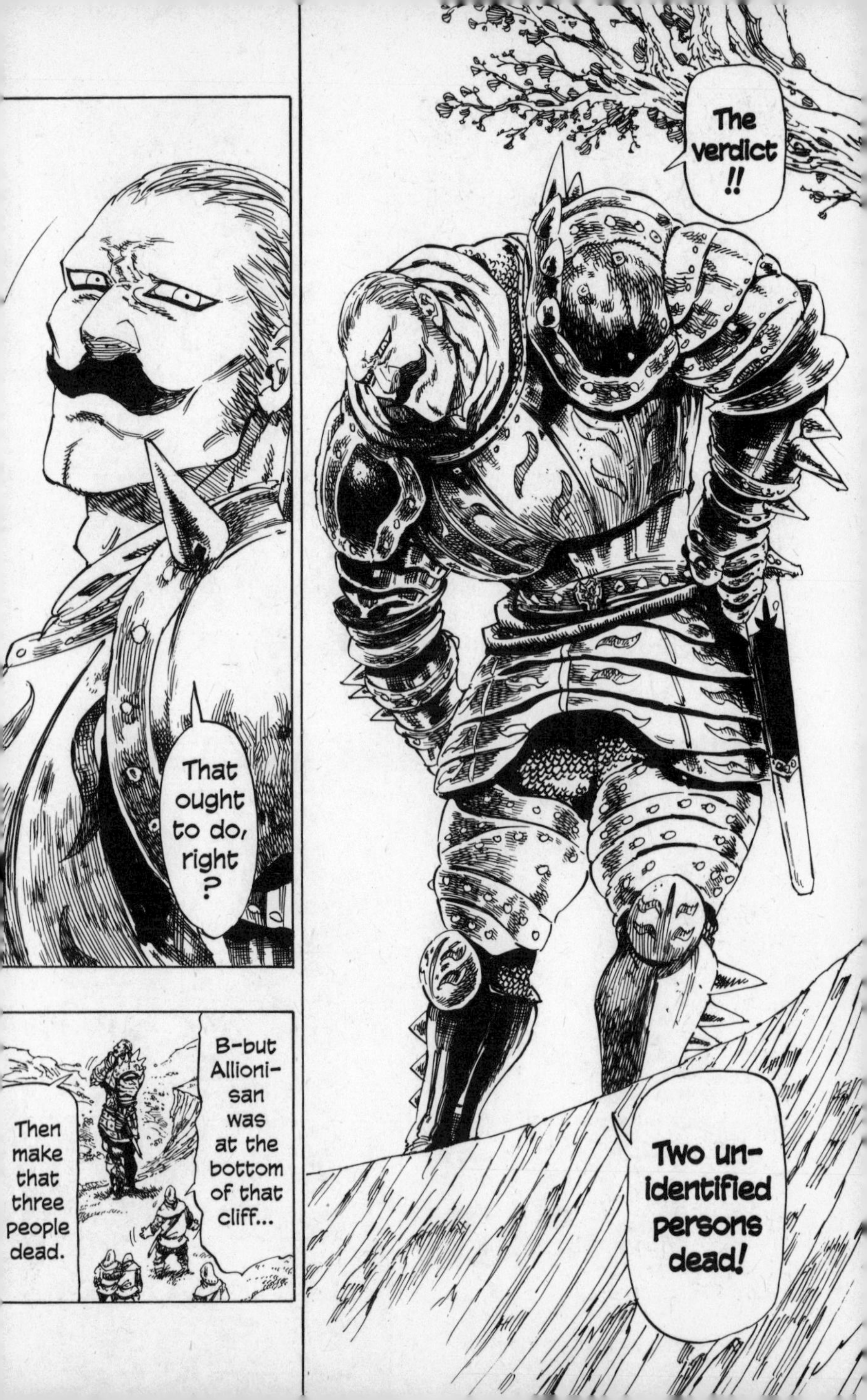
The verdict!!
Two un-identified persons dead!
That ought to do, right?
B-but Allioni-san was at the bottom of that cliff...
Then make that three people dead.

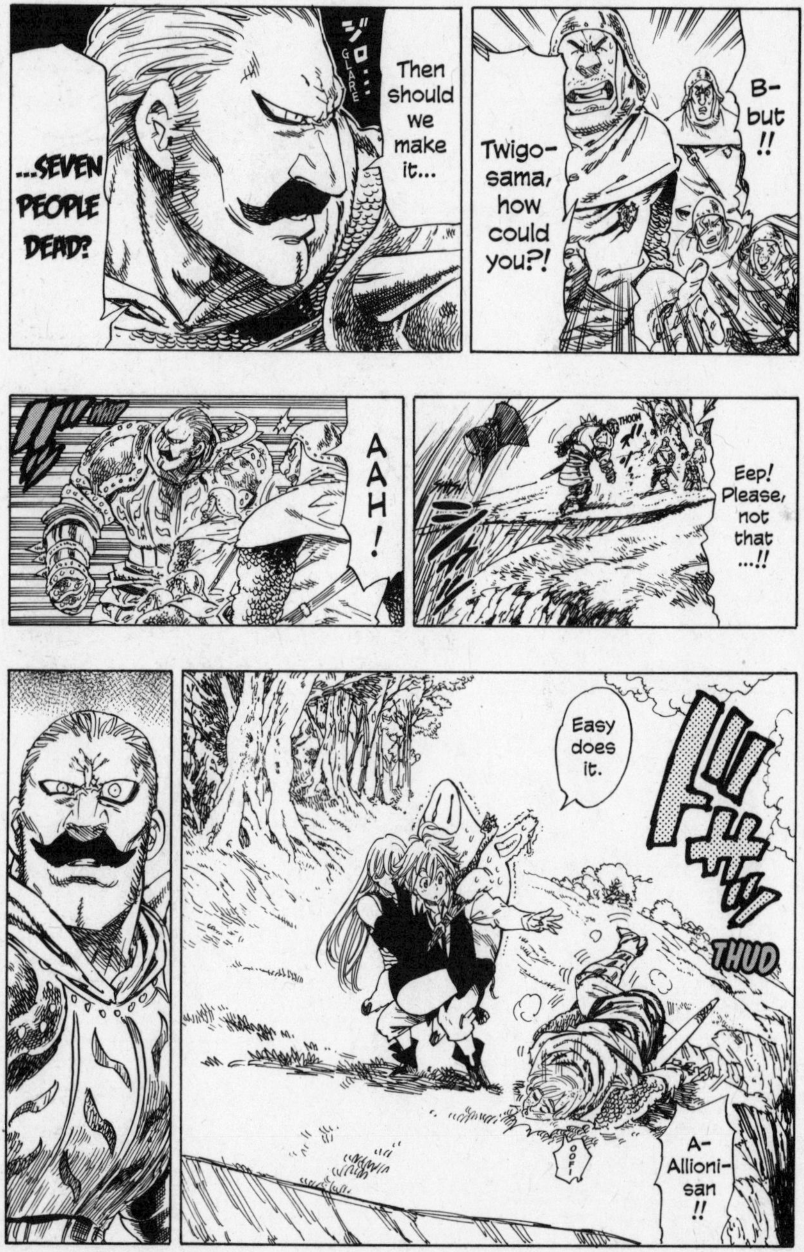
B-but!!
Twigo-sama, how could you?!
Then should we make it...
ジロ…
GLARE
...SEVEN PEOPLE DEAD?
THOOM
Eep! Please, not that...!!
AAH!
Easy does it.
THUD
A-Allioni-san!!
OOF!

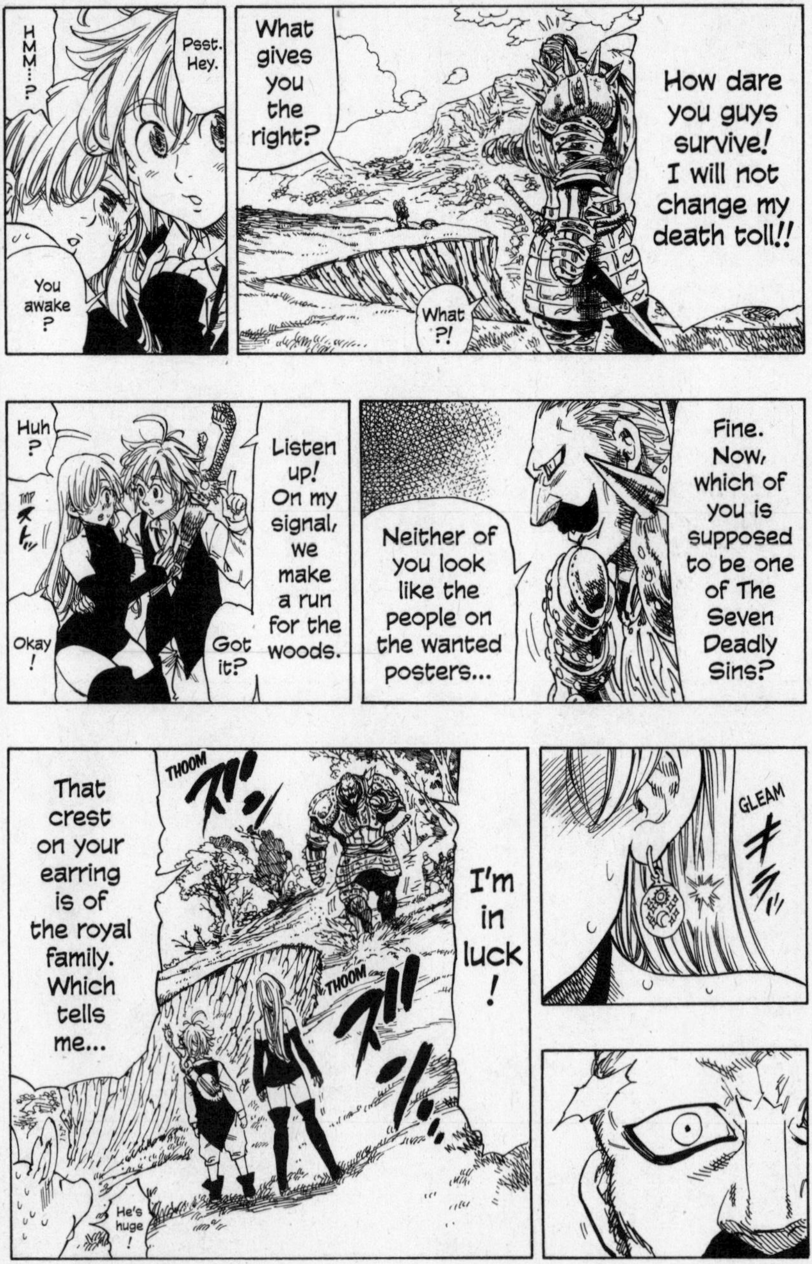
How dare you guys survive! I will not change my death toll!!
What gives you the right?
What?!
Psst. Hey.
HMM...?
You awake?
Fine. Now, which of you is supposed to be one of The Seven Deadly Sins?
Neither of you look like the people on the wanted posters...
Listen up! On my signal, we make a run for the woods.
Huh?
TMP
Got it?
Okay!
GLEAM
THOOM
I'm in luck!
That crest on your earring is of the royal family. Which tells me...
THOOM
He's huge!

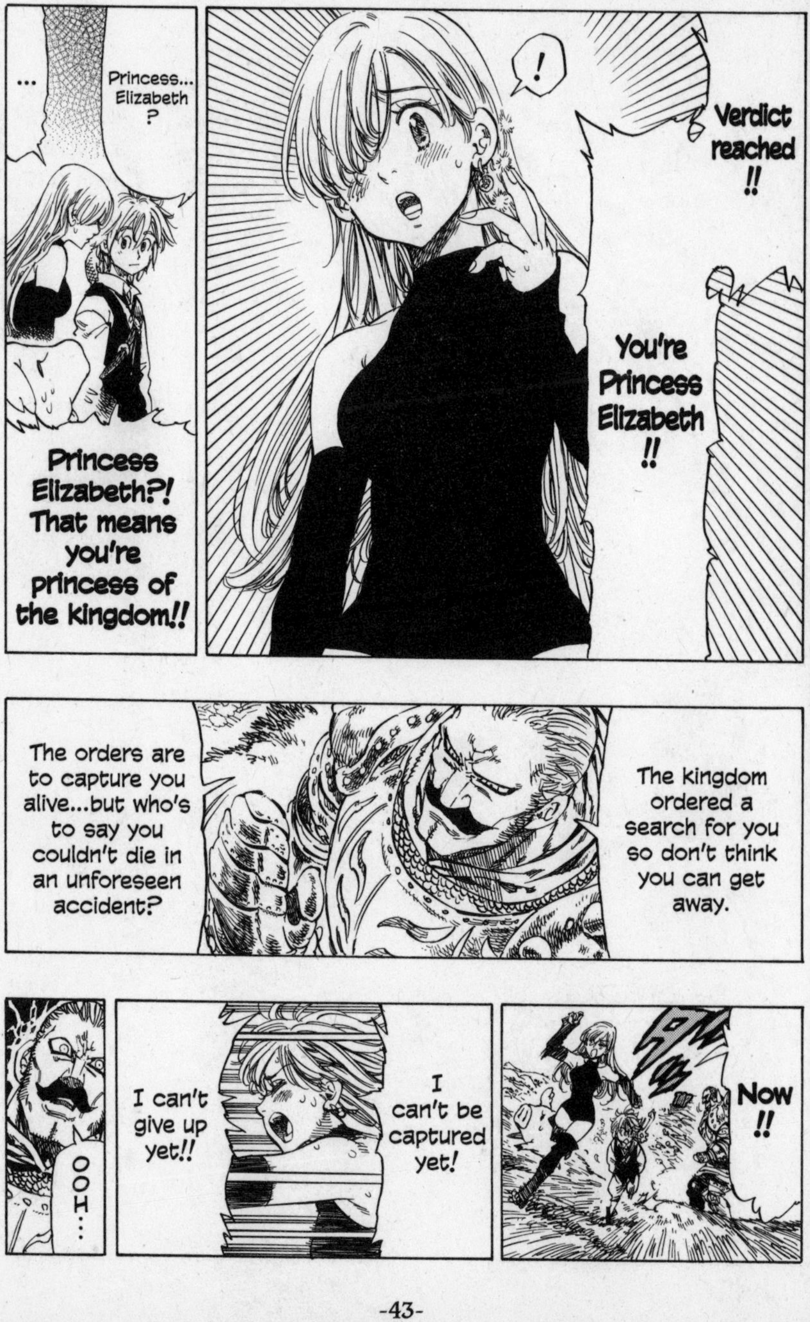
Verdict reached !!
!
You're Princess Elizabeth !!
Princess... Elizabeth ?
...
Princess Elizabeth?! That means you're princess of the kingdom!!
The kingdom ordered a search for you so don't think you can get away.
The orders are to capture you alive...but who's to say you couldn't die in an unforeseen accident?
Now !!
I can't be captured yet!
I can't give up yet!!
OOH...

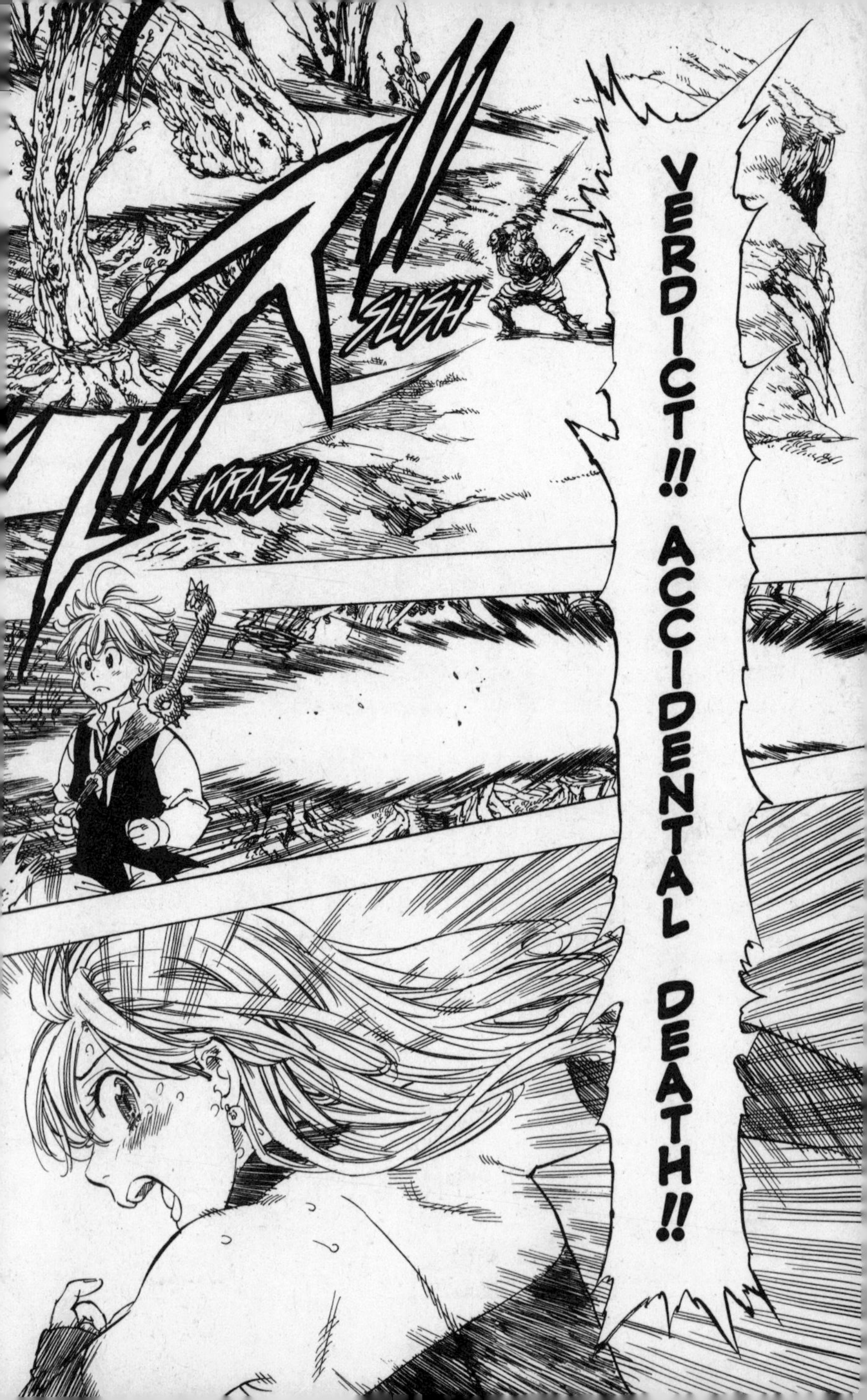
VERDICT!! ACCIDENTAL DEATH!!
SLUSH
KRASH

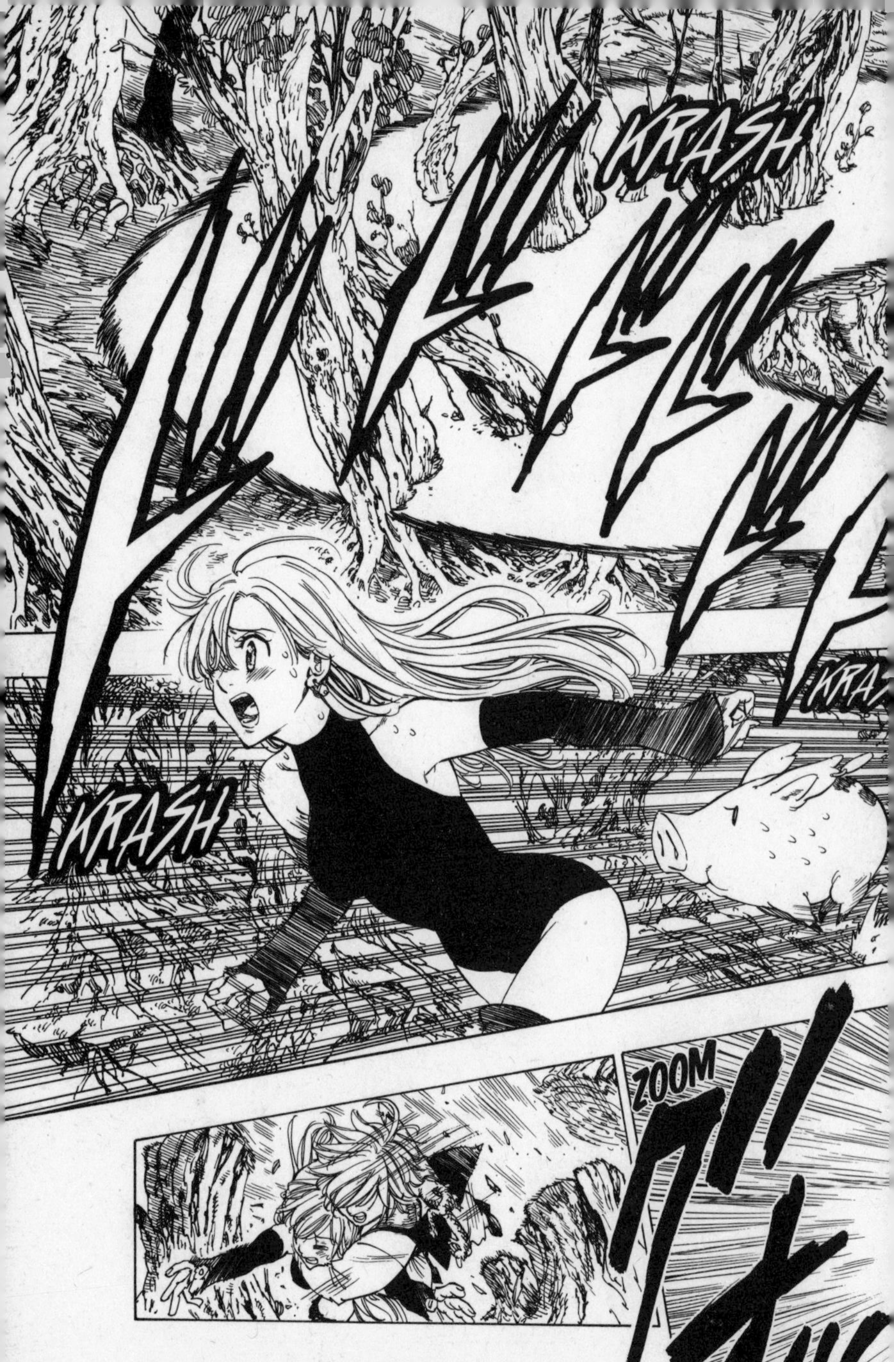
KRASH
KRA
KRASH
ZOOM

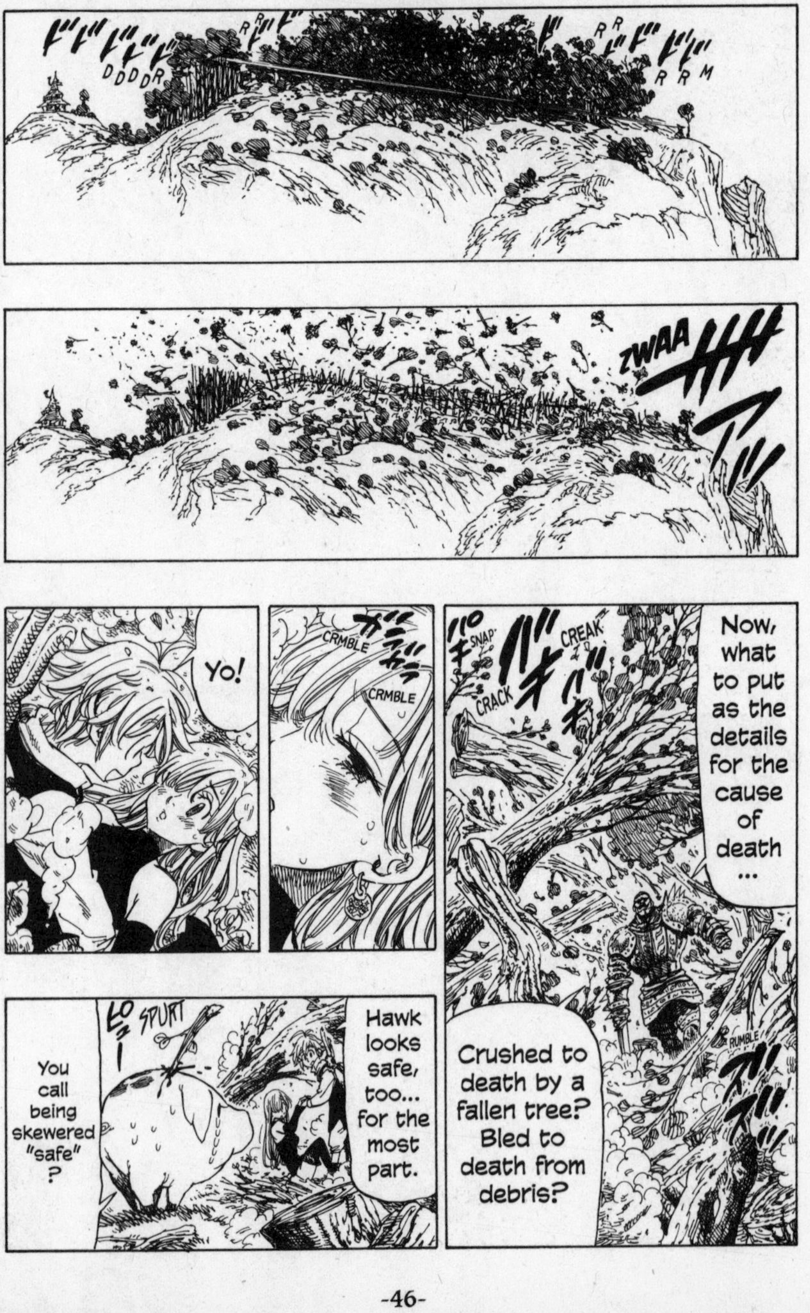
DDDDR
RR
RR
RRM
ZWAA
SNAP
CREAK
CRACK
Now, what to put as the details for the cause of death ...
Crushed to death by a fallen tree? Bled to death from debris?
RUMBLE
CRMBLE
CRMBLE
Yo!
Hawk looks safe, too... for the most part.
SPURT
You call being skewered "safe" ?

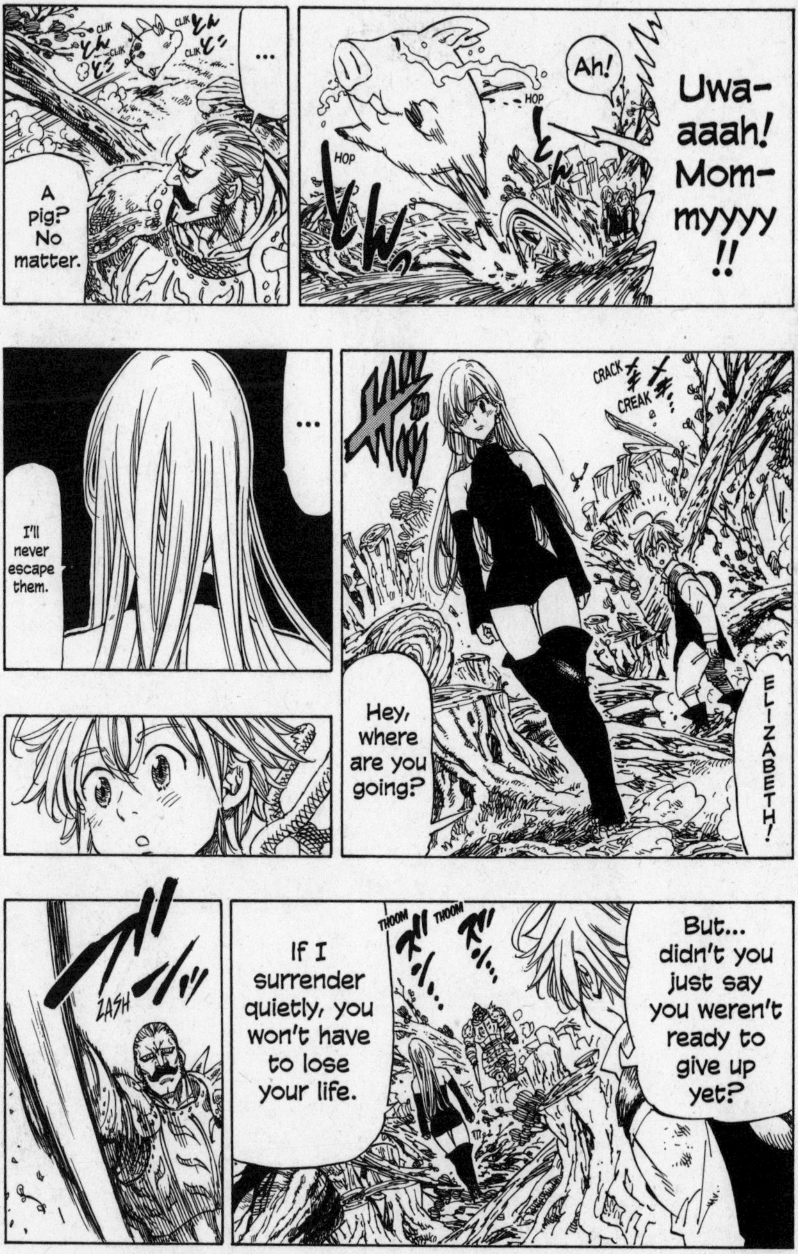
Uwa-aaah! Mommyyyy!!
Ah!
HOP
HOP
CLIK
CLIK
CLIK
CLIK
...
A pig? No matter.
ELIZABETH!
CRACK
CREAK
Hey, where are you going?
...
I'll never escape them.
But... didn't you just say you weren't ready to give up yet?
THOOM
THOOM
If I surrender quietly, you won't have to lose your life.
ZASH

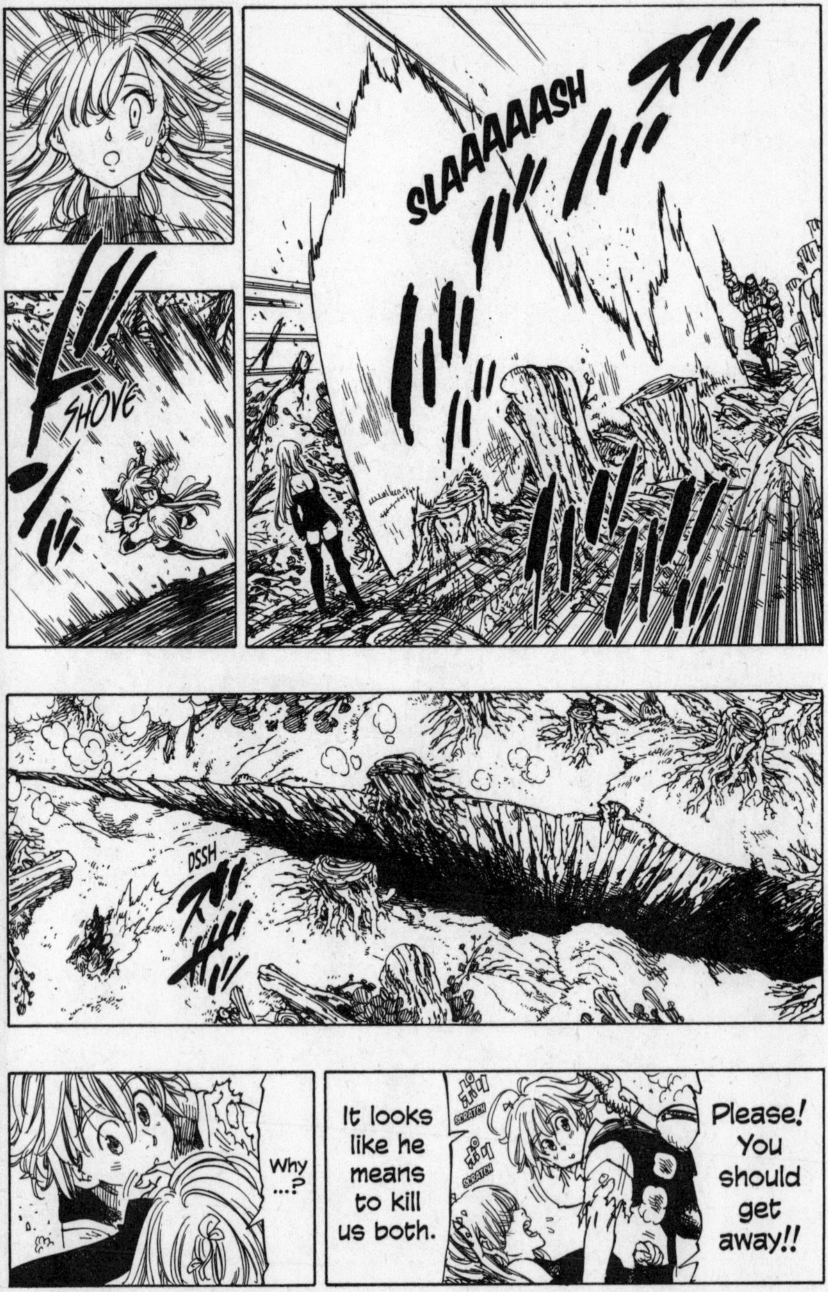
SLAAAAASH
SHOVE
DSSH
Please! You should get away!!
SCRATCH
SCRATCH
It looks like he means to kill us both.
Why ...?

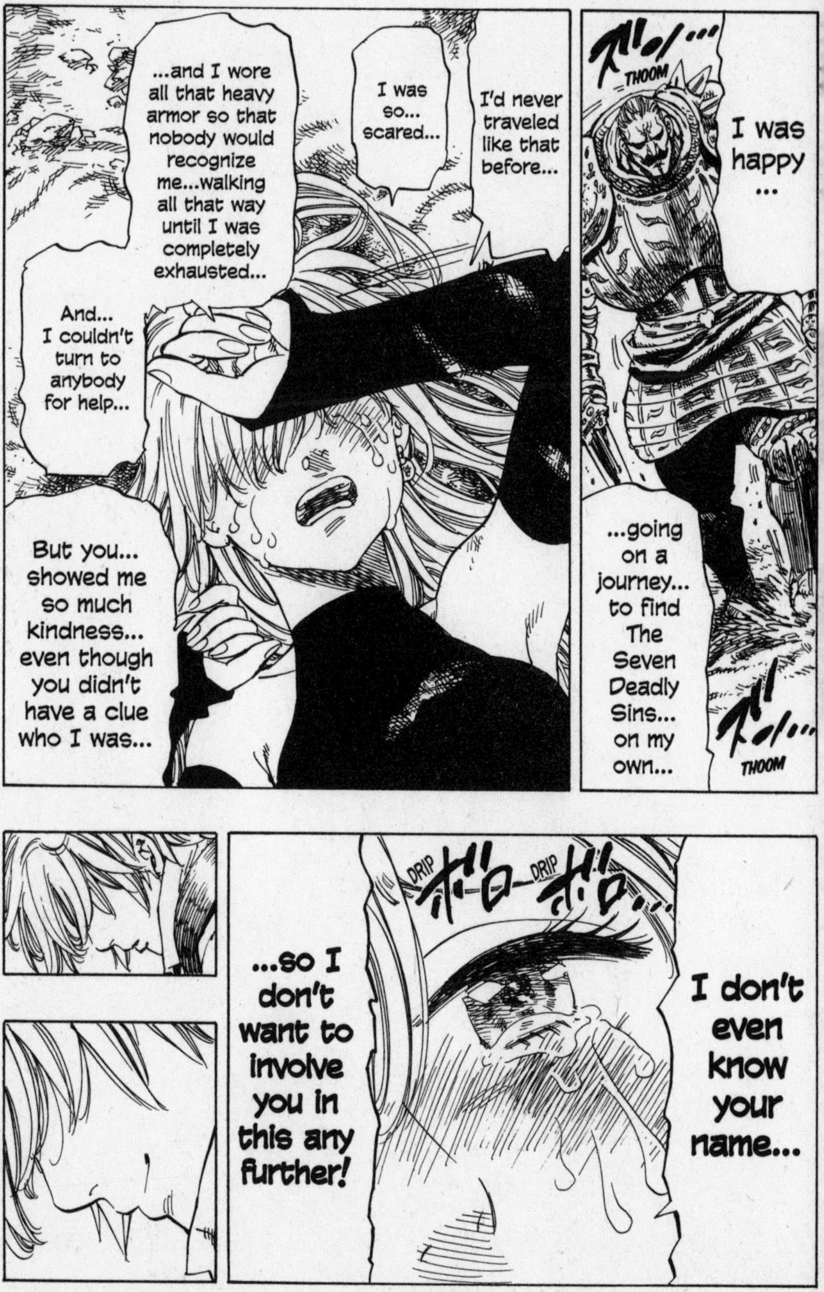
THOOM
I was happy...
...going on a journey... to find The Seven Deadly Sins... on my own...
THOOM
I'd never traveled like that before...
I was so... scared...
...and I wore all that heavy armor so that nobody would recognize me...walking all that way until I was completely exhausted...
And... I couldn't turn to anybody for help...
But you... showed me so much kindness... even though you didn't have a clue who I was...
DRIP
DRIP
I don't even know your name...
...so I don't want to involve you in this any further!

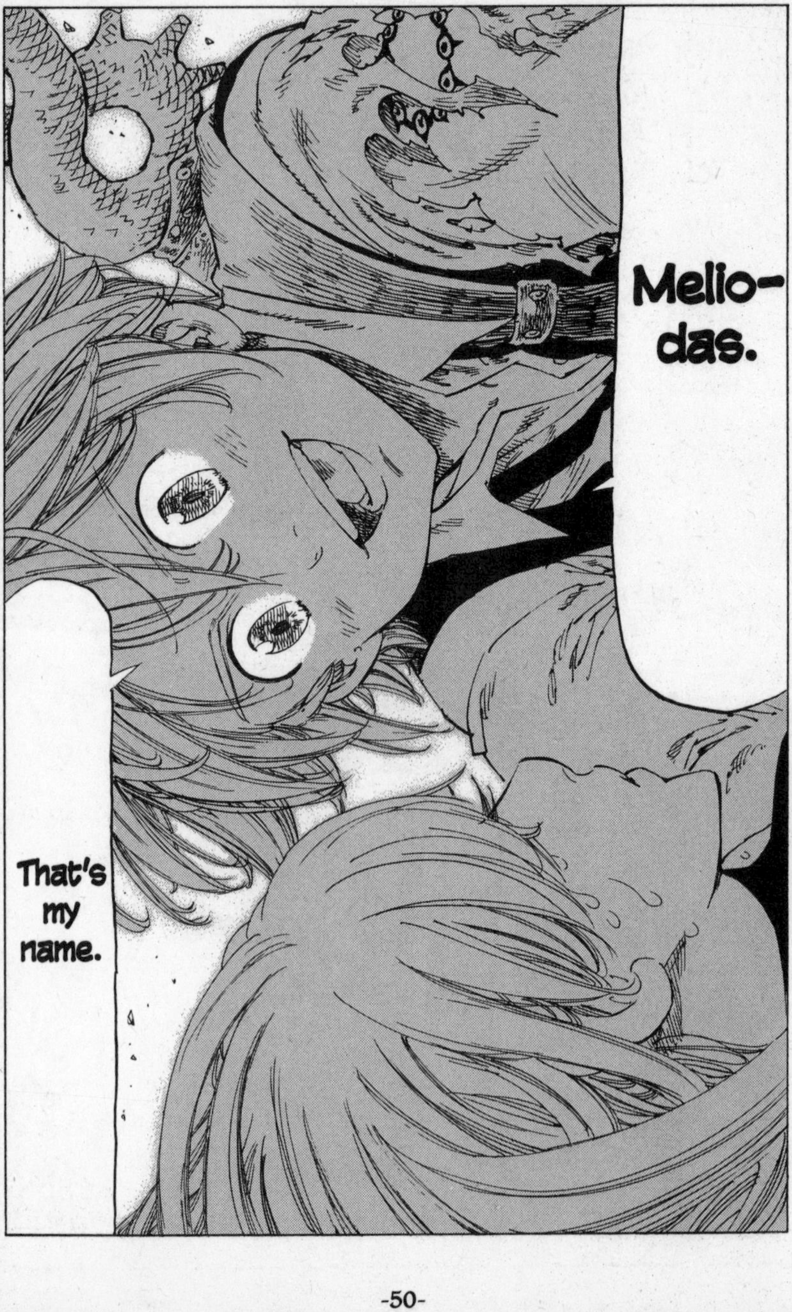
Melio-das.
That's my name.

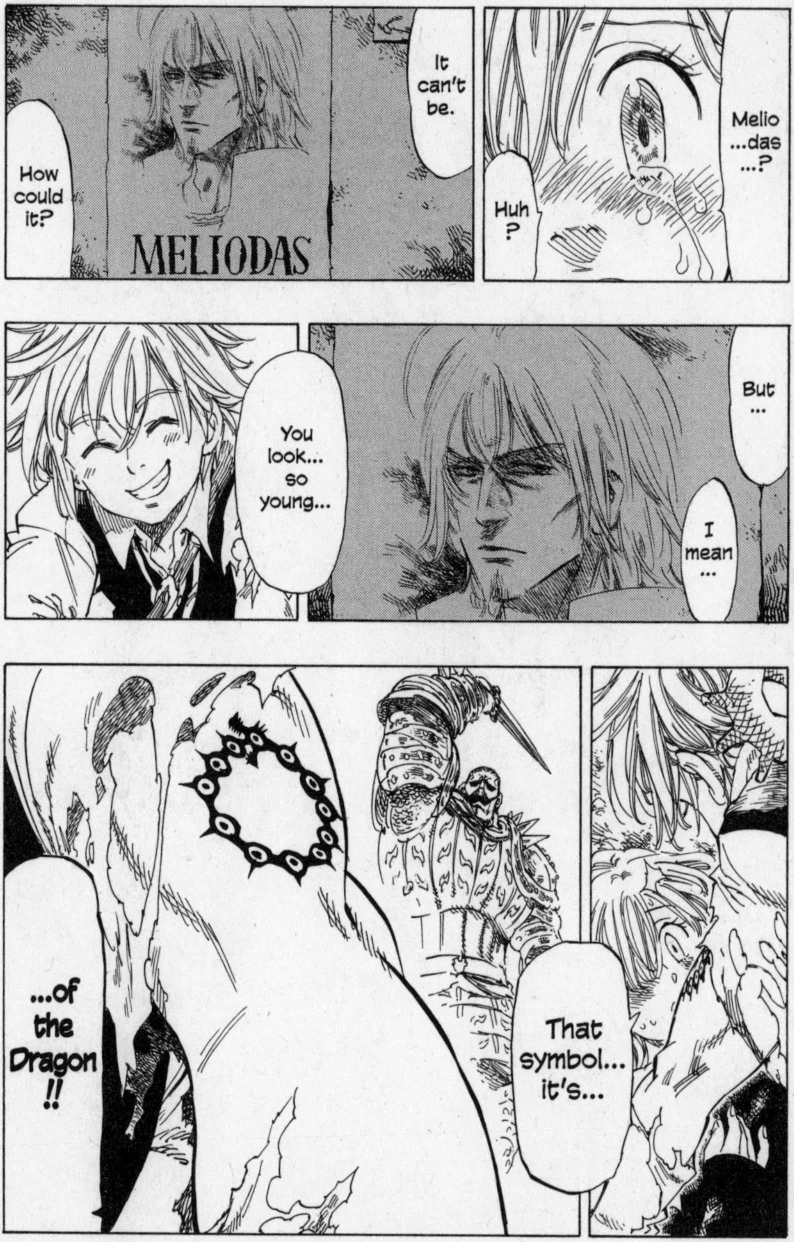
Melio ...das ...?
Huh ?
It can't be.
How could it?
MELIODAS
But ...
I mean ...
You look... so young...
That symbol... it's...
...of the Dragon !!

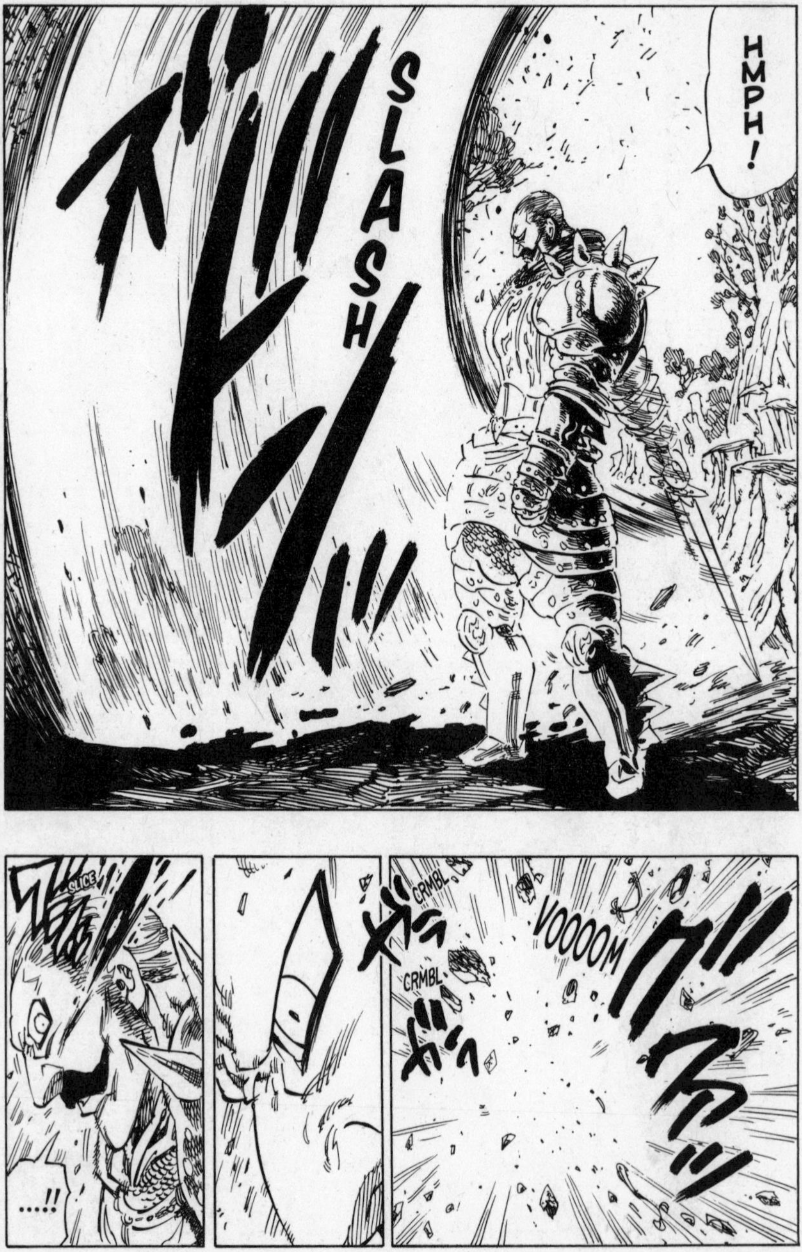
HMPH!
SLASH
VOOOOM
CRMBL
CRMBL
SLICE
....!!

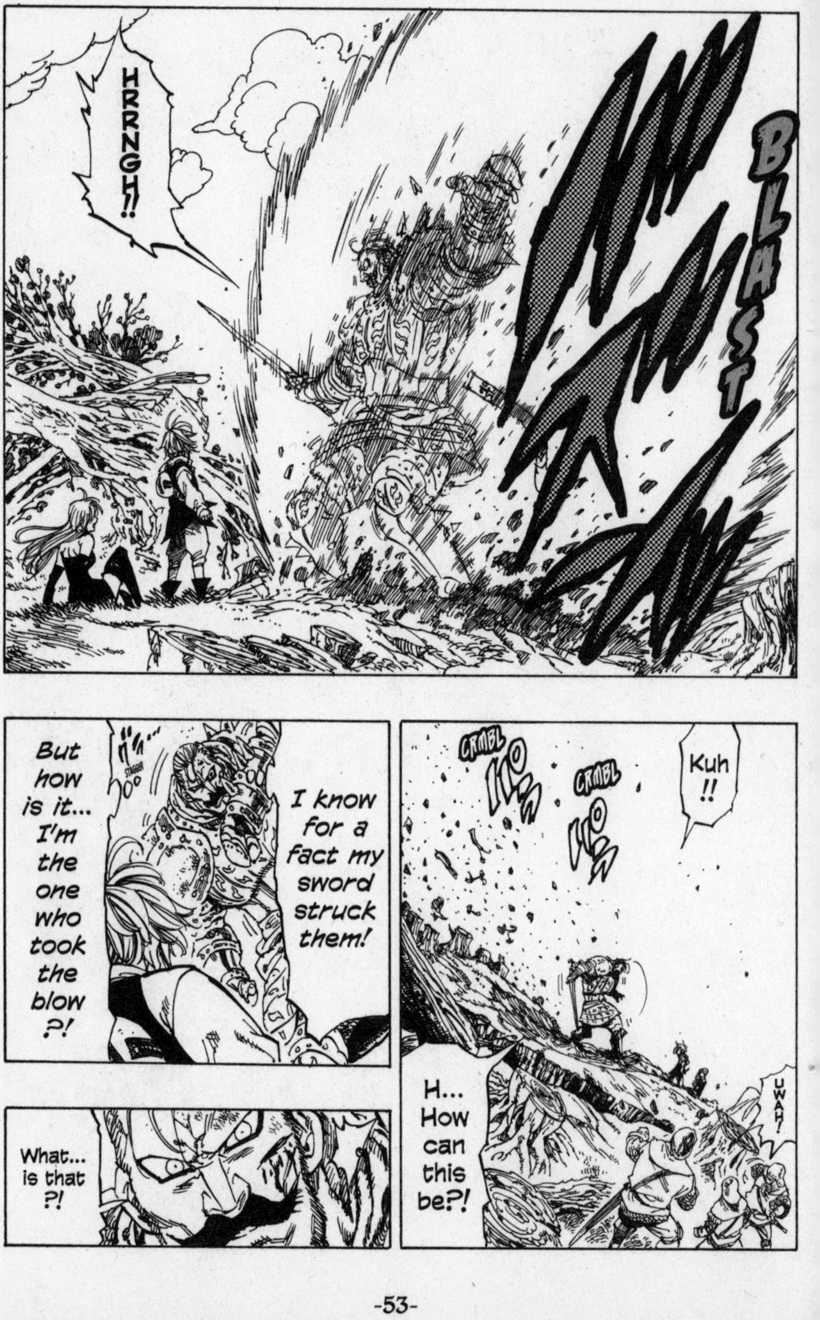
BLAST
HRRNGH!!
Kuh!!
CRMBL
CRMBL
UWAH!
H... How can this be?!
I know for a fact my sword struck them!
STAGGER
But how is it... I'm the one who took the blow?!
What... is that?!

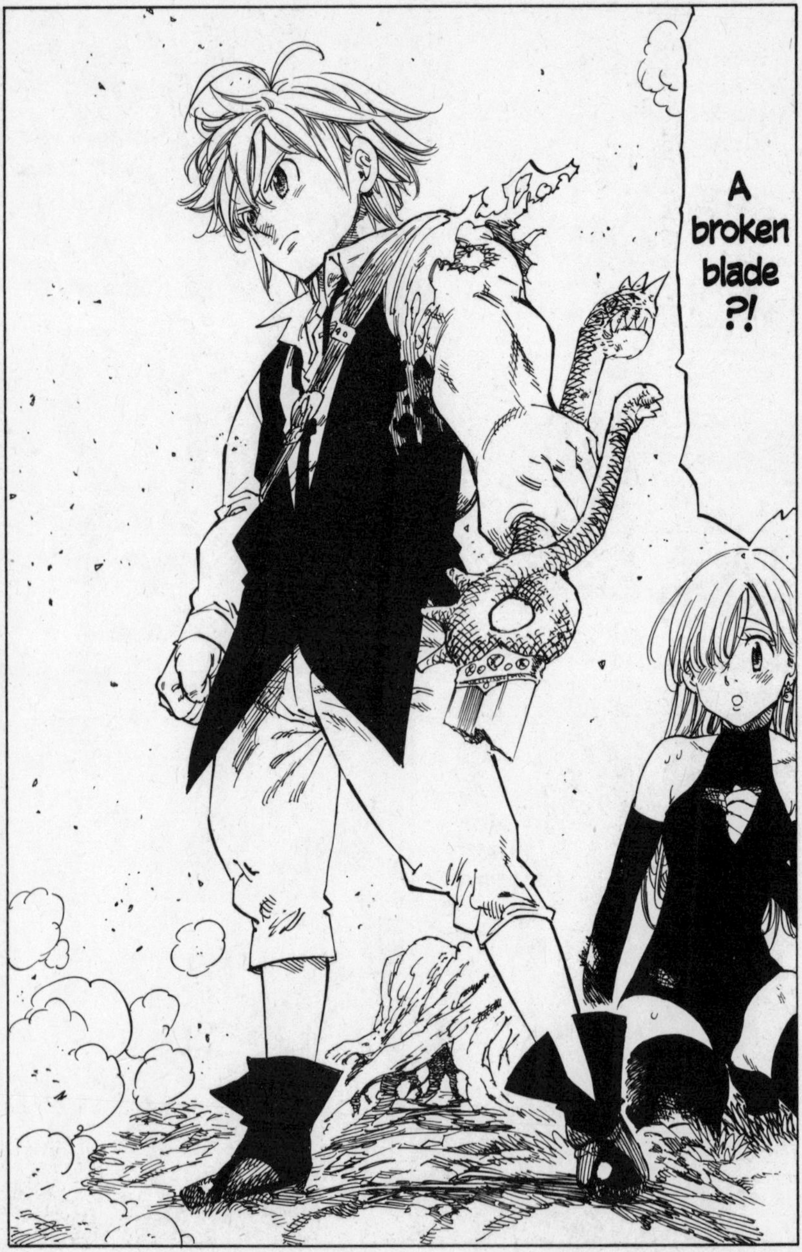
A broken blade ?!

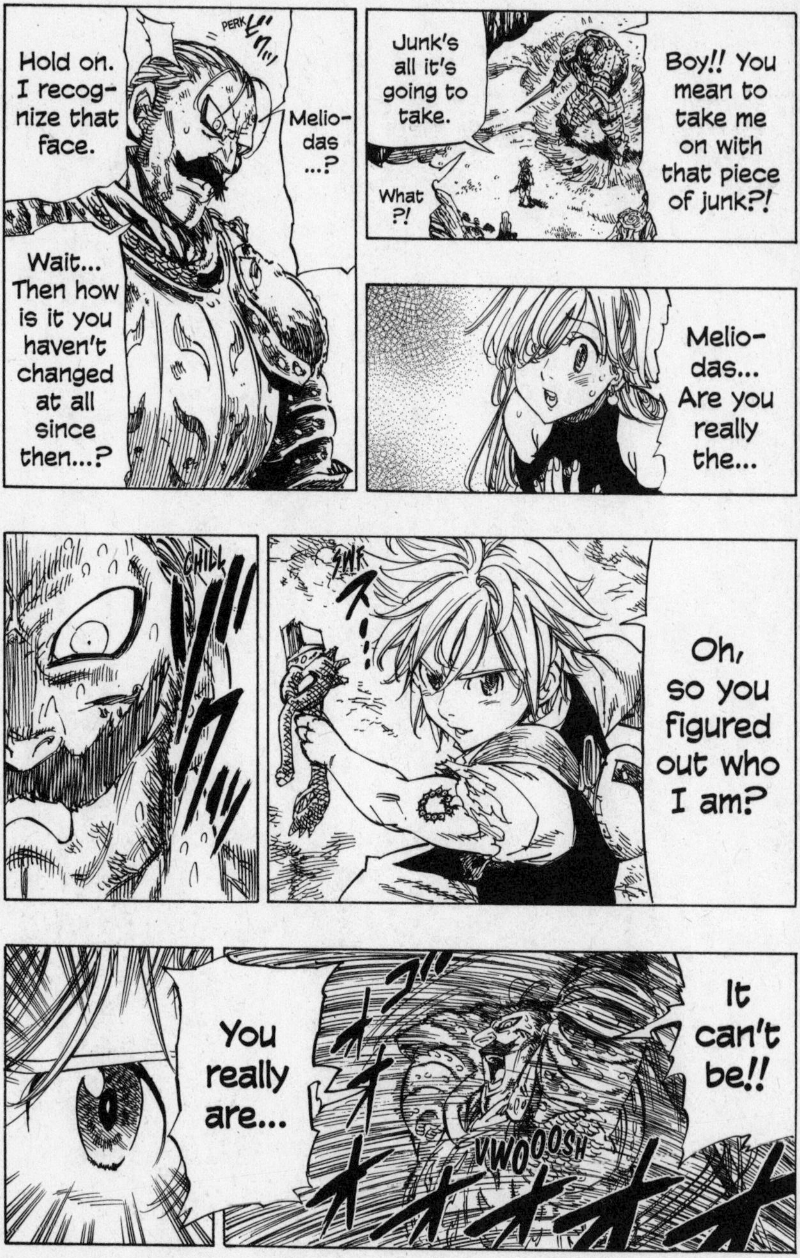
Boy!! You mean to take me on with that piece of junk?!
Junk's all it's going to take.
What ?!
Melio-das... Are you really the...
PERK
Melio-das ...?
Hold on. I recog-nize that face.
Wait... Then how is it you haven't changed at all since then...?
SWF
Oh, so you figured out who I am?
CHILL
It can't be!!
VWOOOSH
You really are...

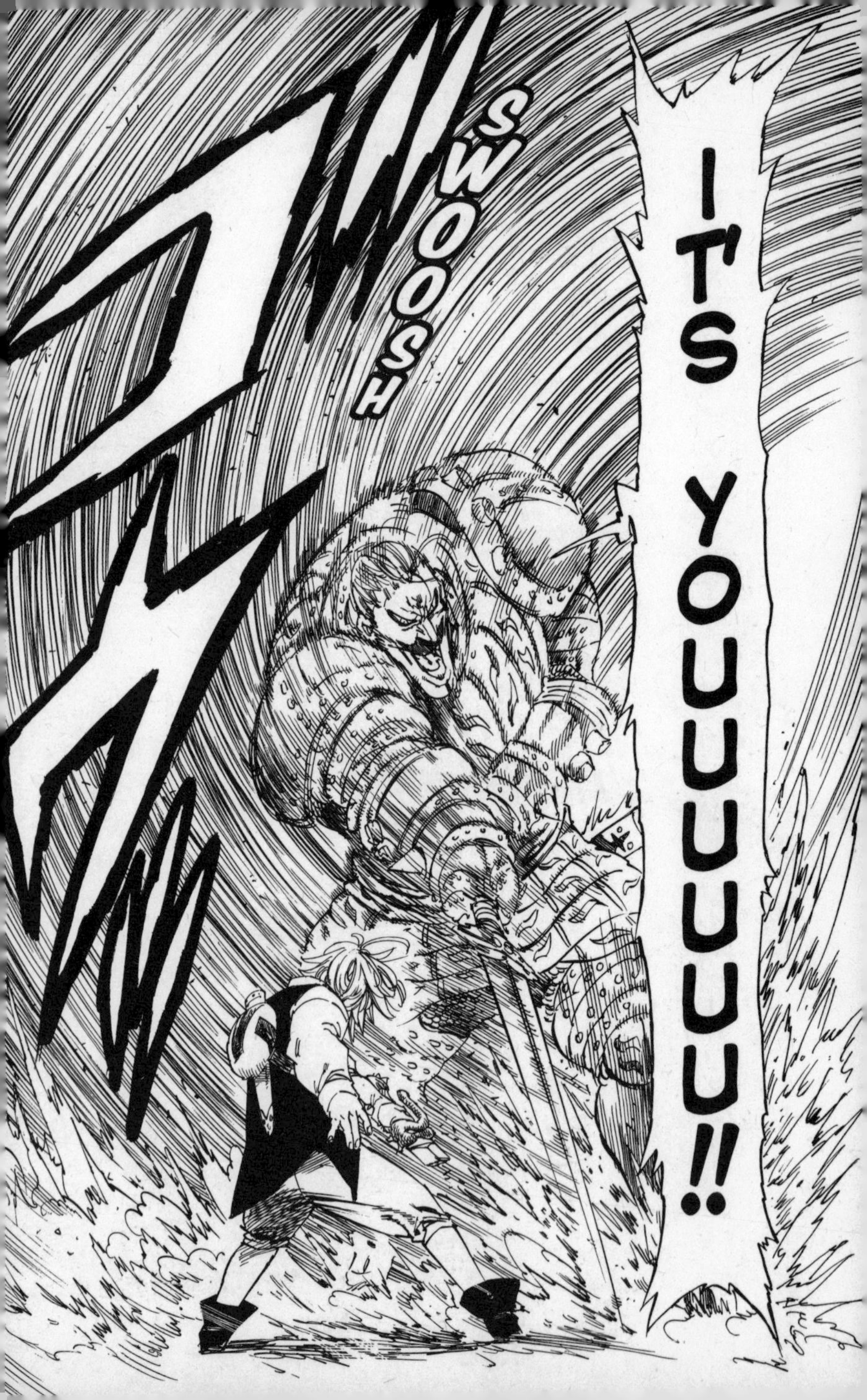
IT'S YOUUUUU!!
SWOOSH

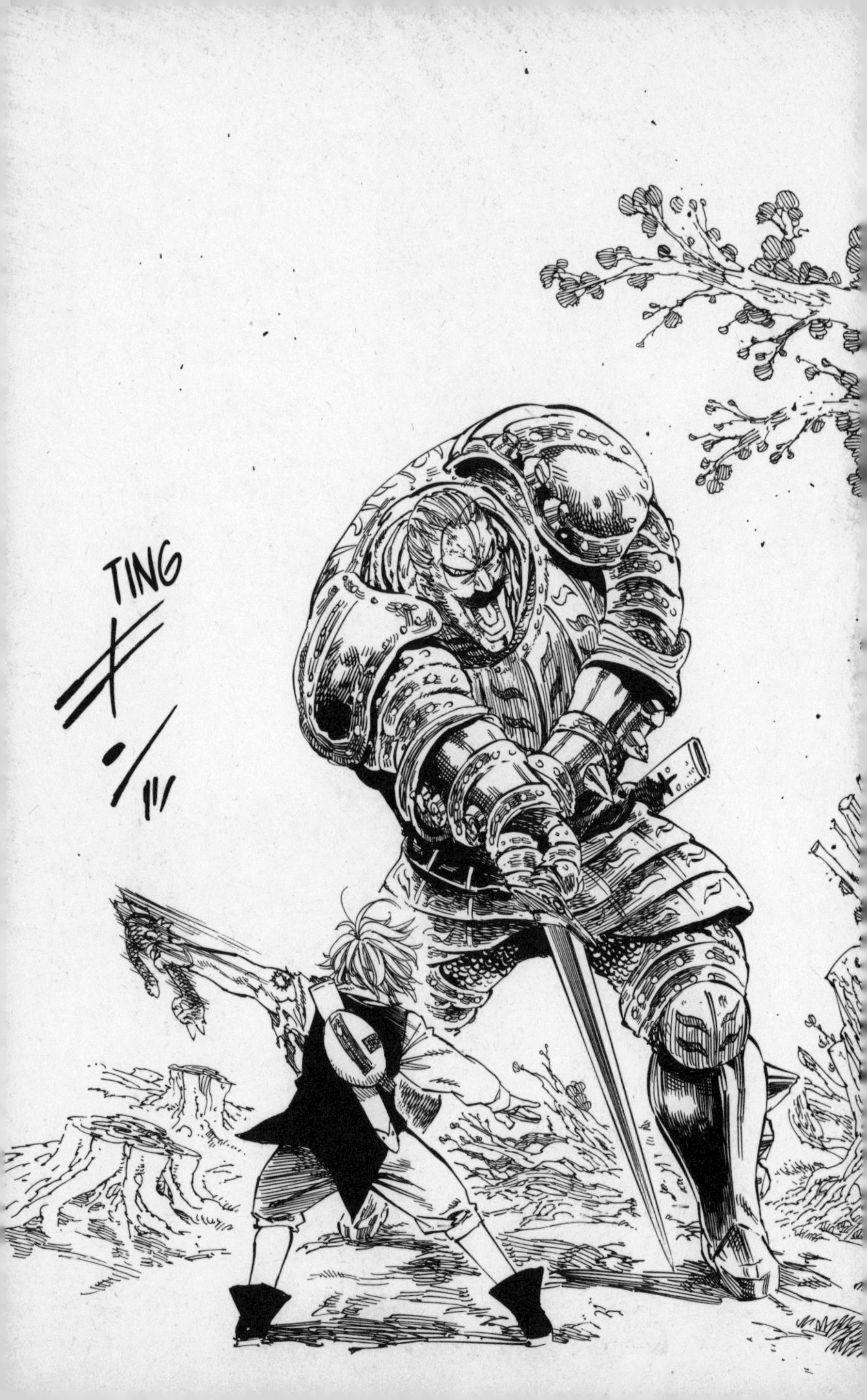
TING

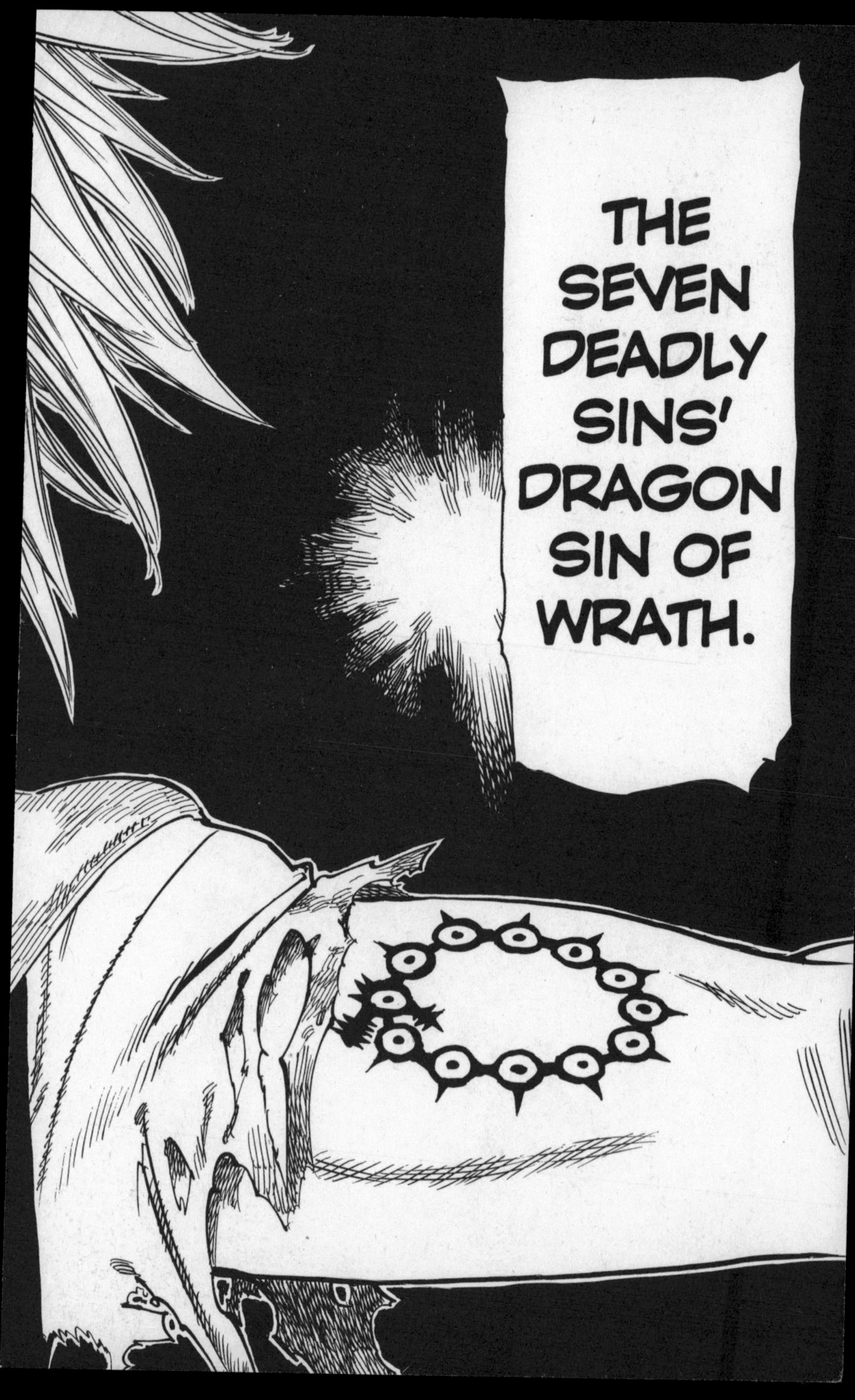
THE SEVEN DEADLY SINS' DRAGON SIN OF WRATH.

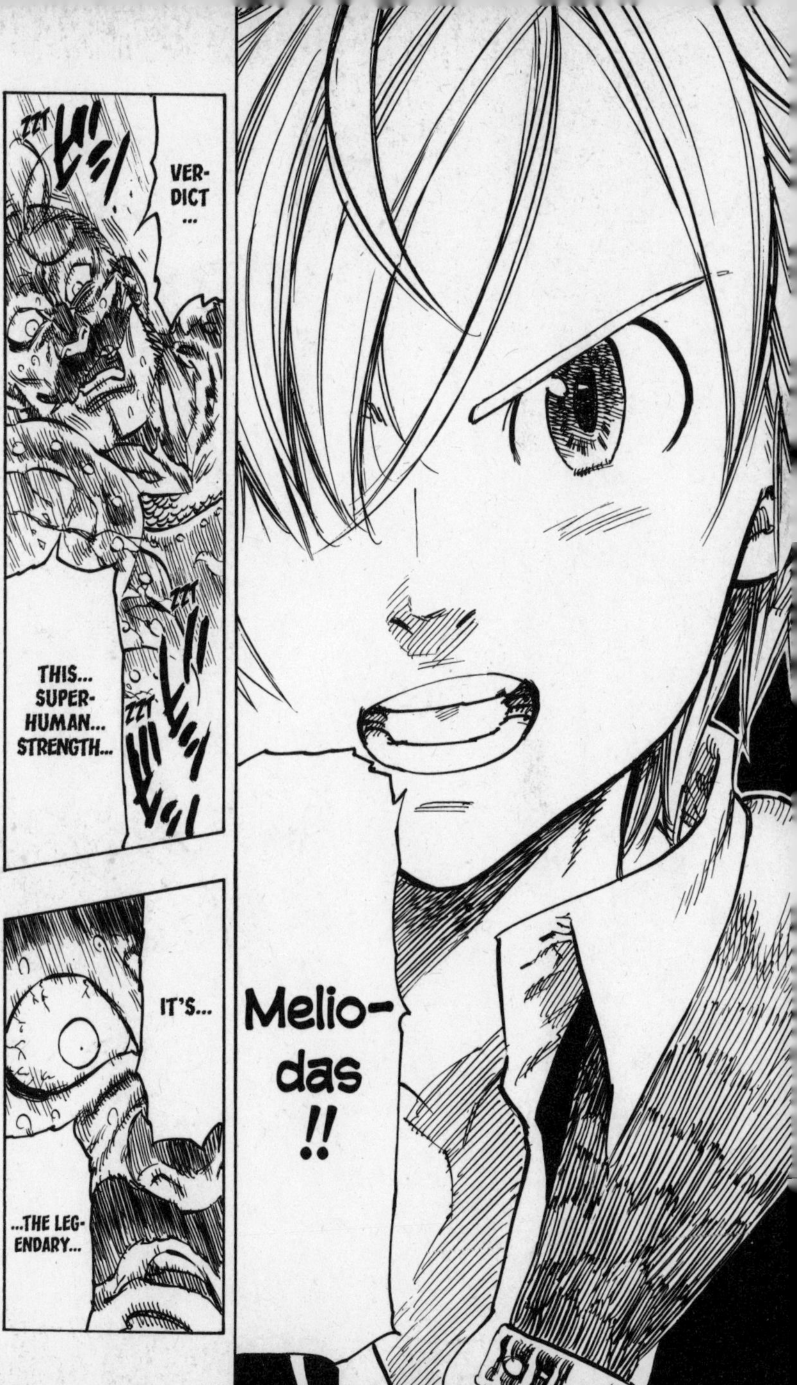
ZZT
VER-DICT...
ZZT
ZZT
THIS... SUPER-HUMAN... STRENGTH...
IT'S...
...THE LEG-ENDARY...
Melio-das!!

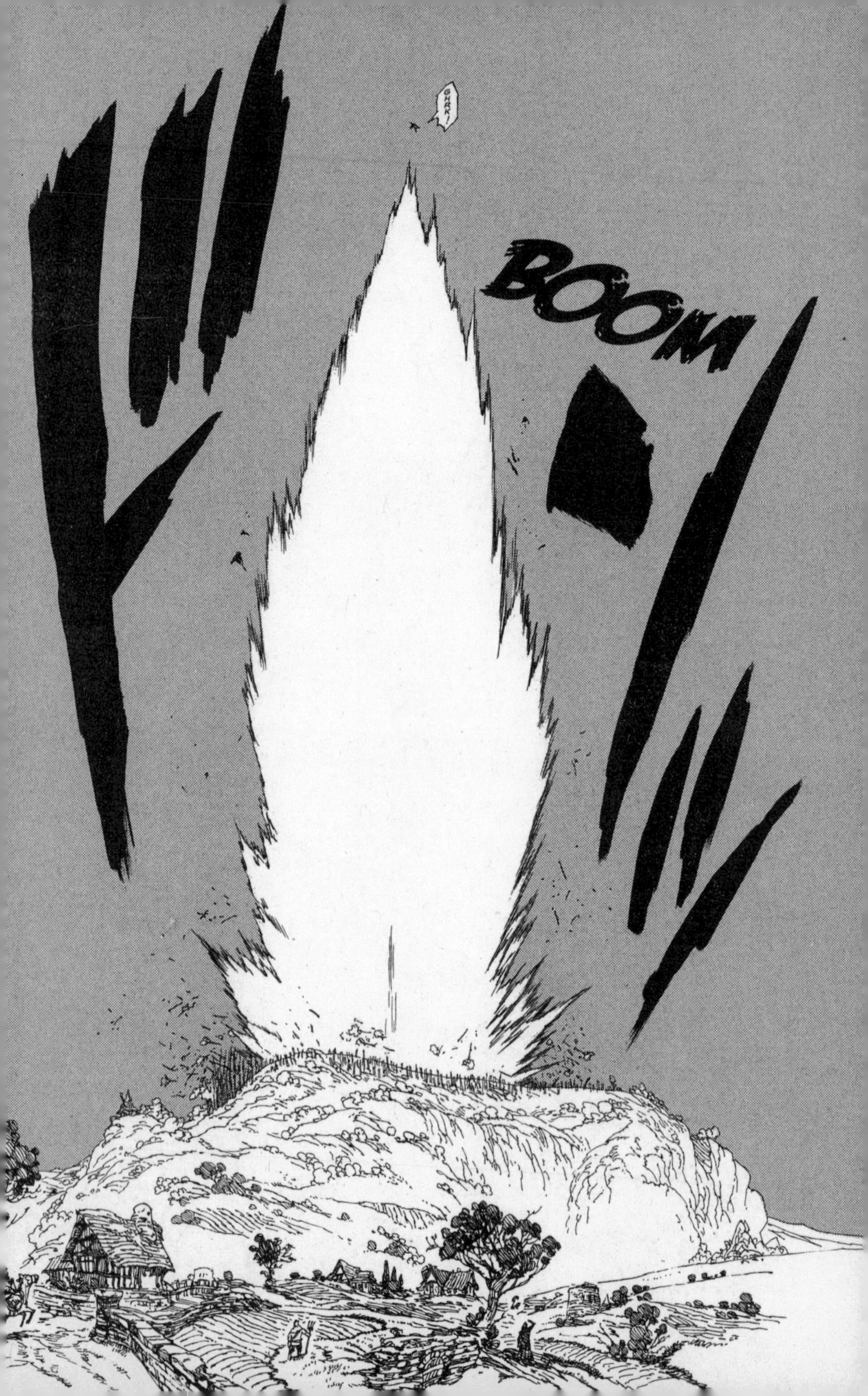
GHRK!
BOOM

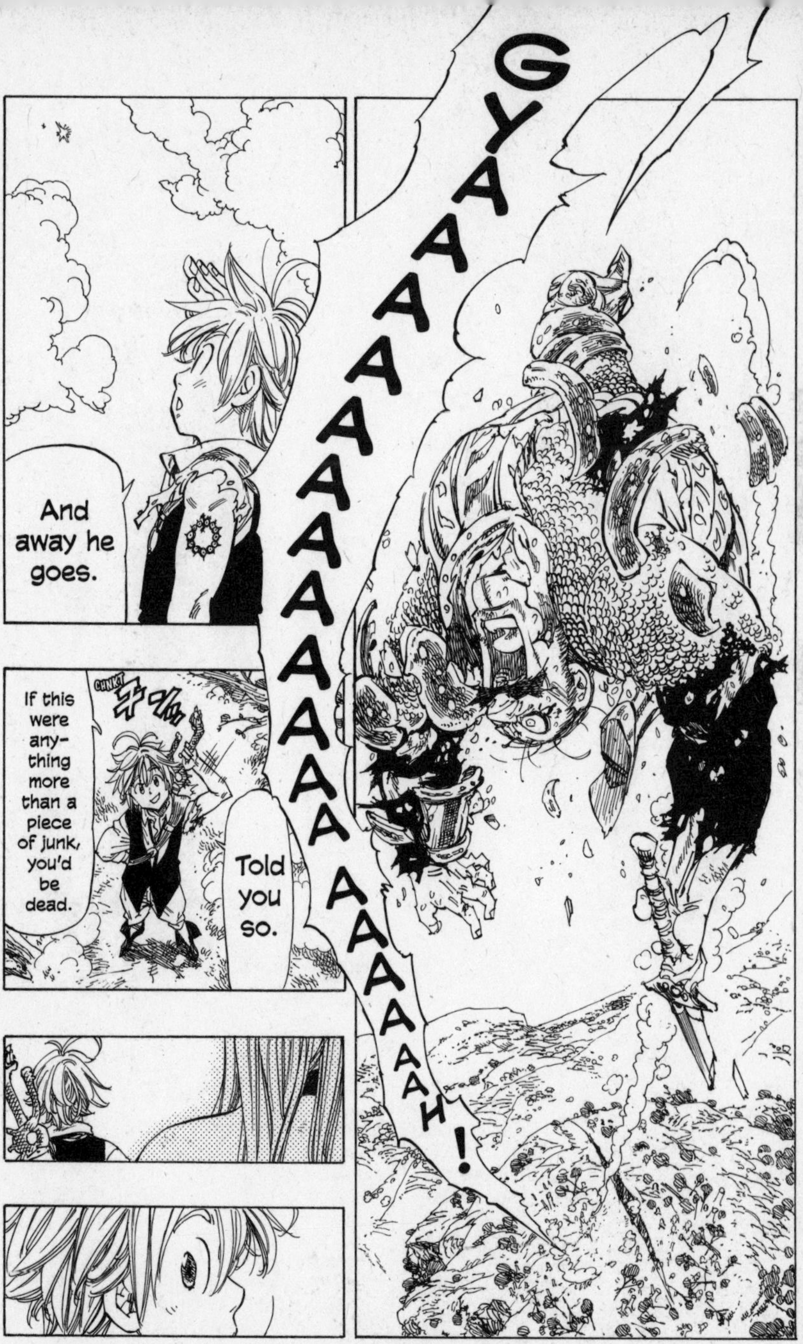
GYAAAAAAAAAAAAAAAAAAAH!
And away he goes.
Told you so.
CHNK
If this were anything more than a piece of junk, you'd be dead.

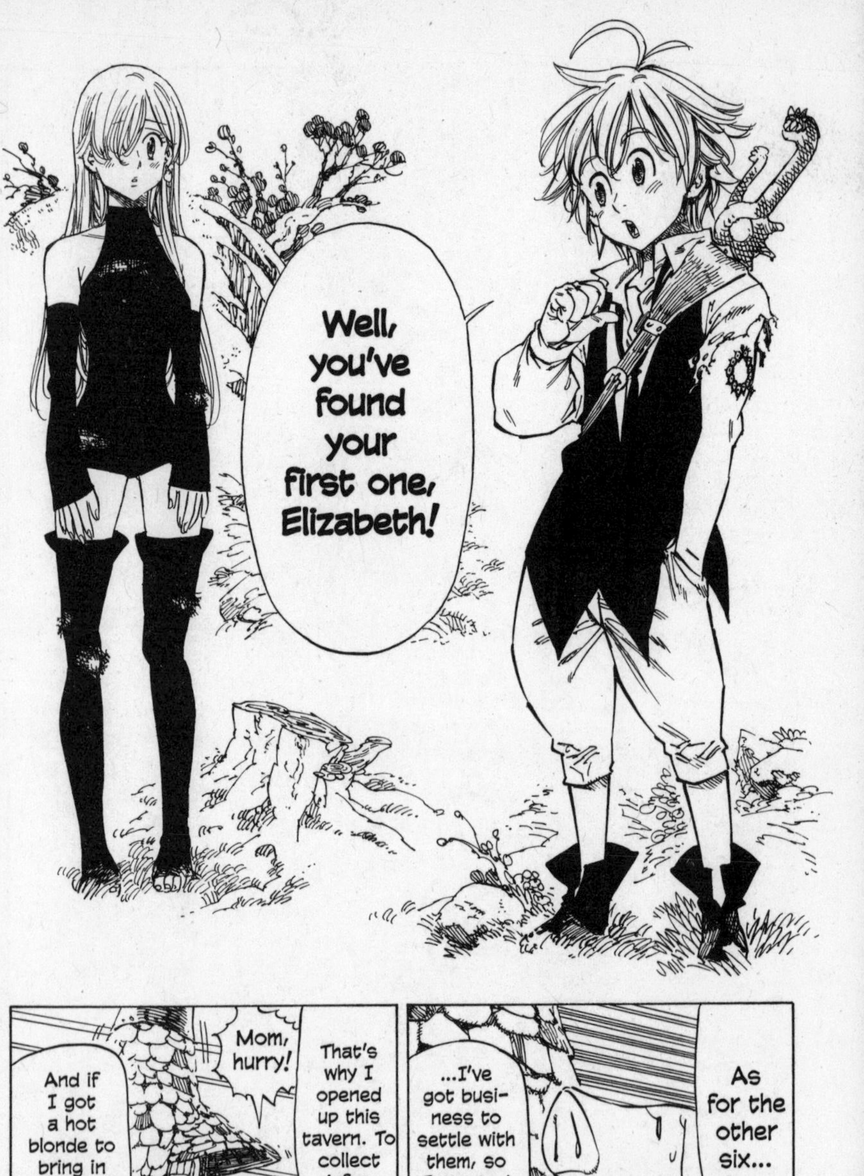
Well, you've found your first one, Elizabeth!
As for the other six...
...I've got business to settle with them, so I started looking for them recently, too.
That's why I opened up this tavern. To collect information.
Mom, hurry!
And if I got a hot blonde to bring in more customers, I'd get even more info.

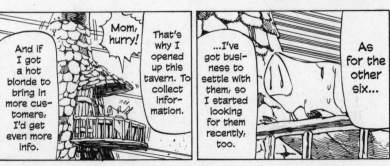

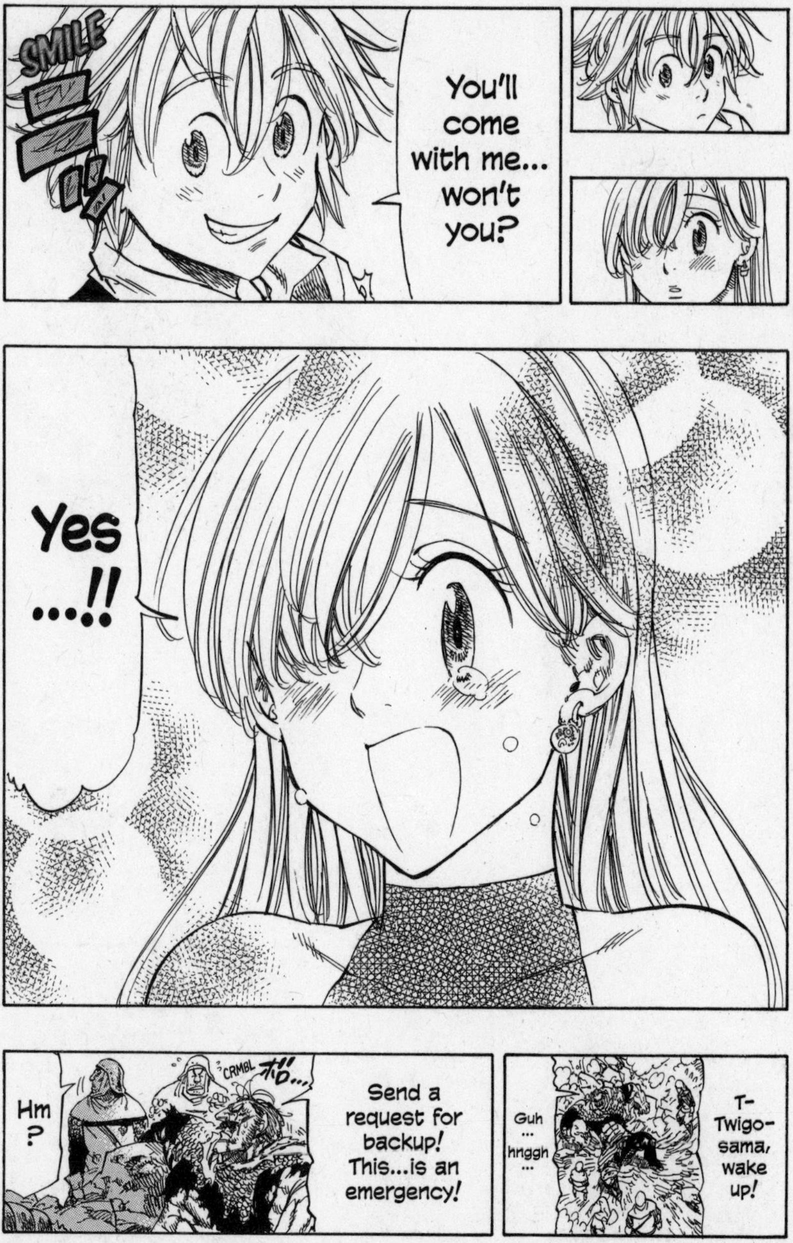
SMILE
You'll come with me... won't you?
Yes ...!!
T-Twigo-sama, wake up!
Guh ... hnggh ...
Send a request for backup! This...is an emergency!
CRMBL
Hm?

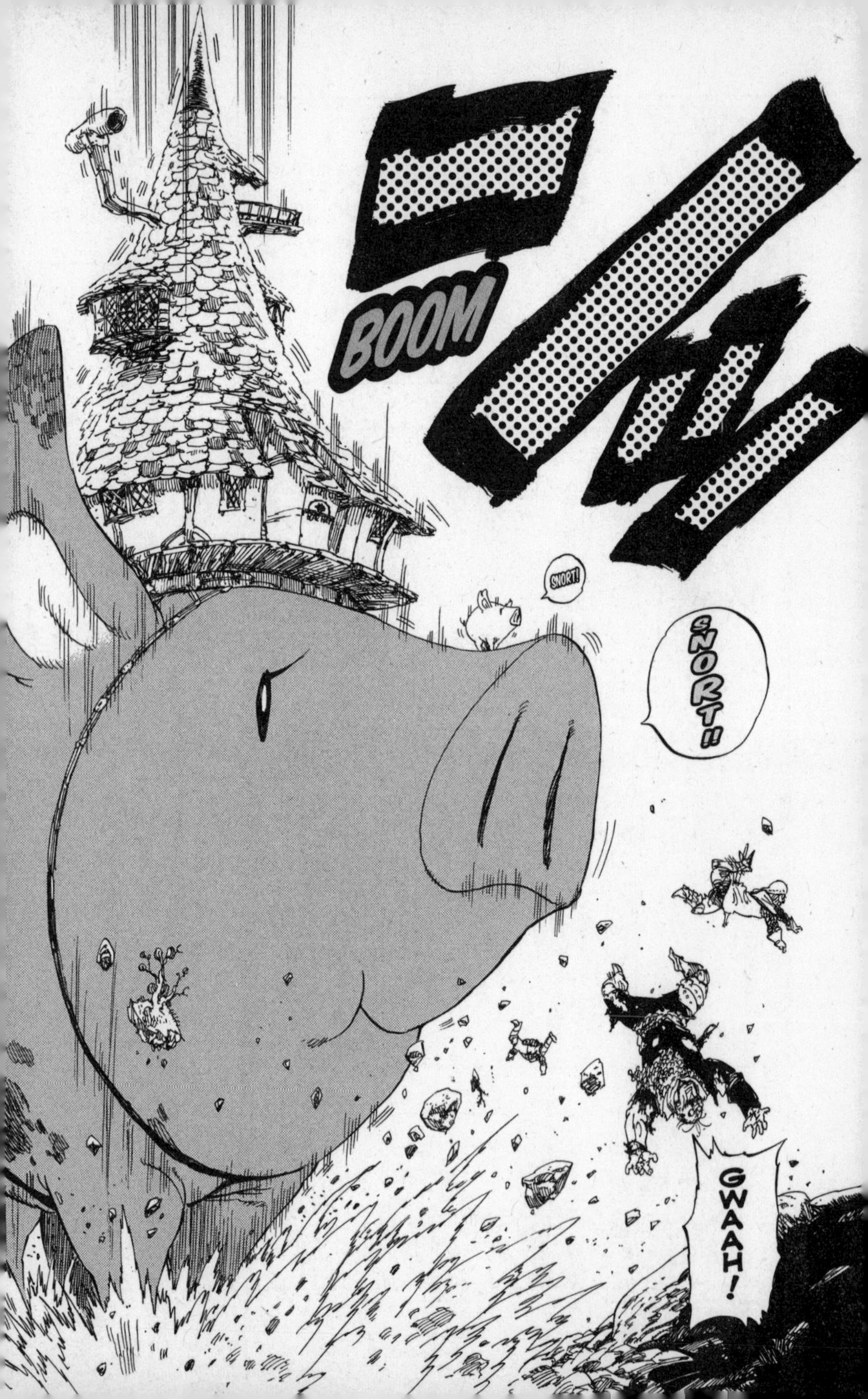
BOOM
SNORT!!
SNORT!
GWAAH!

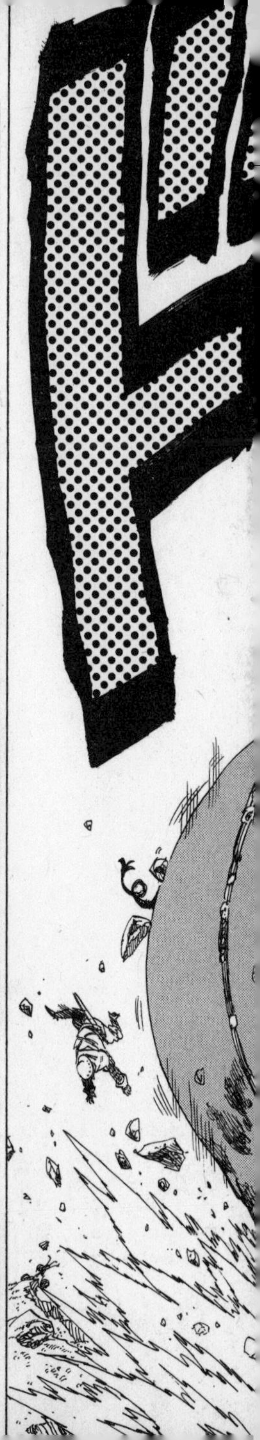
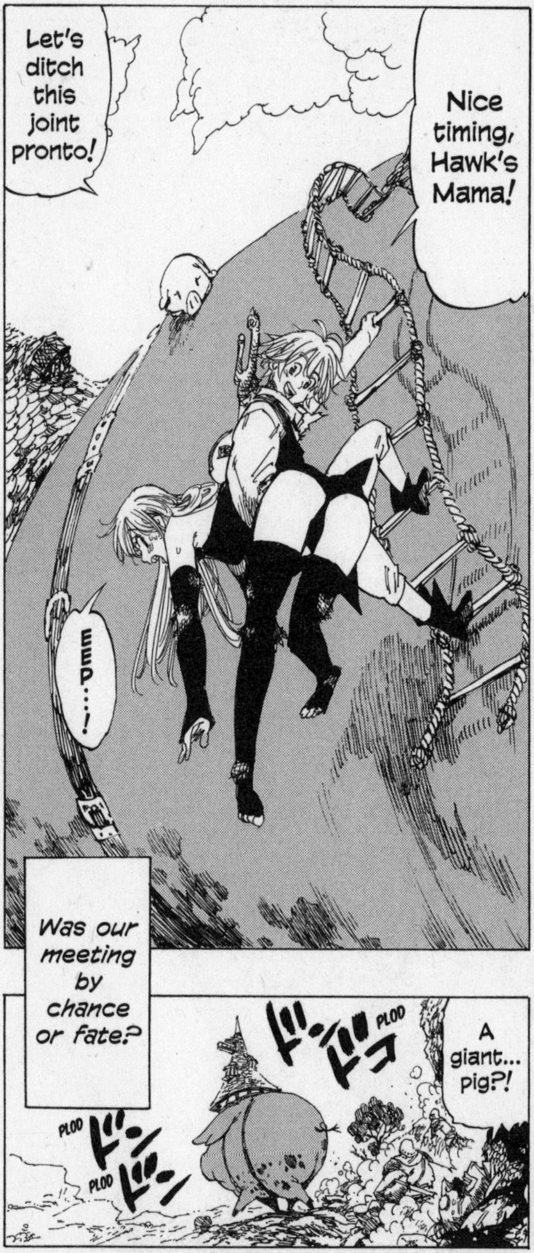
Nice timing, Hawk's Mama!
Let's ditch this joint pronto!
EEP...!
Was our meeting by chance or fate?
A giant... pig?!
PLOO
PLOO
PLOO

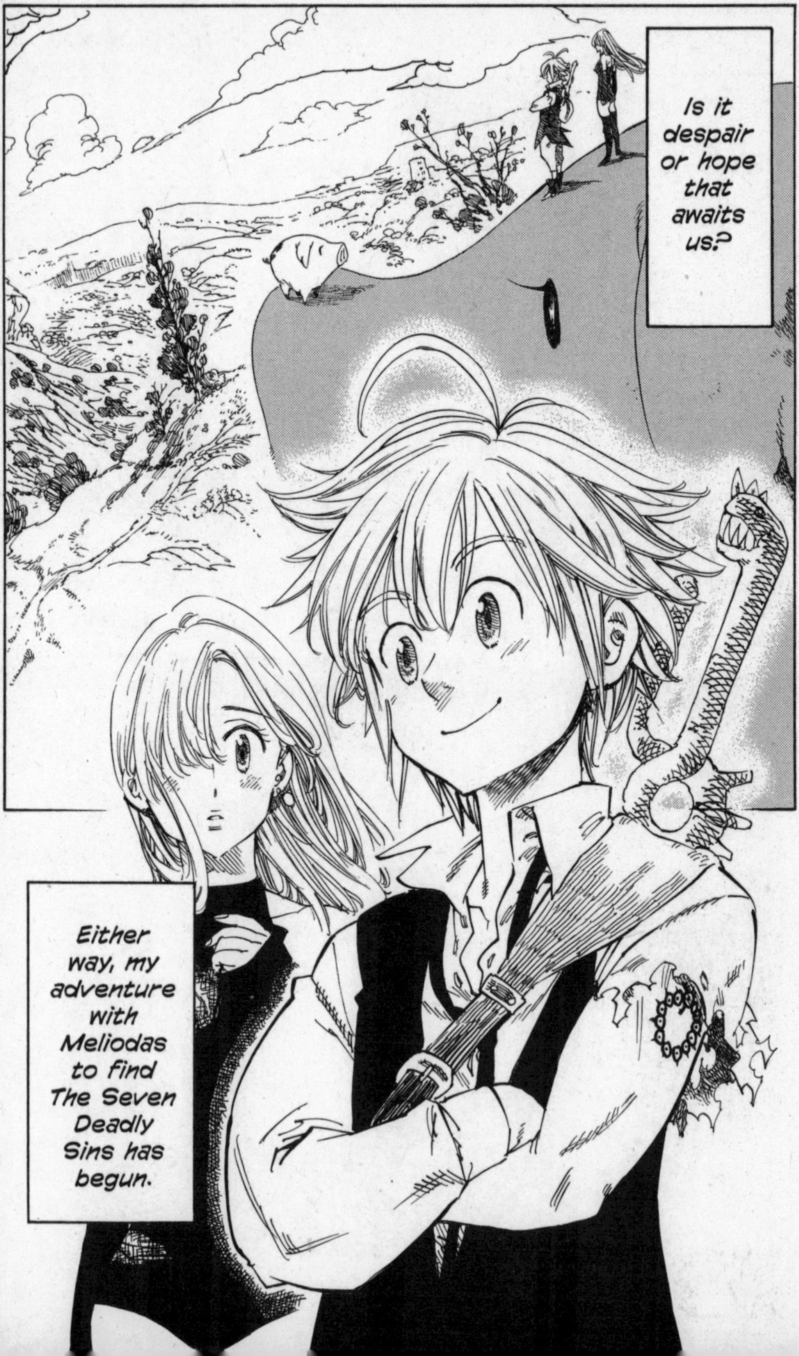
Is it despair or hope that awaits us?
Either way, my adventure with Meliodas to find The Seven Deadly Sins has begun.

Chapter 2 - The Holy Knight's Sword

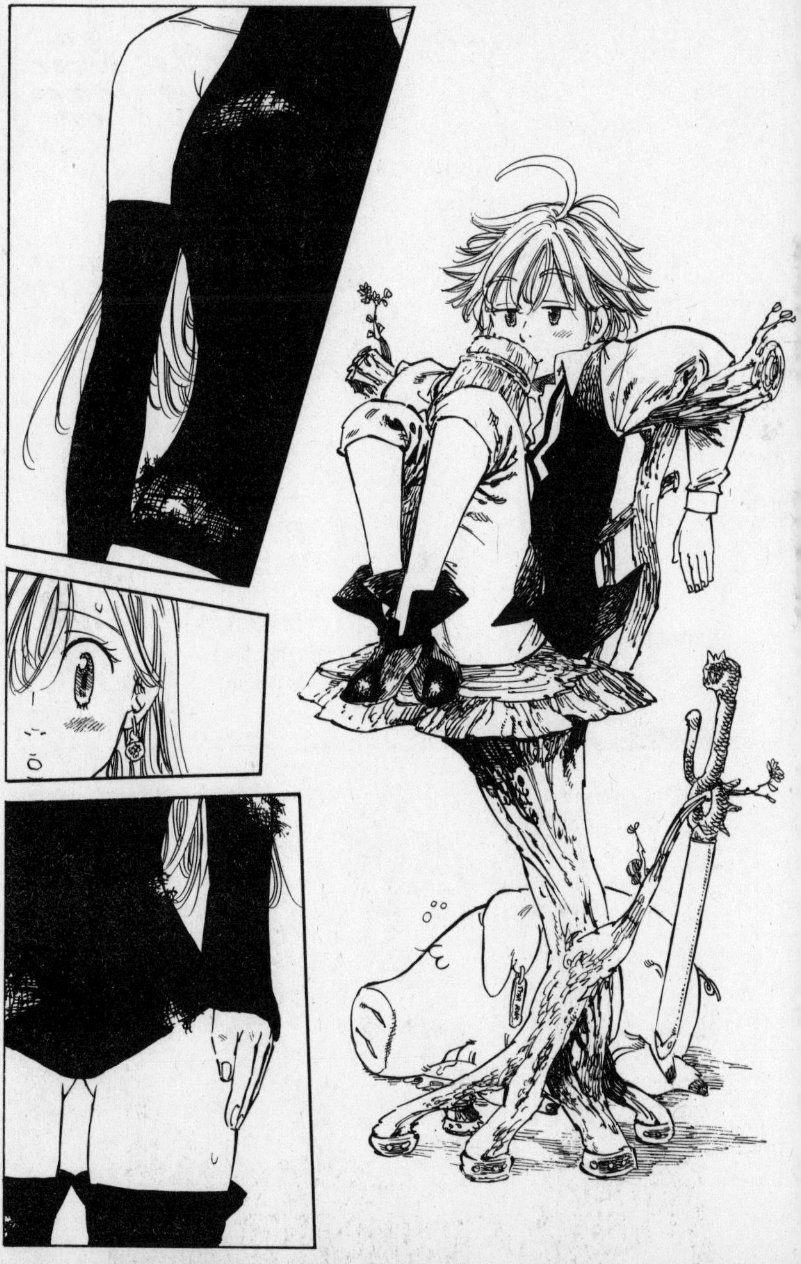

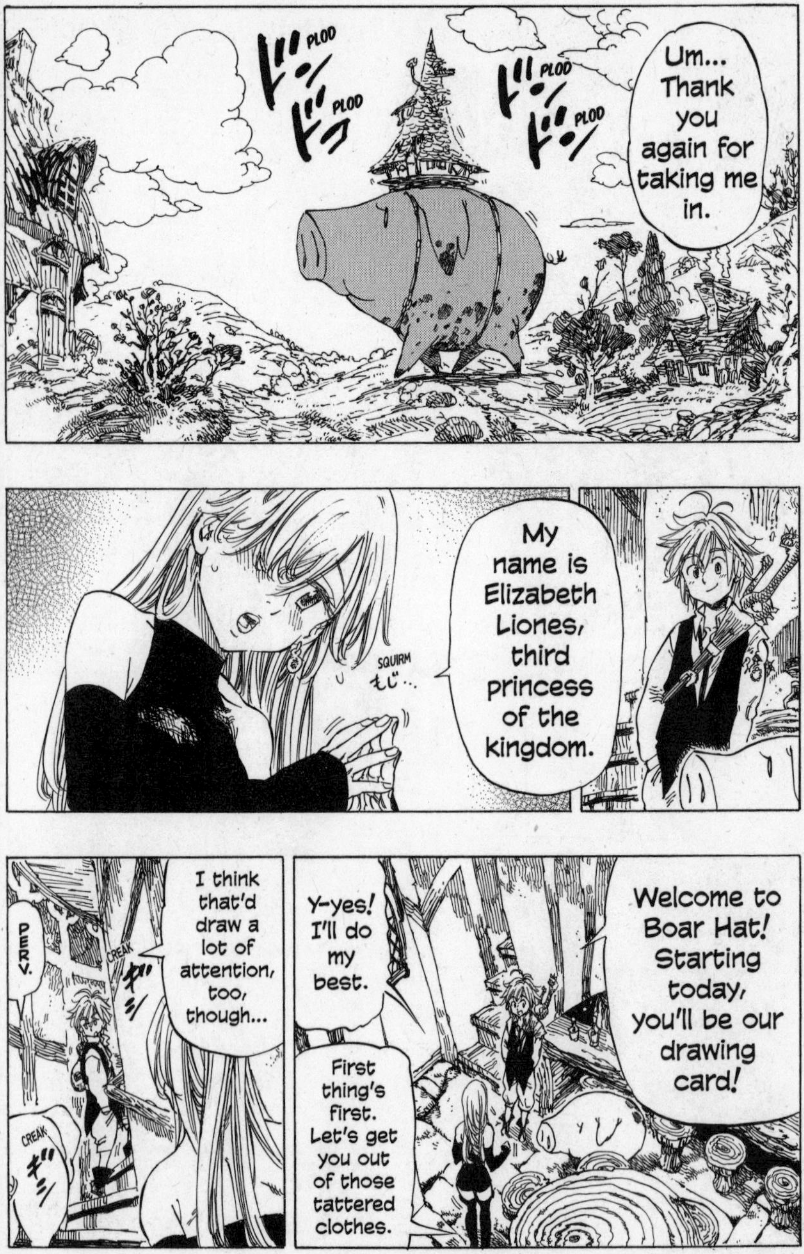
Um... Thank you again for taking me in.
PLOO
PLOO
PLOO
PLOO
My name is Elizabeth Liones, third princess of the kingdom.
SQUIRM
もじ…
Welcome to Boar Hat! Starting today, you'll be our drawing card!
Y-yes! I'll do my best.
First thing's first. Let's get you out of those tattered clothes.
I think that'd draw a lot of attention, too, though...
CREAK
PERV.
CREAK

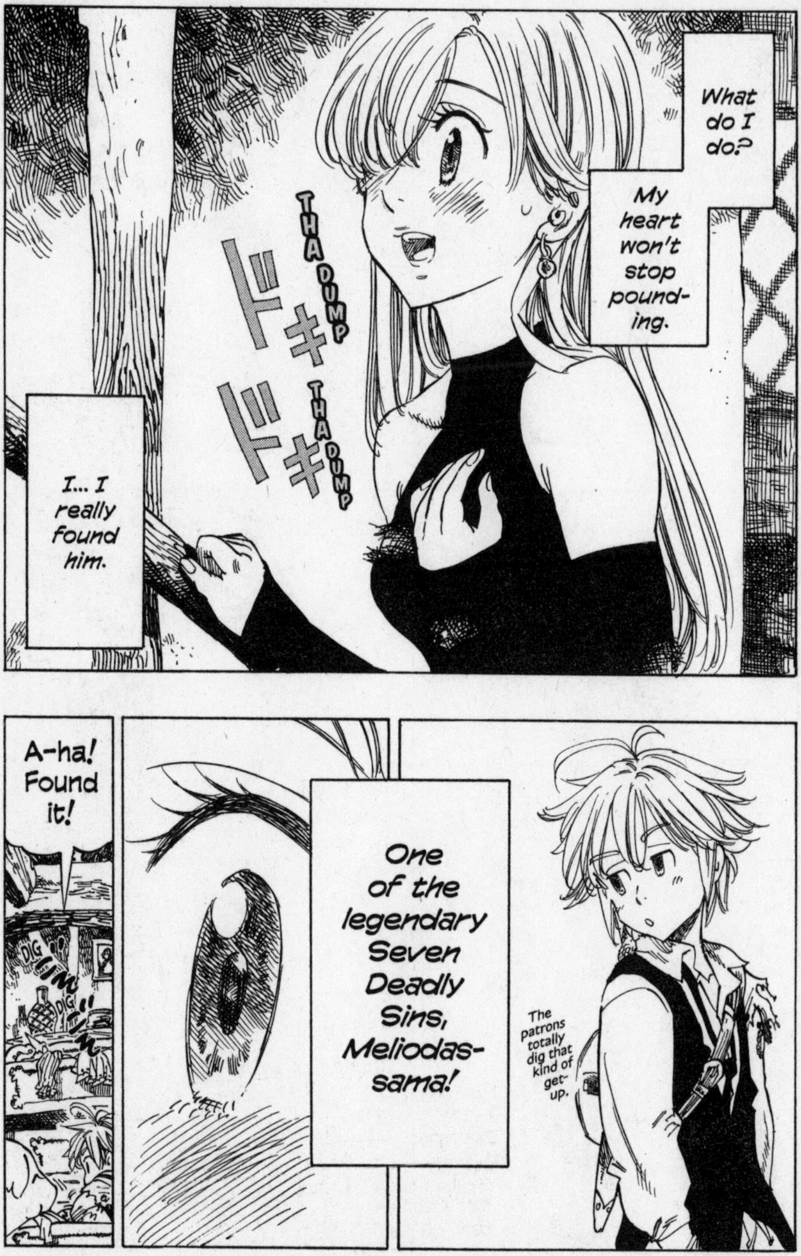
What do I do?
My heart won't stop pound-ing.
THA DUMP
ドキ
THA DUMP
ドキ
I... I really found him.
The patrons totally dig that kind of get-up.
One of the legendary Seven Deadly Sins, Meliodas-sama!
A-ha! Found it!
DIG
DIG

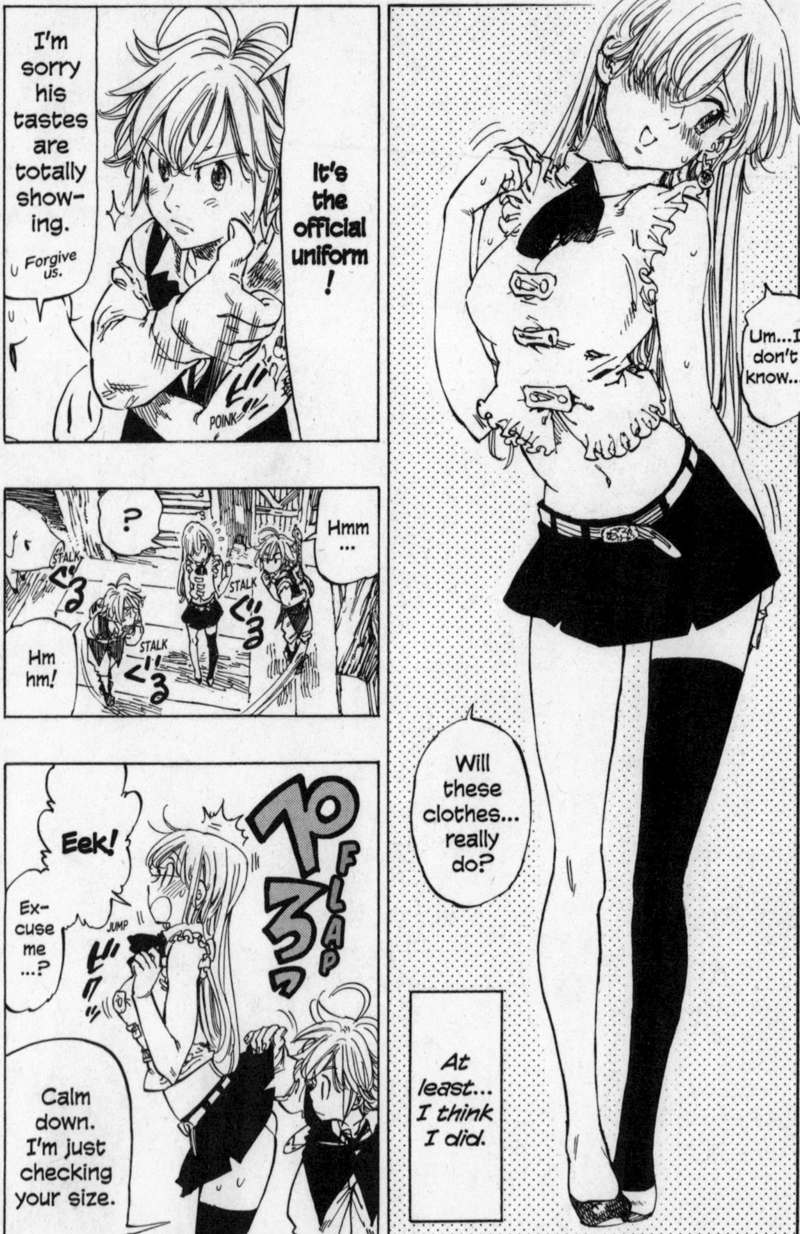

Um...I don't know...
Will these clothes... really do?
At least... I think I did.
It's the official uniform!
I'm sorry his tastes are totally show-ing.
Forgive us.
POINK
Hmm ...
STALK
?
STALK
Hm hm!
STALK
FLAP
Eek!
JUMP
Ex-cuse me ...?
Calm down. I'm just checking your size.

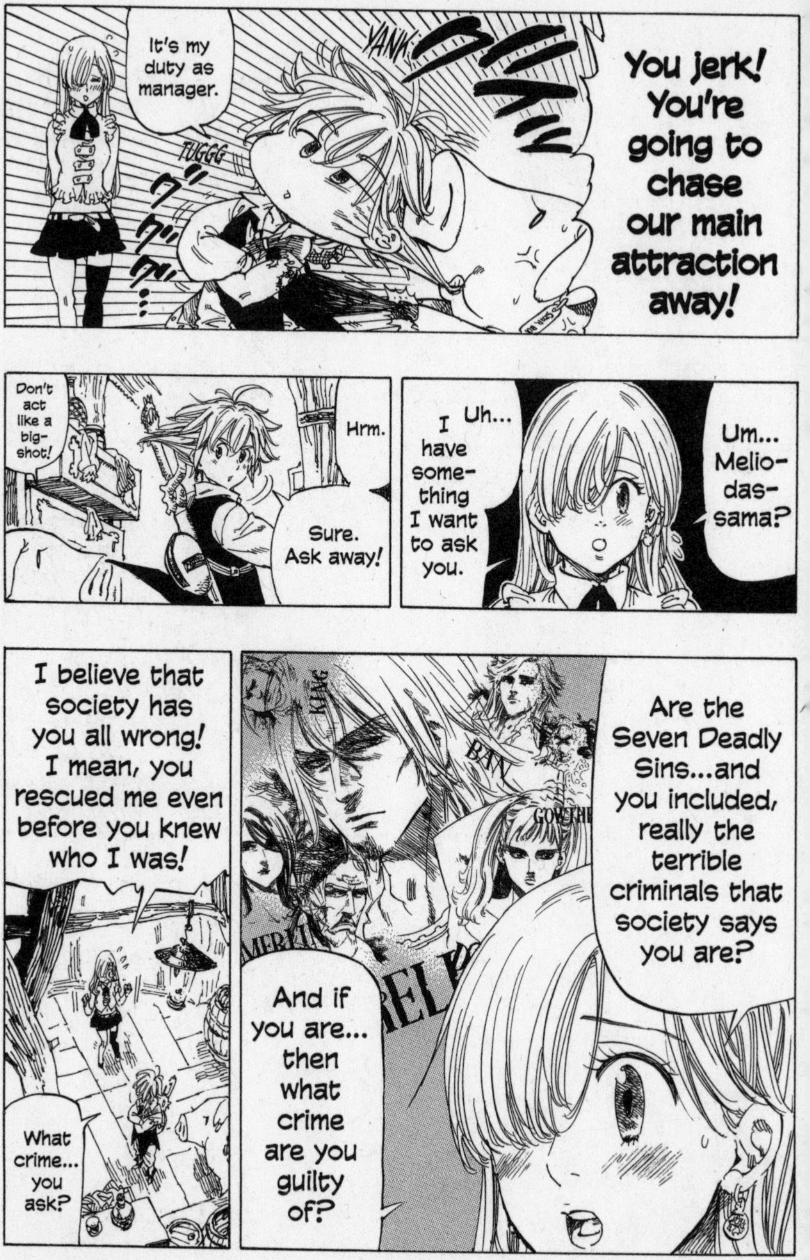

You jerk! You're going to chase our main attraction away!
YANK
TUGGG
It's my duty as manager.
Um... Melio-das-sama?
Uh... I have some-thing I want to ask you.
Hrm.
Sure. Ask away!
Don't act like a big-shot!
Are the Seven Deadly Sins...and you included, really the terrible criminals that society says you are?
KING
BAN
And if you are... then what crime are you guilty of?
I believe that society has you all wrong! I mean, you rescued me even before you knew who I was!
What crime... you ask?

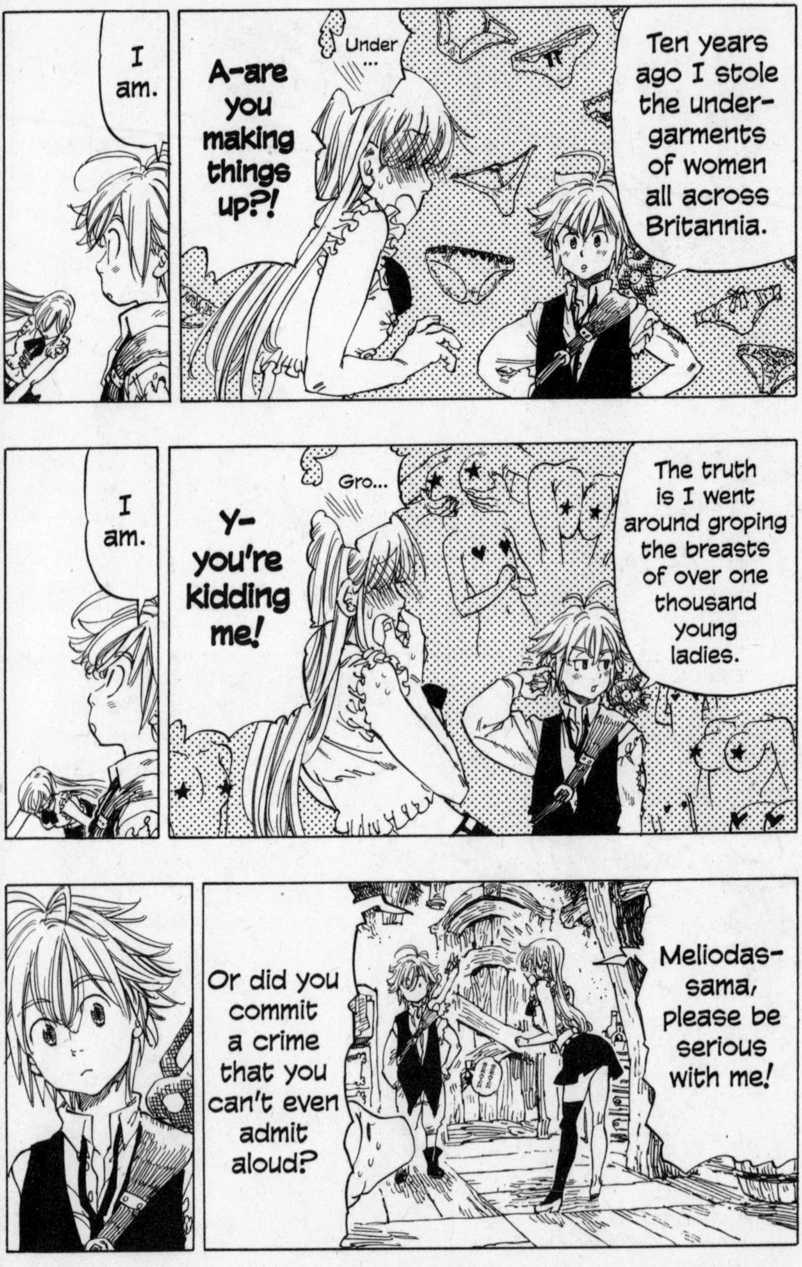
Ten years ago I stole the under-garments of women all across Britannia.
Under...
A-are you making things up?!
I am.
The truth is I went around groping the breasts of over one thousand young ladies.
Gro...
Y-you're kidding me!
I am.
Meliodas-sama, please be serious with me!
Or did you commit a crime that you can't even admit aloud?

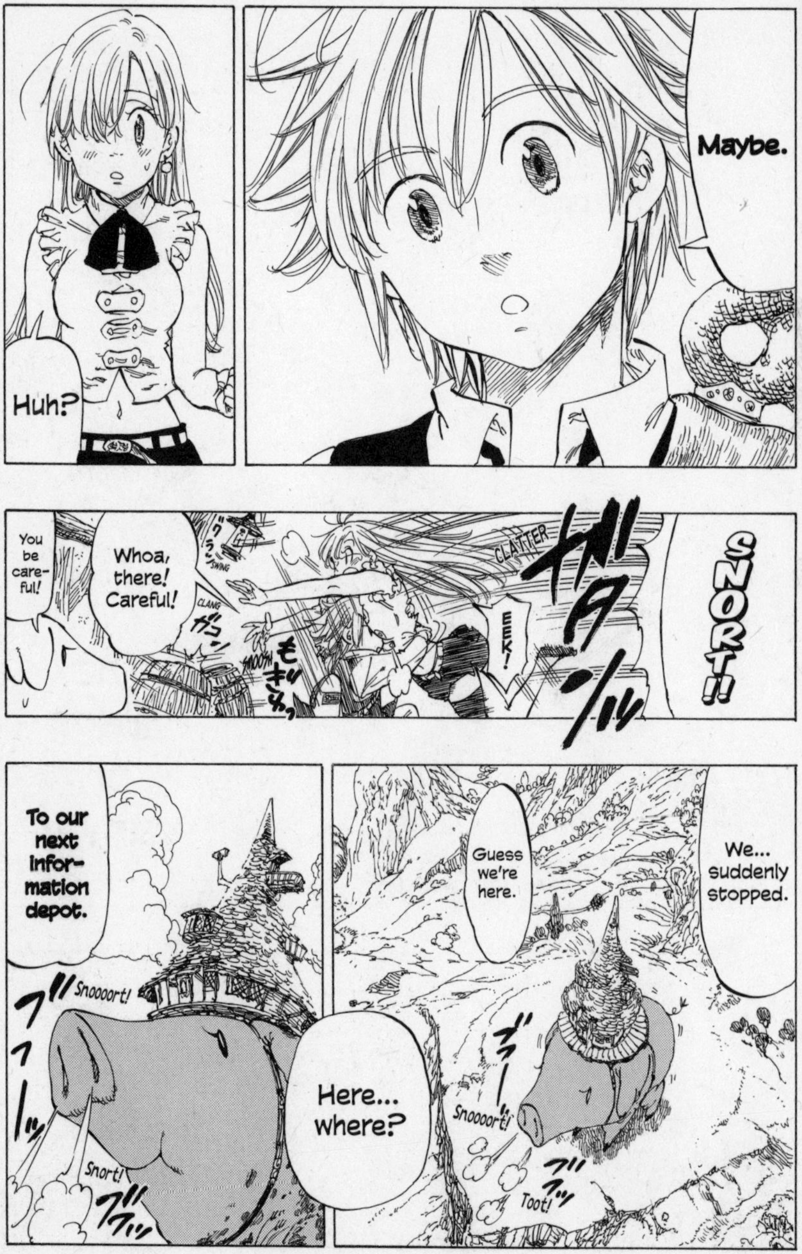
Maybe.
Huh?
SNORT!!
CLATTER
EEK!
SMOOSH
SWING
CLANG
Whoa, there! Careful!
You be careful!
We... suddenly stopped.
Guess we're here.
Snoooort!
Toot!
To our next information depot.
Here... where?
Snoooort!
Snort!

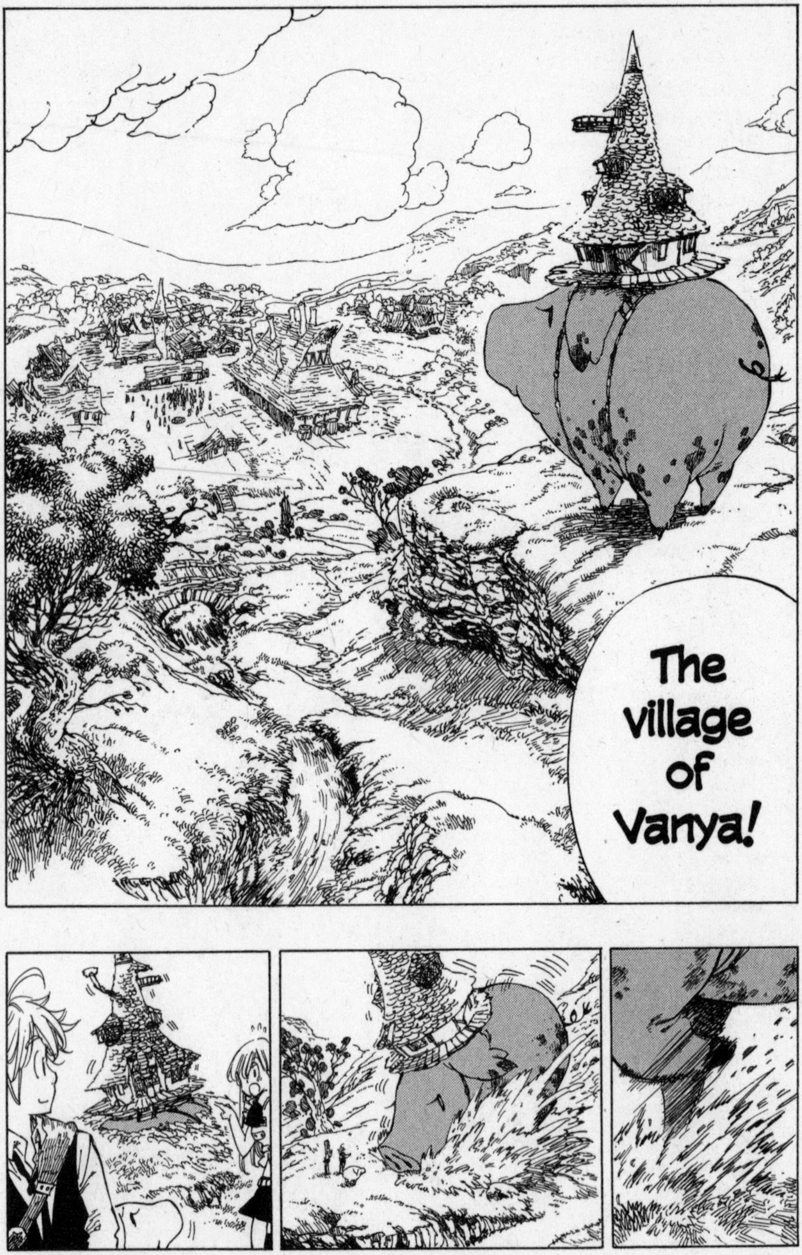
The village of Vanya!

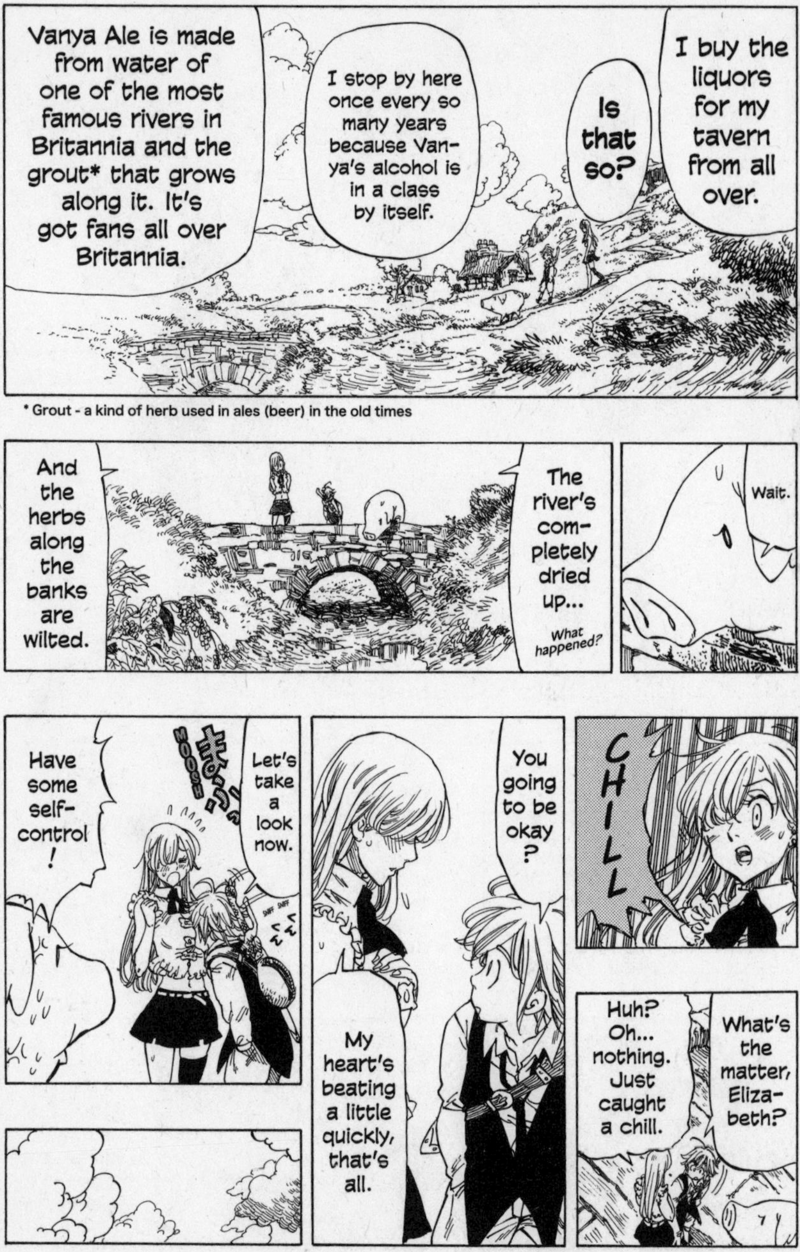
I buy the liquors for my tavern from all over.
Is that so?
I stop by here once every so many years because Vanya's alcohol is in a class by itself.
Vanya Ale is made from water of one of the most famous rivers in Britannia and the grout* that grows along it. It's got fans all over Britannia.
Wait.
The river's completely dried up...
What happened?
And the herbs along the banks are wilted.
CHILL
What's the matter, Elizabeth?
Huh? Oh... nothing. Just caught a chill.
You going to be okay?
My heart's beating a little quickly, that's all.
Let's take a look now.
MOOSH
SNIFF SNIFF
Have some self-control!

* Grout - a kind of herb used in ales (beer) in the old times

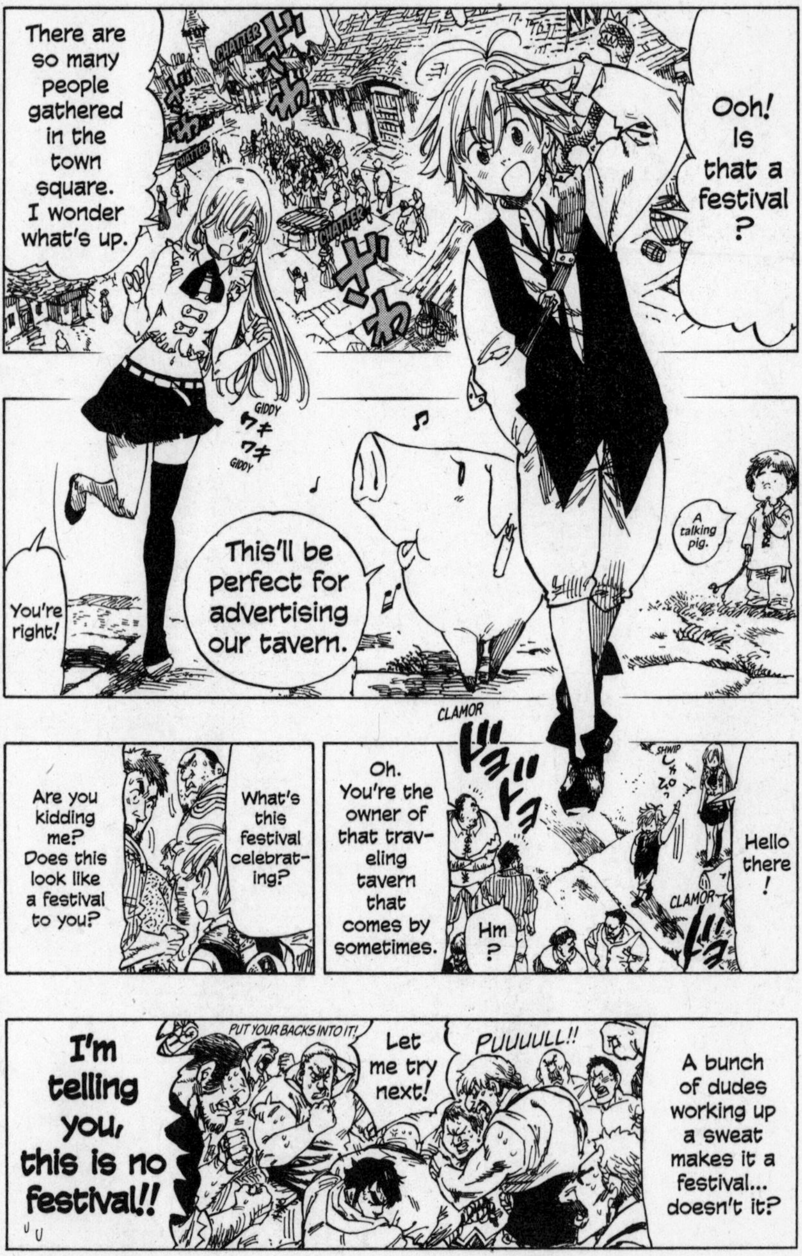
Ooh! Is that a festival?
There are so many people gathered in the town square. I wonder what's up.
CHATTER
CHATTER
CHATTER
A talking pig.
This'll be perfect for advertising our tavern.
GIDDY
GIDDY
You're right!
CLAMOR
Hello there!
SHWIP
CLAMOR
Hm?
Oh. You're the owner of that traveling tavern that comes by sometimes.
What's this festival celebrating?
Are you kidding me? Does this look like a festival to you?
A bunch of dudes working up a sweat makes it a festival... doesn't it?
PUUUULL!!
Let me try next!
PUT YOUR BACKS INTO IT!
I'm telling you, this is no festival!!

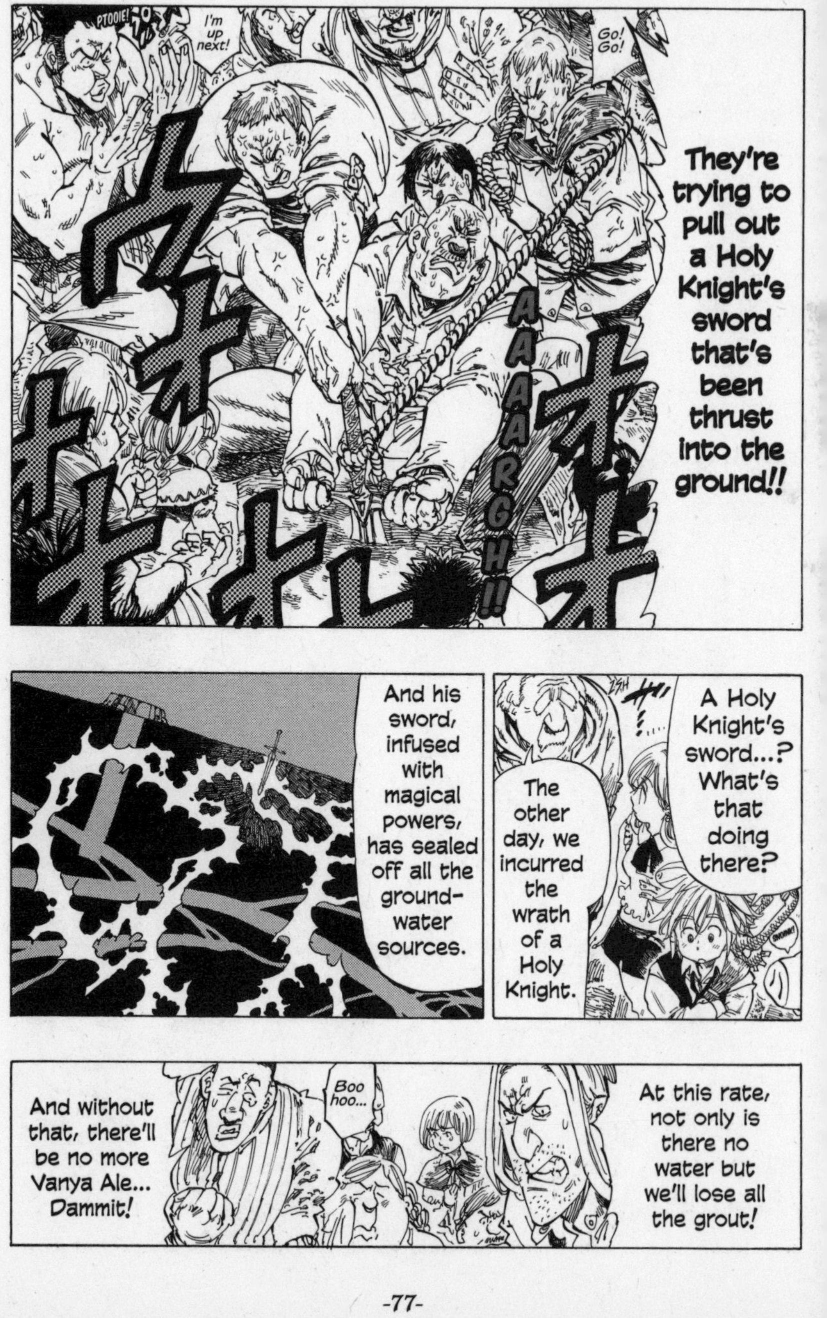

Go! Go!
They're trying to pull out a Holy Knight's sword that's been thrust into the ground!!
I'm up next!
PTOOIE!
AAAAARGH!!
A Holy Knight's sword...? What's that doing there?
The other day, we incurred the wrath of a Holy Knight.
And his sword, infused with magical powers, has sealed off all the groundwater sources.
At this rate, not only is there no water but we'll lose all the grout!
Boo hoo...
And without that, there'll be no more Vanya Ale... Dammit!

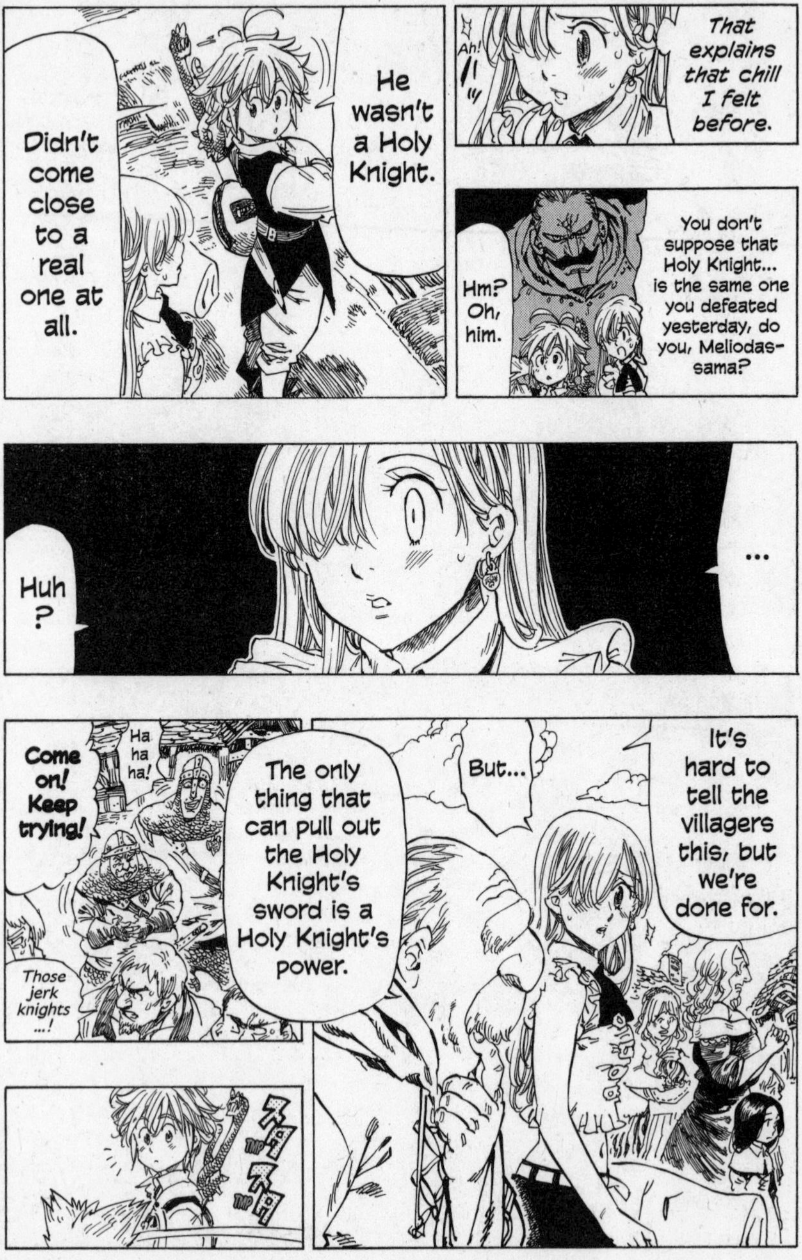

That explains that chill I felt before.
Ah!
You don't suppose that Holy Knight... is the same one you defeated yesterday, do you, Meliodas-sama?
Hm? Oh, him.
He wasn't a Holy Knight.
Didn't come close to a real one at all.
...
Huh?
It's hard to tell the villagers this, but we're done for.
But...
The only thing that can pull out the Holy Knight's sword is a Holy Knight's power.
Ha ha ha!
Come on! Keep trying!
Those jerk knights ...!
TMP
TMP

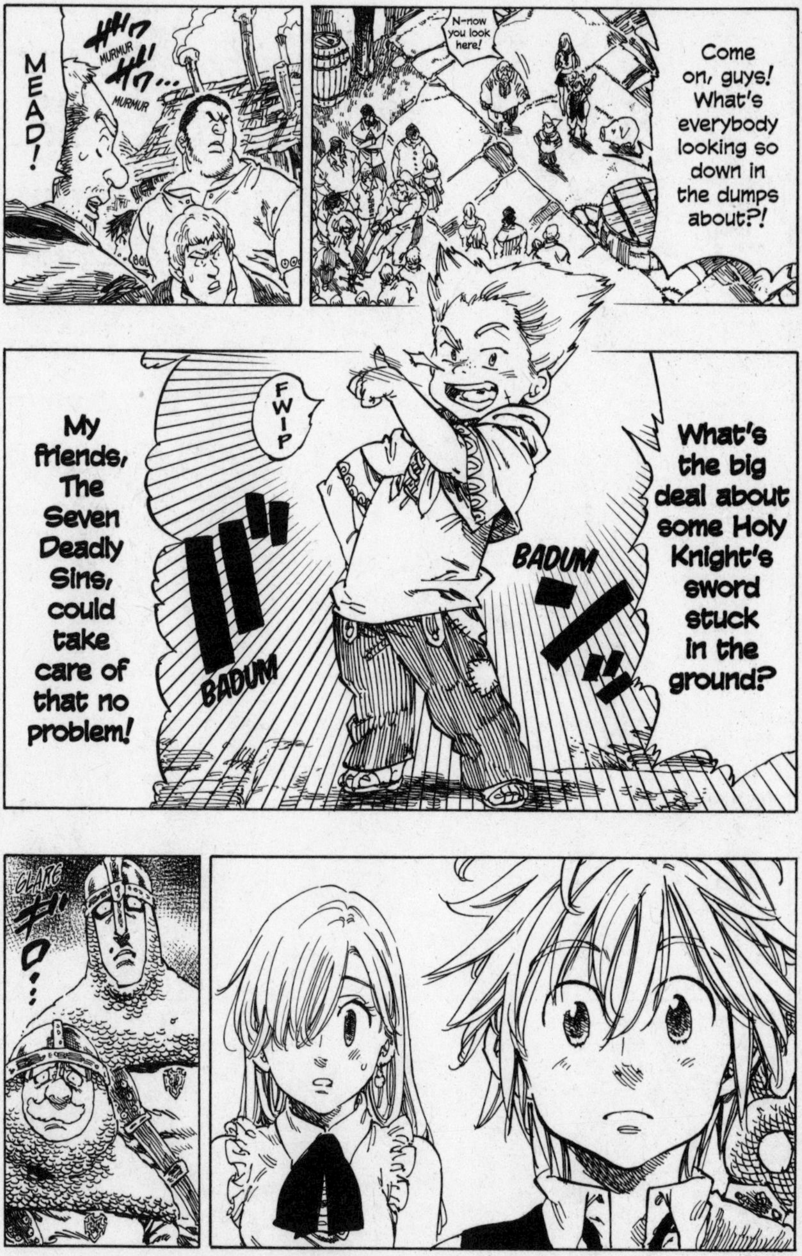

Come on, guys! What's everybody looking so down in the dumps about?!
N-now you look here!
MURMUR
MURMUR
MEAD!
What's the big deal about some Holy Knight's sword stuck in the ground?
BADUM
FWIP
My friends, The Seven Deadly Sins, could take care of that no problem!
BADUM
GLARE

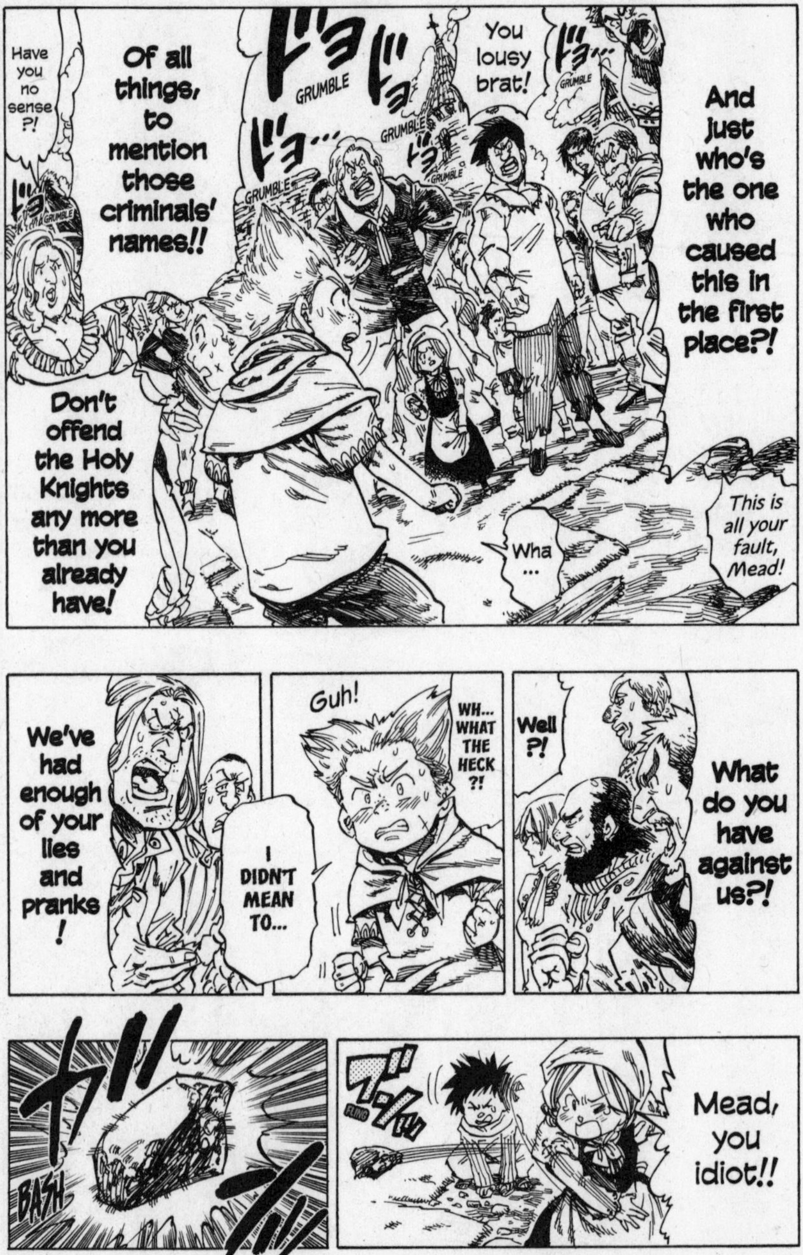
And just who's the one who caused this in the first place?!
You lousy brat!
GRUMBLE
GRUMBLE
GRUMBLE
GRUMBLE
Of all things, to mention those criminals' names!!
Have you no sense?!
GRUMBLE
This is all your fault, Mead!
Wha...
Don't offend the Holy Knights any more than you already have!
What do you have against us?!
Well?!
WH... WHAT THE HECK?!
Guh!
I DIDN'T MEAN TO...
We've had enough of your lies and pranks!
Mead, you idiot!!
FLING
BASH

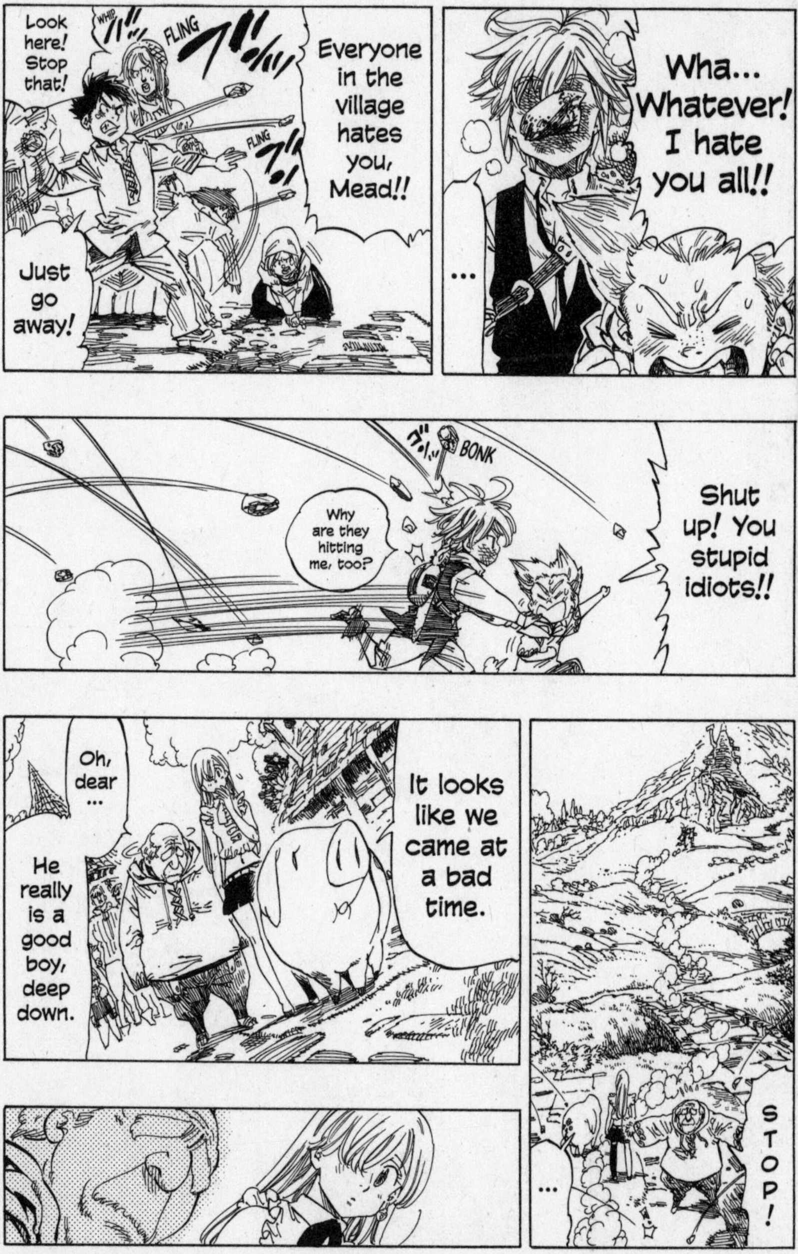
Wha... Whatever! I hate you all!!
...
Everyone in the village hates you, Mead!!
FLING
WHIP
Look here! Stop that!
FLING
Just go away!
Shut up! You stupid idiots!!
BONK
Why are they hitting me, too?
STOP!
...
It looks like we came at a bad time.
Oh, dear ...
He really is a good boy, deep down.

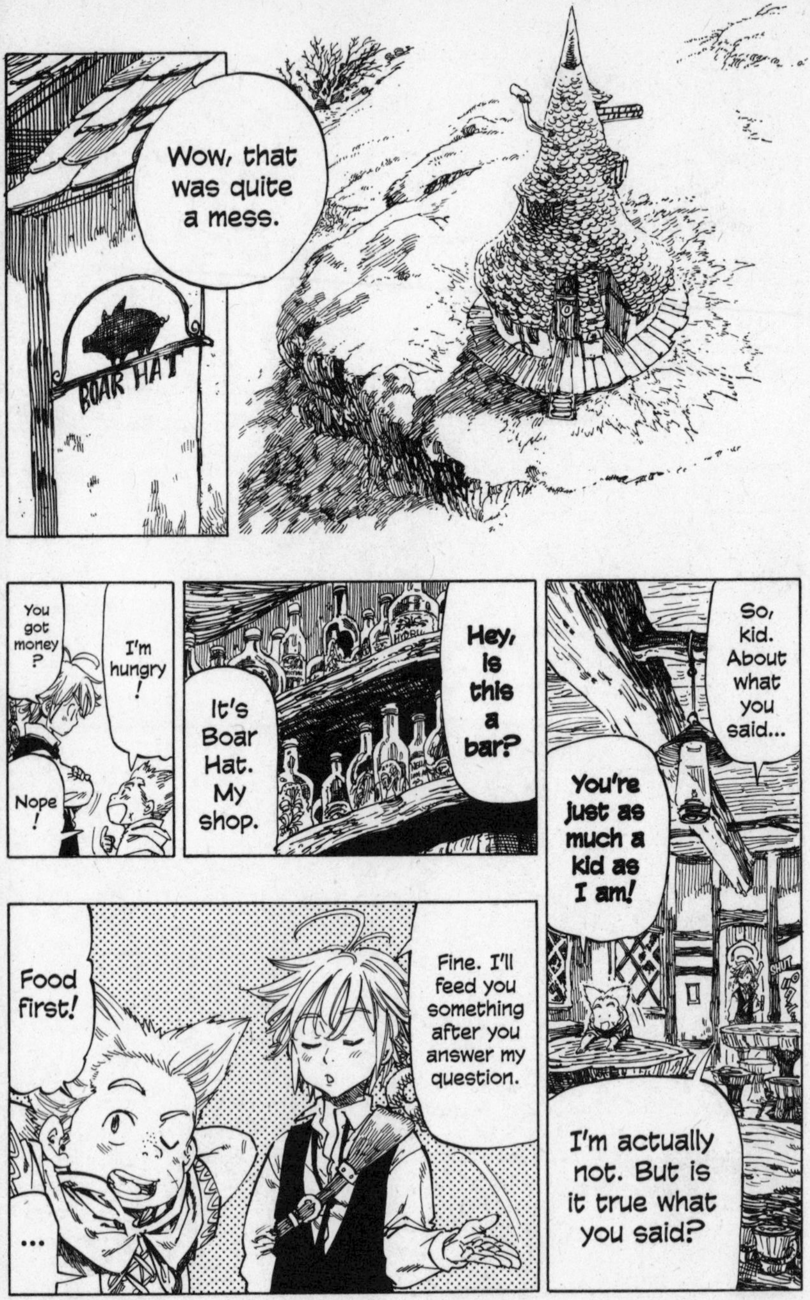
Wow, that was quite a mess.
BOAR HAT
So, kid. About what you said...
You're just as much a kid as I am!
SHUT
I'm actually not. But is it true what you said?
Hey, is this a bar?
It's Boar Hat. My shop.
I'm hungry!
You got money?
Nope!
Fine. I'll feed you something after you answer my question.
Food first!
...

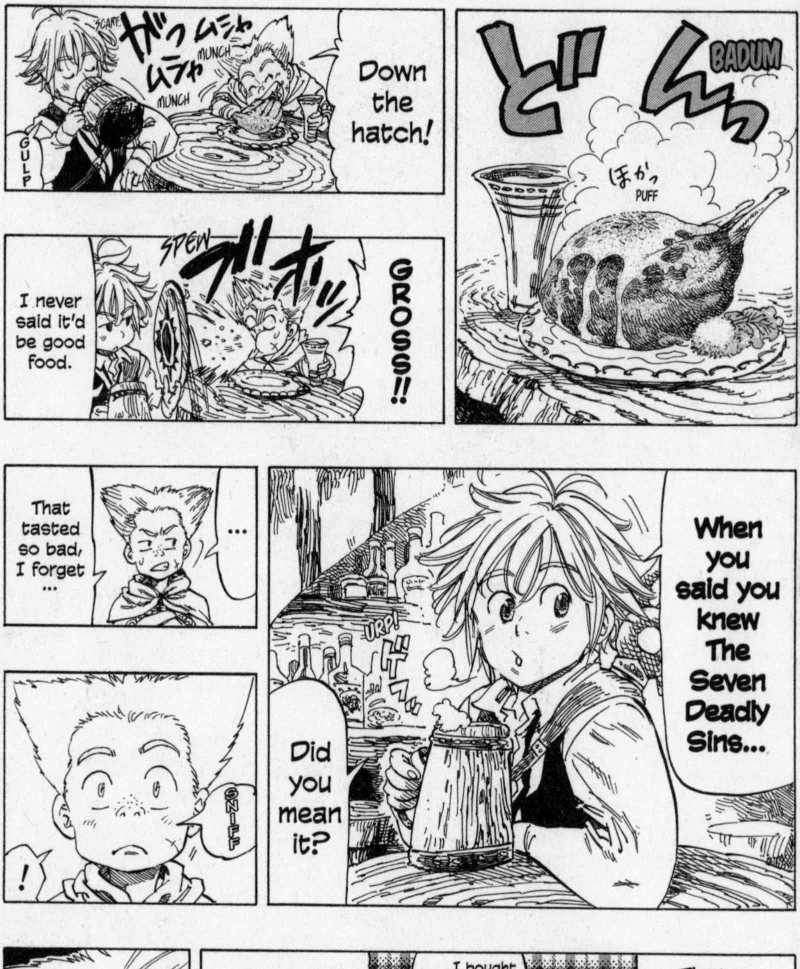
BADUM
PUFF
Down the hatch!
SCARF
MUNCH
MUNCH
GULP
GROSS!!
SPEW
I never said it'd be good food.
When you said you knew The Seven Deadly Sins...
URP!
Did you mean it?
...
That tasted so bad, I forget ...
SNIFF
!
That... That's the smell of Vanya Ale, isn't it?! Should a kid like you be drinking liquor like that?!
I bought that bottle last year.
And I'm no kid.
That's some good stuff, right?! It smells like apples and is sweet and full-bodied. It's the best ale around!!
That's what the adults say.

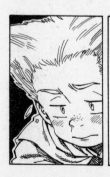

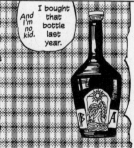

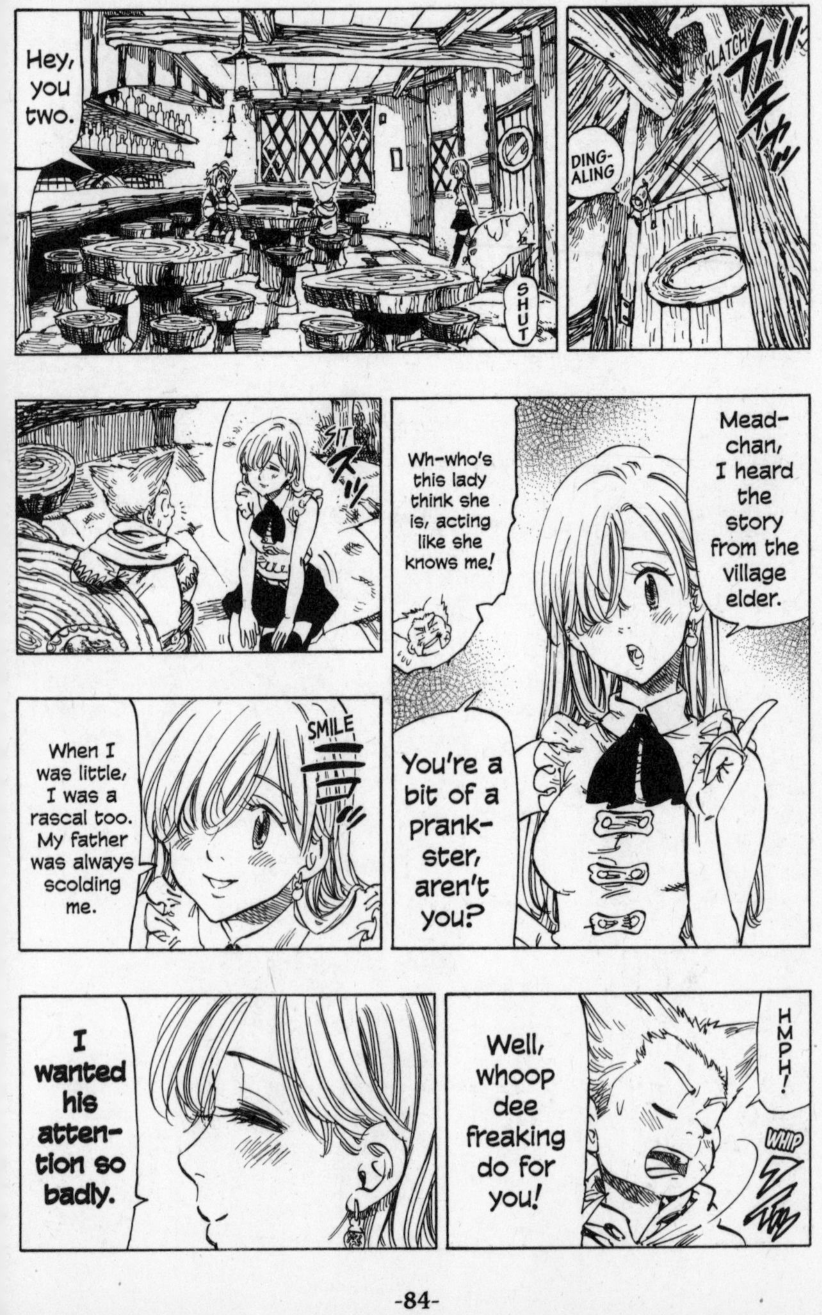
KLATCH
DING-ALING
SHUT
Hey, you two.
Mead-chan, I heard the story from the village elder.
Wh-who's this lady think she is, acting like she knows me!
You're a bit of a prank-ster, aren't you?
SIT
SMILE
When I was little, I was a rascal too. My father was always scolding me.
HMPH!
Well, whoop dee freaking do for you!
WHIP
I wanted his atten-tion so badly.

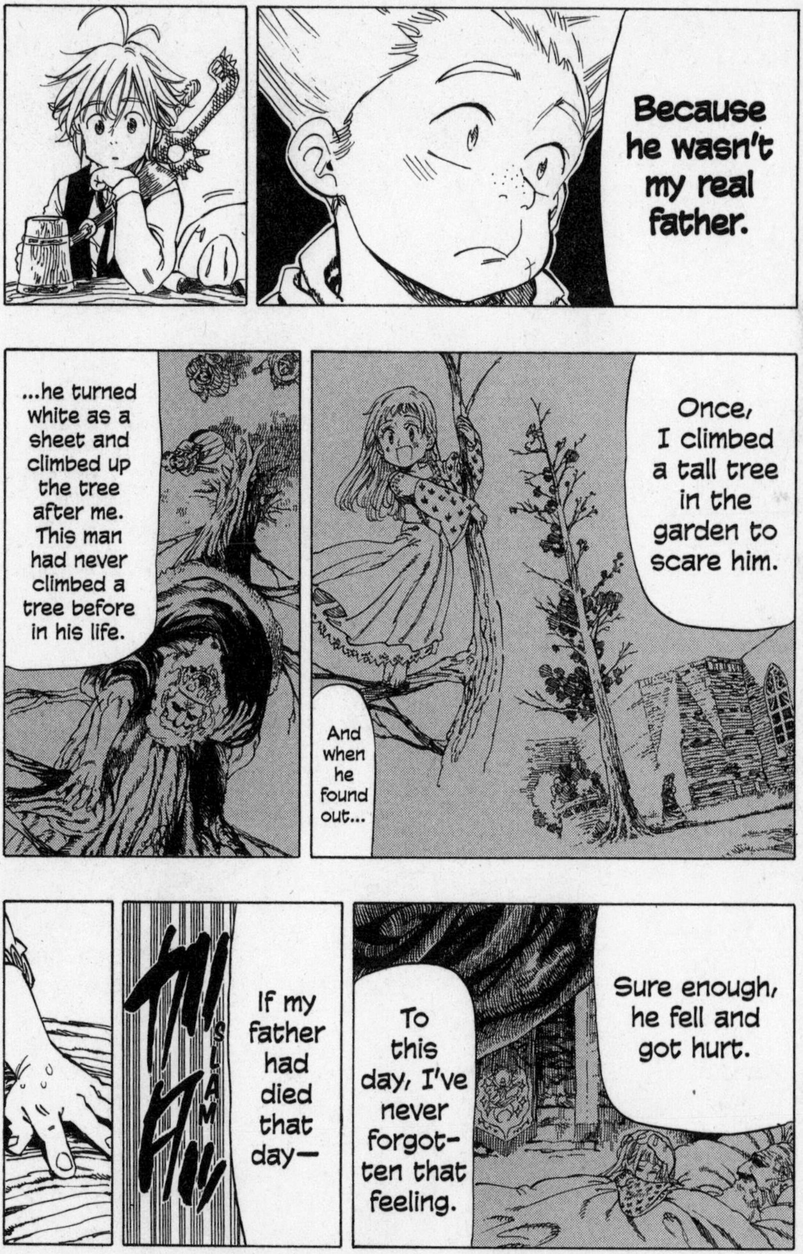
Because he wasn't my real father.
Once, I climbed a tall tree in the garden to scare him.
And when he found out...
...he turned white as a sheet and climbed up the tree after me. This man had never climbed a tree before in his life.
Sure enough, he fell and got hurt.
To this day, I've never forgotten that feeling.
If my father had died that day—
SLAM

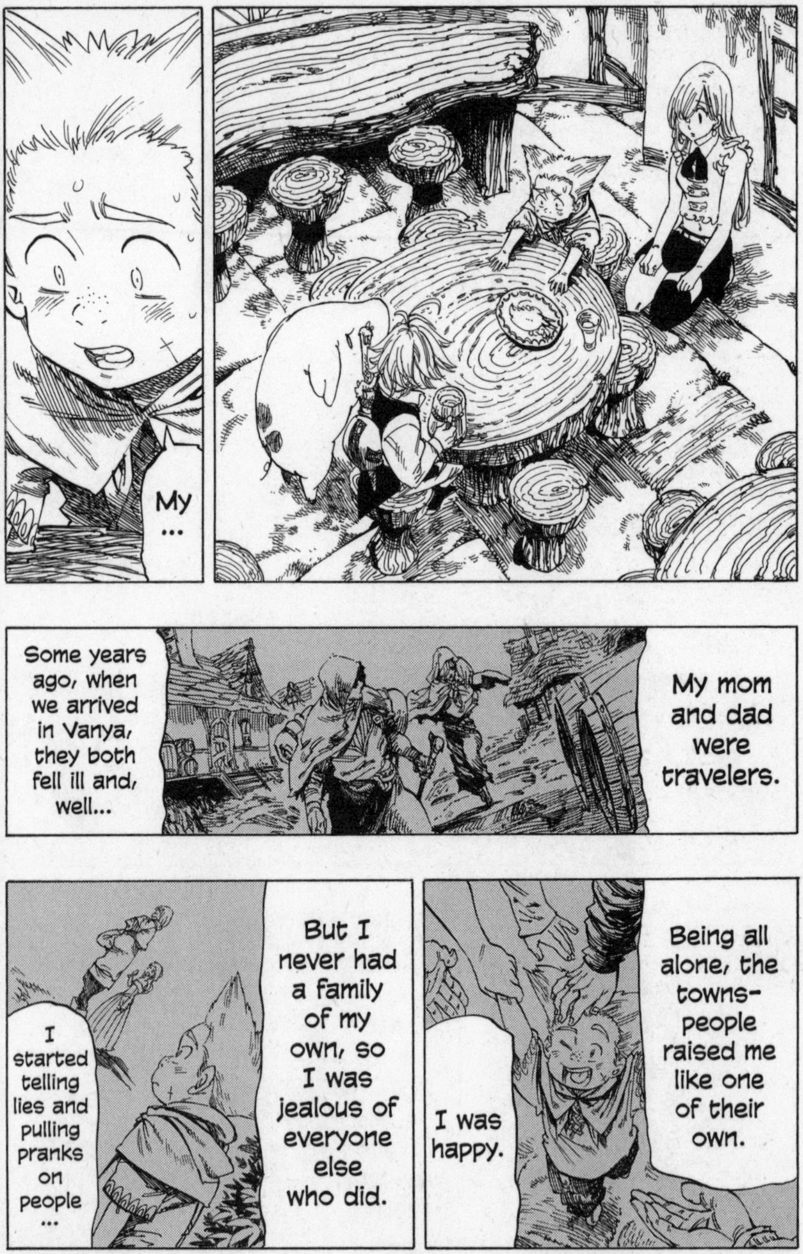
My ...
My mom and dad were travelers.
Some years ago, when we arrived in Vanya, they both fell ill and, well...
Being all alone, the towns-people raised me like one of their own.
I was happy.
But I never had a family of my own, so I was jealous of everyone else who did.
I started telling lies and pulling pranks on people ...

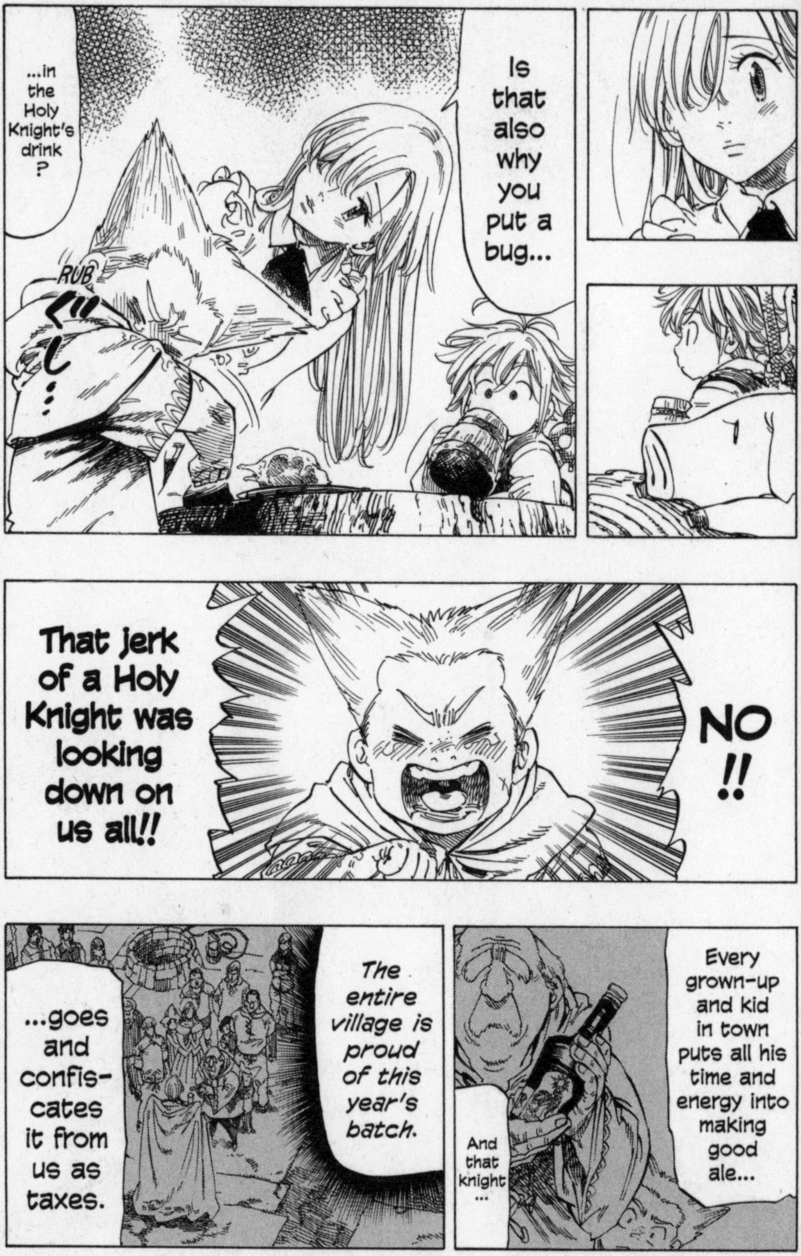
Is that also why you put a bug...
...in the Holy Knight's drink?
RUB
NO!!
That jerk of a Holy Knight was looking down on us all!!
Every grown-up and kid in town puts all his time and energy into making good ale...
And that knight...
The entire village is proud of this year's batch.
...goes and confiscates it from us as taxes.

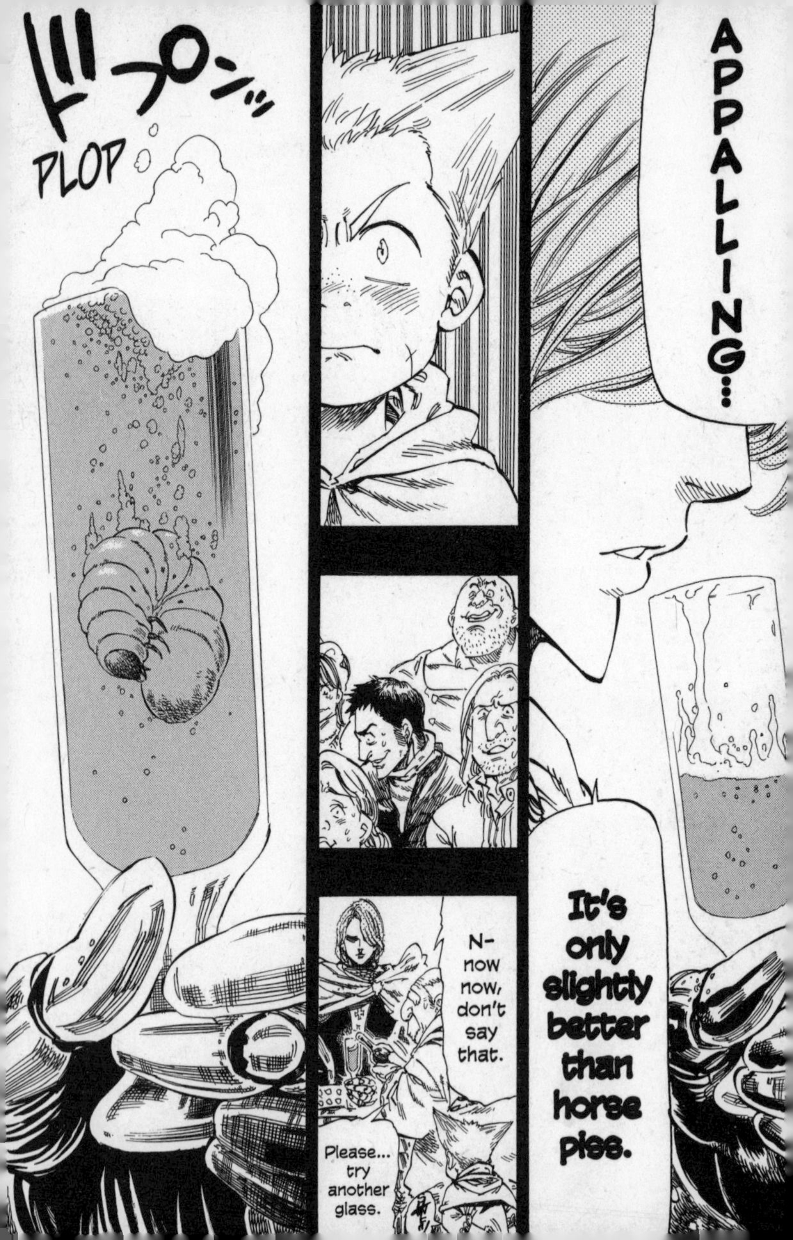
APPALLING...
It's only slightly better than horse piss.
N-now now, don't say that.
Please... try another glass.
PLOP

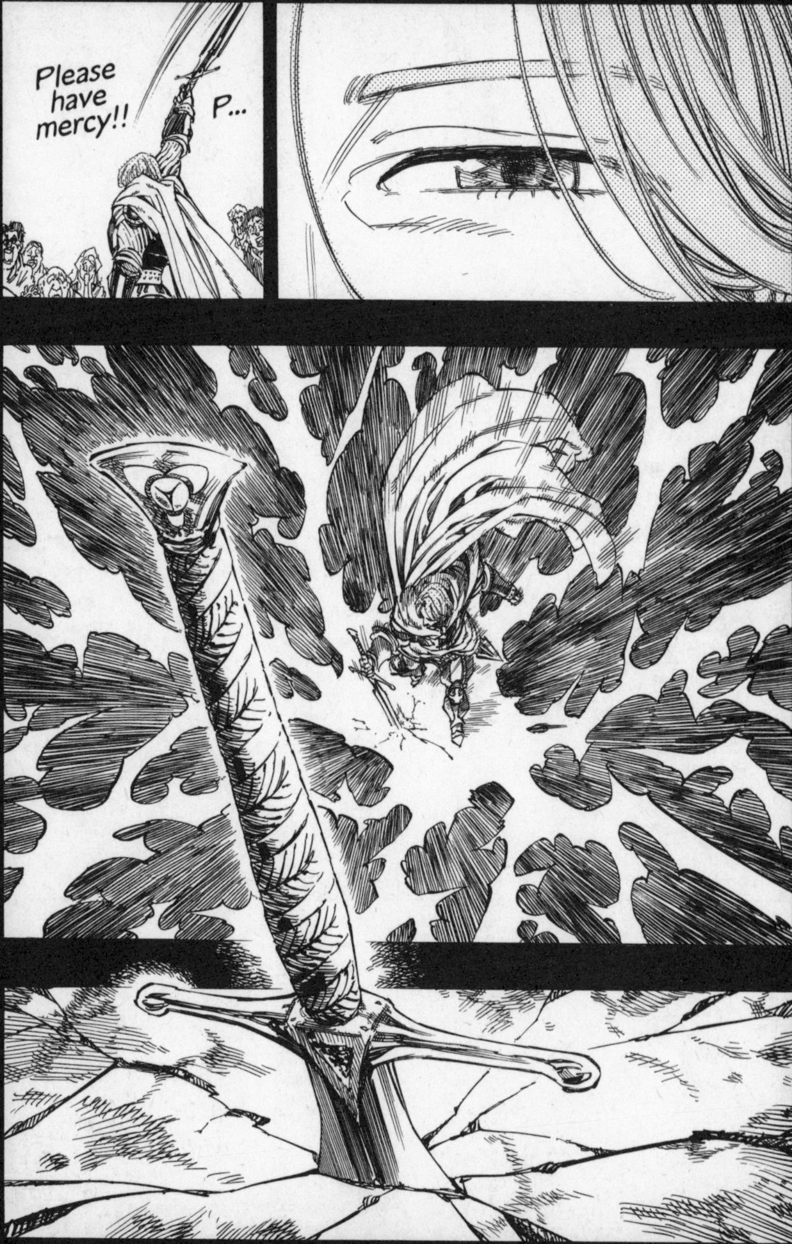
P...
Please have mercy!!

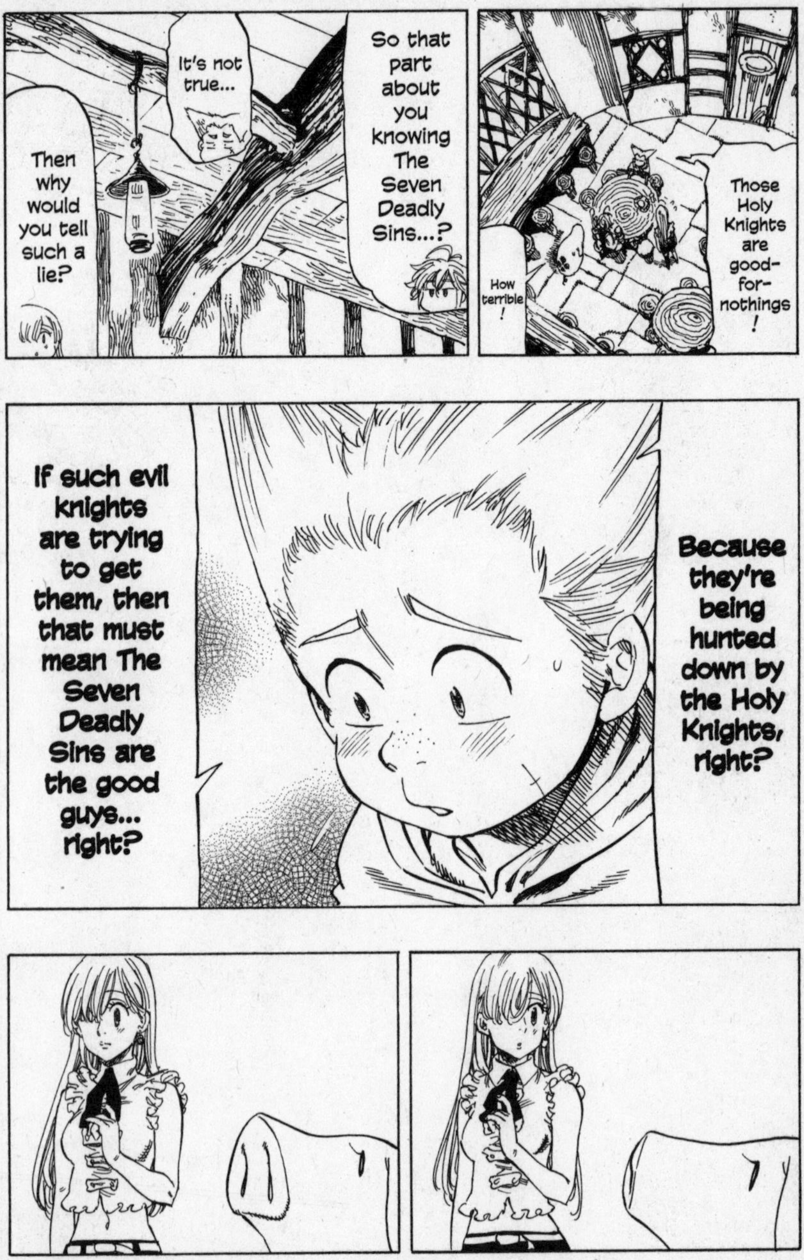
Those Holy Knights are good-for-nothings!
How terrible!
So that part about you knowing The Seven Deadly Sins...?
It's not true...
Then why would you tell such a lie?
Because they're being hunted down by the Holy Knights, right?
If such evil knights are trying to get them, then that must mean The Seven Deadly Sins are the good guys... right?

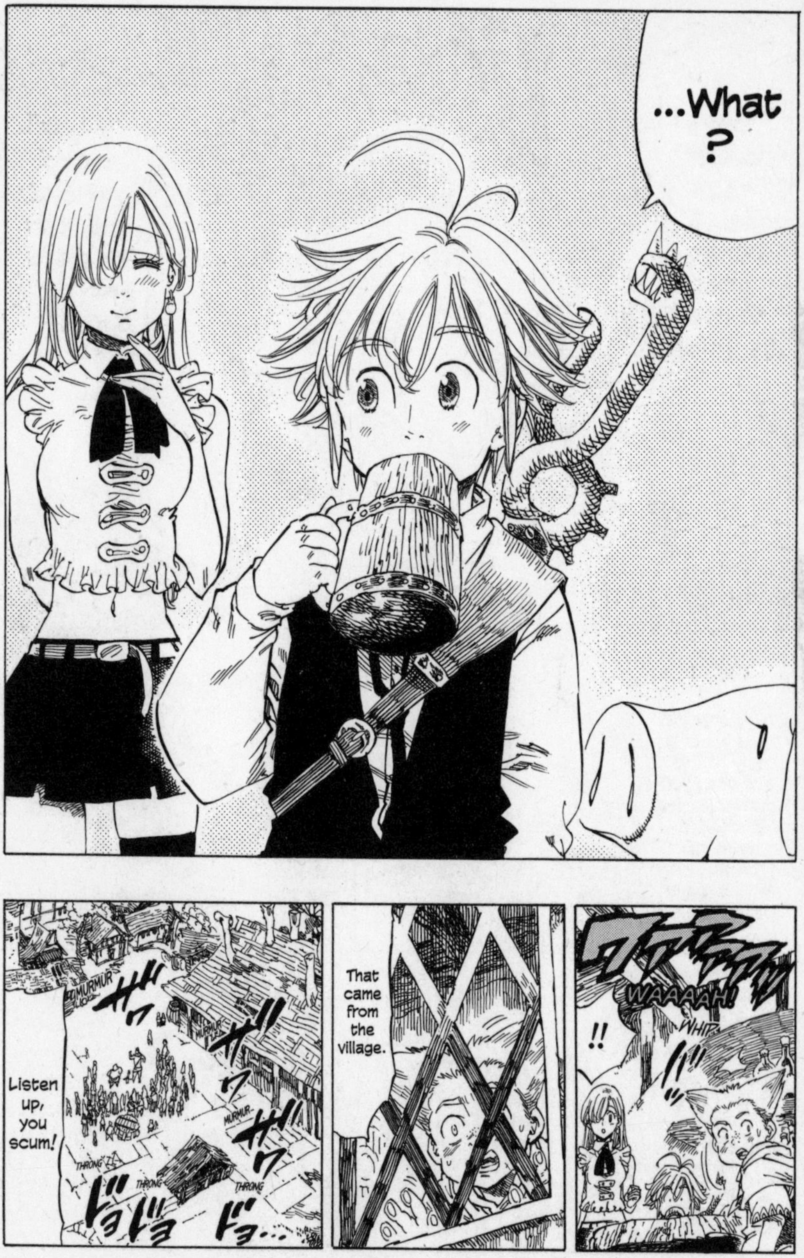
...What?
WAAAAH!
WHIP
!!
That came from the village.
MURMUR
MURMUR
MURMUR
THRONG
THRONG
THRONG
Listen up, you scum!

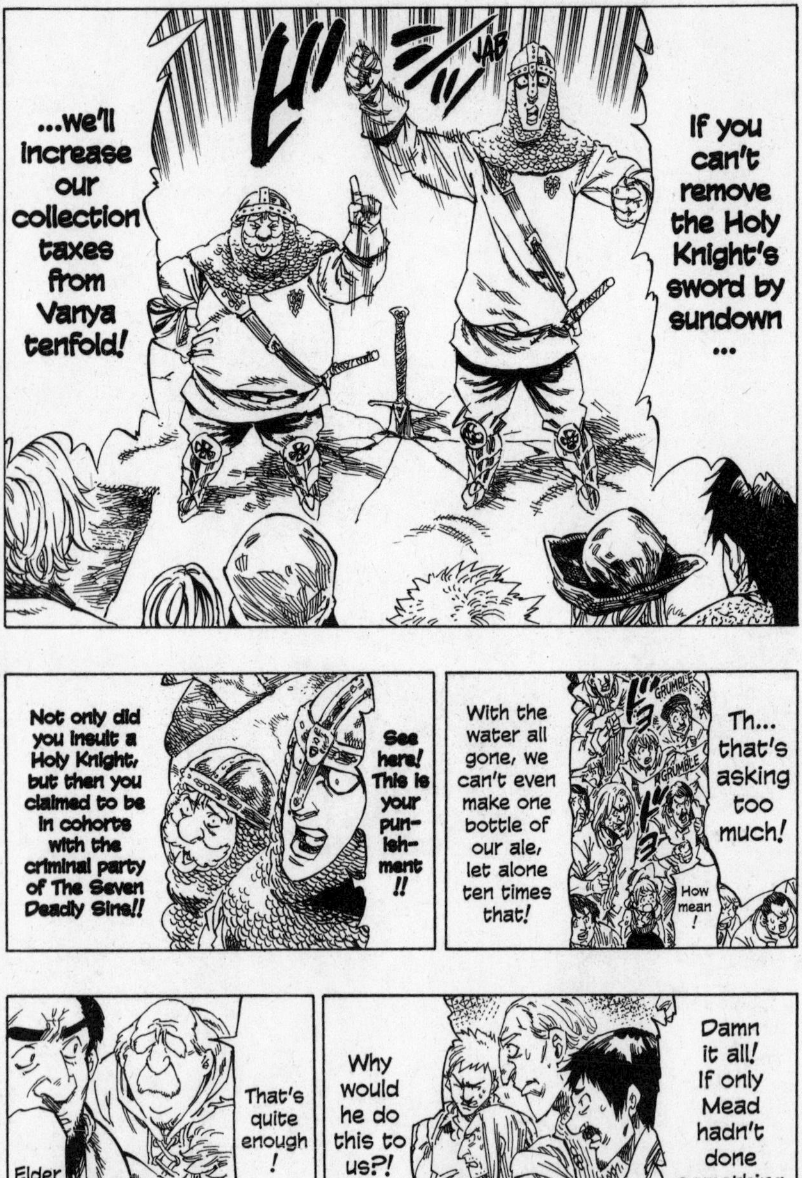
JAB
If you can't remove the Holy Knight's sword by sundown...
...we'll increase our collection taxes from Vanya tenfold!
Th... that's asking too much!
GRUMBLE
GRUMBLE
How mean!
With the water all gone, we can't even make one bottle of our ale, let alone ten times that!
See here! This is your punishment!!
Not only did you insult a Holy Knight, but then you claimed to be in cohorts with the criminal party of The Seven Deadly Sins!!
Damn it all! If only Mead hadn't done something so stupid!
Why would he do this to us?!
That's quite enough!
Elder...

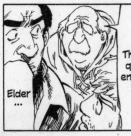

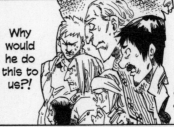

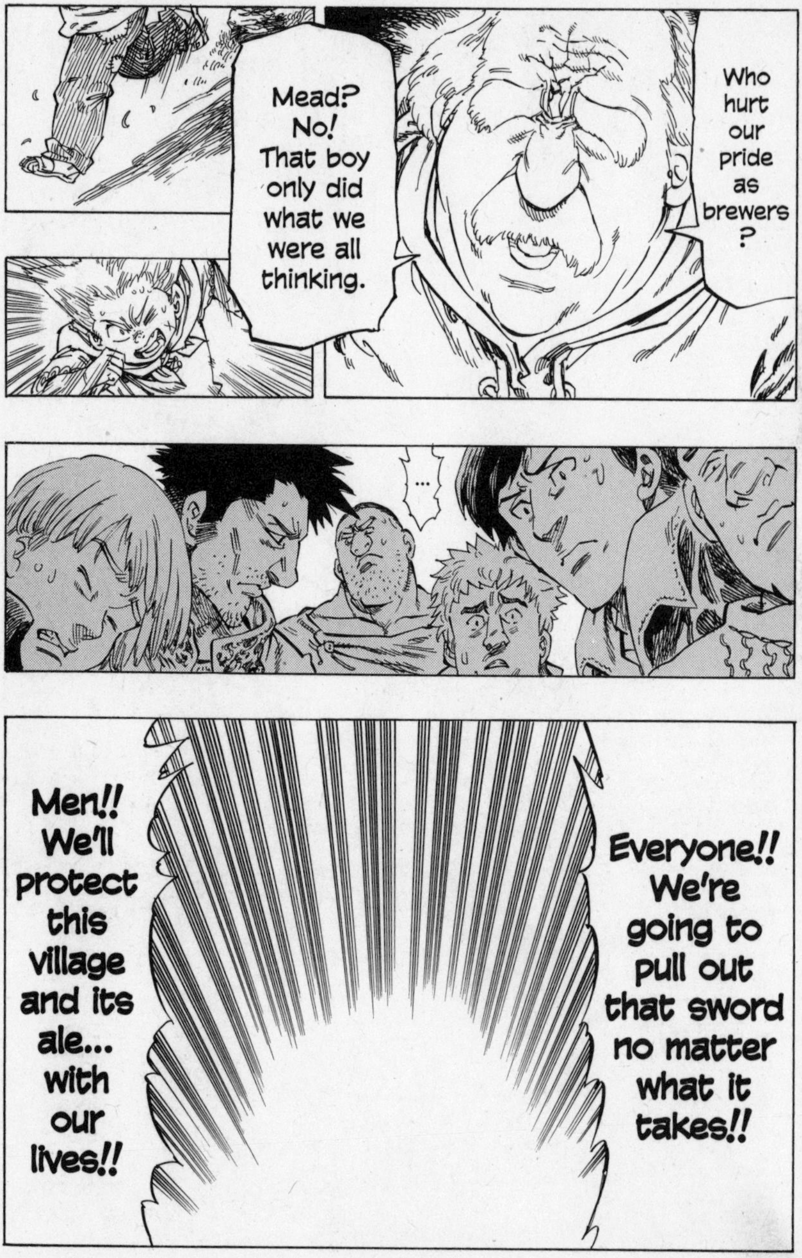
Who hurt our pride as brewers?
Mead? No! That boy only did what we were all thinking.
...
Everyone!! We're going to pull out that sword no matter what it takes!!
Men!! We'll protect this village and its ale... with our lives!!

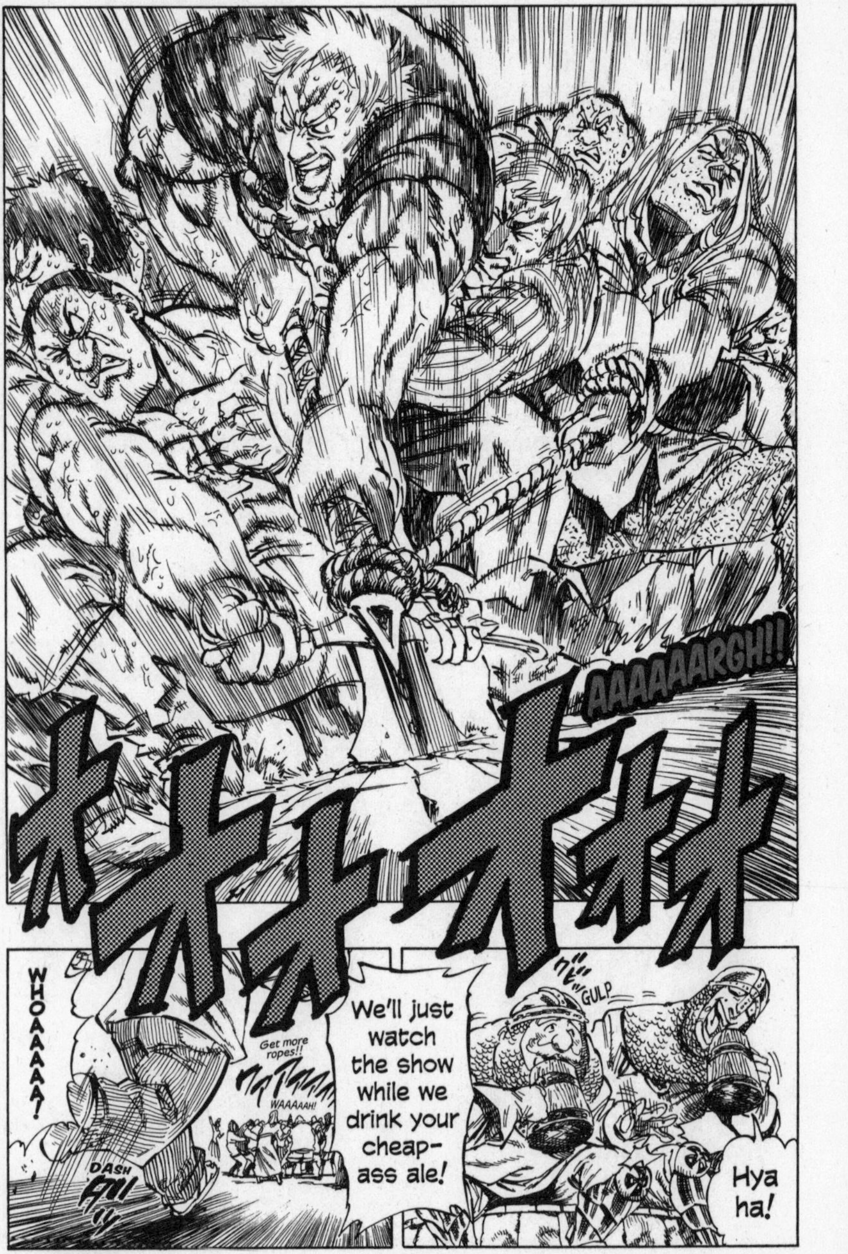
AAAAAARGH!!
We'll just watch the show while we drink your cheap-ass ale!
GULP
Hya ha!
WHOAAAAAA!
Get more ropes!!
WAAAAAH!
DASH

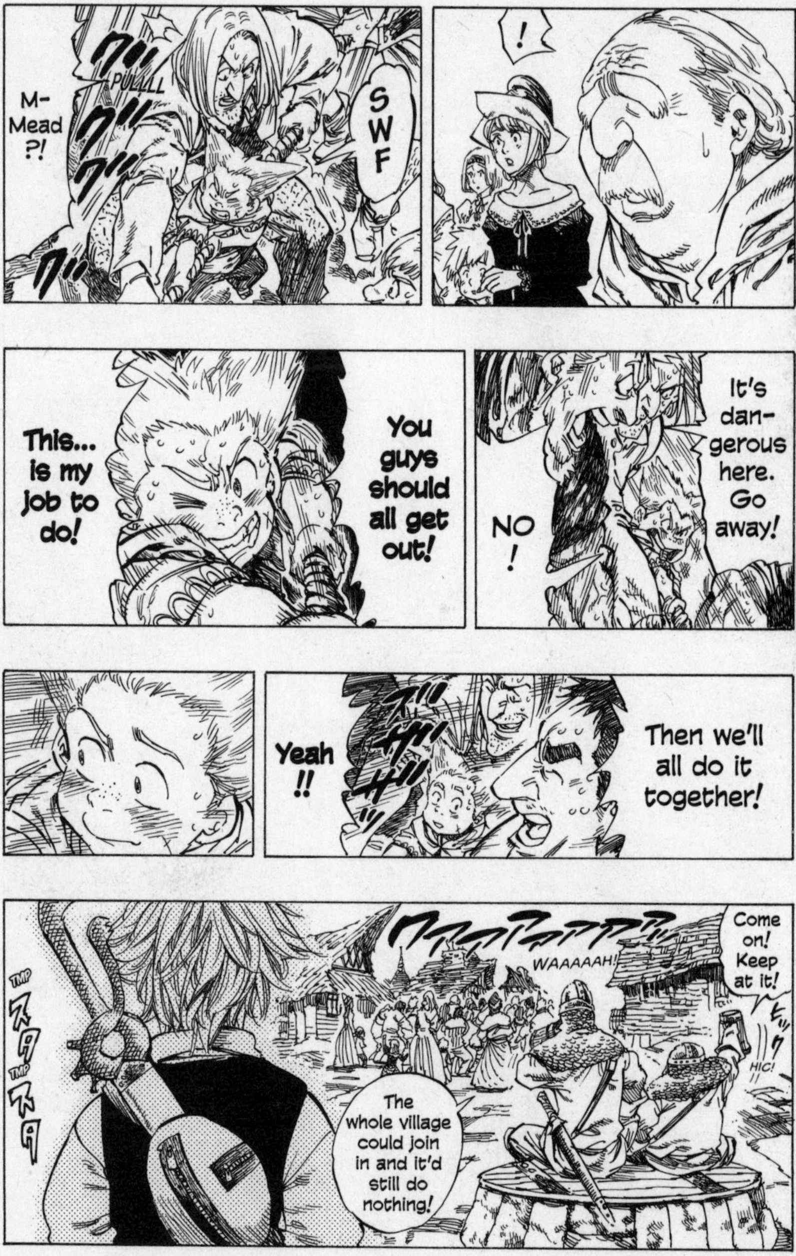
!
SWF
PULLLL
M-Mead?!
It's dangerous here. Go away!
NO!
You guys should all get out!
This... is my job to do!
Then we'll all do it together!
Yeah!!
Come on! Keep at it!
HIC!
WAAAAAH!
The whole village could join in and it'd still do nothing!
TMP
TMP

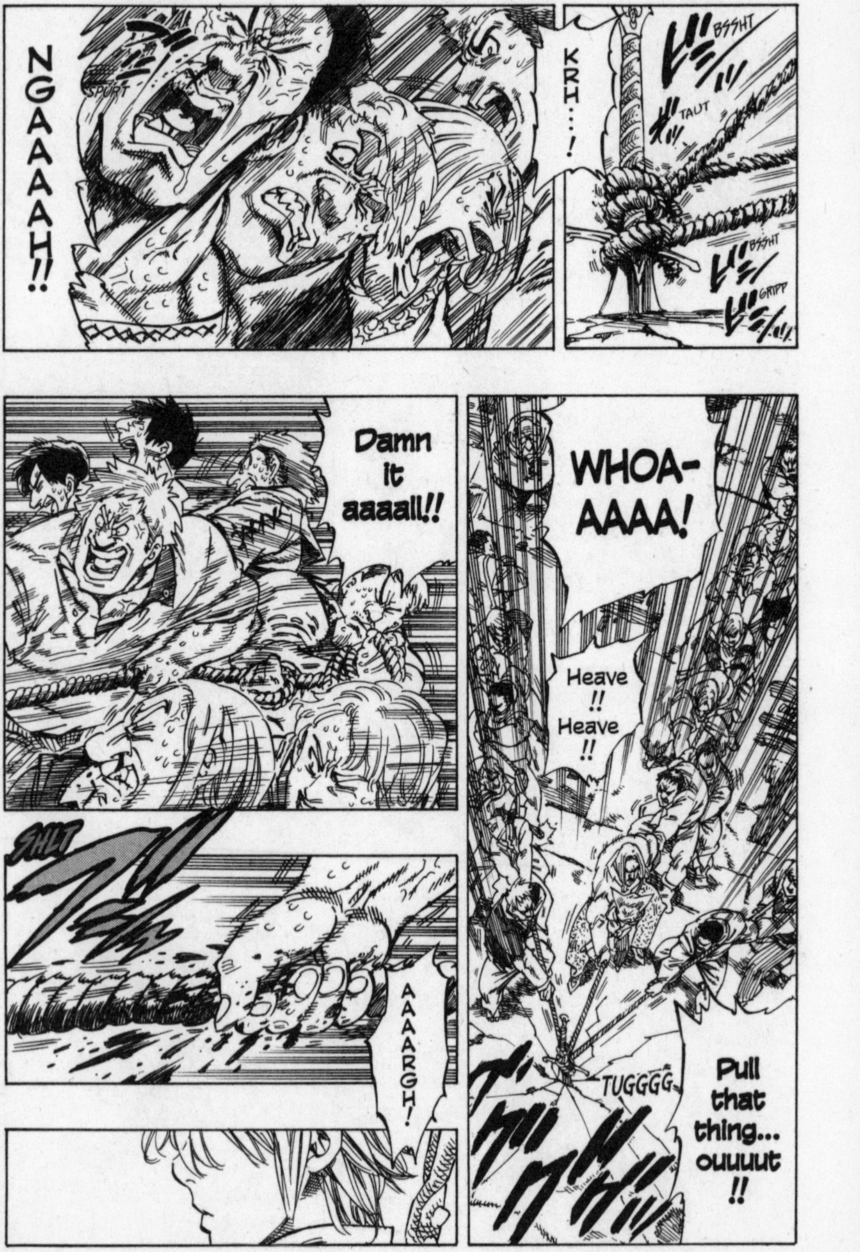
KRH...!
BSSHT
TAUT
BSSHT
GRIPP
NGAAAAAH!!
SPURT
WHOA-AAAA!
Heave!! Heave!!
TUGGGG
Pull that thing... ouuuut!!
Damn it aaaall!!
SHLT
AAAARGH!

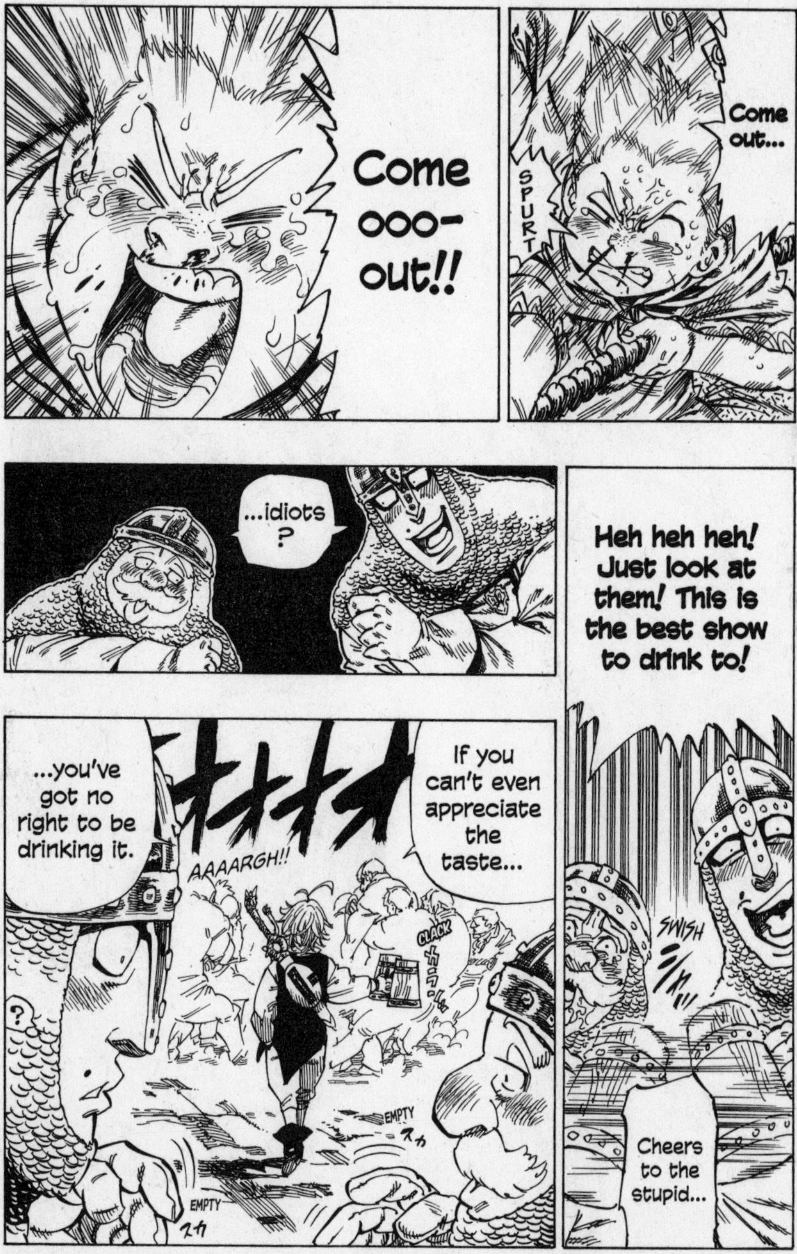
Come out...
SPURT
Come ooo-out!!
Heh heh heh! Just look at them! This is the best show to drink to!
SWISH
Cheers to the stupid...
...idiots?
If you can't even appreciate the taste...
...you've got no right to be drinking it.
AAAARGH!!
CLACK
EMPTY
EMPTY
?

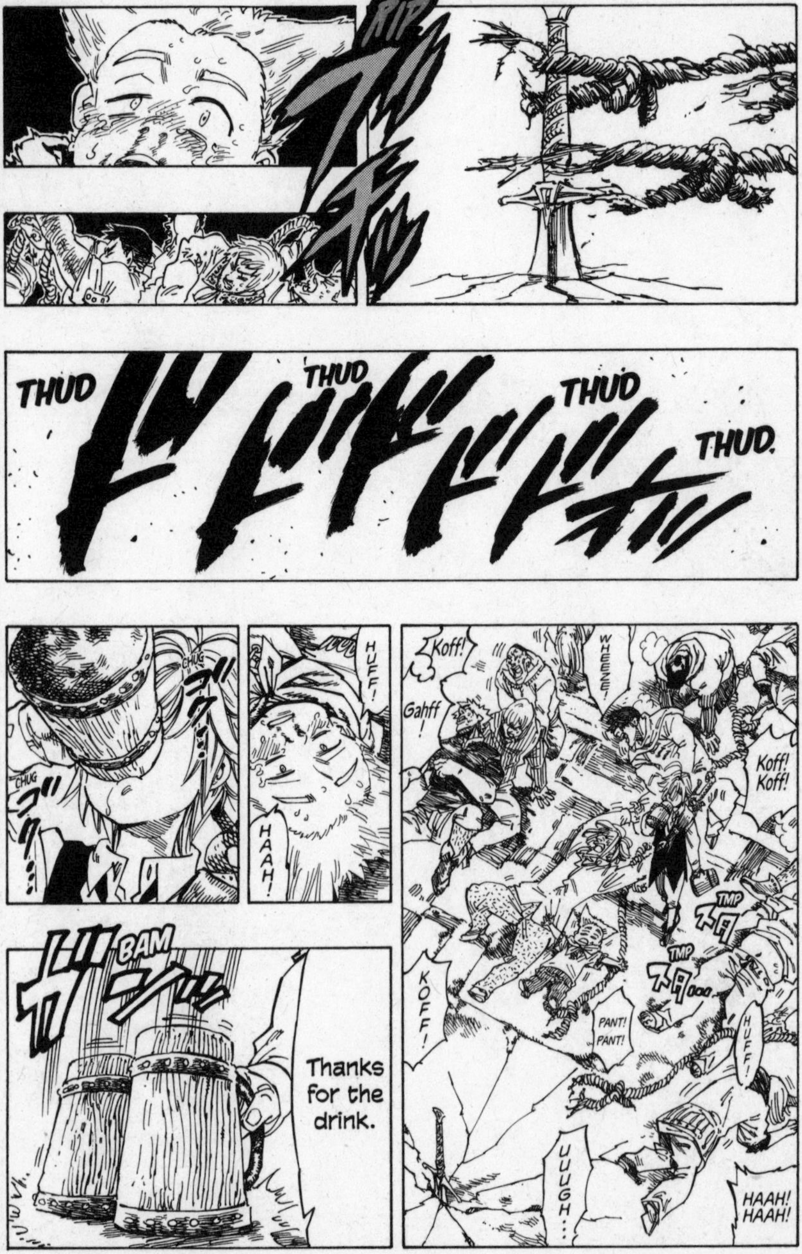
RIP
THUD
THUD
THUD
THUD.
Koff!
WHEEZE!
Koff! Koff!
Gahff!
TMP
TMP
KOFF!
PANT! PANT!
HUFF!
UUUGH...
HAAH! HAAH!
HUFF!
HAAH!
CHUG
CHUG
BAM
Thanks for the drink.

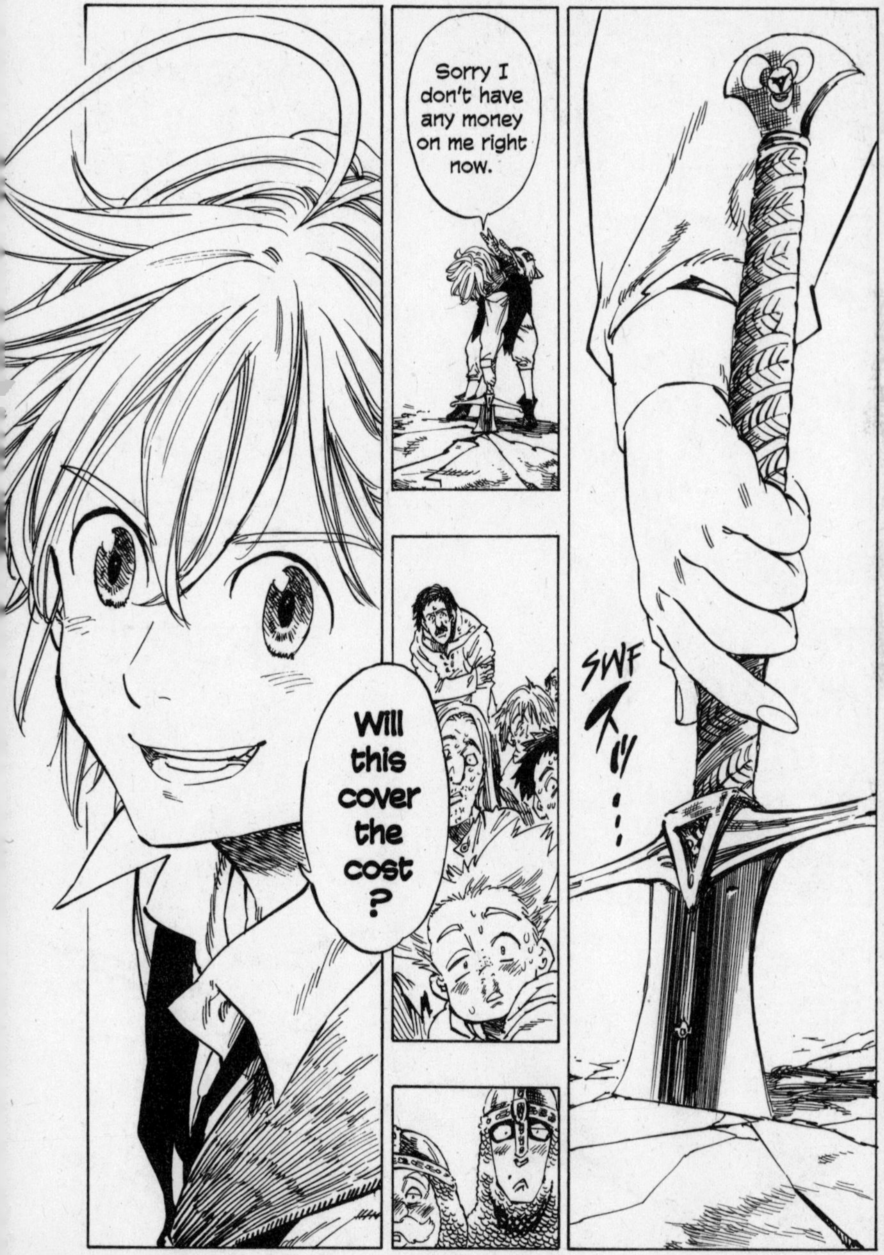
SWF
スッ…
Sorry I don't have any money on me right now.
Will this cover the cost?

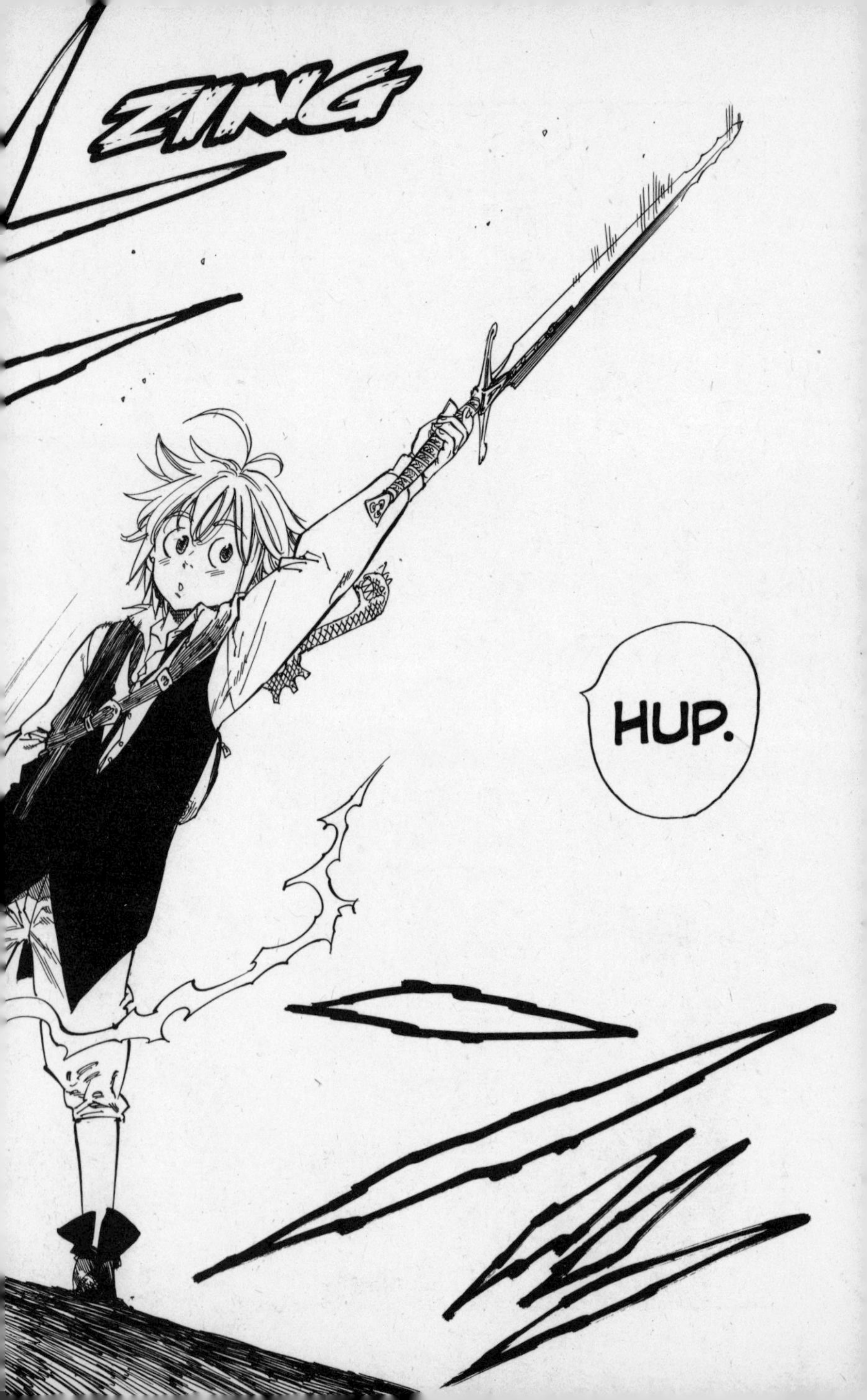
ZING
HUP.

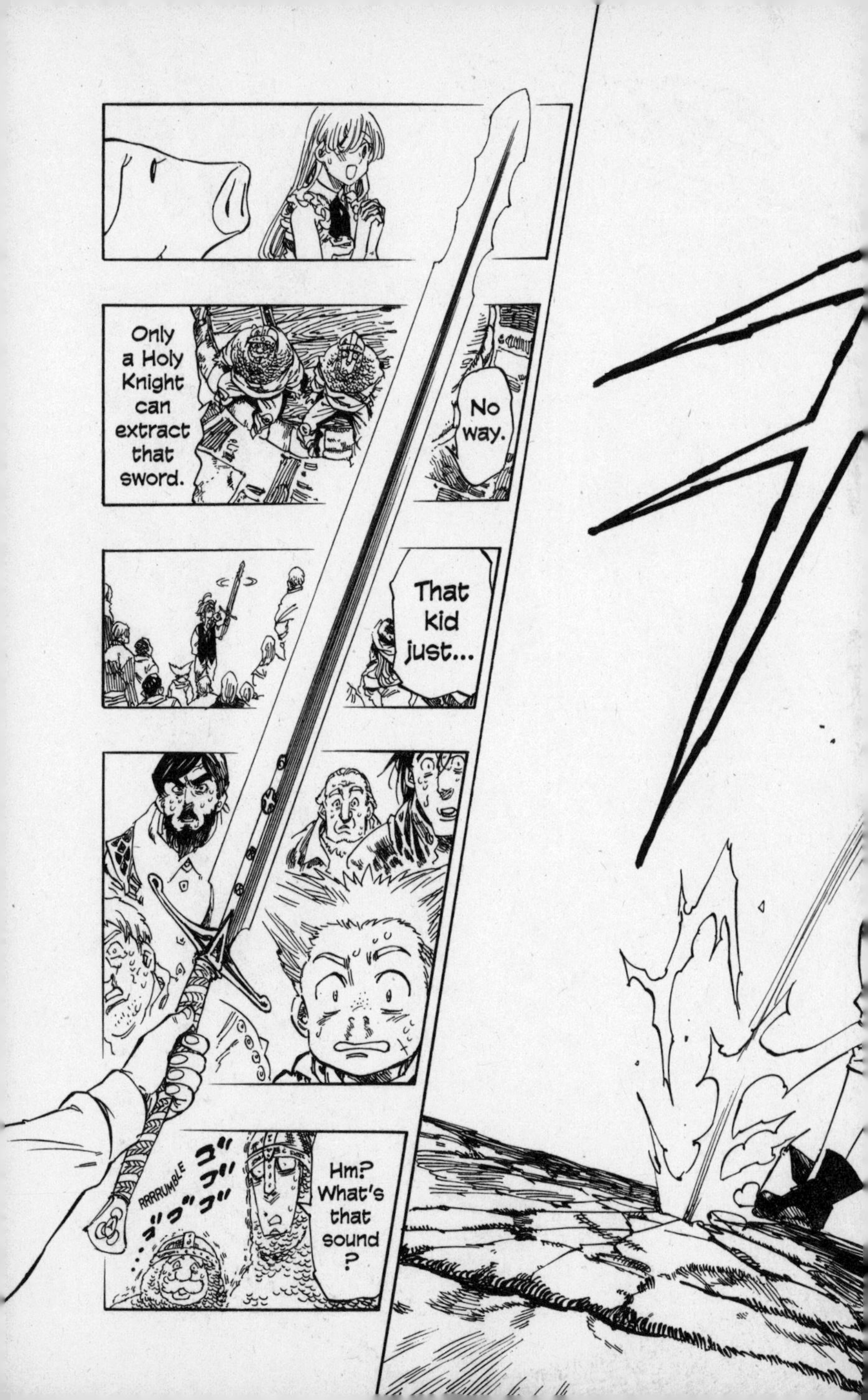
No way.
Only a Holy Knight can extract that sword.
That kid just...
Hm? What's that sound?
RRRRUMBLE

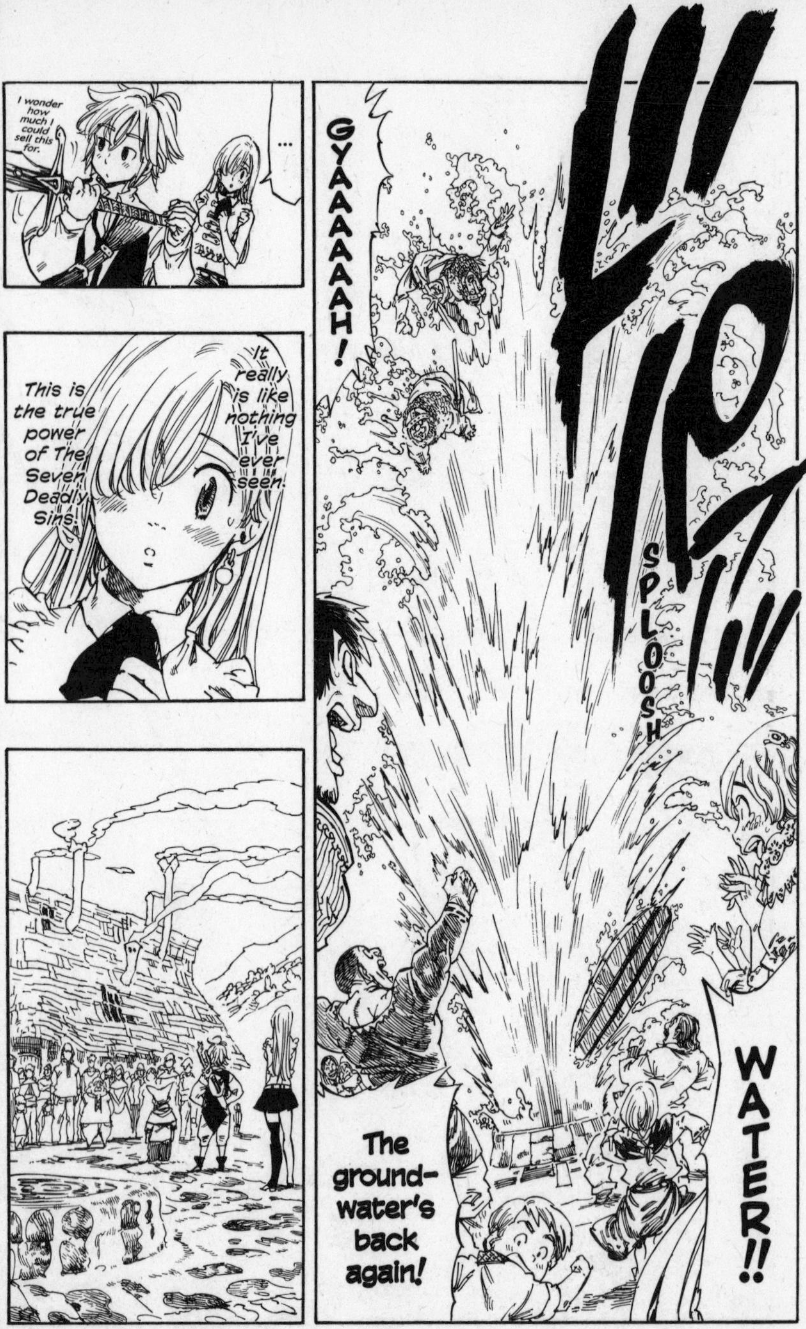

GYAAAAAAH!
SPLOOSH
WATER!!
The ground-water's back again!
I wonder how much I could sell this for.
...
It really is like nothing I've ever seen.
This is the true power of The Seven Deadly Sins.

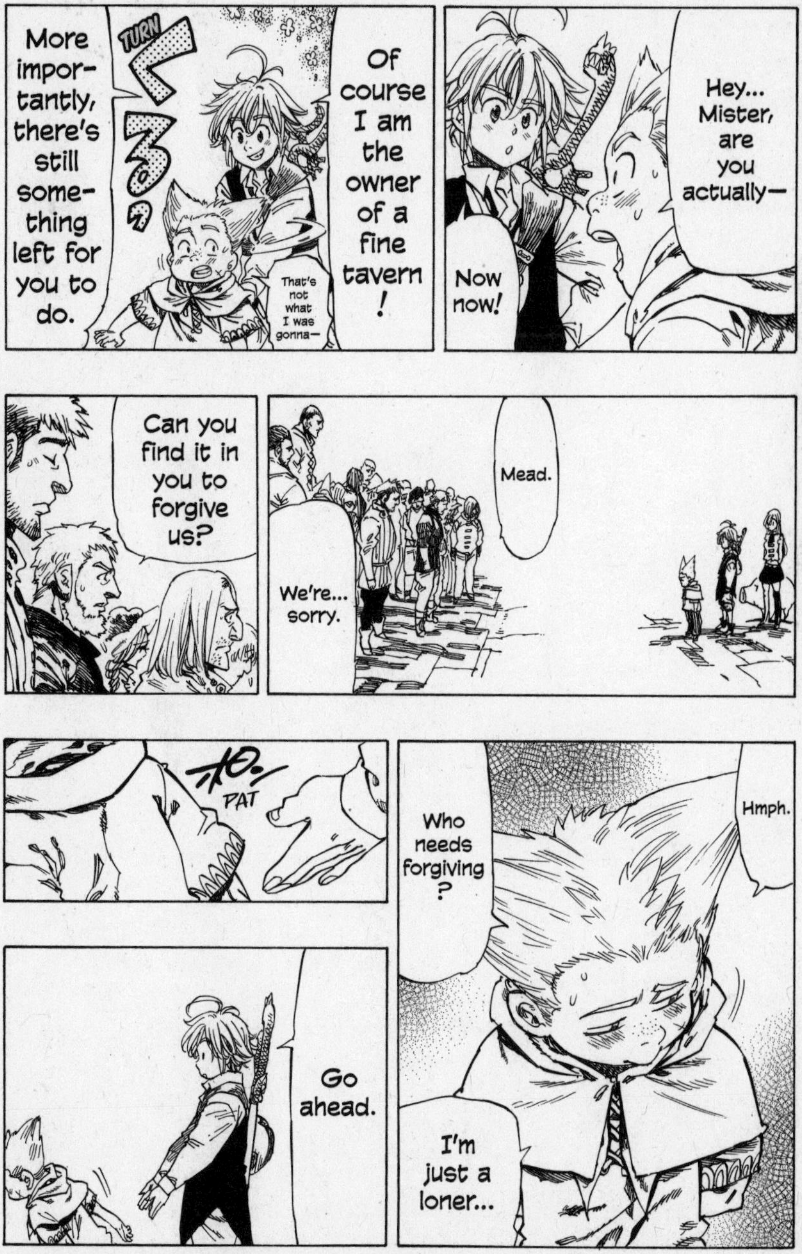
Hey... Mister, are you actually—
Now now!
Of course I am the owner of a fine tavern!
That's not what I was gonna—
TURN
More importantly, there's still something left for you to do.
Mead.
We're... sorry.
Can you find it in you to forgive us?
Hmph.
Who needs forgiving?
I'm just a loner...
PAT
Go ahead.

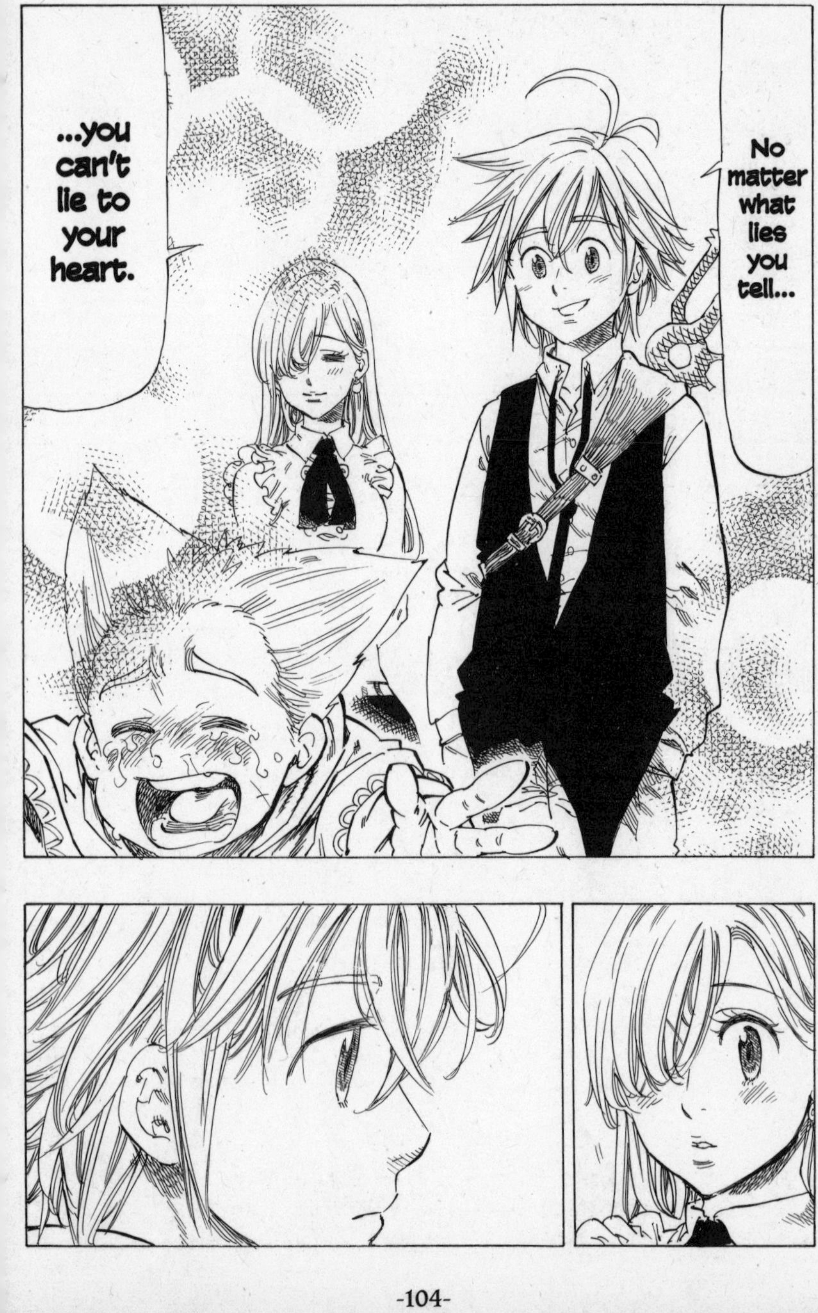
No matter what lies you tell...
...you can't lie to your heart.

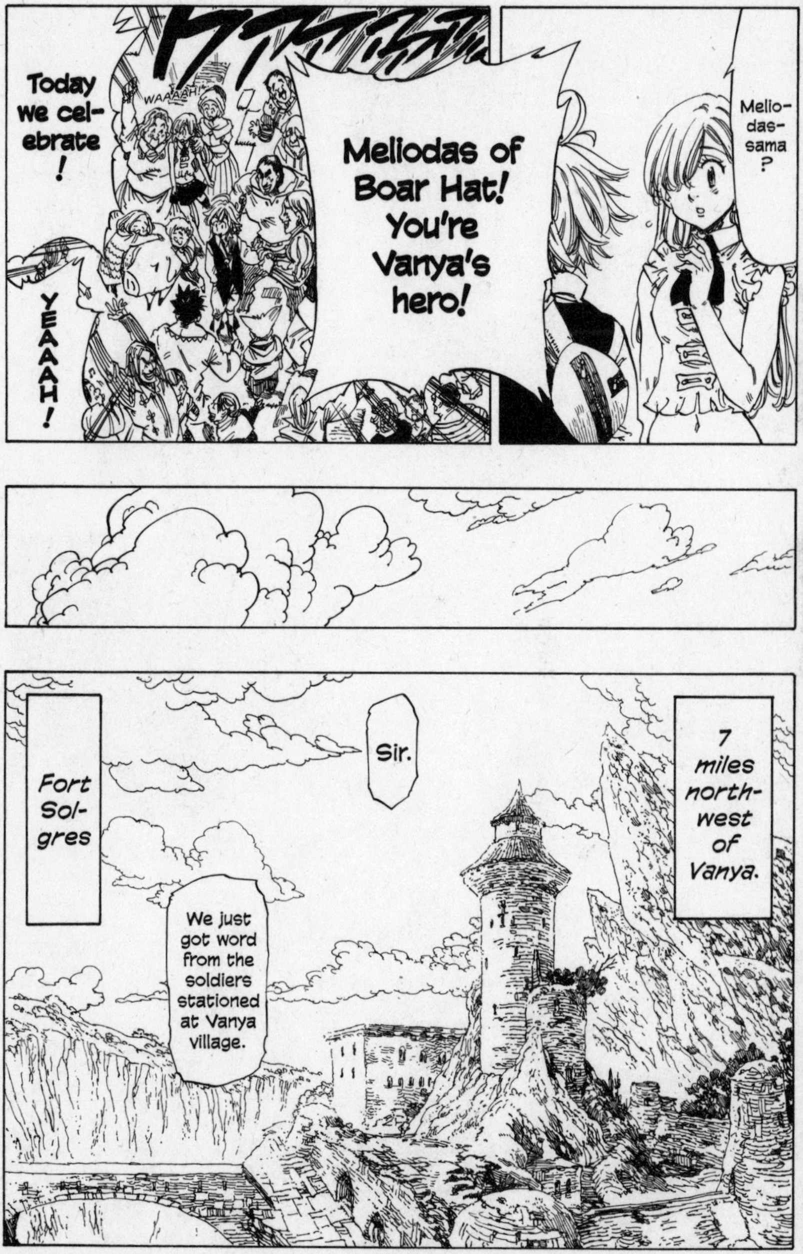
Melio-das-sama?
Today we cel-ebrate!
WAAAAH!
Meliodas of Boar Hat! You're Vanya's hero!
YEAAAAH!
7 miles north-west of Vanya.
Sir.
Fort Sol-gres
We just got word from the soldiers stationed at Vanya village.

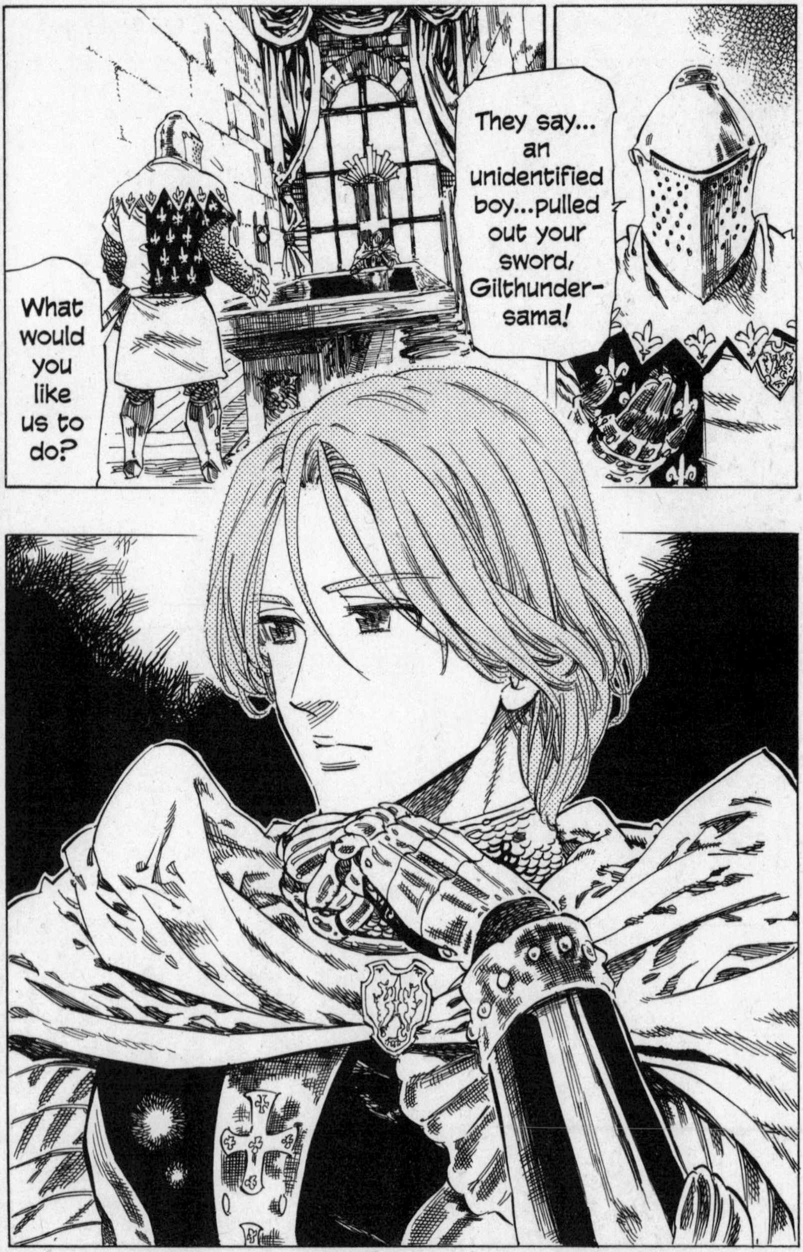
They say... an unidentified boy...pulled out your sword, Gilthunder-sama!
What would you like us to do?

Chapter 3 - What One Must Do

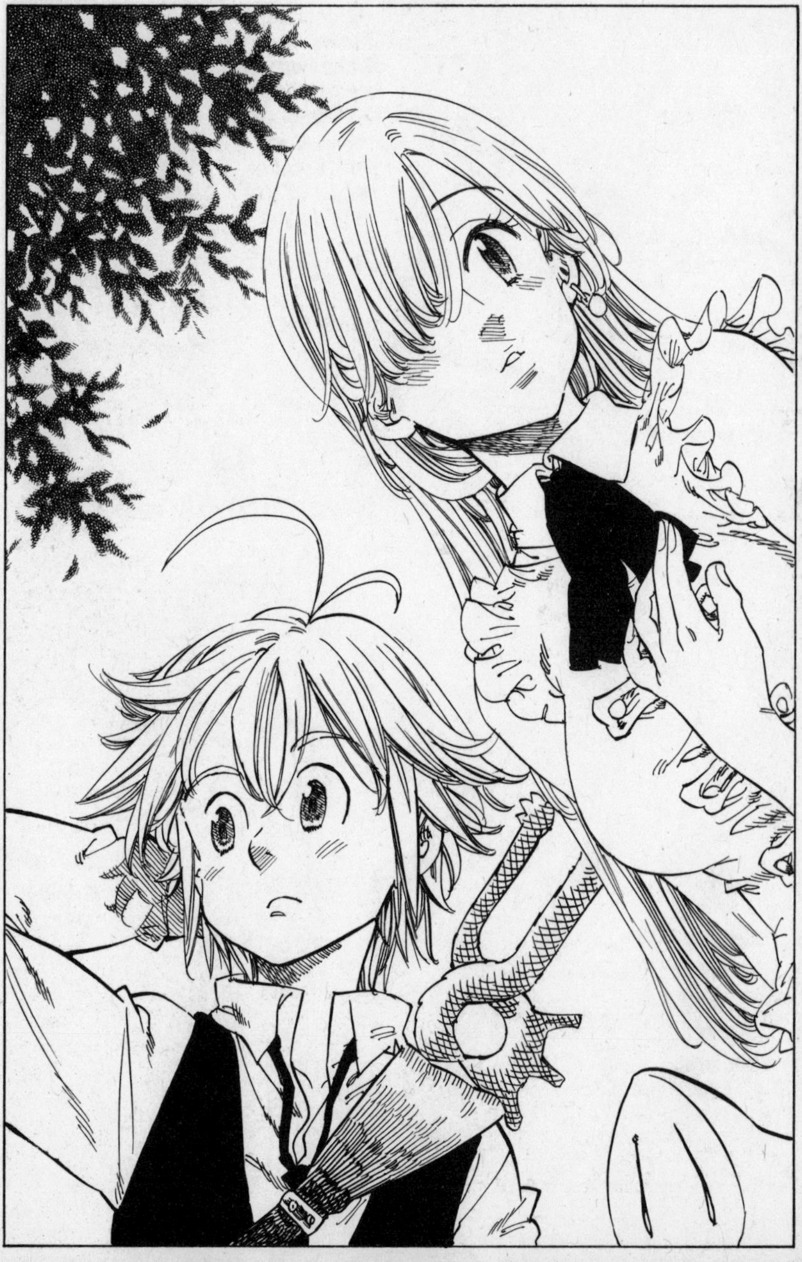

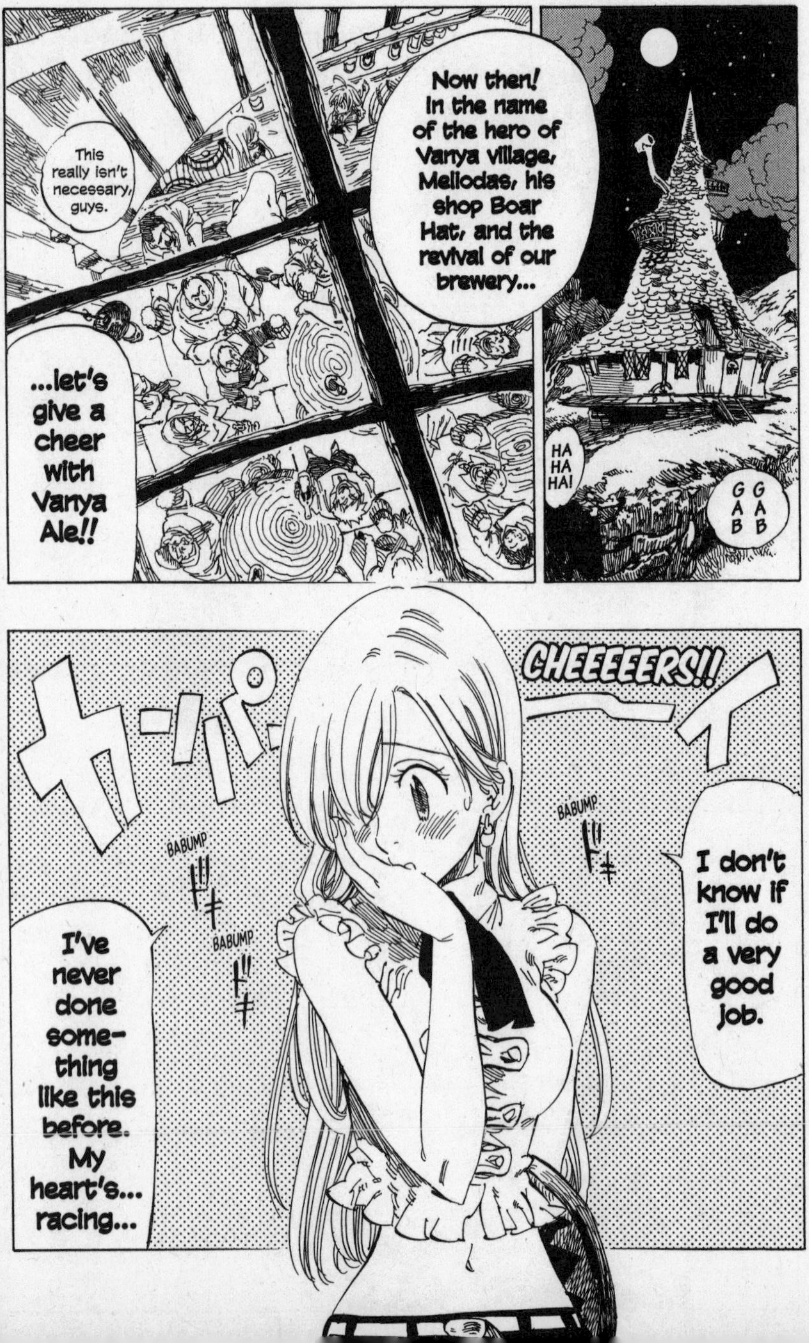
HA HA HA!
GAB GAB
GAB GAB
Now then! In the name of the hero of Vanya village, Meliodas, his shop Boar Hat, and the revival of our brewery...
This really isn't necessary, guys.
...let's give a cheer with Vanya Ale!!
CHEEEEERS!!
BABUMP
I don't know if I'll do a very good job.
BABUMP
BABUMP
I've never done some-thing like this before. My heart's... racing...

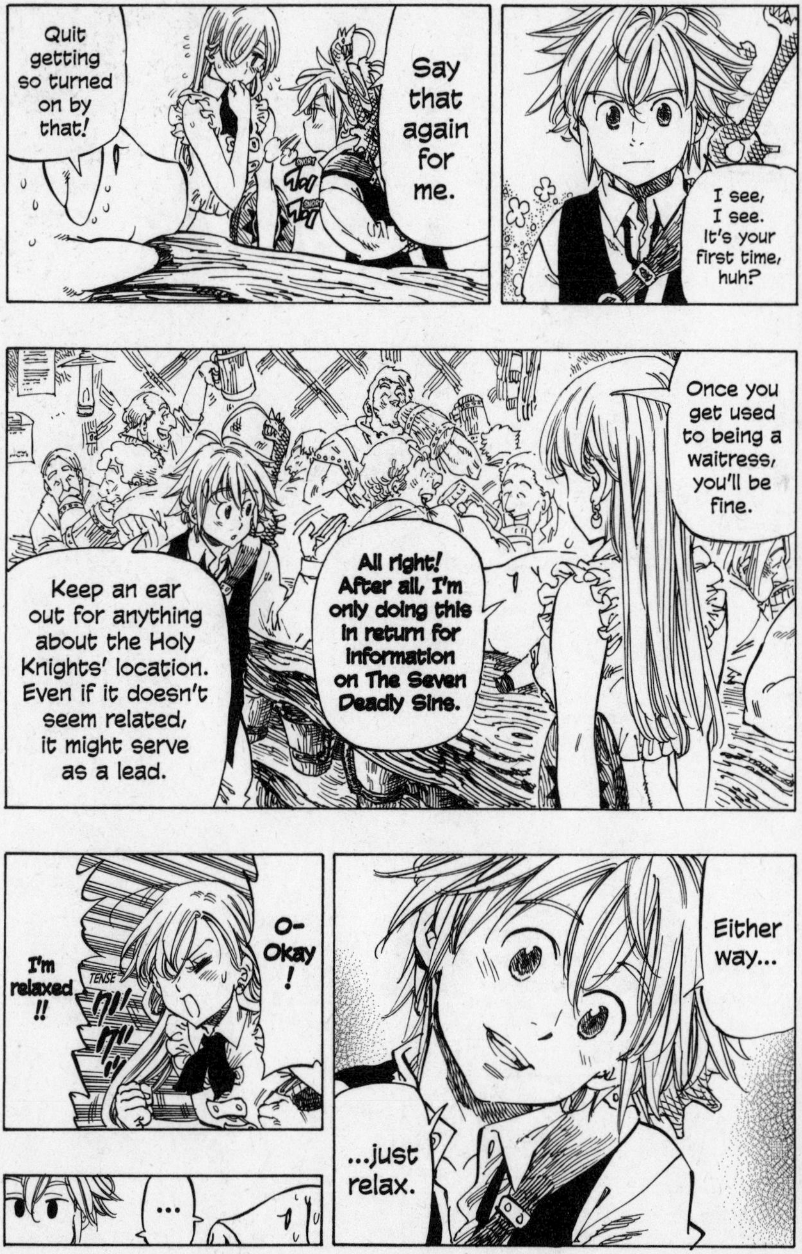
I see, I see. It's your first time, huh?
Say that again for me.
SNORT
SNORT
Quit getting so turned on by that!
Once you get used to being a waitress, you'll be fine.
All right! After all, I'm only doing this in return for information on The Seven Deadly Sins.
Keep an ear out for anything about the Holy Knights' location. Even if it doesn't seem related, it might serve as a lead.
Either way...
...just relax.
O-Okay!
TENSE
I'm relaxed!!
...

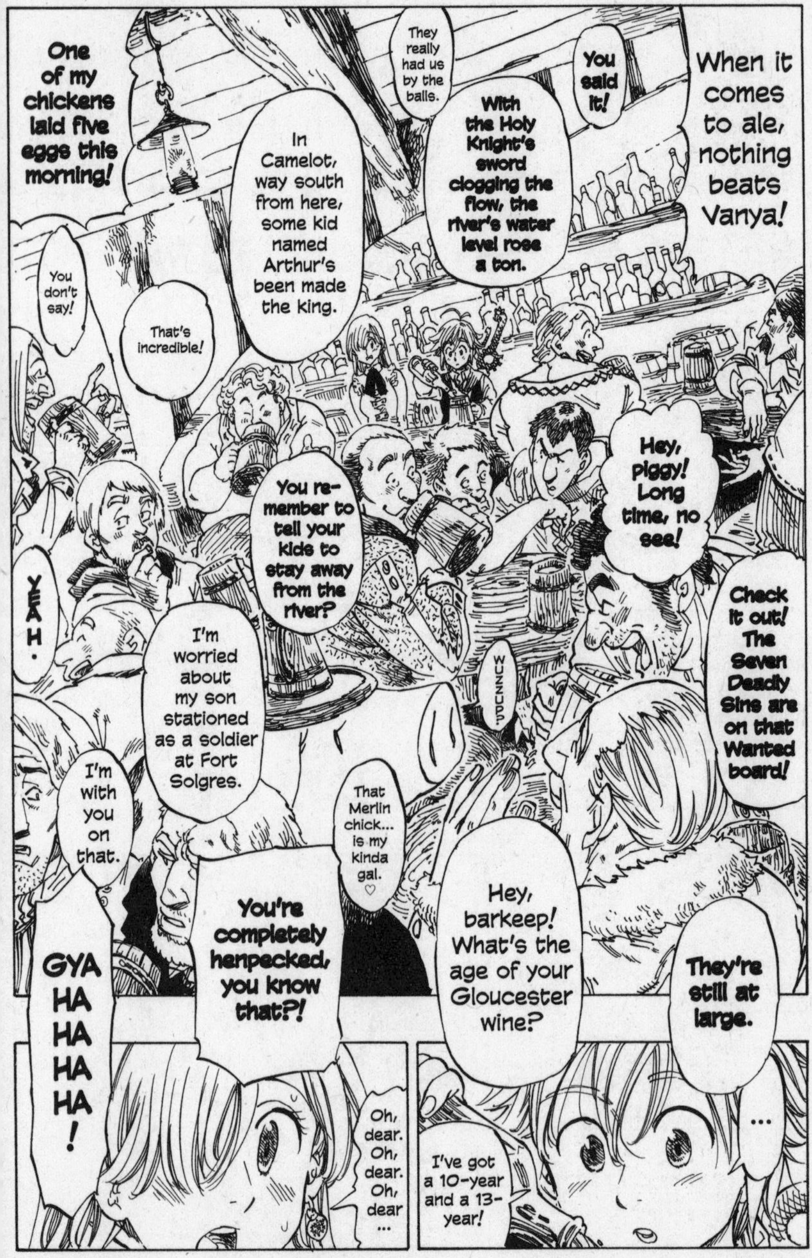

When it comes to ale, nothing beats Vanya!
You said it!
With the Holy Knight's sword clogging the flow, the river's water level rose a ton.
They really had us by the balls.
In Camelot, way south from here, some kid named Arthur's been made the king.
One of my chickens laid five eggs this morning!
You don't say!
That's incredible!
Hey, piggy! Long time, no see!
You remember to tell your kids to stay away from the river?
YEAH.
Check it out! The Seven Deadly Sins are on that Wanted board!
WUZZUP?
I'm worried about my son stationed as a soldier at Fort Solgres.
I'm with you on that.
They're still at large.
Hey, barkeep! What's the age of your Gloucester wine?
That Merlin chick... is my kinda gal. ♡
You're completely henpecked, you know that?!
GYA HA HA HA HA!
...
I've got a 10-year and a 13-year!
Oh, dear. Oh, dear. Oh, dear...

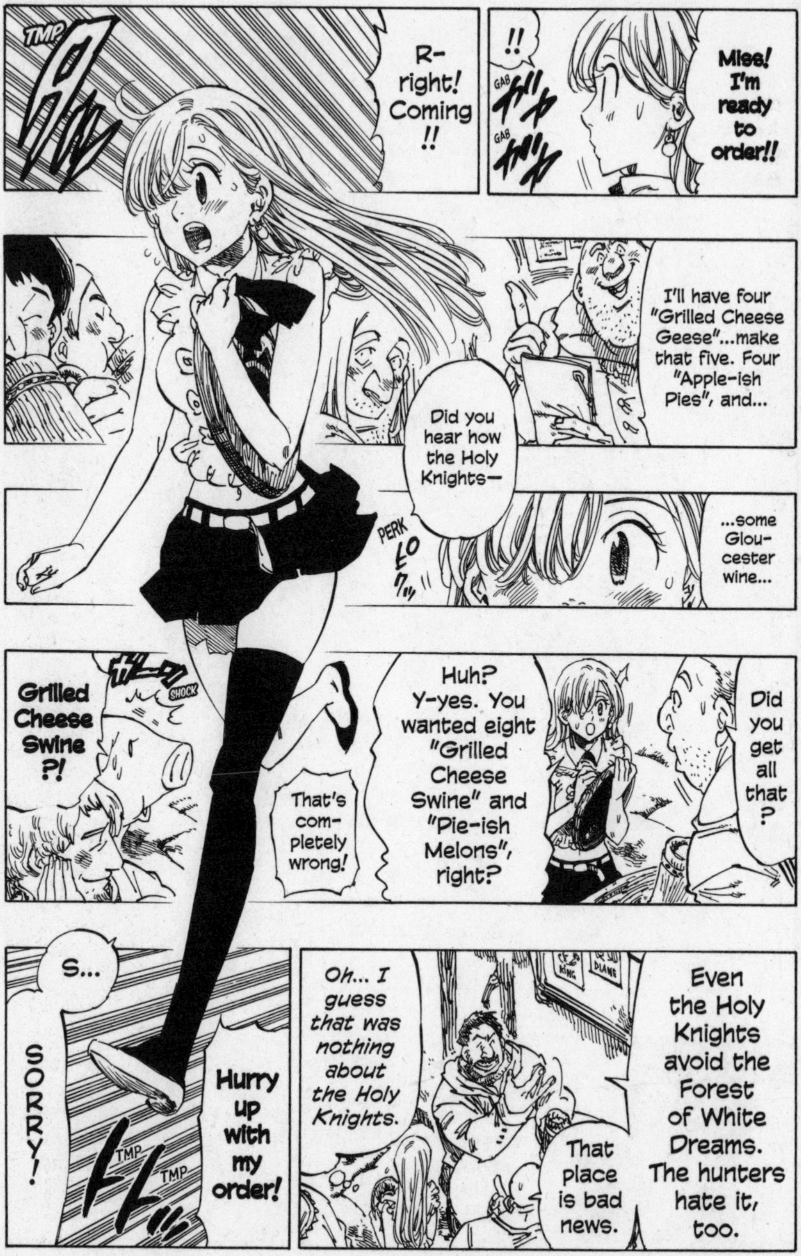
Miss! I'm ready to order!!
!!
GAB
GAB
R-right! Coming!!
TMP
I'll have four "Grilled Cheese Geese"...make that five. Four "Apple-ish Pies", and...
Did you hear how the Holy Knights—
...some Glou-cester wine...
PERK
Did you get all that?
Huh? Y-yes. You wanted eight "Grilled Cheese Swine" and "Pie-ish Melons", right?
That's com-pletely wrong!
Grilled Cheese Swine?!
SHOCK
Even the Holy Knights avoid the Forest of White Dreams. The hunters hate it, too.
That place is bad news.
Oh... I guess that was nothing about the Holy Knights.
Hurry up with my order!
S...
SORRY!
TMP
TMP

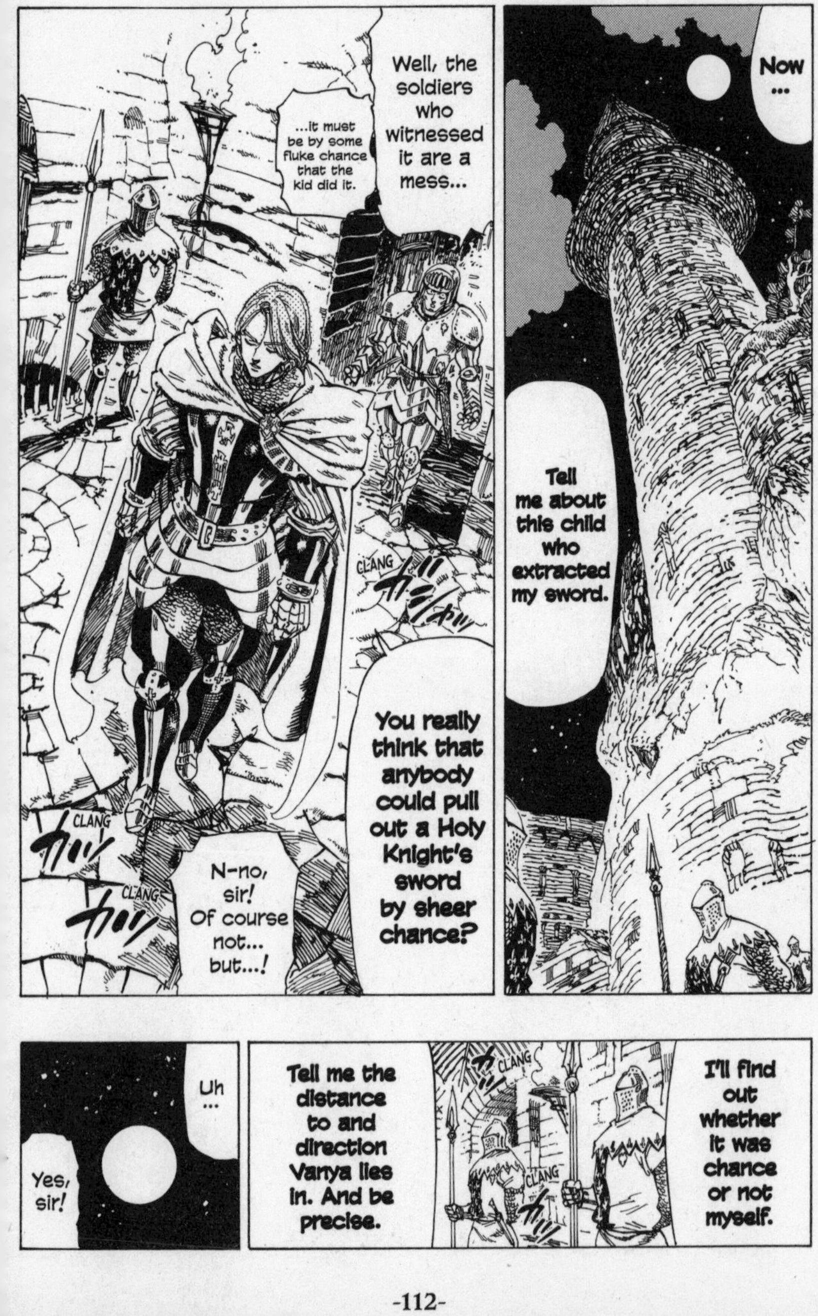

Now ...
Tell me about this child who extracted my sword.
Well, the soldiers who witnessed it are a mess...
...it must be by some fluke chance that the kid did it.
CLANG
You really think that anybody could pull out a Holy Knight's sword by sheer chance?
CLANG
CLANG
N-no, sir! Of course not... but...!
I'll find out whether it was chance or not myself.
CLANG
CLANG
Tell me the distance to and direction Vanya lies in. And be precise.
Uh ...
Yes, sir!

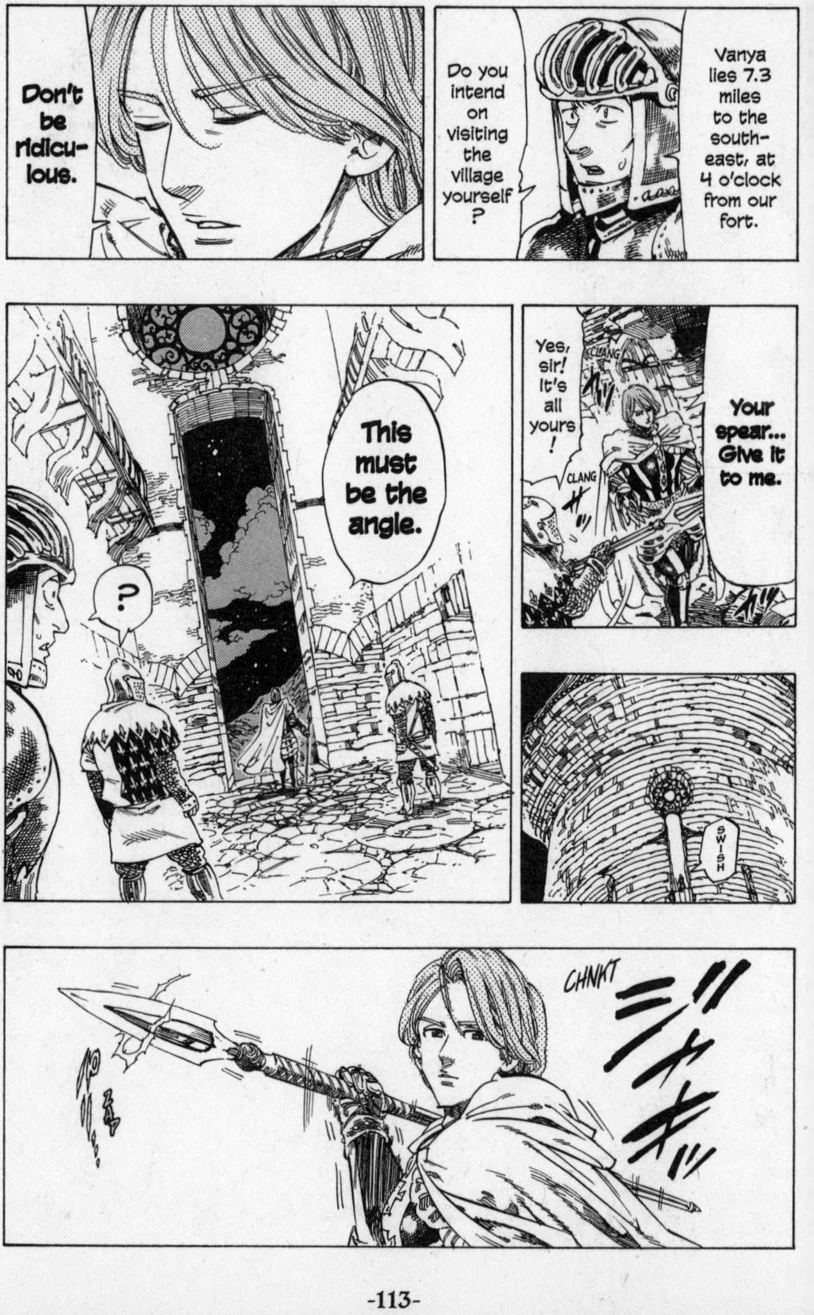
Vanya lies 7.3 miles to the south-east, at 4 o'clock from our fort.
Do you intend on visiting the village yourself?
Don't be ridicu-lous.
Your spear... Give it to me.
CLANG
Yes, sir! It's all yours!
CLANG
SWISH
This must be the angle.
?
CHNKT

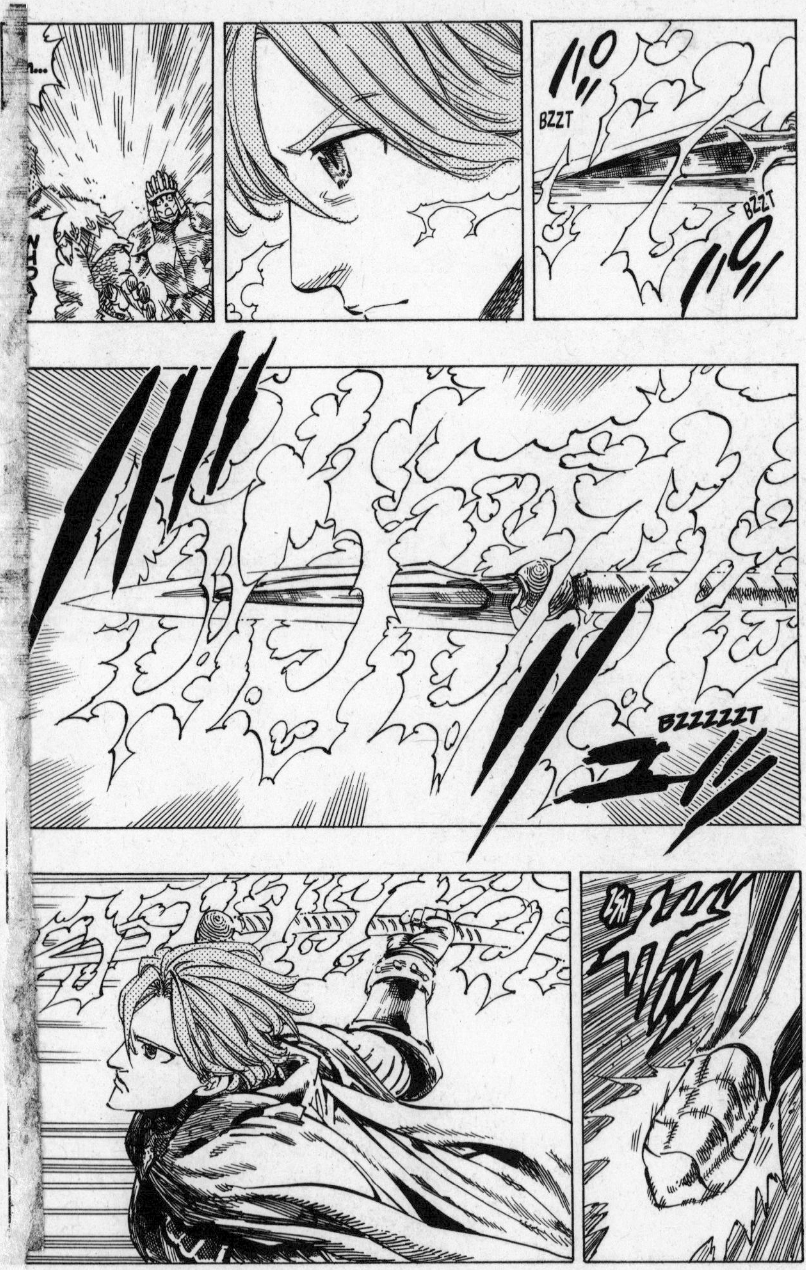
BZZT
BZZT
n...
WHOA!
BZZZZZT
ZSH

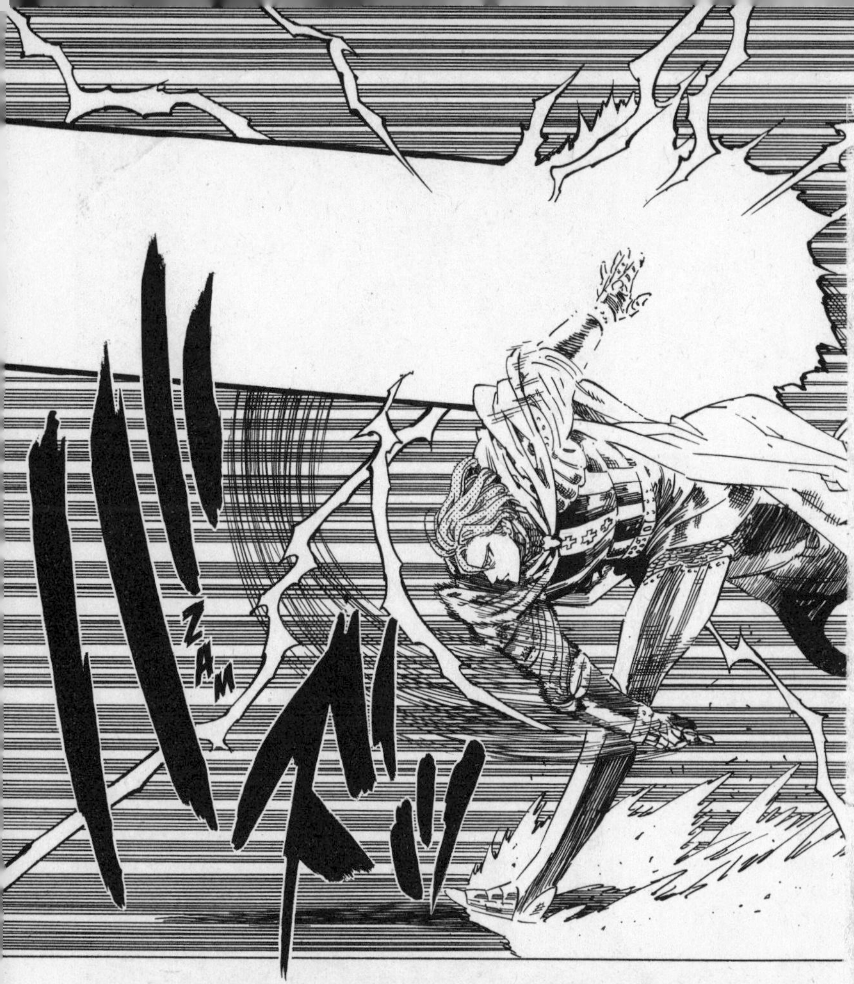
ZAM
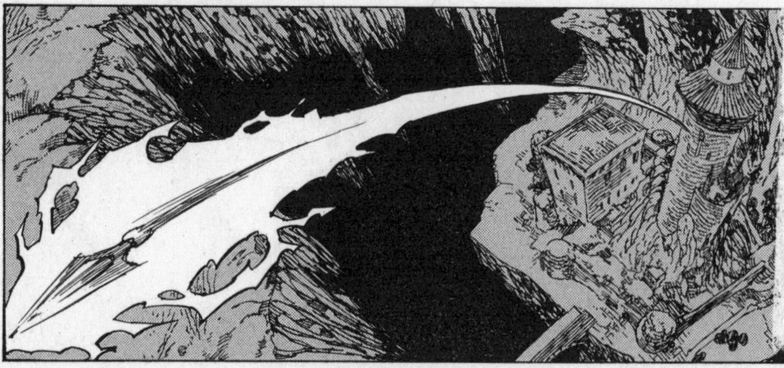

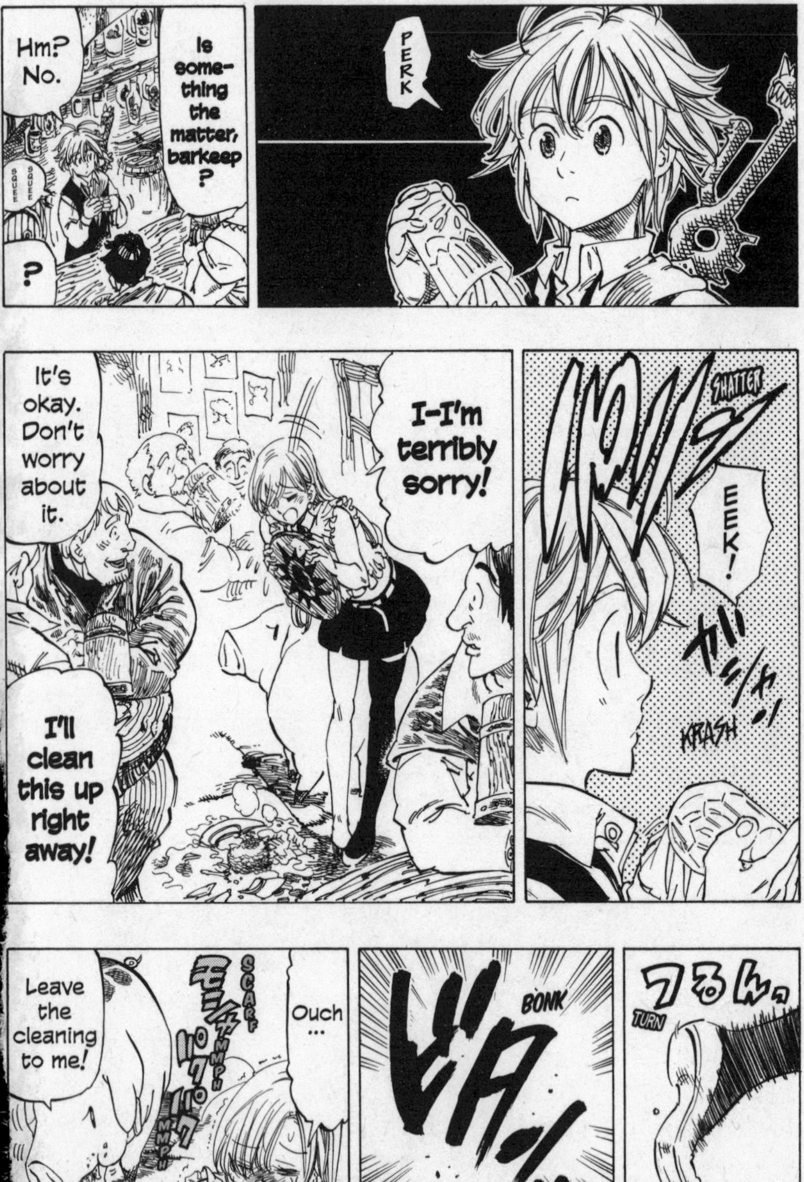
PERK
Is something the matter, barkeep?
Hm? No.
SQUEE
SQUEE
?
SHATTER
EEK!
KRASH
I-I'm terribly sorry!
It's okay. Don't worry about it.
I'll clean this up right away!
TURN
BONK
SCARF
MMPH
MMPH
Ouch ...
Leave the cleaning to me!

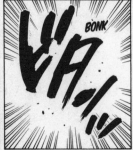

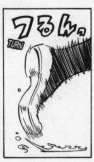

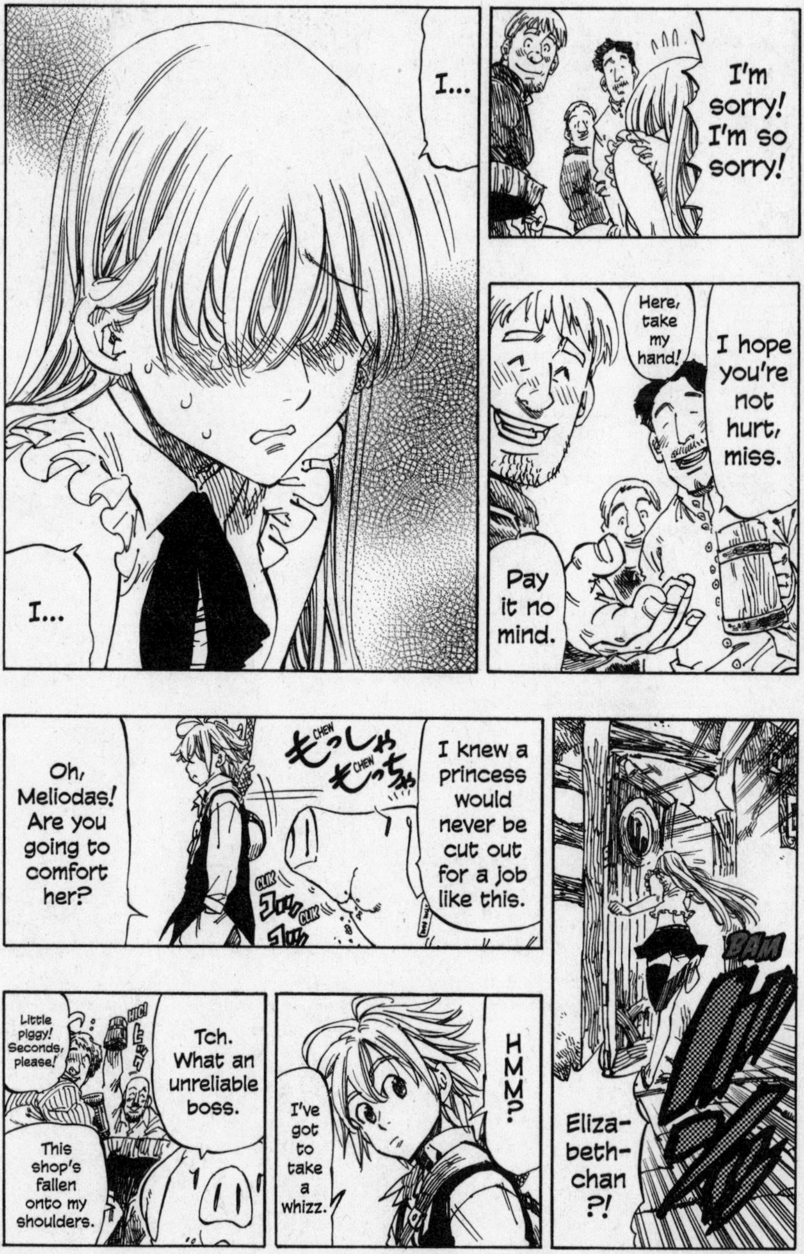
I'm sorry! I'm so sorry!
I hope you're not hurt, miss.
Here, take my hand!
Pay it no mind.
I...
I...
BAM
Eliza-beth-chan?!
I knew a princess would never be cut out for a job like this.
CHEW CHEW
Oh, Meliodas! Are you going to comfort her?
CLIK CLIK
HMM?
I've got to take a whizz.
Tch. What an unreliable boss.
HIC!
Little piggy! Seconds, please!
This shop's fallen onto my shoulders.

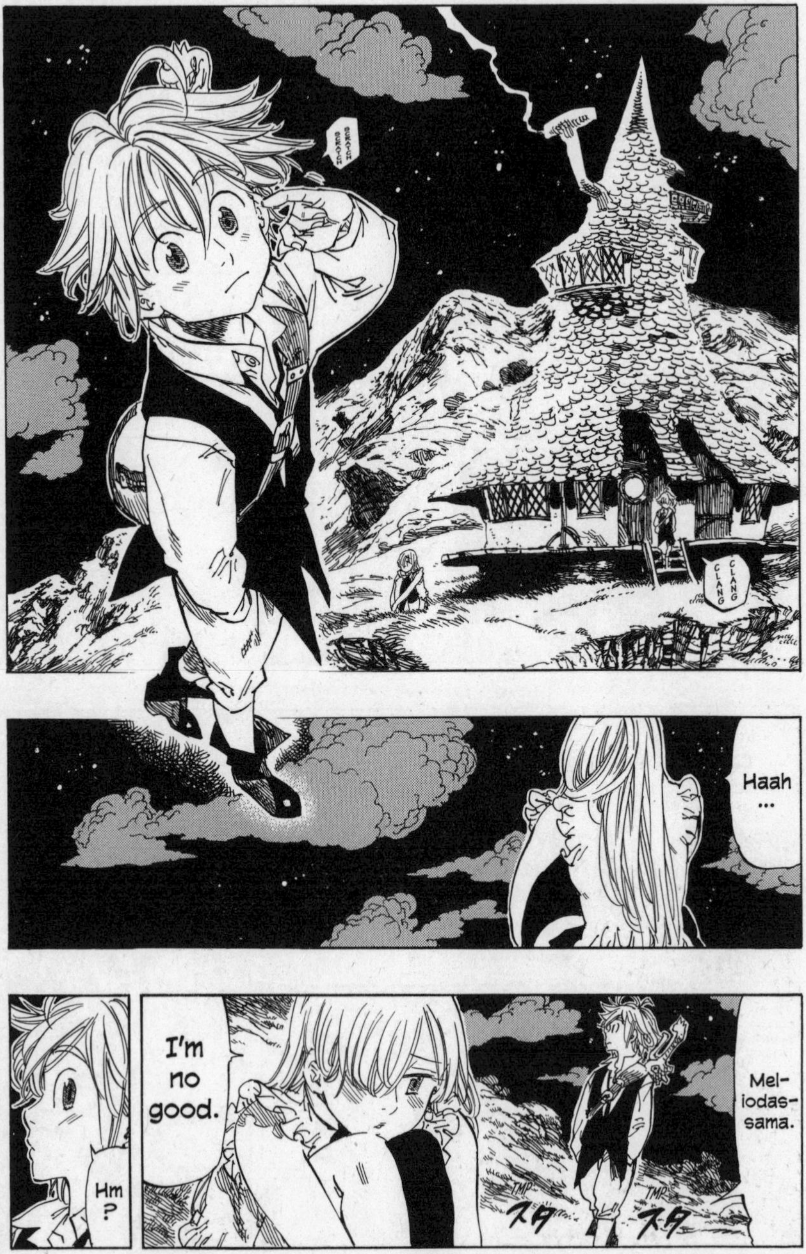
SCRATCH SCRATCH
CLANG CLANG
Haah ...
Mel-iodas-sama.
TMP
TMP
I'm no good.
Hm?

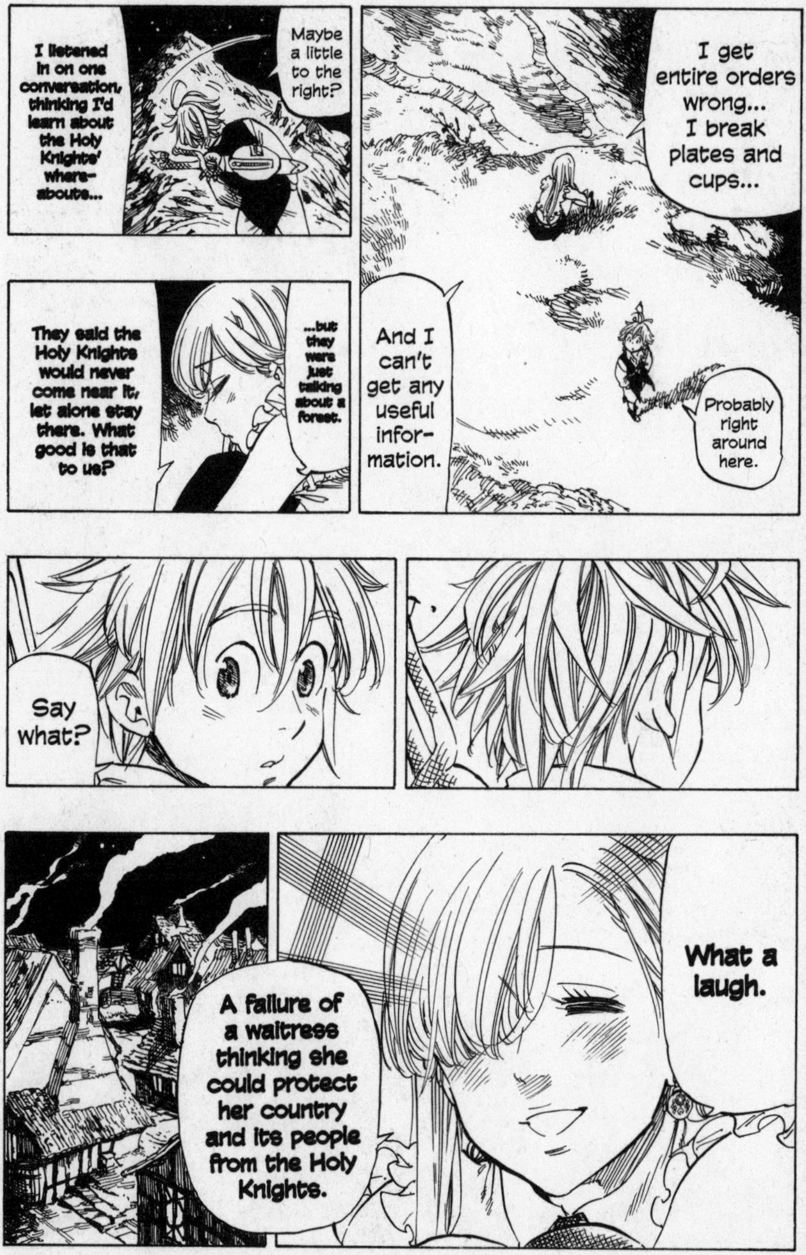

I get entire orders wrong... I break plates and cups...
And I can't get any useful information.
Probably right around here.
Maybe a little to the right?
I listened in on one conversation, thinking I'd learn about the Holy Knights' whereabouts...
...but they were just talking about a forest.
They said the Holy Knights would never come near it, let alone stay there. What good is that to us?
Say what?
What a laugh.
A failure of a waitress thinking she could protect her country and its people from the Holy Knights.

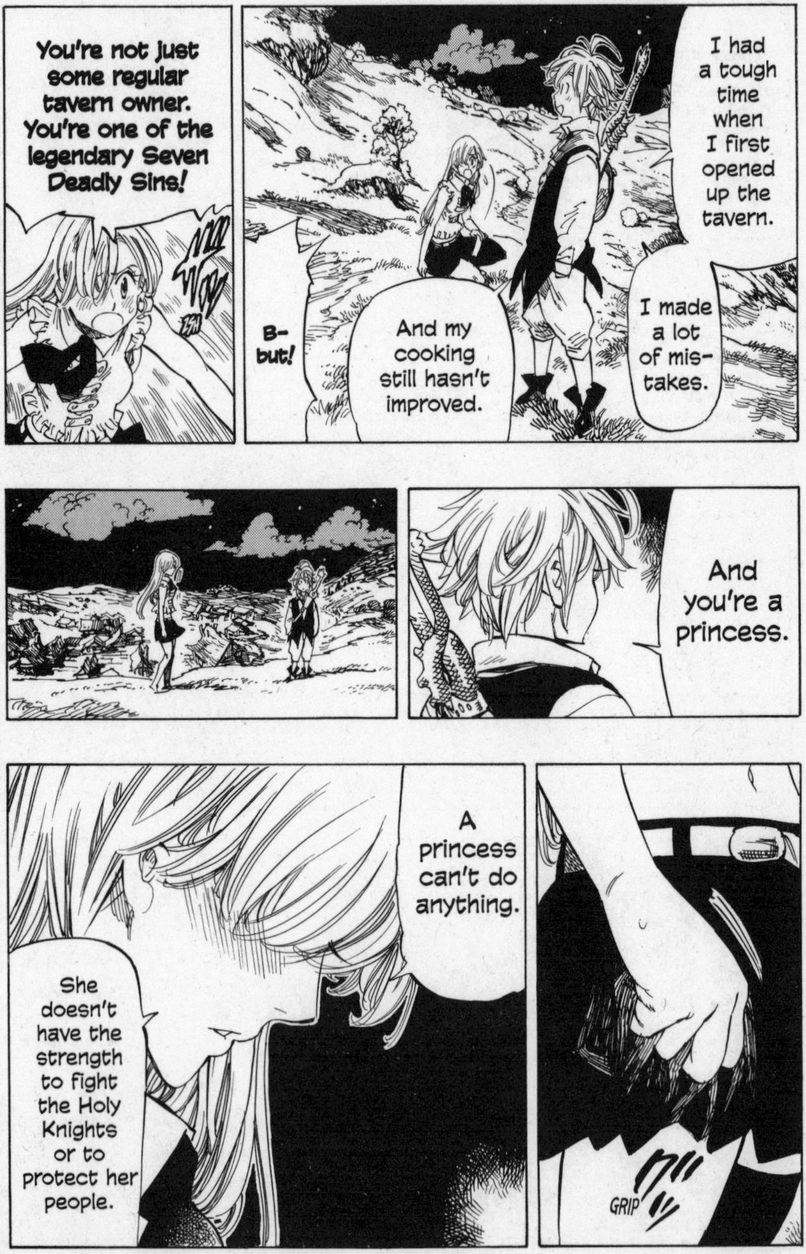
I had a tough time when I first opened up the tavern.
I made a lot of mistakes.
And my cooking still hasn't improved.
B-but!
You're not just some regular tavern owner. You're one of the legendary Seven Deadly Sins!
And you're a princess.
GRIP
A princess can't do anything.
She doesn't have the strength to fight the Holy Knights or to protect her people.

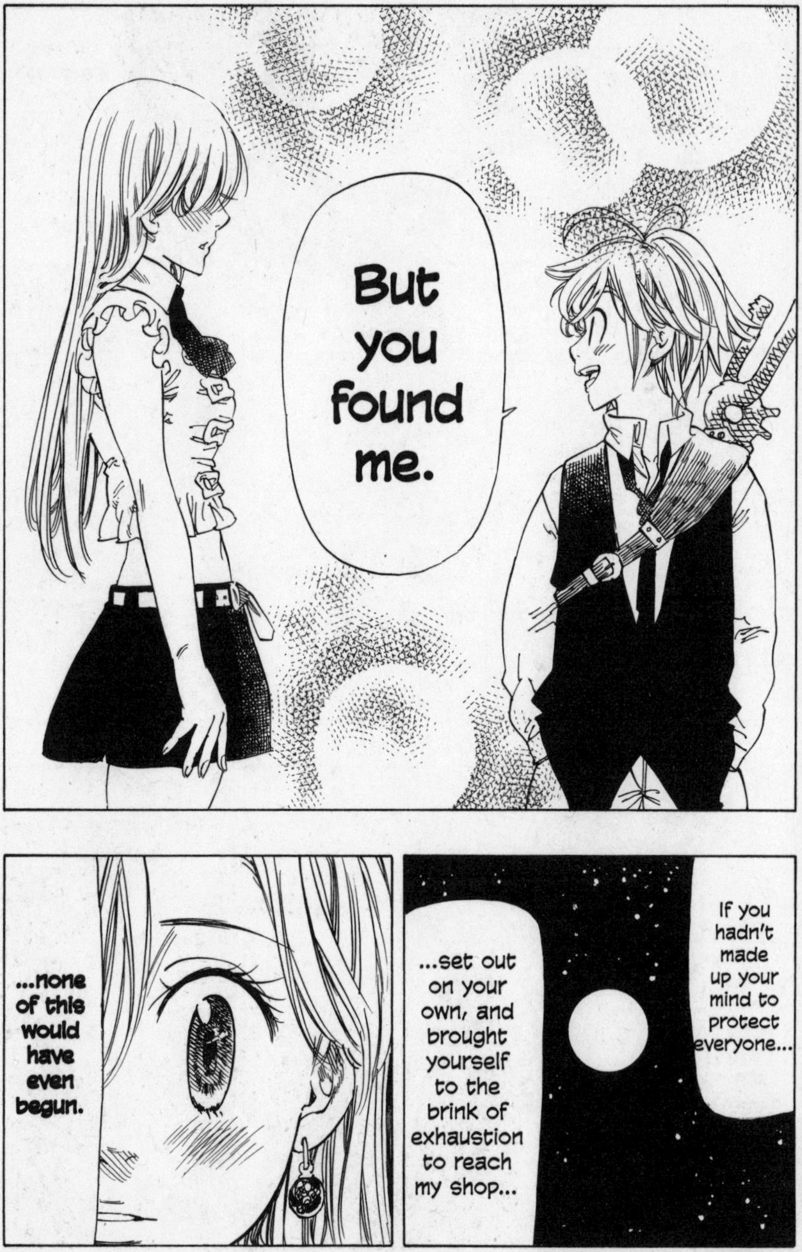

But you found me.
If you hadn't made up your mind to protect everyone...
...set out on your own, and brought yourself to the brink of exhaustion to reach my shop...
...none of this would have even begun.

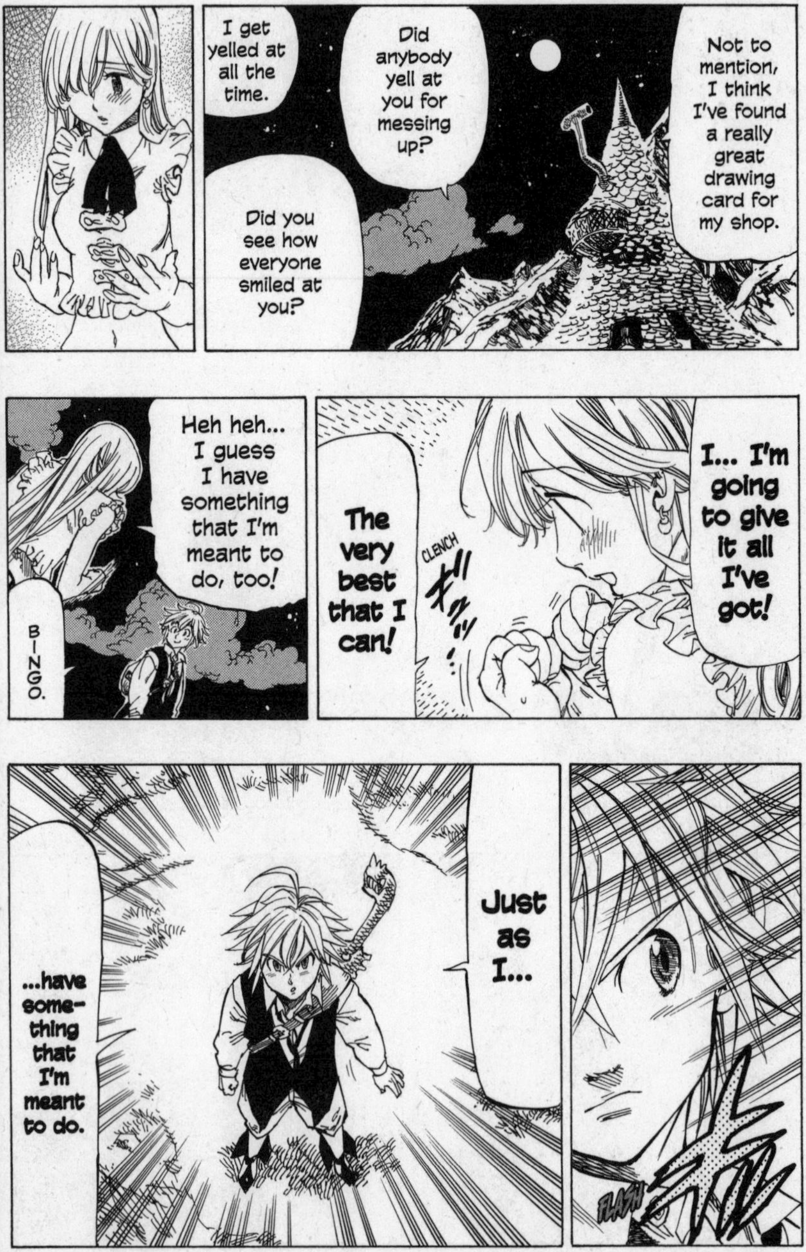
Not to mention, I think I've found a really great drawing card for my shop.
Did anybody yell at you for messing up?
I get yelled at all the time.
Did you see how everyone smiled at you?
I... I'm going to give it all I've got!
CLENCH
The very best that I can!
Heh heh... I guess I have something that I'm meant to do, too!
BINGO.
FLASH
Just as I...
...have something that I'm meant to do.

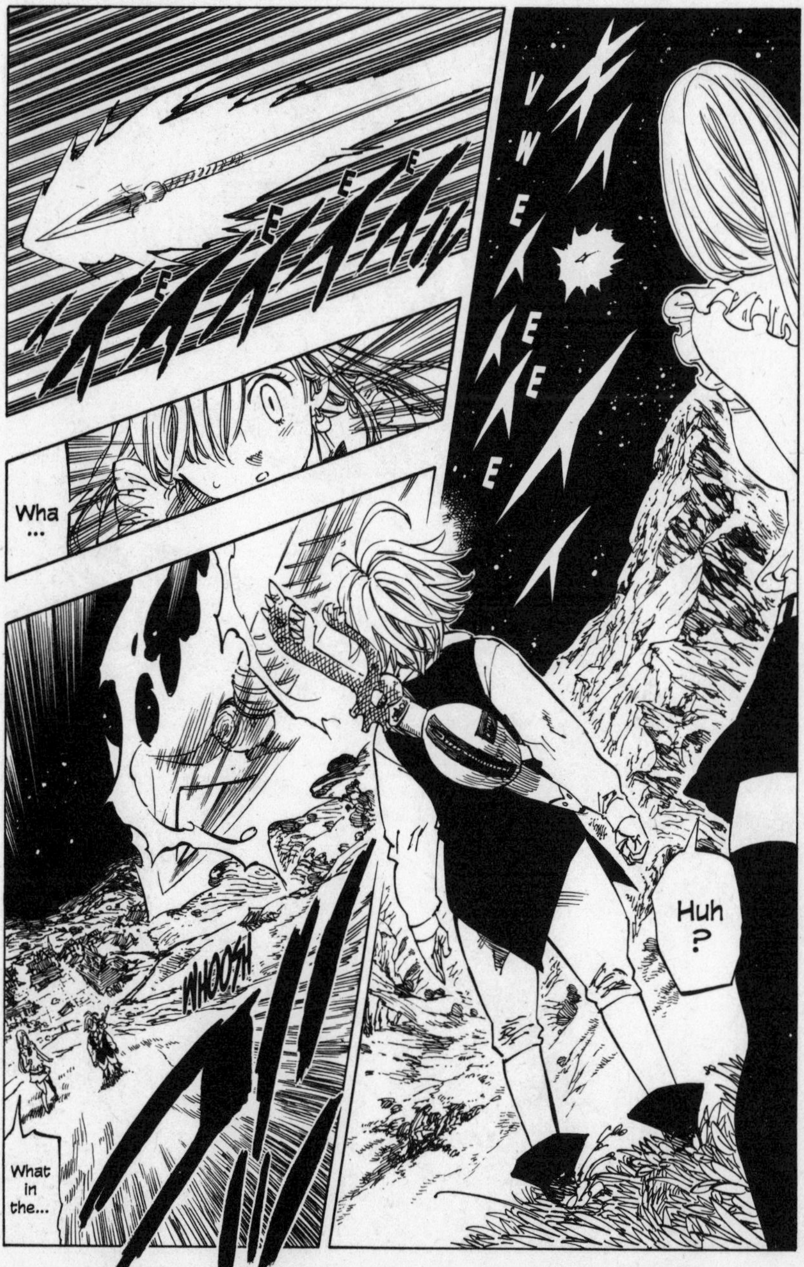
VWEEEEE
Huh?
EEEE
Wha...
WHOOSH!!
What in the...

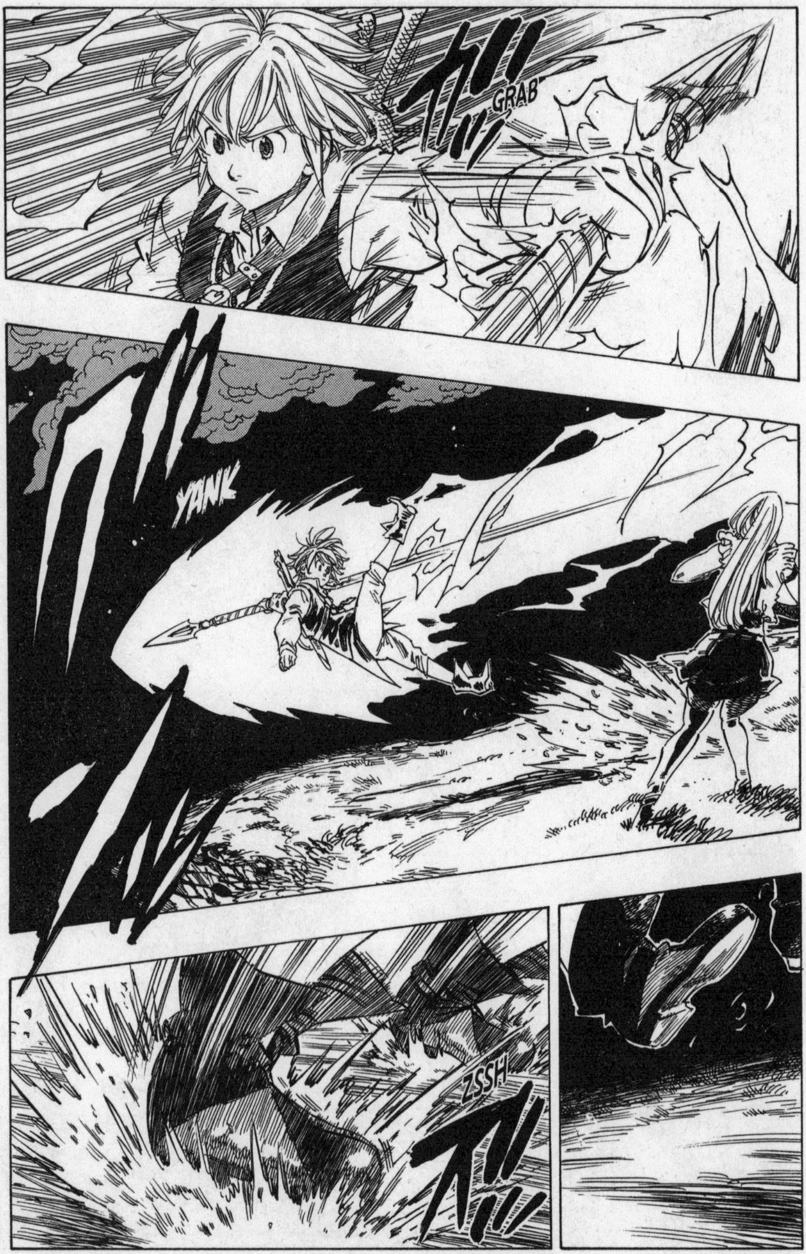
GRAB
YANK
ZSSH

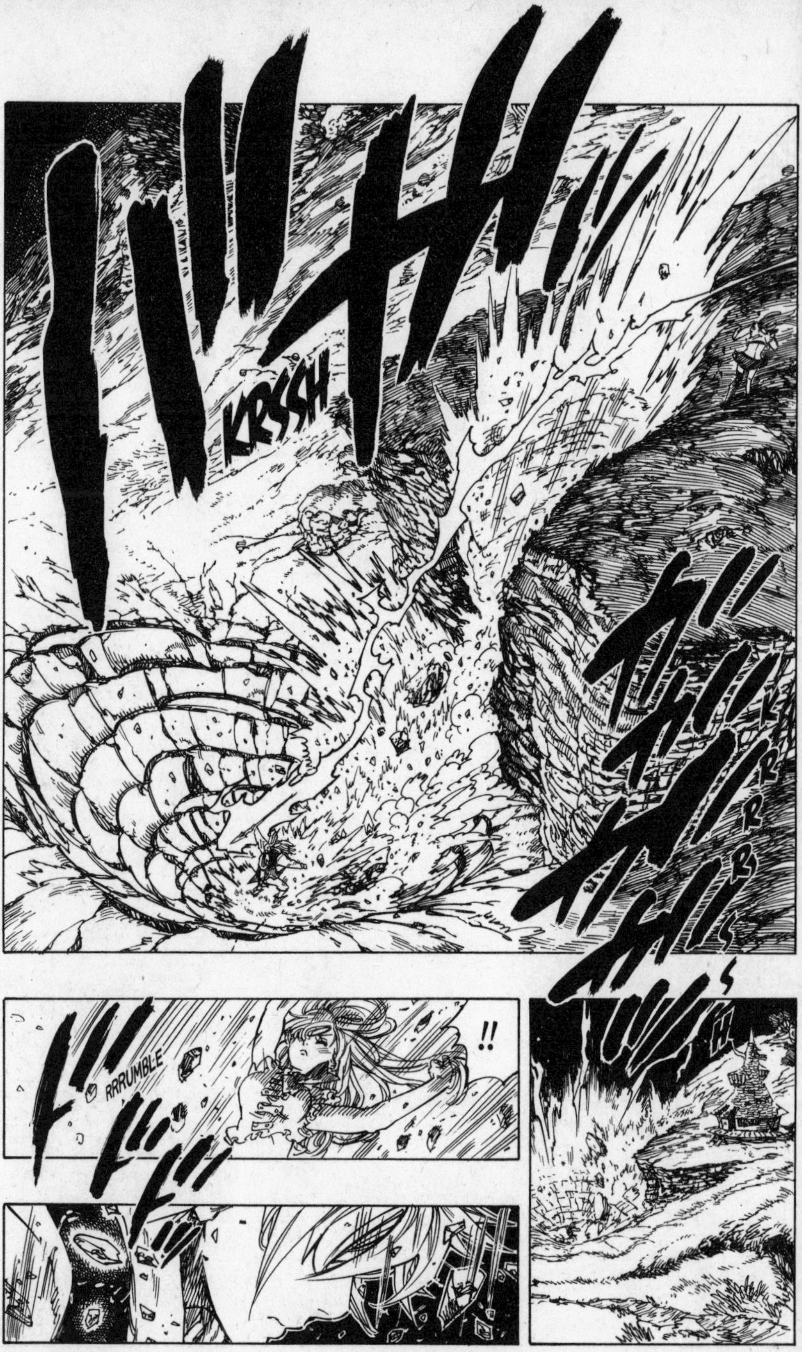
KRSSH
KRRRRSSSH
!!
RRRUMBLE

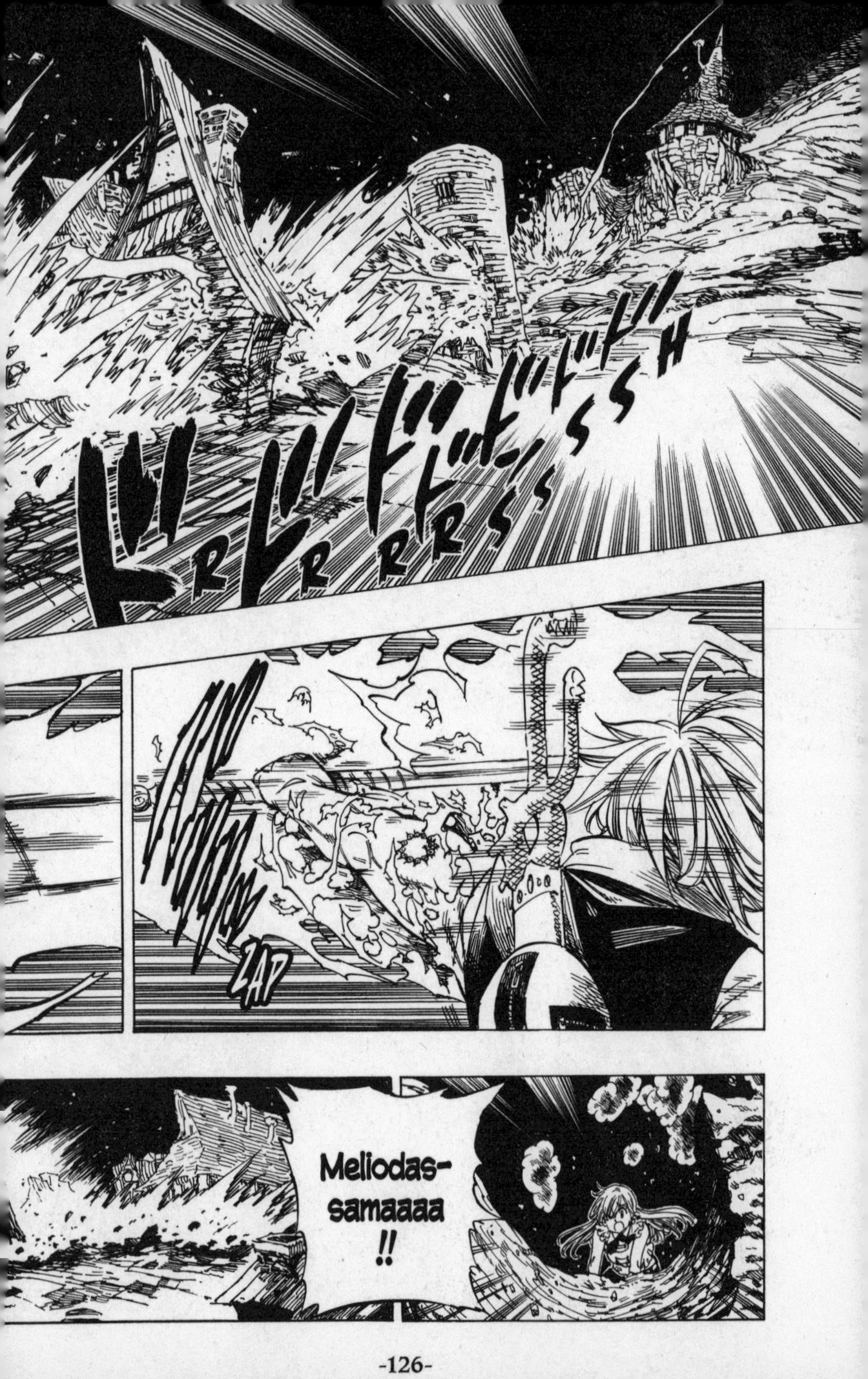
RRRRSSSSH
ZAP
Meliodas-samaaaa!!

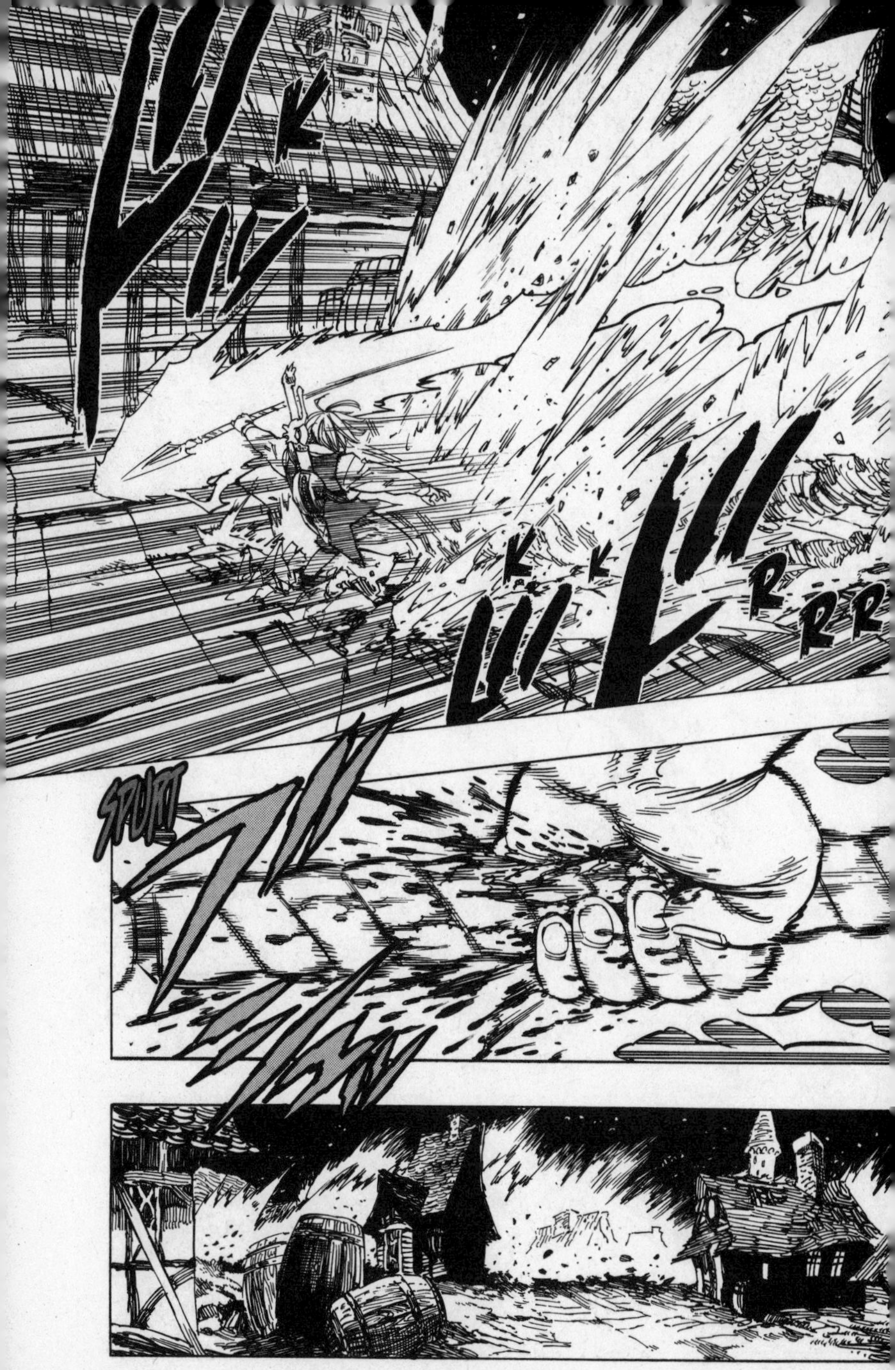
SPURT

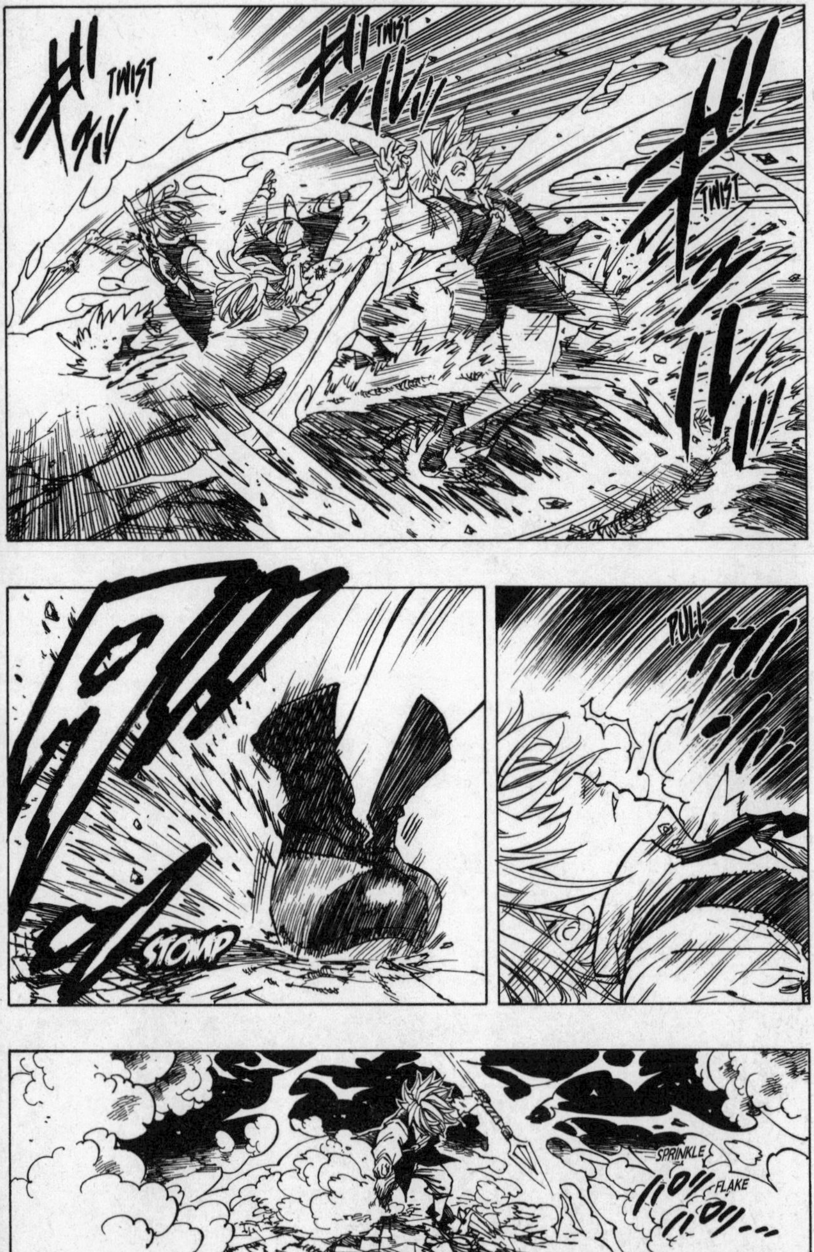
TWIST
TWIST
TWIST
PULL
STOMP
SPRINKLE
FLAKE

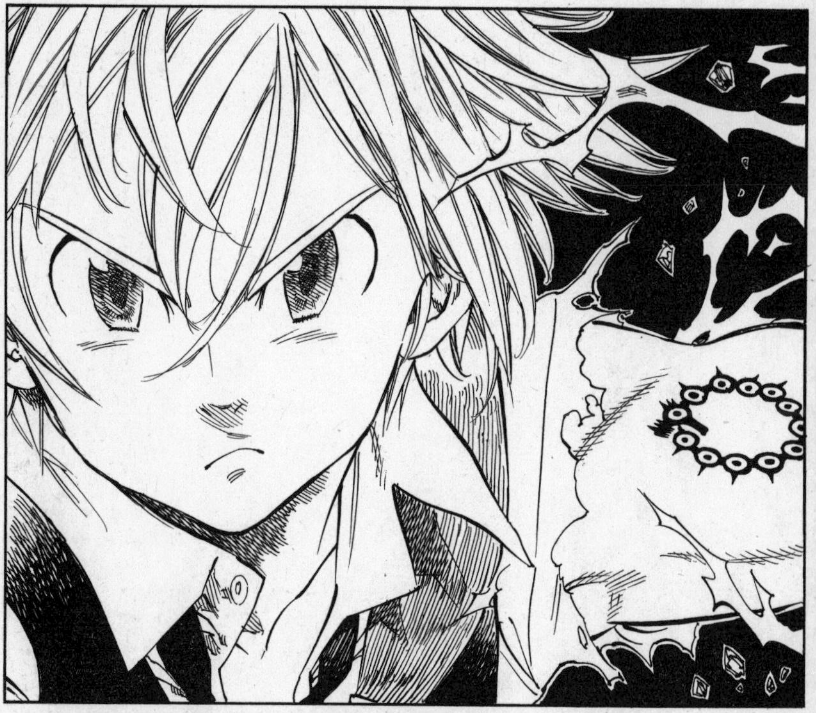

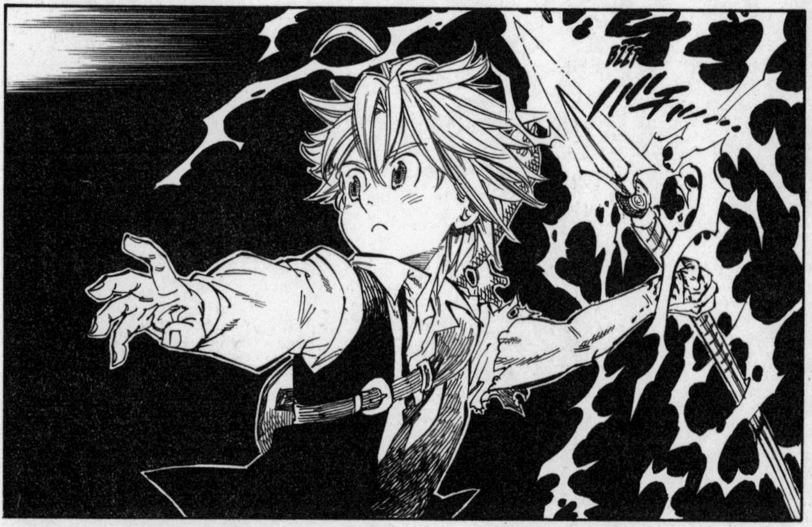
BZZT
バチィ……

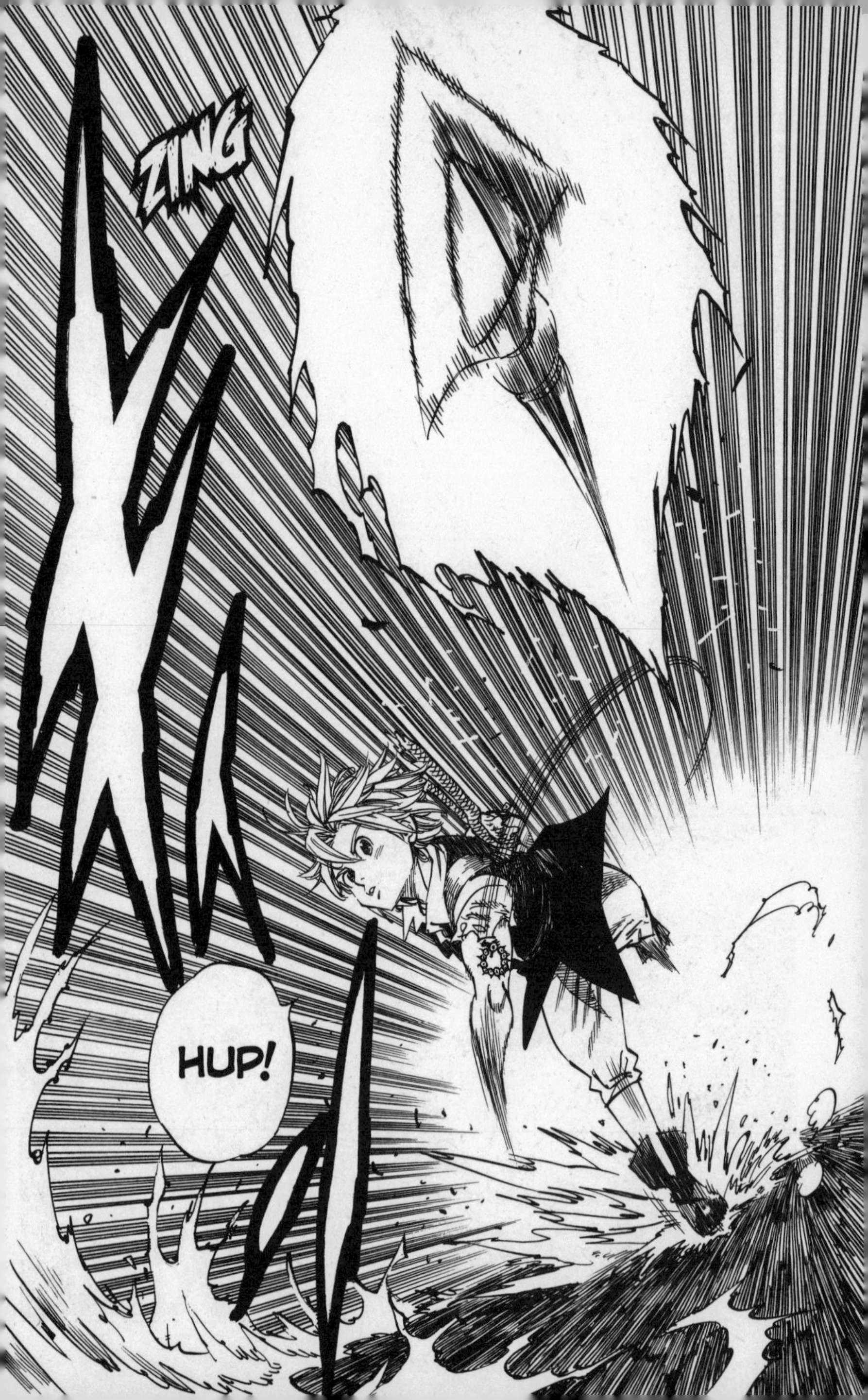
ZING
HUP!

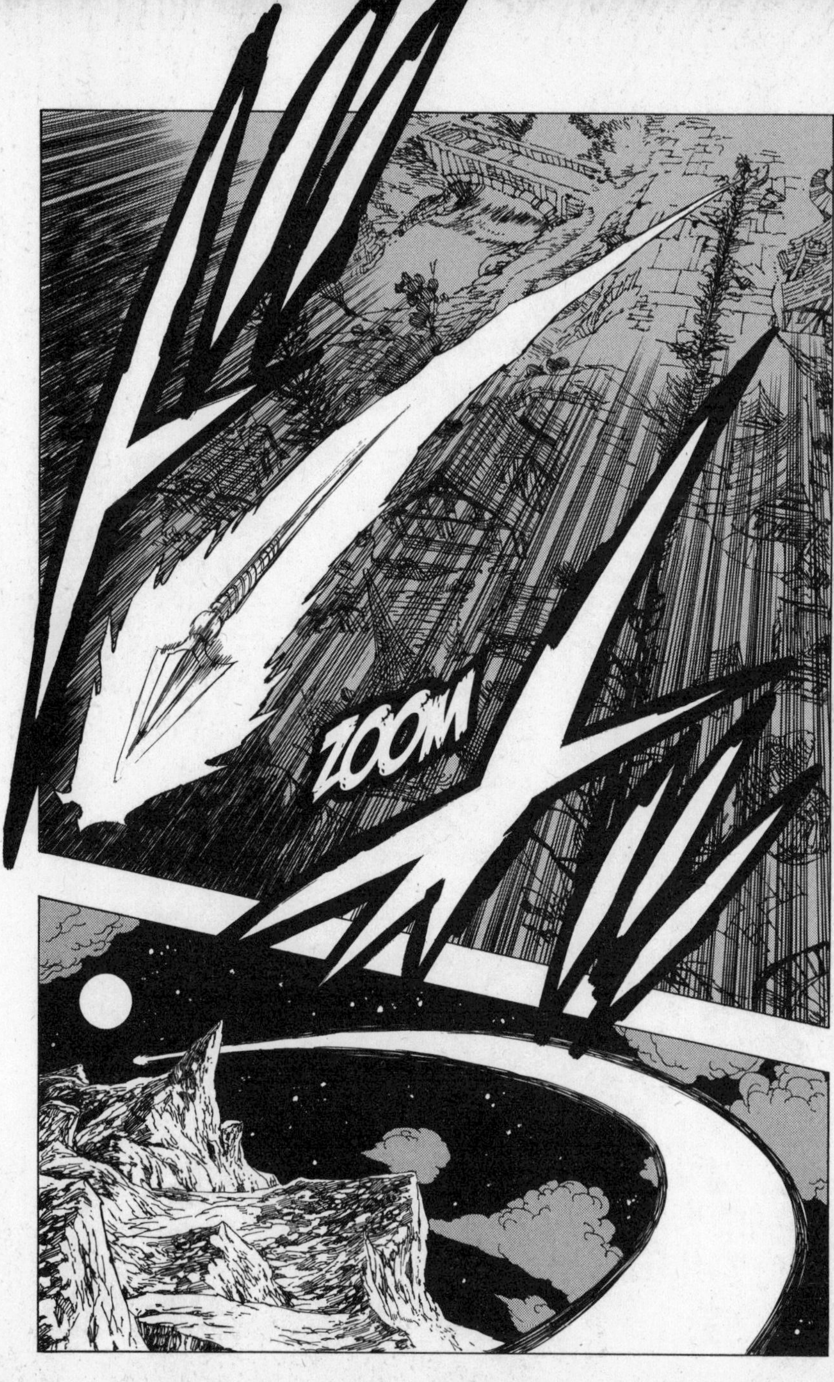
ZOOM

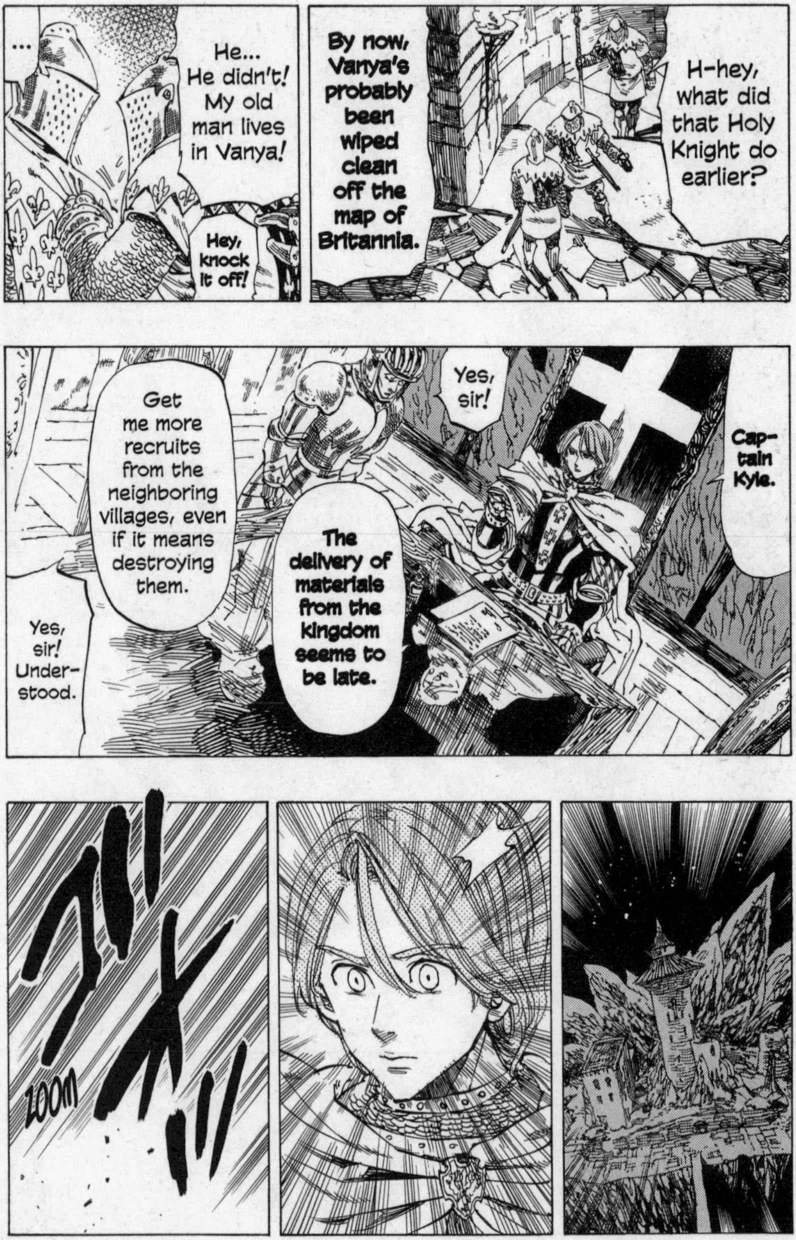
H-hey, what did that Holy Knight do earlier?
By now, Vanya's probably been wiped clean off the map of Britannia.
He... He didn't! My old man lives in Vanya!
Hey, knock it off!
...
Captain Kyle.
Yes, sir!
The delivery of materials from the kingdom seems to be late.
Get me more recruits from the neighboring villages, even if it means destroying them.
Yes, sir! Understood.
ZOOM

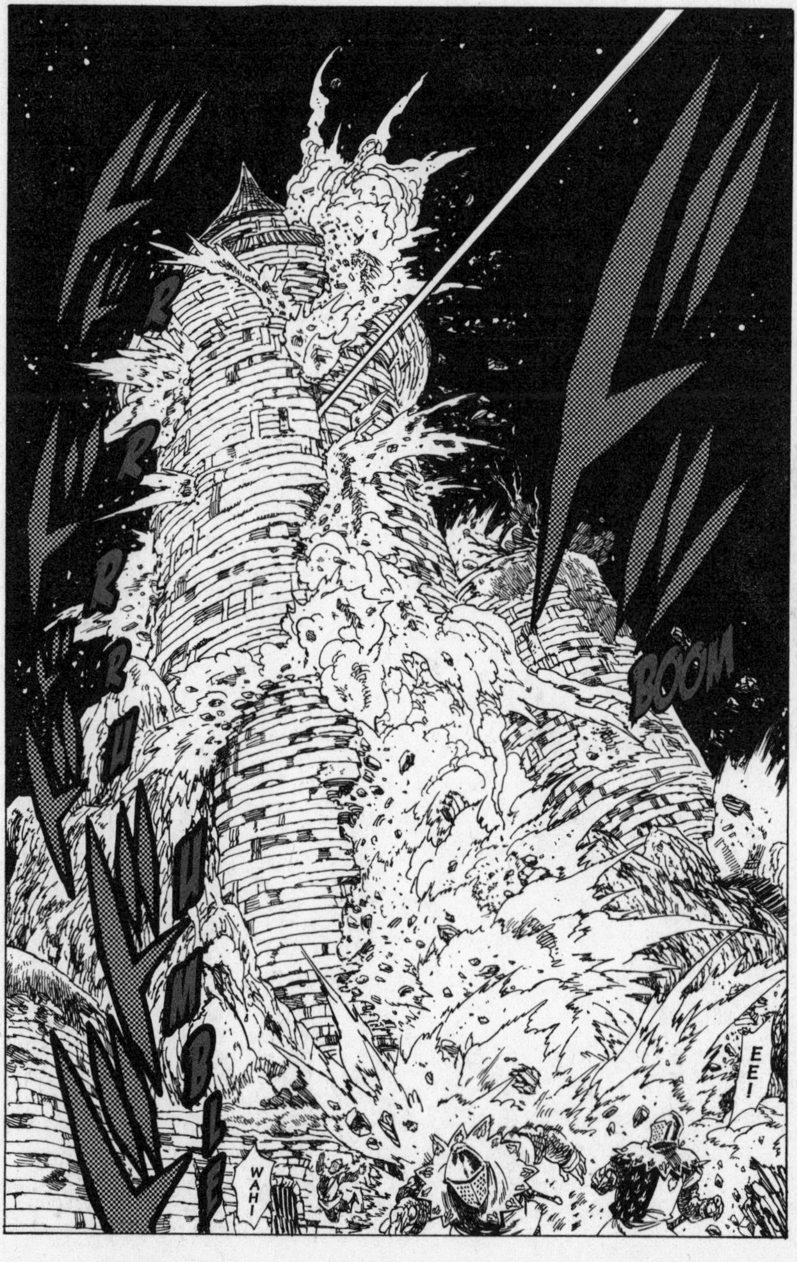
BOOM
EE!
RRRRUMMBLE
WAH!

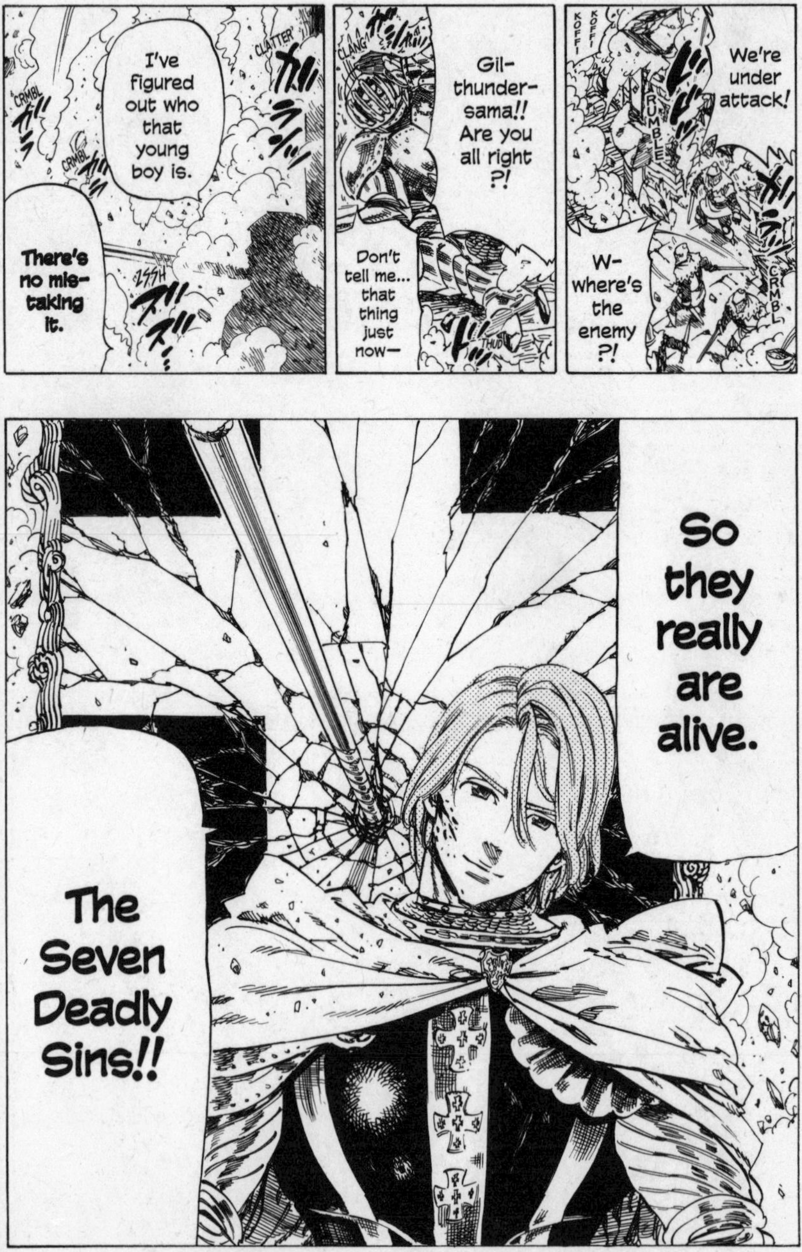
KOFF
KOFF
We're under attack!
RUMBLE
W-where's the enemy?!
CRMBL
CLANG
Gil-thunder-sama!! Are you all right?!
Don't tell me... that thing just now—
THUD
CLATTER
I've figured out who that young boy is.
CRMBL
CRMBL
There's no mistaking it.
ZSSH
So they really are alive.
The Seven Deadly Sins!!

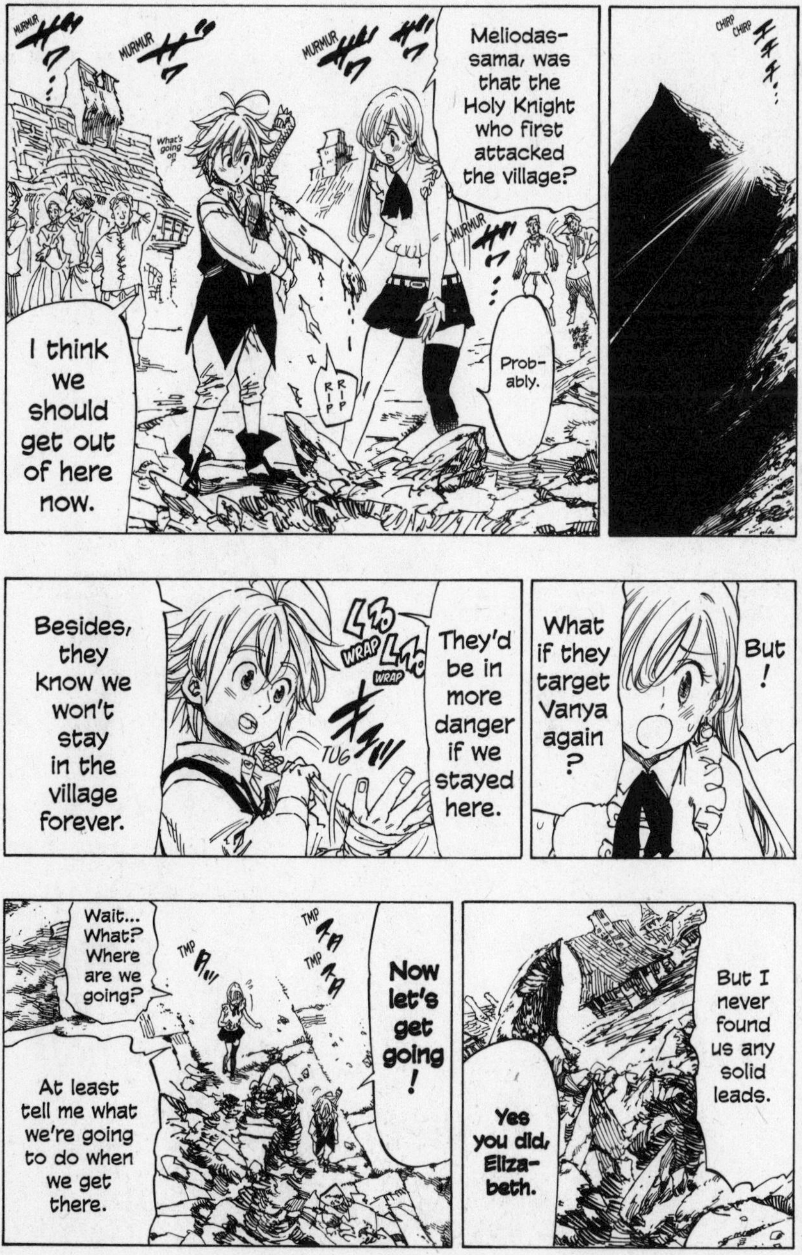
CHIRP CHIRP
Meliodas-sama, was that the Holy Knight who first attacked the village?
MURMUR
MURMUR
MURMUR
MURMUR
What's going on?
Probably.
RIP RIP
I think we should get out of here now.
But!
What if they target Vanya again?
They'd be in more danger if we stayed here.
WRAP
WRAP
TUG
Besides, they know we won't stay in the village forever.
But I never found us any solid leads.
Yes you did, Elizabeth.
Now let's get going!
TMP
TMP
TMP
Wait... What? Where are we going?
At least tell me what we're going to do when we get there.

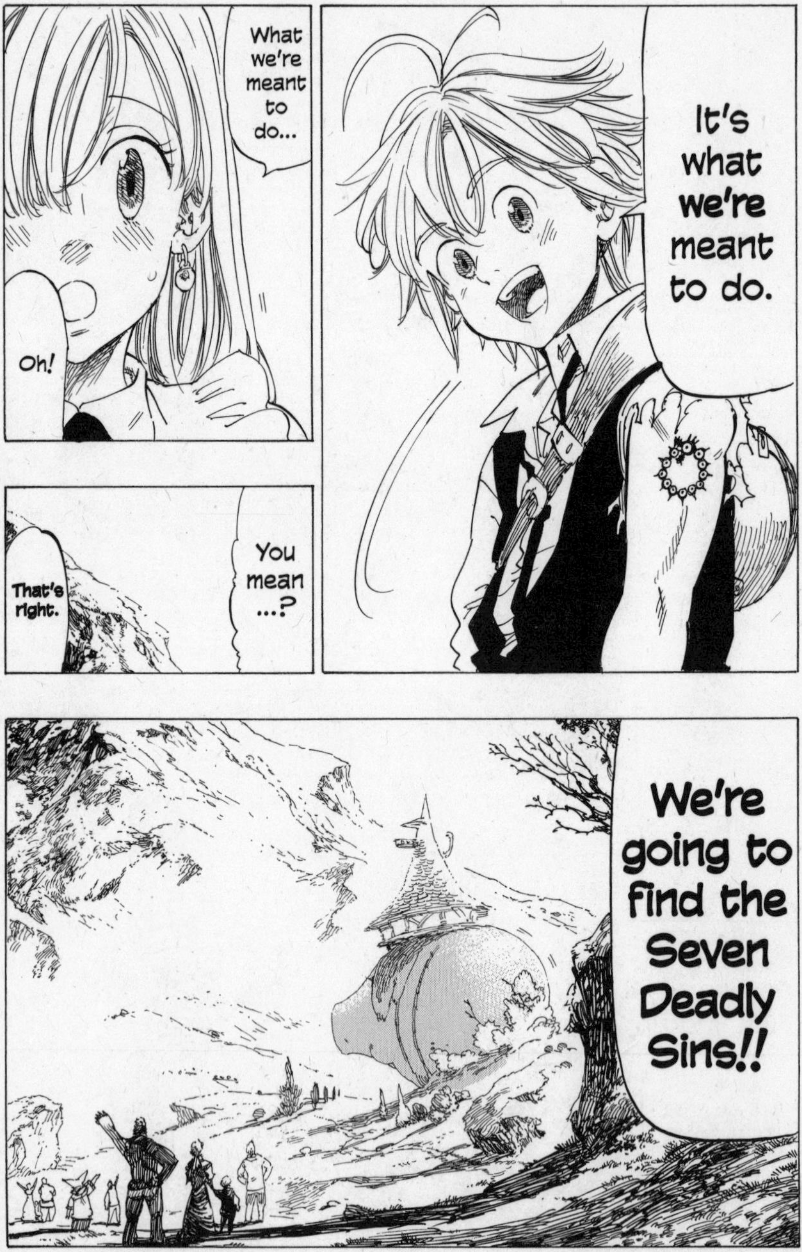
It's what we're meant to do.
What we're meant to do...
Oh!
You mean ...?
That's right.
We're going to find the Seven Deadly Sins!!

Chapter 4 - The Sin in the Sleeping Forest

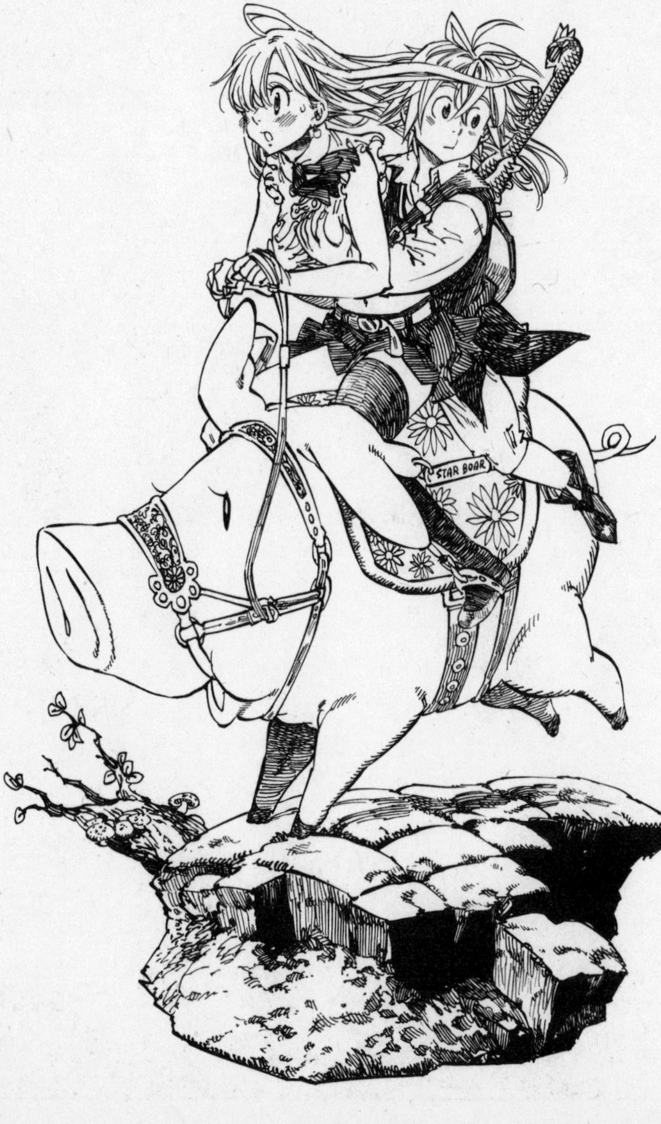
STAR BOAR

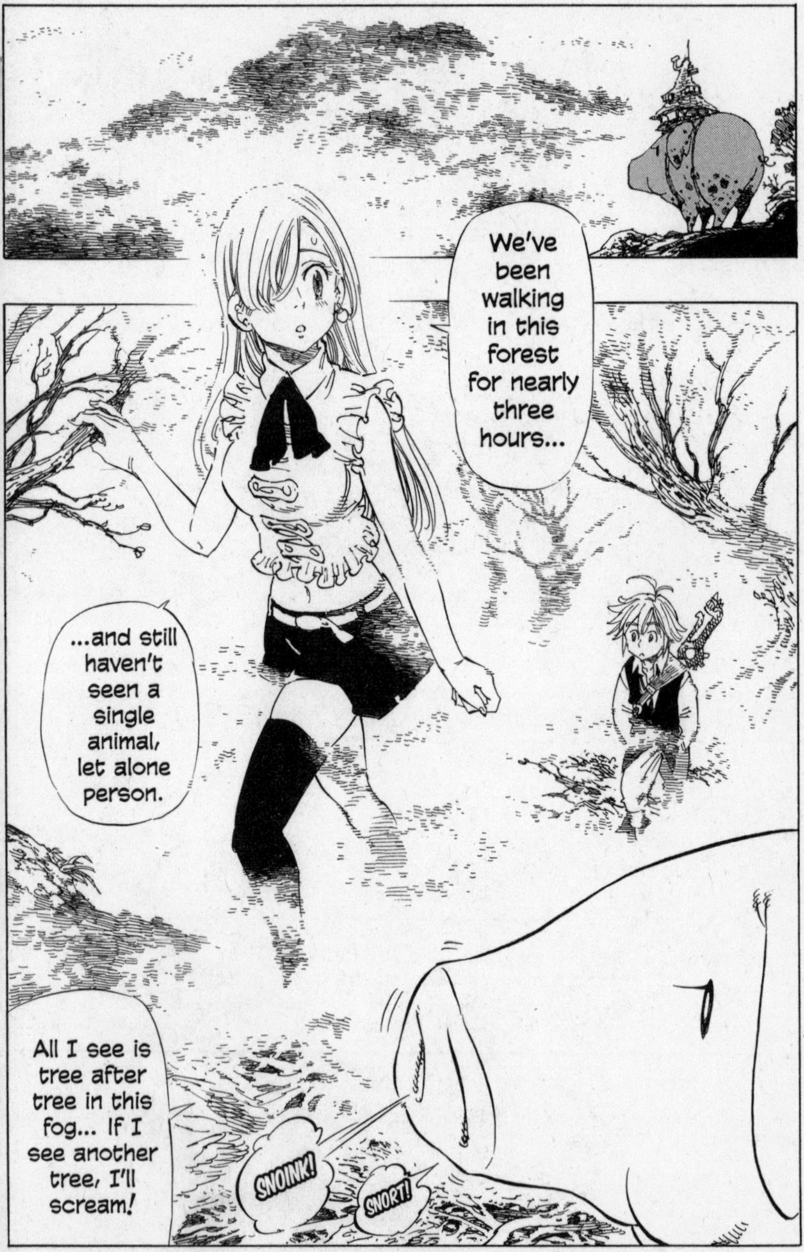
We've been walking in this forest for nearly three hours...
...and still haven't seen a single animal, let alone person.
All I see is tree after tree in this fog... If I see another tree, I'll scream!
SNOINK!
SNORT!

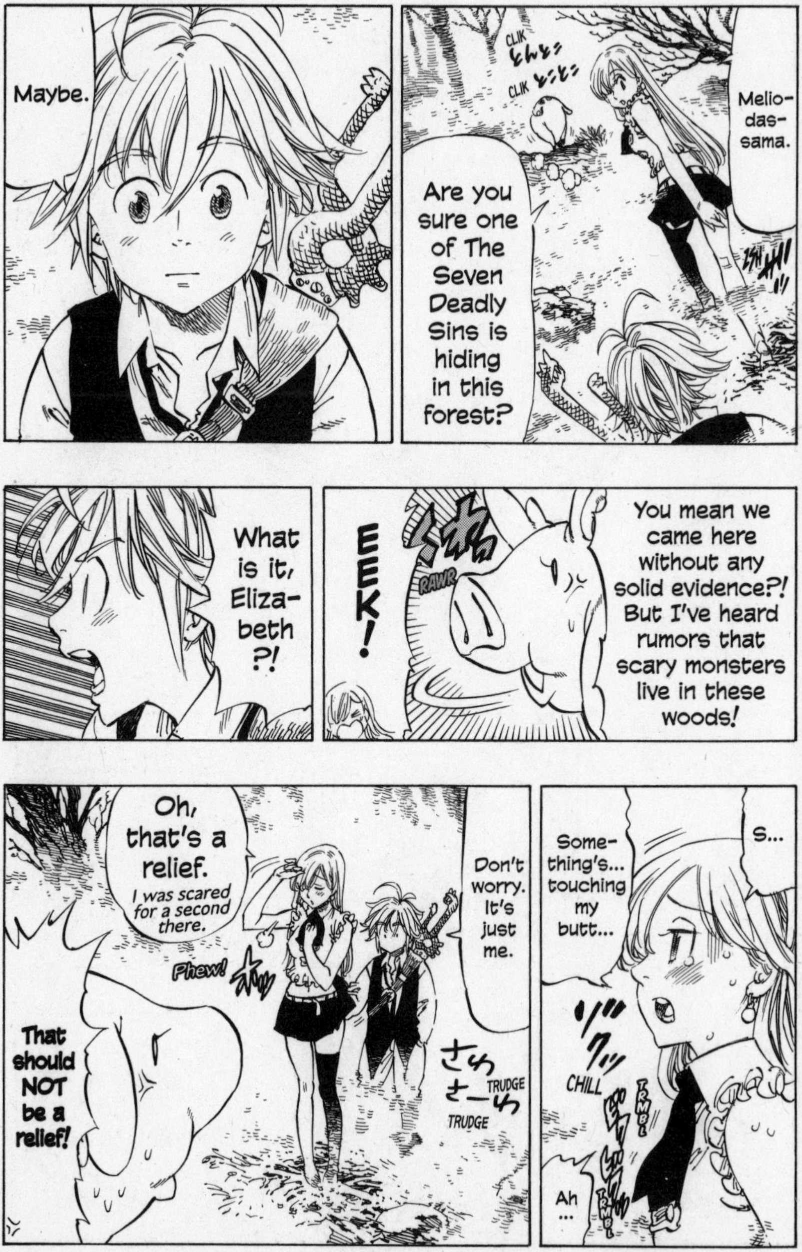
Melio-das-sama.
CLIK
CLIK
Are you sure one of The Seven Deadly Sins is hiding in this forest?
Maybe.
You mean we came here without any solid evidence?! But I've heard rumors that scary monsters live in these woods!
RAWR
EEK!
What is it, Eliza-beth?!
S...
Some-thing's... touching my butt...
CHILL
TRMBL
TRMBL
Ah ...
Don't worry. It's just me.
Oh, that's a relief. I was scared for a second there.
Phew!
TRUDGE
TRUDGE
That should NOT be a relief!

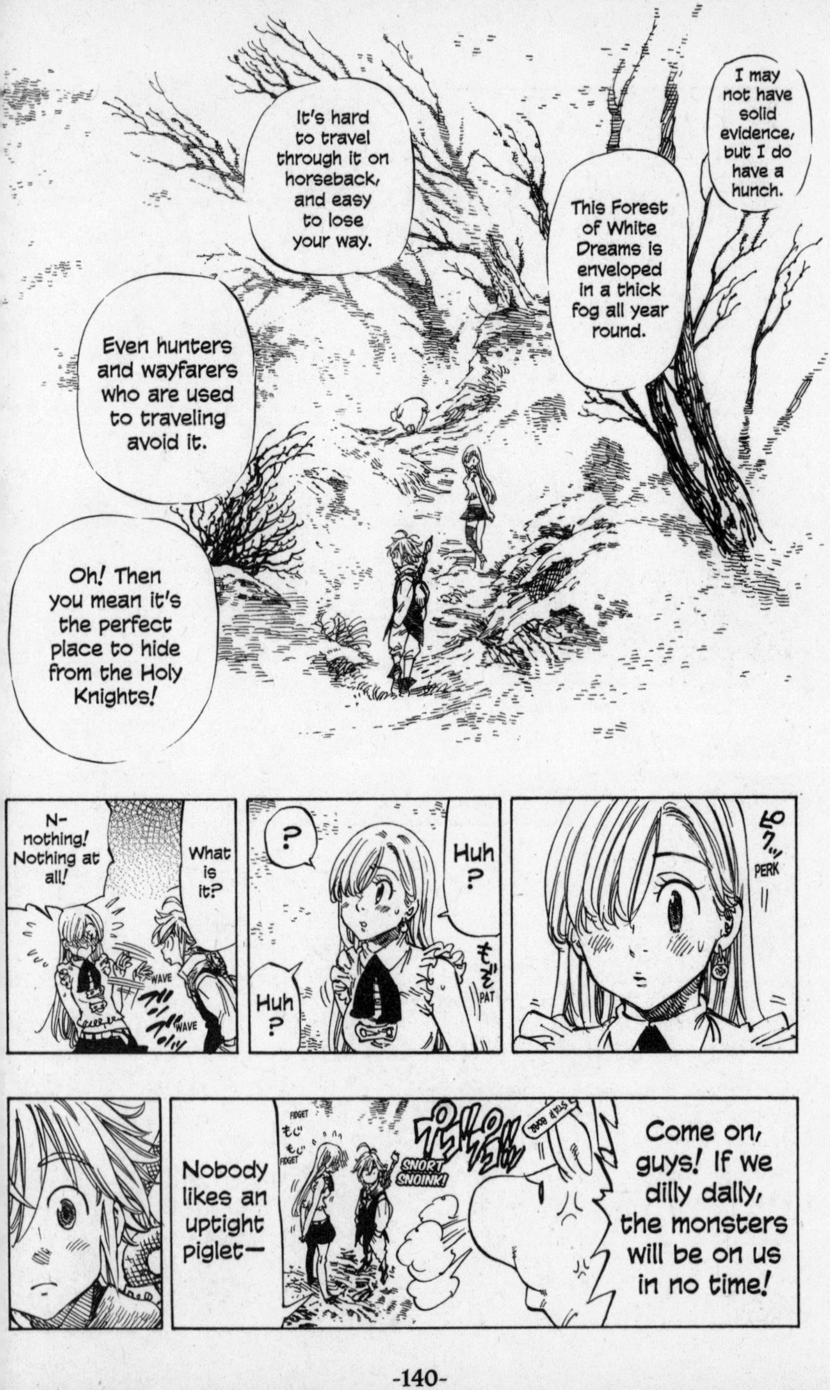
I may not have solid evidence, but I do have a hunch.
This Forest of White Dreams is enveloped in a thick fog all year round.
It's hard to travel through it on horseback, and easy to lose your way.
Even hunters and wayfarers who are used to traveling avoid it.
Oh! Then you mean it's the perfect place to hide from the Holy Knights!
PERK
Huh?
?
PAT
Huh?
What is it?
N-nothing! Nothing at all!
WAVE
WAVE
Come on, guys! If we dilly dally, the monsters will be on us in no time!
SNORT SNOINK!
Nobody likes an uptight piglet—
FIDGET
もじ
もじ
FIDGET

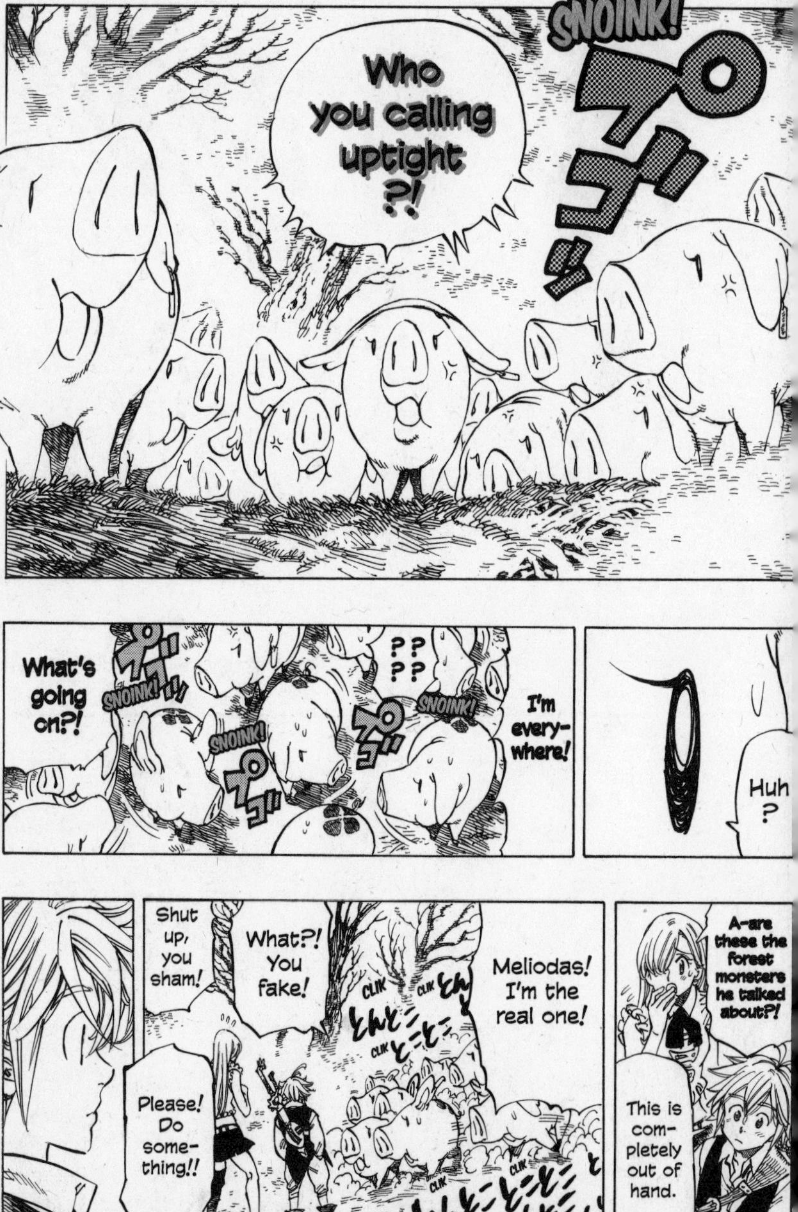

SNOINK!
Who you calling uptight?!
Huh?
??
??
I'm everywhere!
SNOINK!
SNOINK!
SNOINK!
What's going on?!
A-are these the forest monsters he talked about?!
This is completely out of hand.
Meliodas! I'm the real one!
CLIK
CLIK
CLIK
CLIK
CLIK
What?! You fake!
Shut up, you sham!
Please! Do something!!

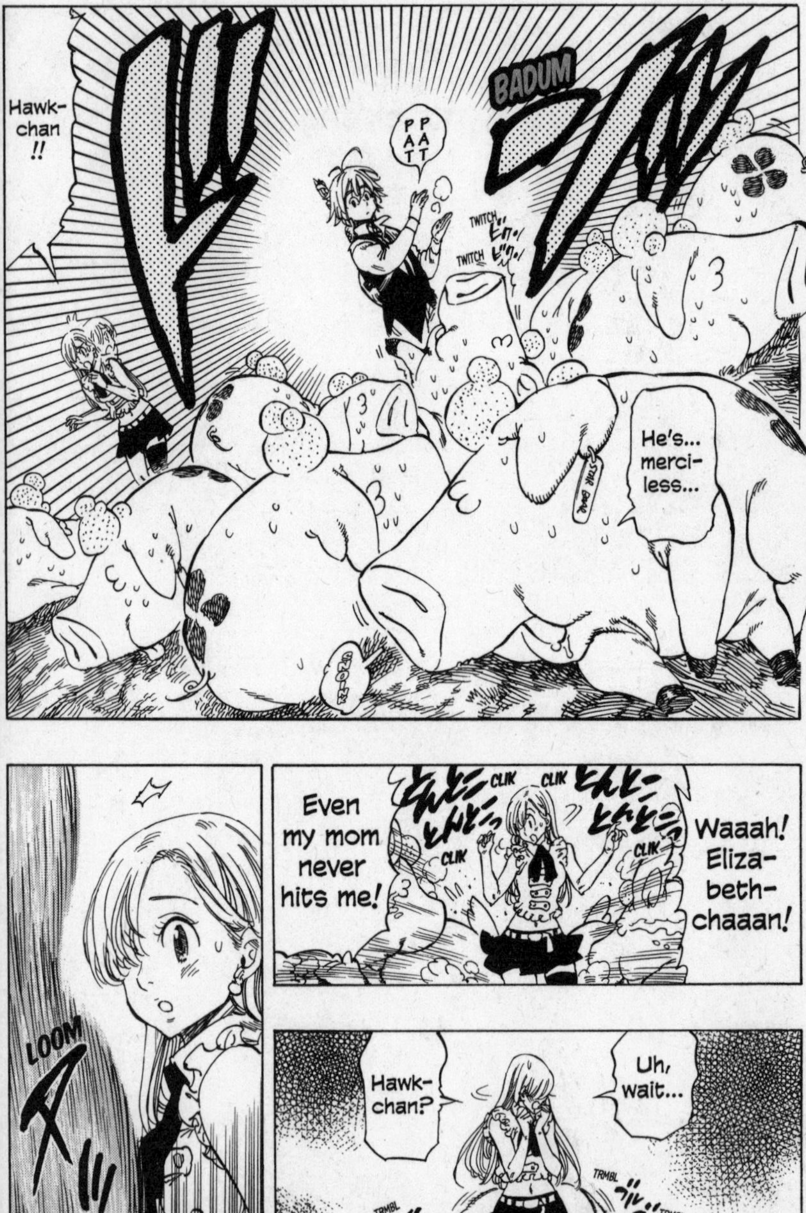
BADUM
TWITCH
TWITCH
PAT PAT
He's... merciless...
Hawk-chan!!
Waaah! Eliza-beth-chaaan!
CLIK
CLIK
CLIK
CLIK
Even my mom never hits me!
Uh, wait...
TRMBL
TRMBL
TRMBL
Hawk-chan?
LOOM

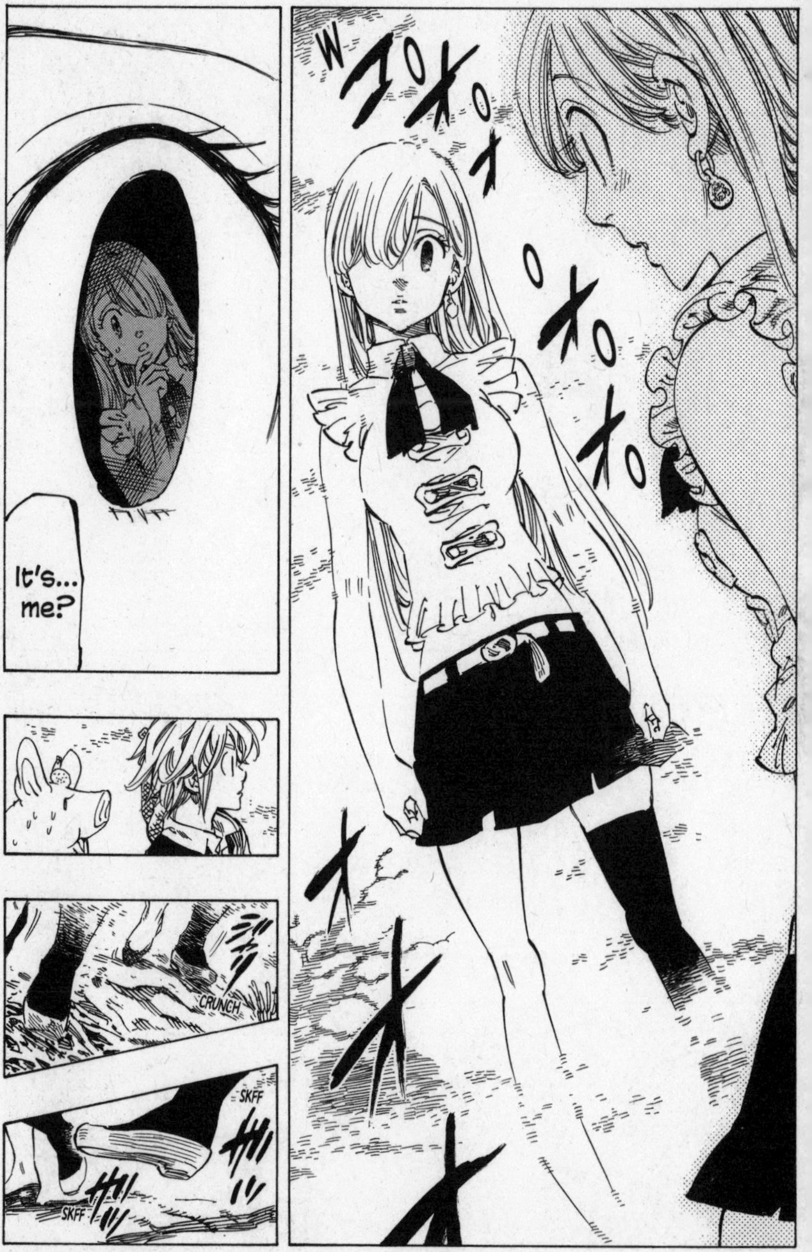
W
It's... me?
CRUNCH
SKFF
SKFF

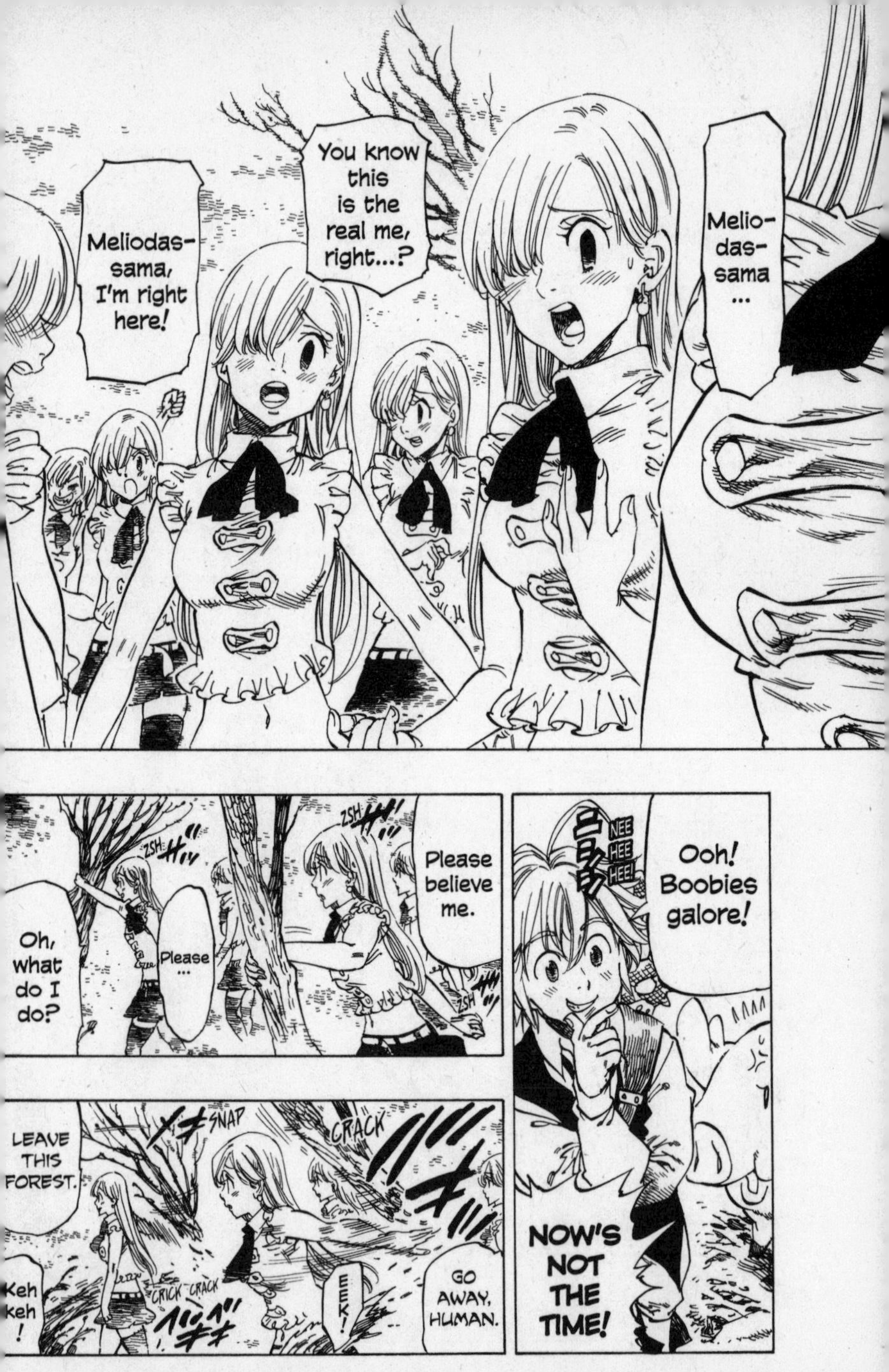
Melio-das-sama ...
You know this is the real me, right...?
Meliodas-sama, I'm right here!
Ooh! Boobies galore!
NEE HEE HEE!
NOW'S NOT THE TIME!
ZSH
Please believe me.
ZSH
ZSH
Please ...
Oh, what do I do?
CRACK
SNAP
LEAVE THIS FOREST.
GO AWAY, HUMAN.
EEK!
CRICK CRACK
Keh keh!

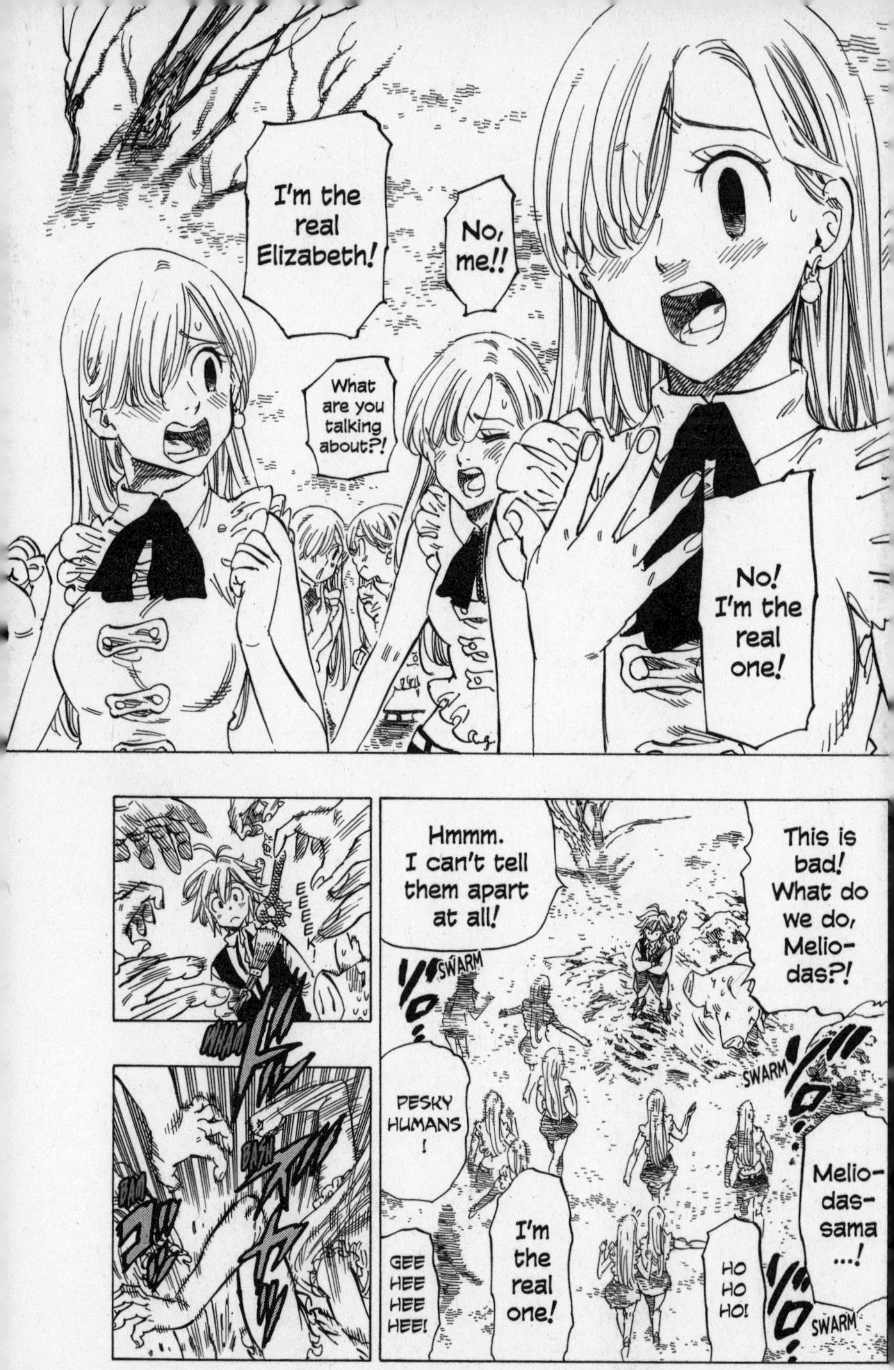
I'm the real Elizabeth!
No, me!!
What are you talking about?!
No! I'm the real one!
This is bad! What do we do, Melio-das?!
Hmmm. I can't tell them apart at all!
SWARM
SWARM
Melio-das-sama ...!
HO HO HO!
I'm the real one!
PESKY HUMANS!
GEE HEE HEE HEE!
SWARM
EEEEK!
WHAM
BASH

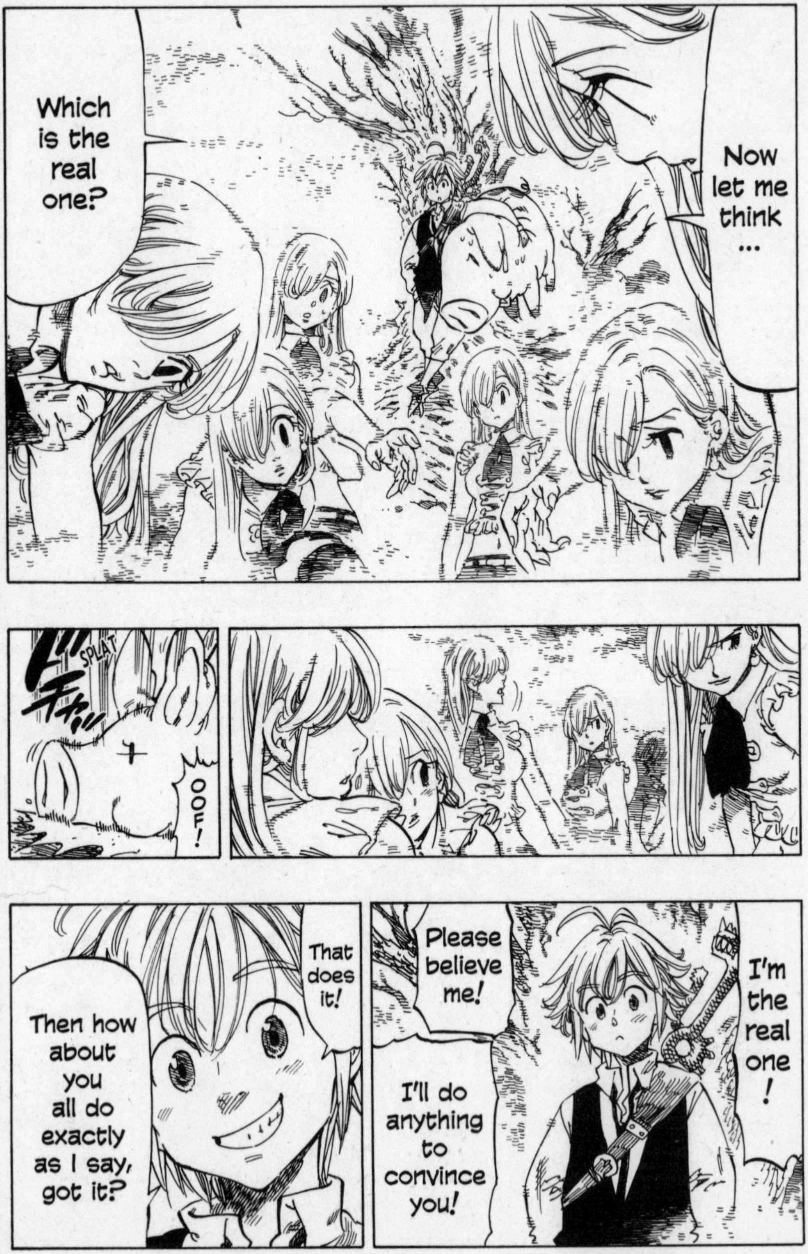
Now let me think ...
Which is the real one?
SPLAT
OOF!
I'm the real one!
Please believe me!
I'll do anything to convince you!
That does it!
Then how about you all do exactly as I say, got it?

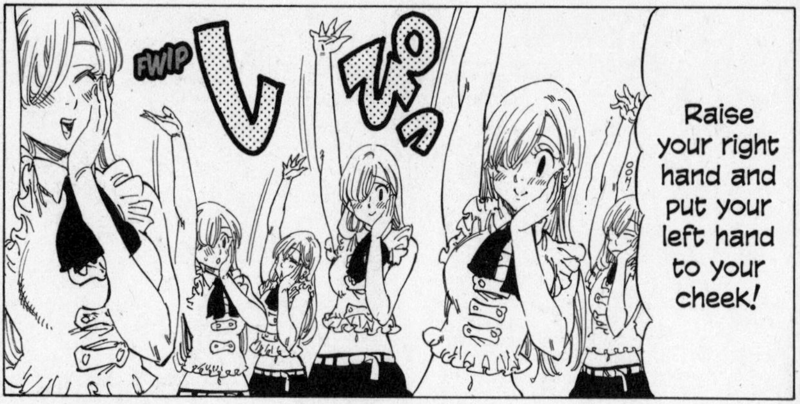
Raise your right hand and put your left hand to your cheek!
OOH!
FWIP

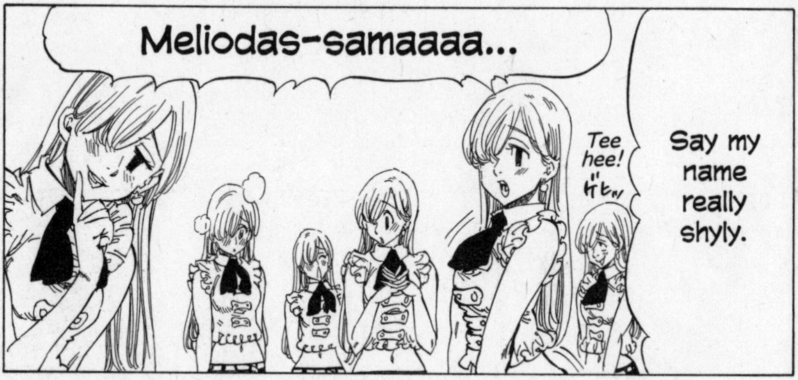
Say my name really shyly.
Tee hee!
Meliodas-samaaaa...

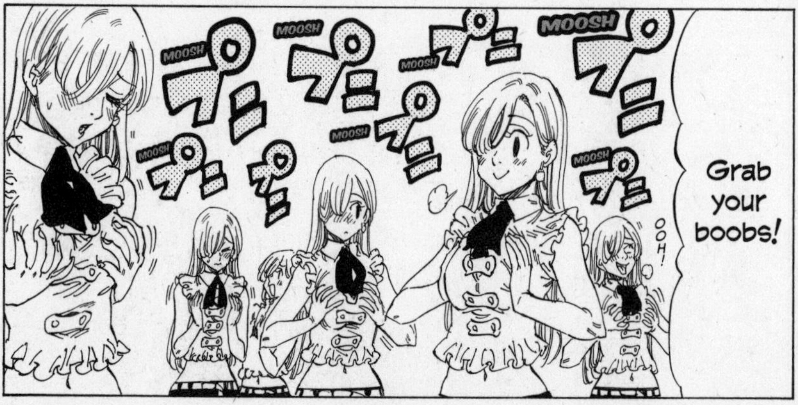
Grab your boobs!
OOH!
MOOSH
MOOSH
MOOSH
MOOSH
MOOSH
MOOSH
MOOSH

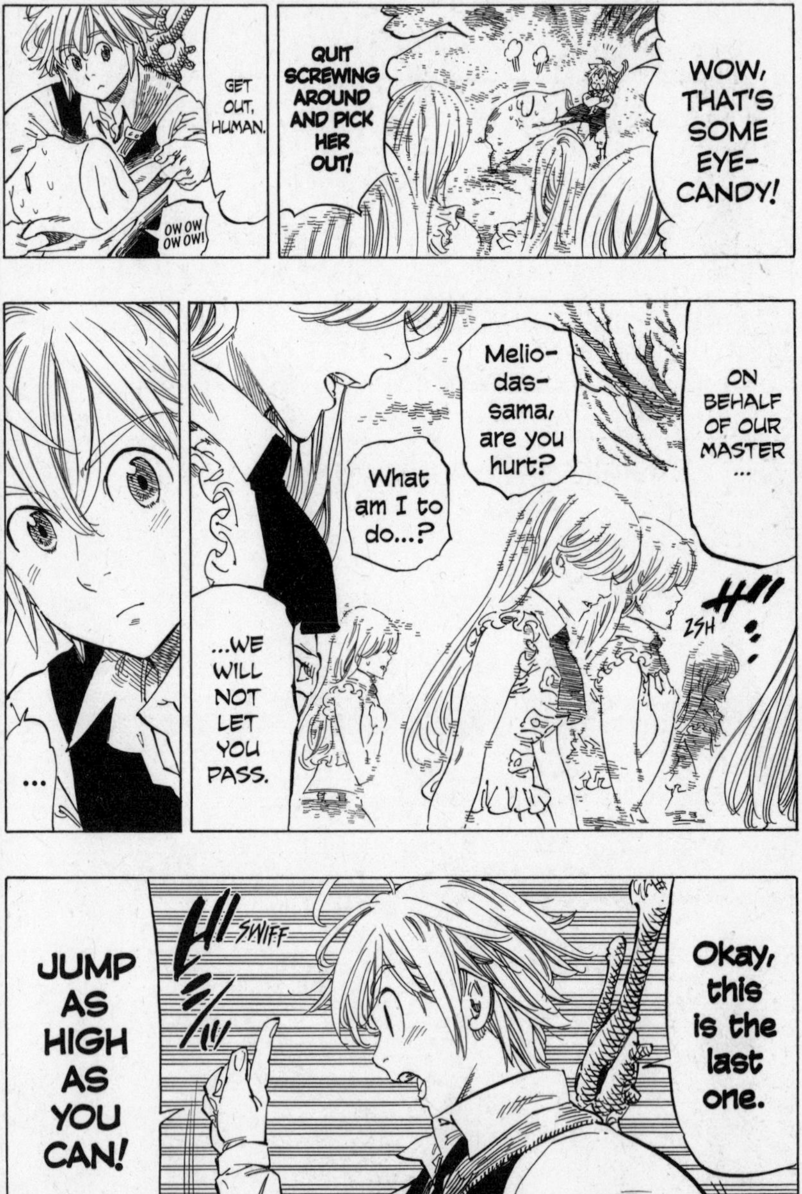
WOW, THAT'S SOME EYE-CANDY!
QUIT SCREWING AROUND AND PICK HER OUT!
GET OUT, HUMAN.
OW OW OW OW!
ON BEHALF OF OUR MASTER ...
Melio-das-sama, are you hurt?
What am I to do...?
ZSH
...WE WILL NOT LET YOU PASS.
...
Okay, this is the last one.
SWIFF
JUMP AS HIGH AS YOU CAN!

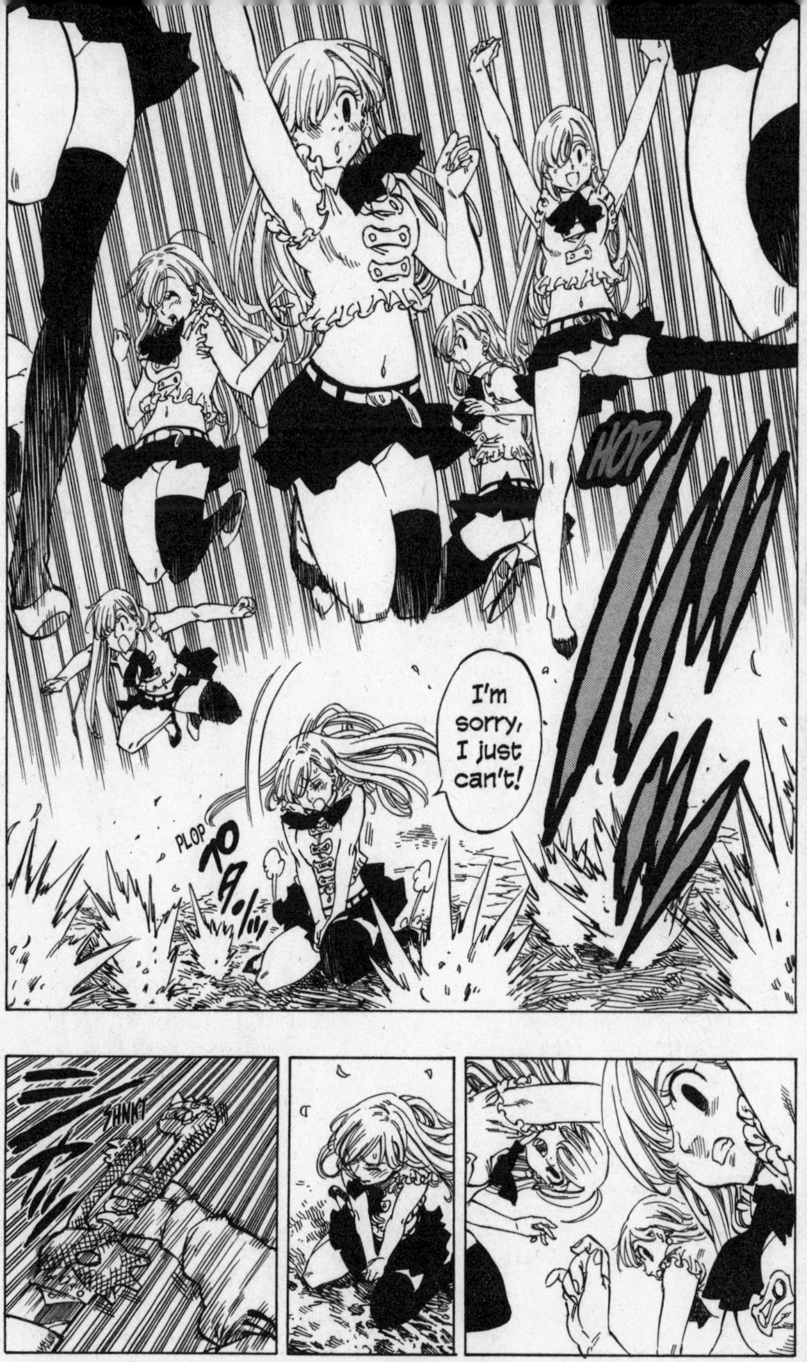
HOP
I'm sorry, I just can't!
PLOP
SHNK!

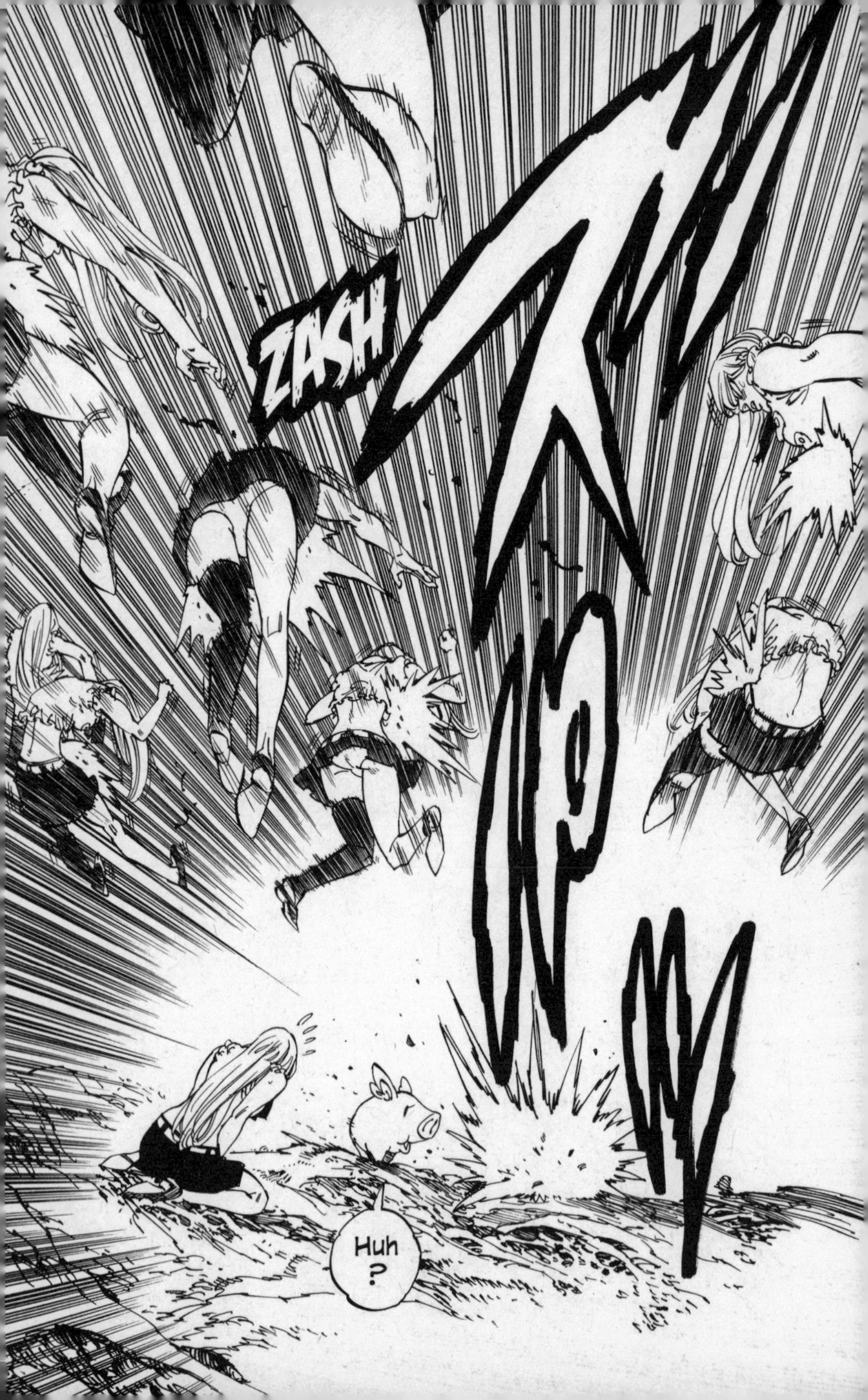
ZASH
Huh?

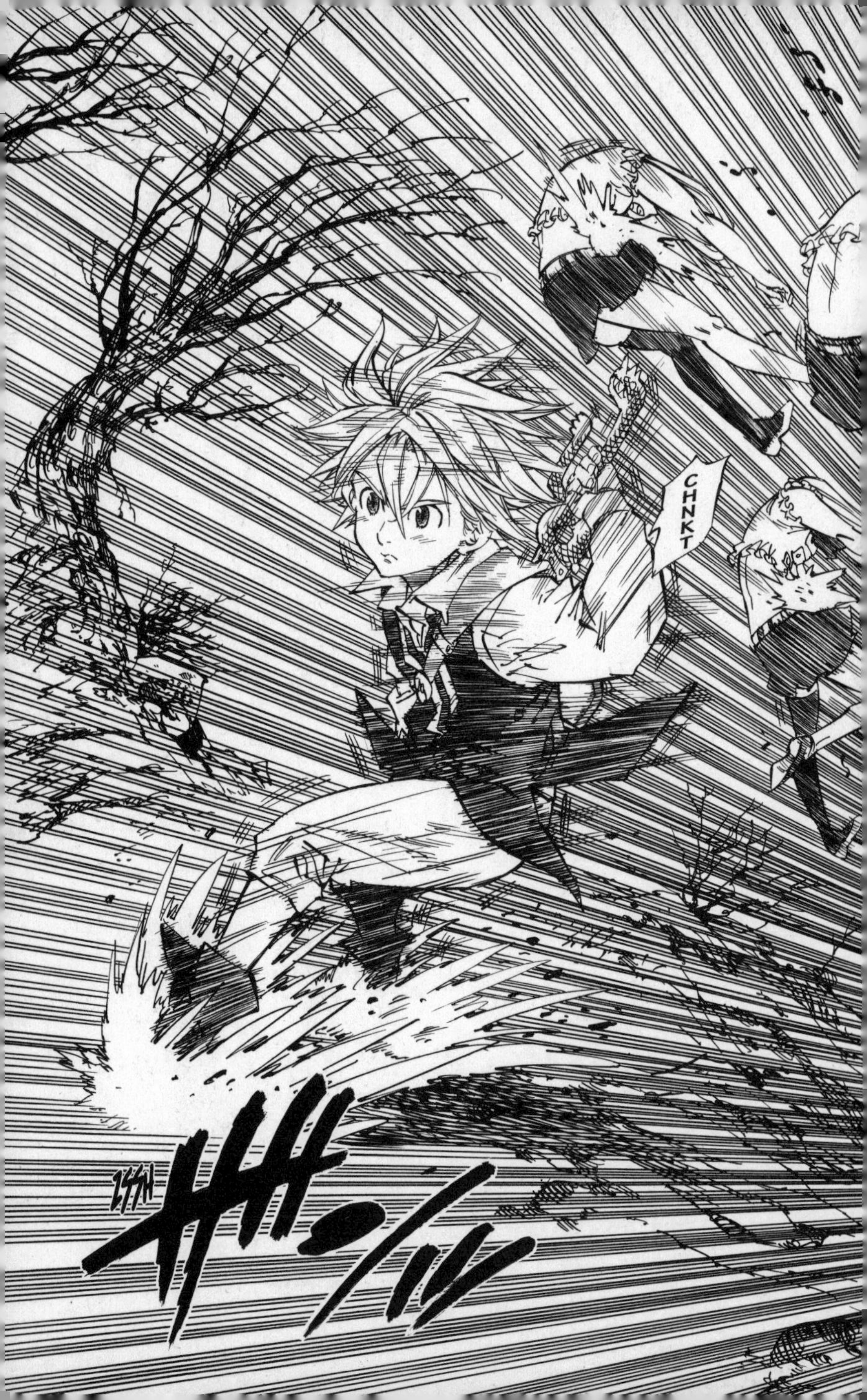
CHNKT
ZSSH

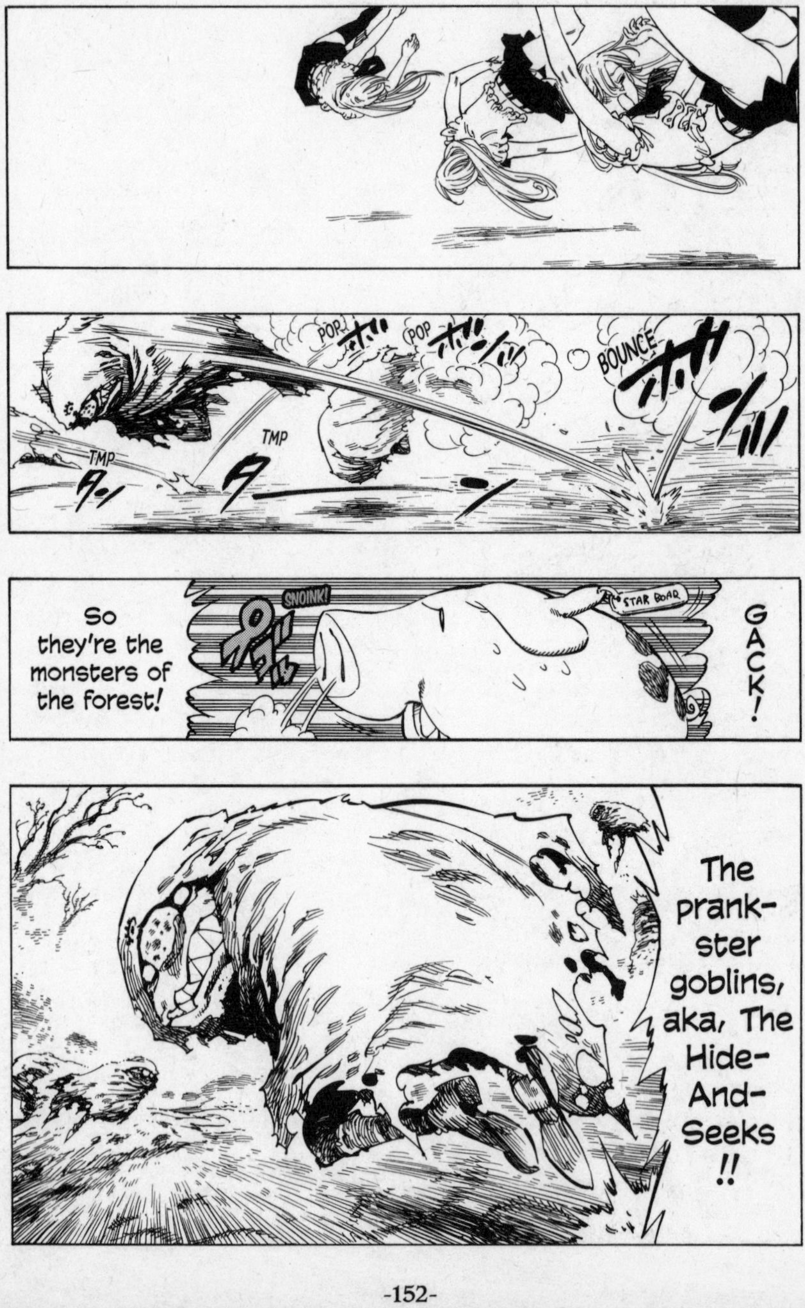
BOUNCE
POP
POP
TMP
TMP
GACK!
STAR BOAR
SNOINK!
So they're the monsters of the forest!
The prank-ster goblins, aka, The Hide-And-Seeks!!

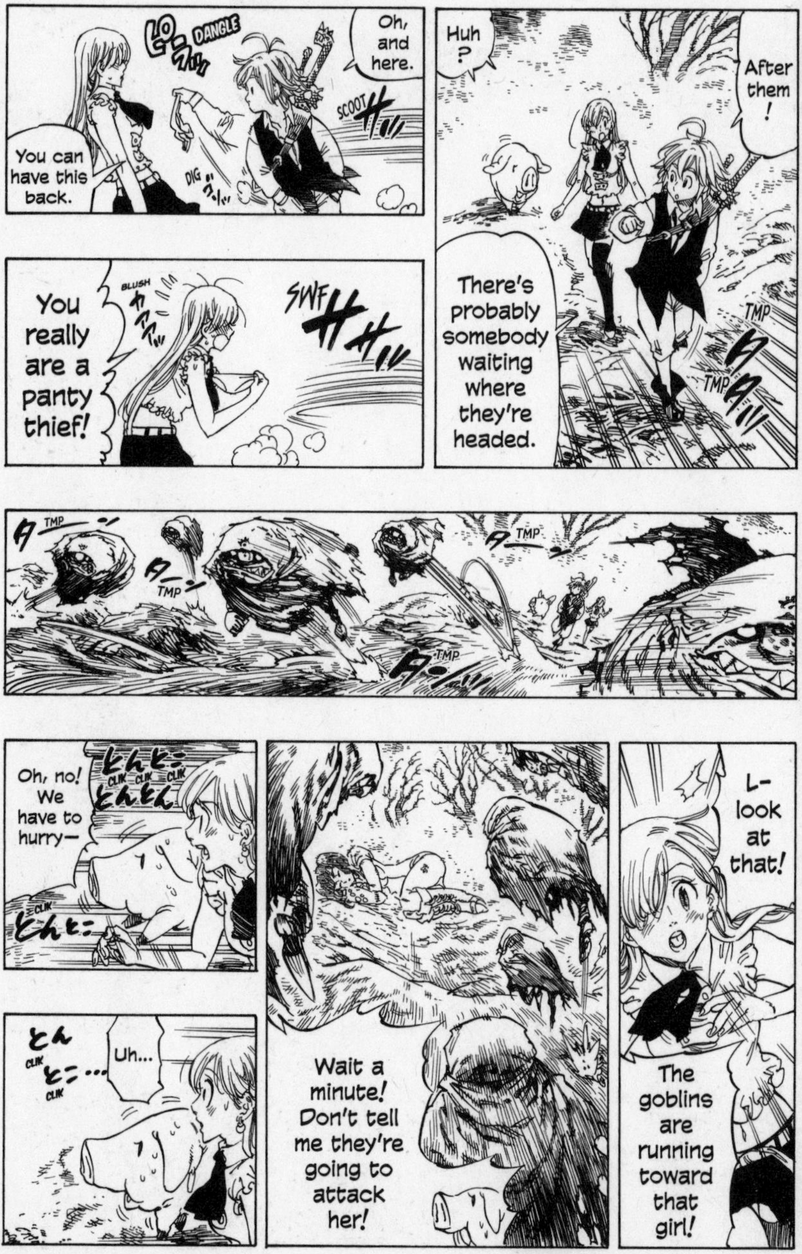
After them!
Huh?
TMP
TMP
There's probably somebody waiting where they're headed.
Oh, and here.
SCOOT
DANGLE
You can have this back.
DIG
SWF
BLUSH
You really are a panty thief!
TMP
TMP
TMP
TMP
L-look at that!
The goblins are running toward that girl!
Wait a minute! Don't tell me they're going to attack her!
CLIK CLIK CLIK
Oh, no! We have to hurry—
CLIK
Uh...
CLIK
CLIK

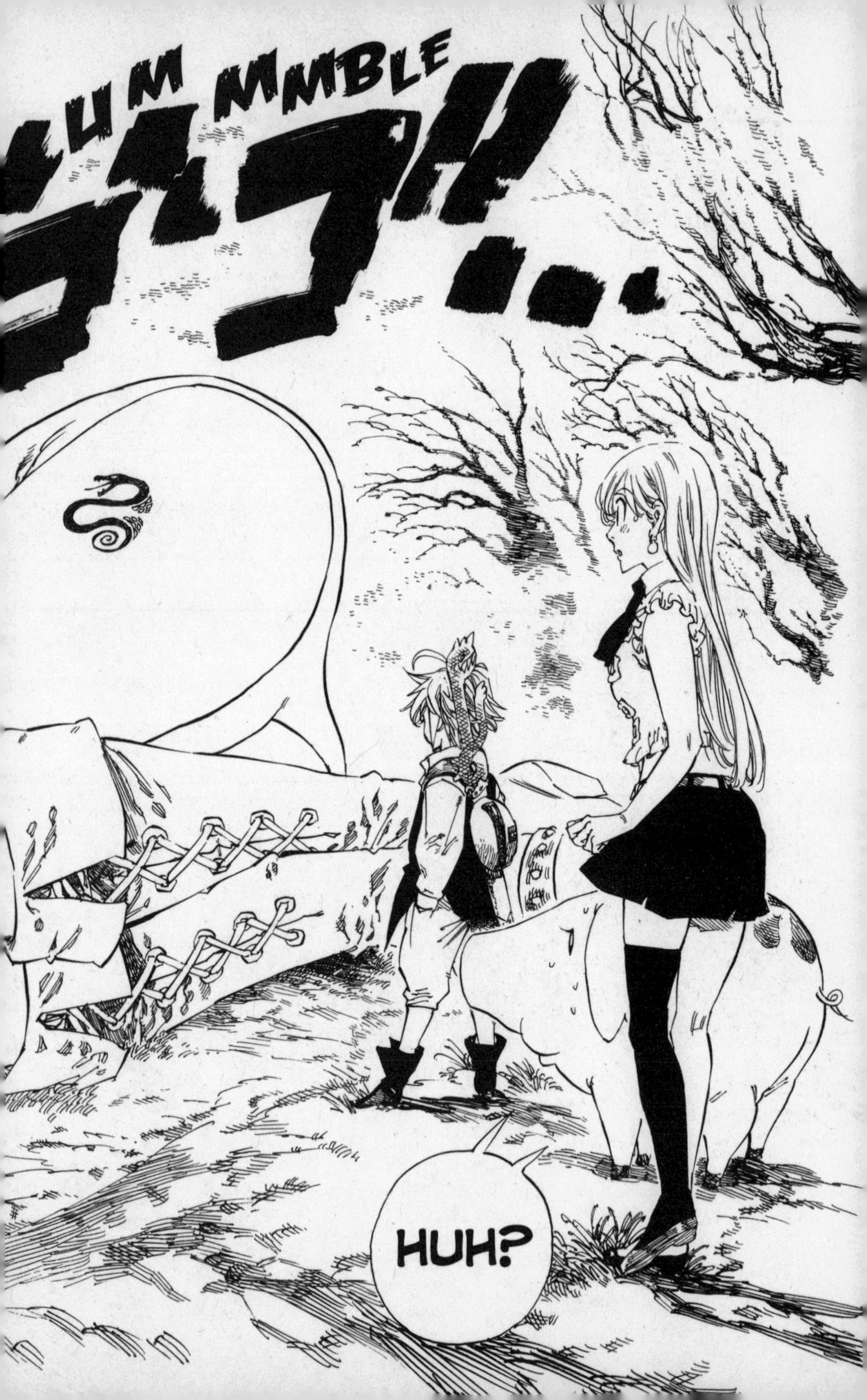
UM MMBLE
HUH?

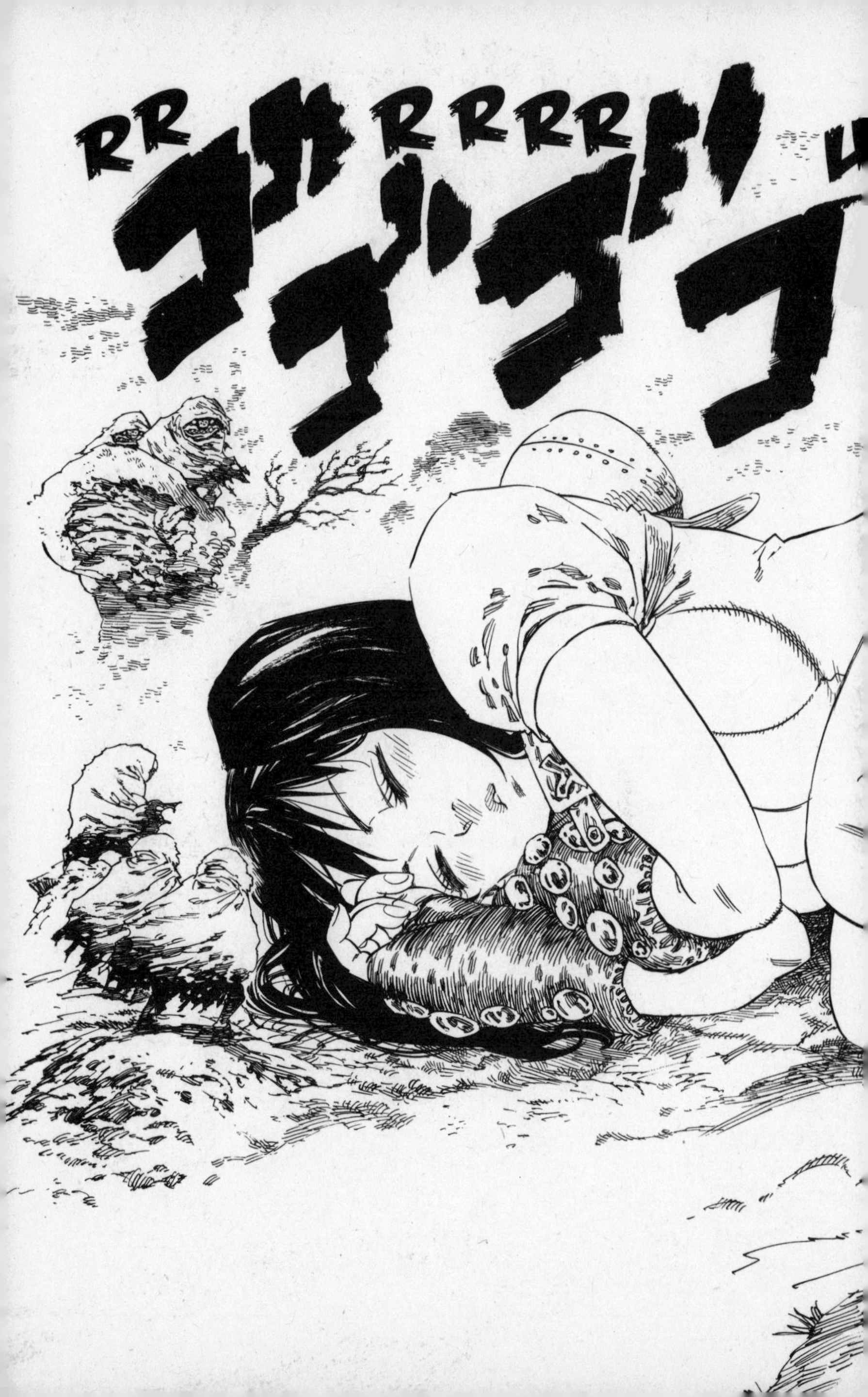
RR
RRRRR
ゴゴゴゴ

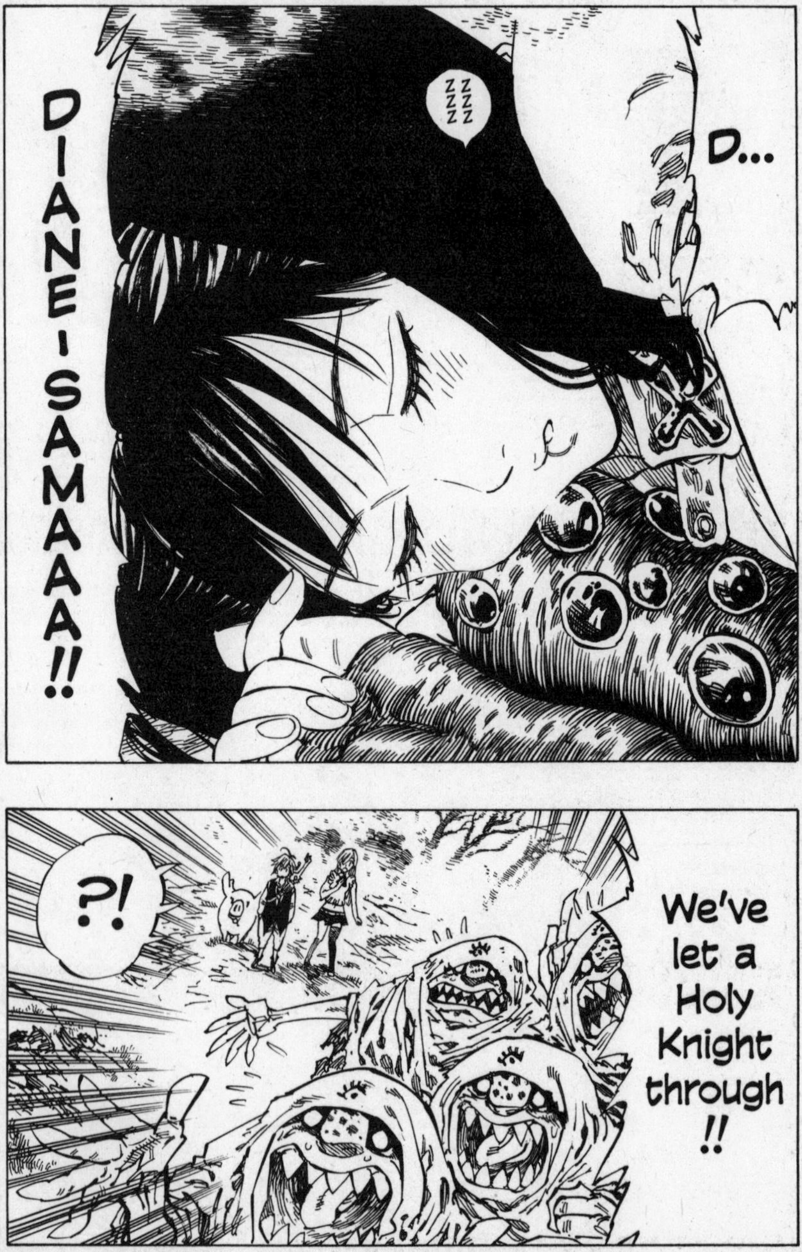
D...
ZZZ ZZZ
DIANE-SAMAAA!!
We've let a Holy Knight through!!
?!

Now Accepting Letters!

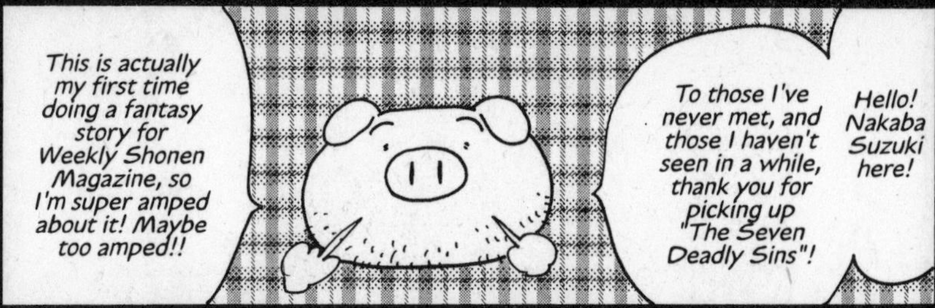

Hello! Nakaba Suzuki here!
To those I've never met, and those I haven't seen in a while, thank you for picking up "The Seven Deadly Sins"!
This is actually my first time doing a fantasy story for Weekly Shonen Magazine, so I'm super amped about it! Maybe too amped!!

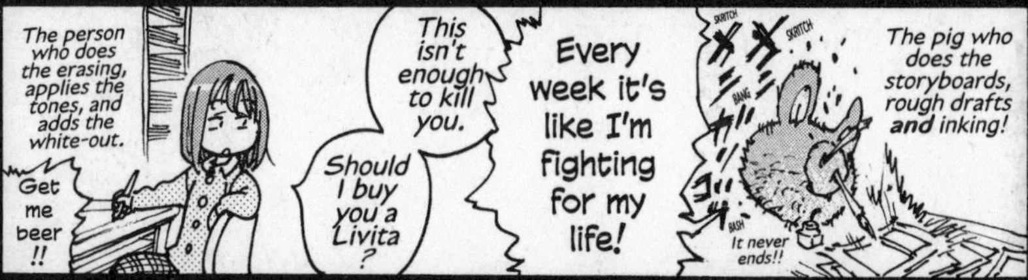

The pig who does the storyboards, rough drafts and inking!
SKRITCH
SKRITCH
BANG
BASH
It never ends!!
Every week it's like I'm fighting for my life!
This isn't enough to kill you.
Should I buy you a Livita?
The person who does the erasing, applies the tones, and adds the white-out.
Get me beer!!

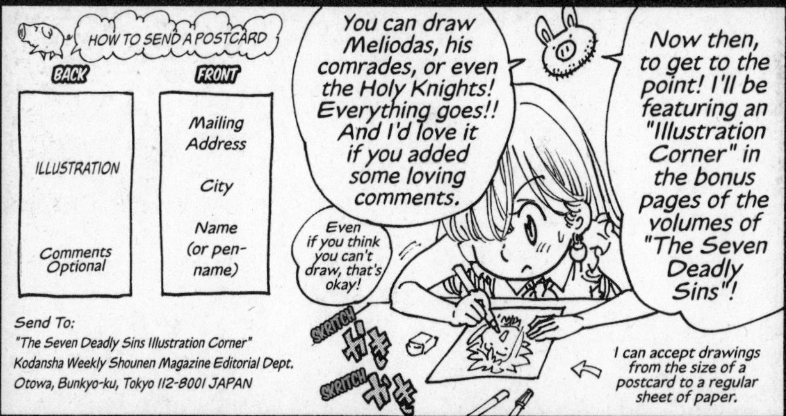

Now then, to get to the point! I'll be featuring an "Illustration Corner" in the bonus pages of the volumes of "The Seven Deadly Sins"!
You can draw Meliodas, his comrades, or even the Holy Knights! Everything goes!! And I'd love it if you added some loving comments.
Even if you think you can't draw, that's okay!
I can accept drawings from the size of a postcard to a regular sheet of paper.
SKRITCH
SKRITCH
HOW TO SEND A POSTCARD
BACK
ILLUSTRATION
Comments Optional
FRONT
Mailing Address
City
Name (or pen-name)
Send To:
"The Seven Deadly Sins Illustration Corner"
Kodansha Weekly Shounen Magazine Editorial Dept.
Otowa, Bunkyo-ku, Tokyo 112-8001 JAPAN

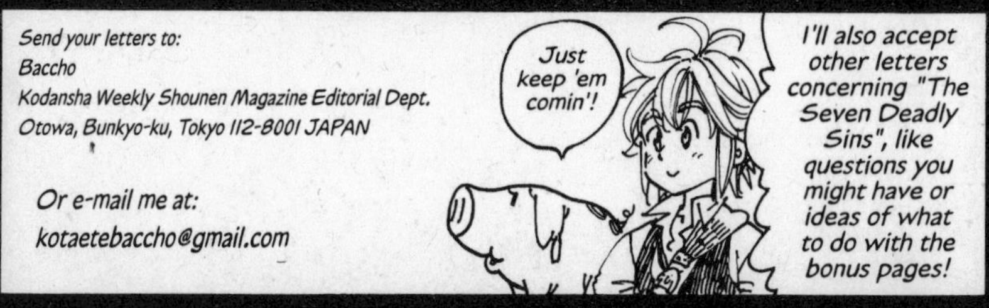

I'll also accept other letters concerning "The Seven Deadly Sins", like questions you might have or ideas of what to do with the bonus pages!
Just keep 'em comin'!
Send your letters to:
Baccho
Kodansha Weekly Shounen Magazine Editorial Dept.
Otowa, Bunkyo-ku, Tokyo 112-8001 JAPAN
Or e-mail me at:
kotaetebaccho@gmail.com

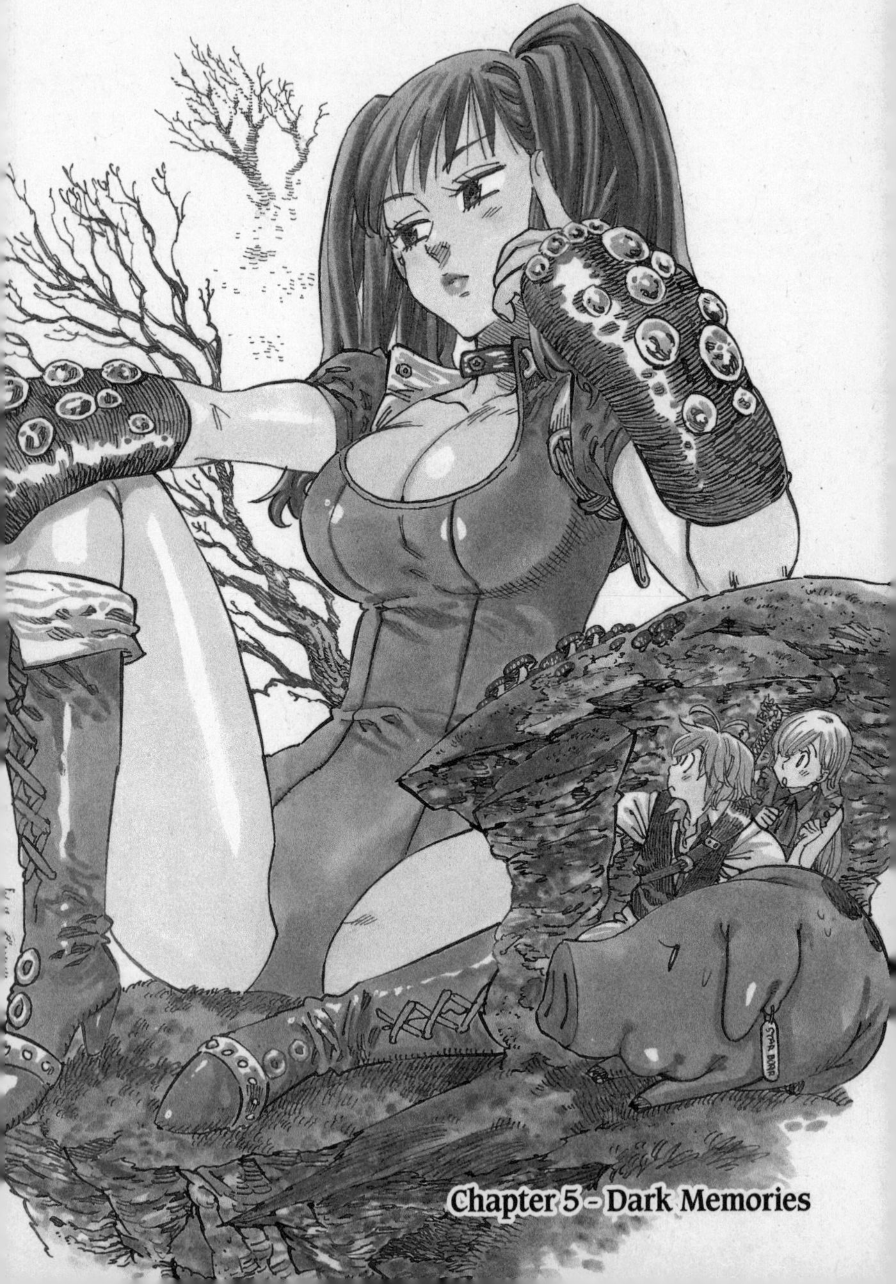
STAR BOAR

Chapter 5 - Dark Memories

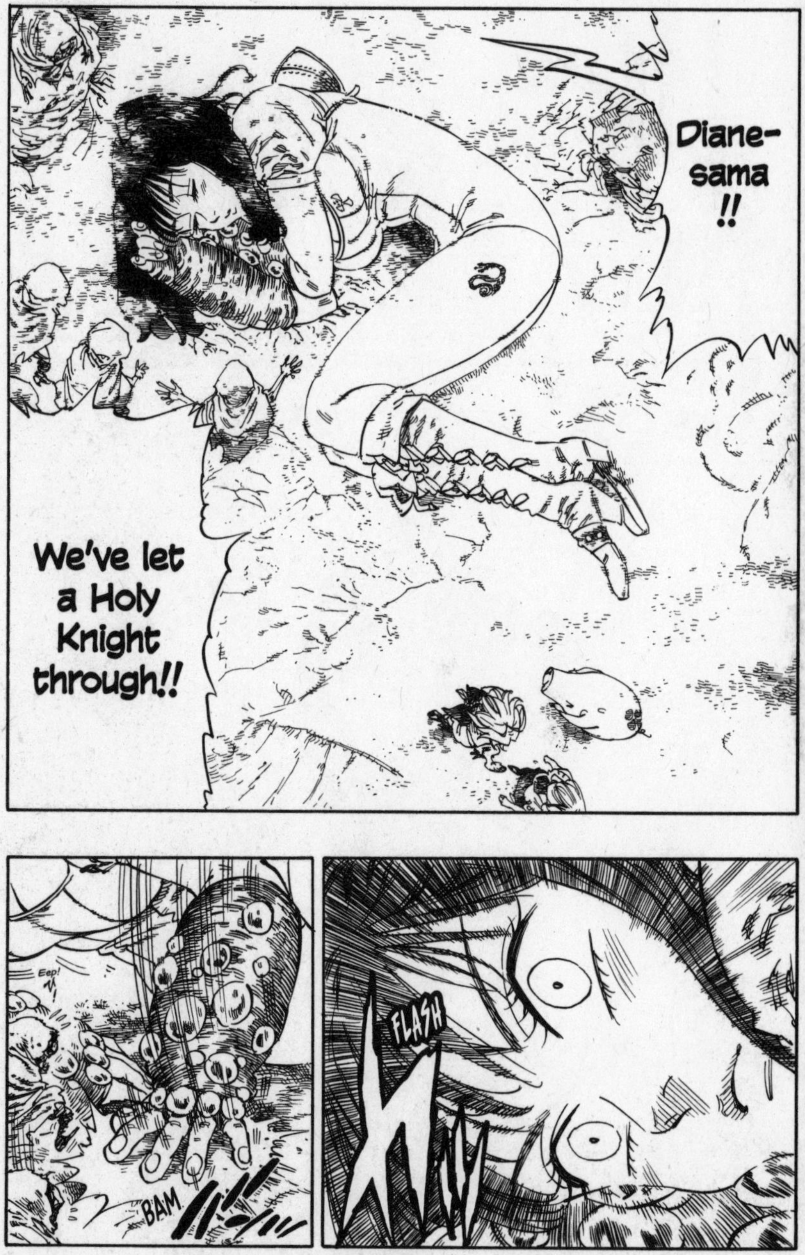
Diane-sama!!
We've let a Holy Knight through!!
FLASH
Eep!
BAM

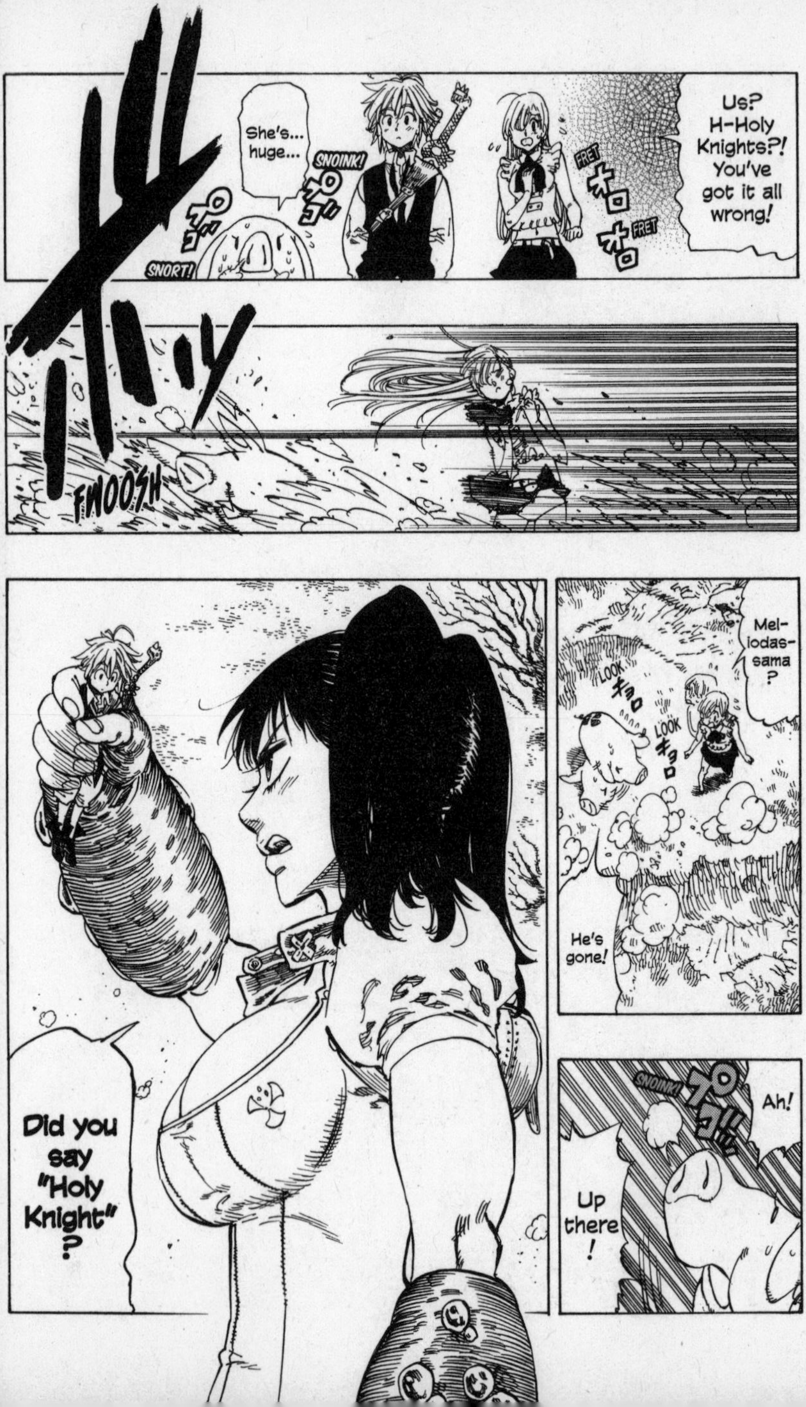
Us? H-Holy Knights?! You've got it all wrong!
FRET
FRET
She's... huge...
SNOINK!
SNORT!
FWOOSH
Mel-iodas-sama?
LOOK
LOOK
He's gone!
Ah!
SNOINK!
Up there!
Did you say "Holy Knight"?

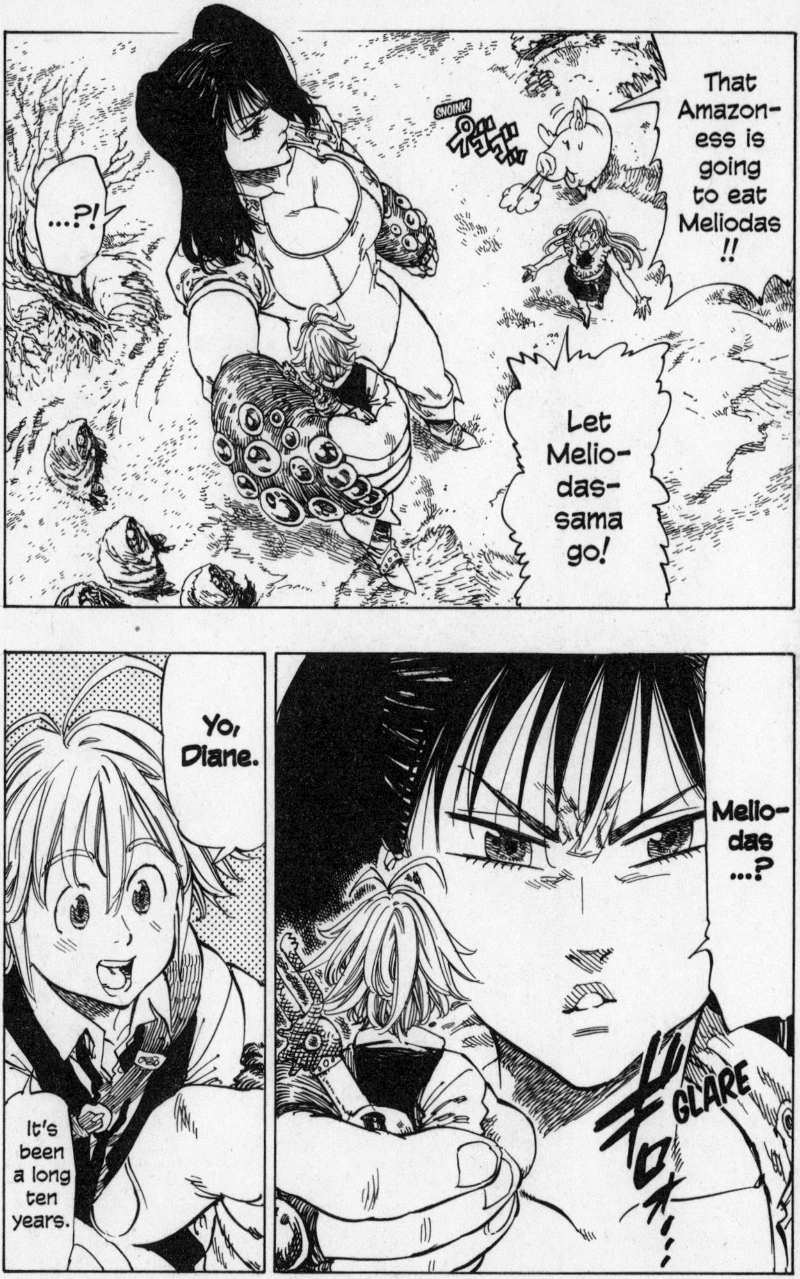
That Amazon-ess is going to eat Meliodas!!
SNOINK!
Let Melio-das-sama go!
...?!
Melio-das ...?
GLARE
Yo, Diane.
It's been a long ten years.

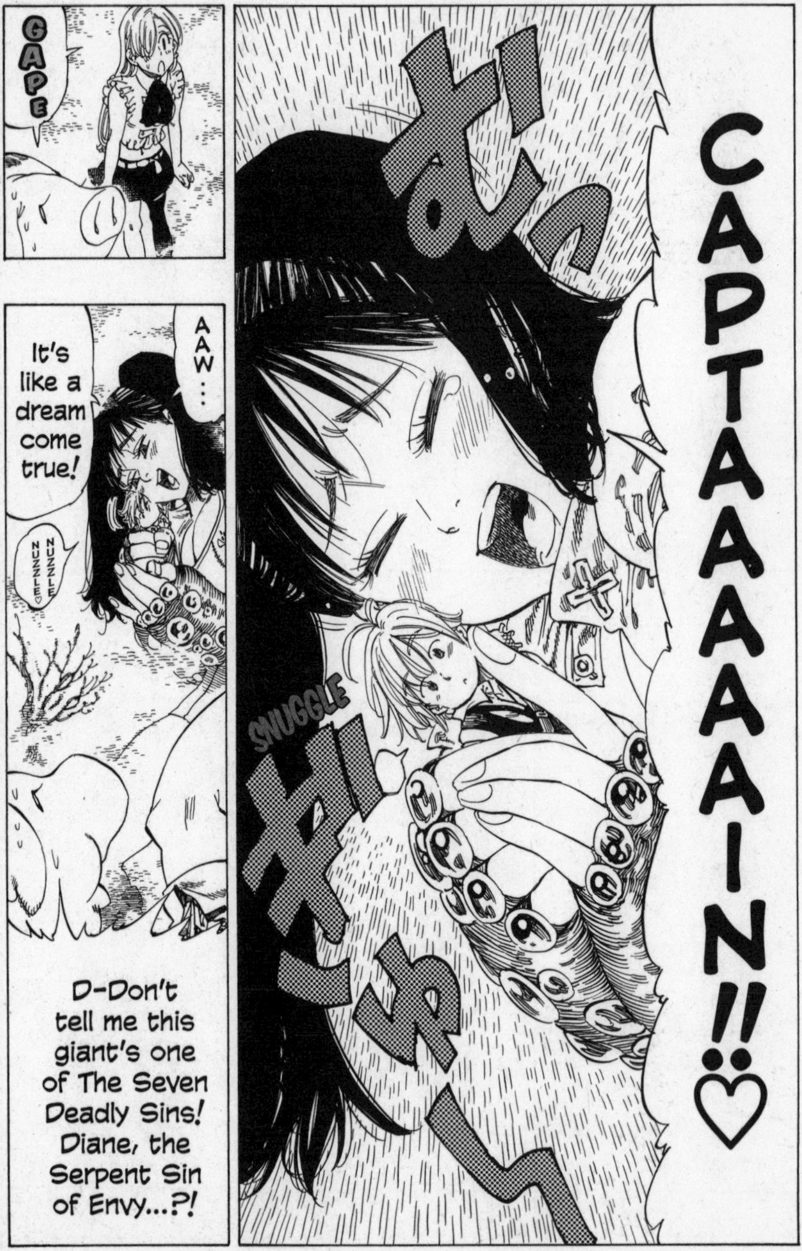
CAPTAAAAIN!!♥
SNUGGLE
GAPE
AAW...
It's like a dream come true!
NUZZLE NUZZLE♥
D-Don't tell me this giant's one of The Seven Deadly Sins! Diane, the Serpent Sin of Envy...?!

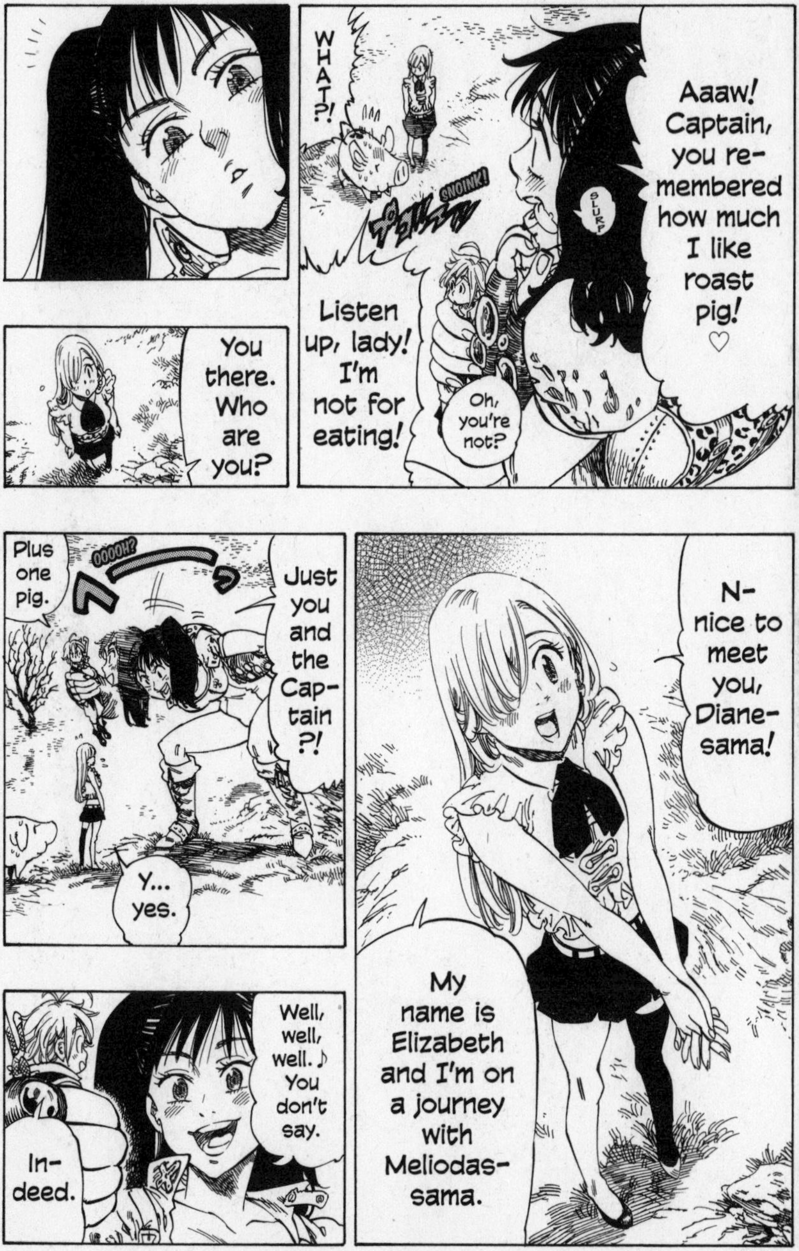
Aaaw! Captain, you remembered how much I like roast pig! ♡
SLURP
WHAT?!
SNOINK!
Listen up, lady! I'm not for eating!
Oh, you're not?
You there. Who are you?
N-nice to meet you, Diane-sama!
My name is Elizabeth and I'm on a journey with Meliodas-sama.
Just you and the Captain?!
OOOOH?
Plus one pig.
Y... yes.
Well, well, well.♪ You don't say.
Indeed.

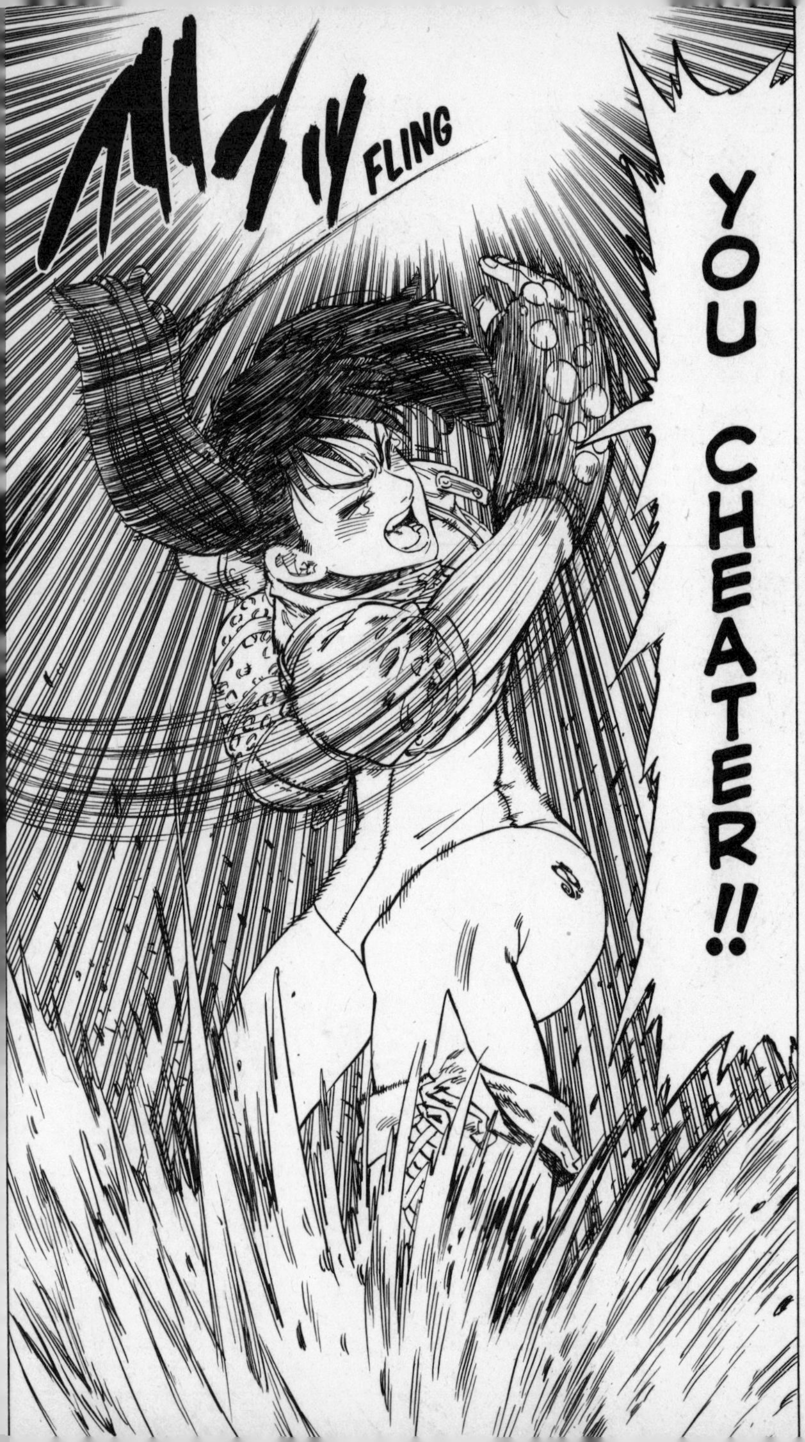
YOU CHEATER!!
FLING

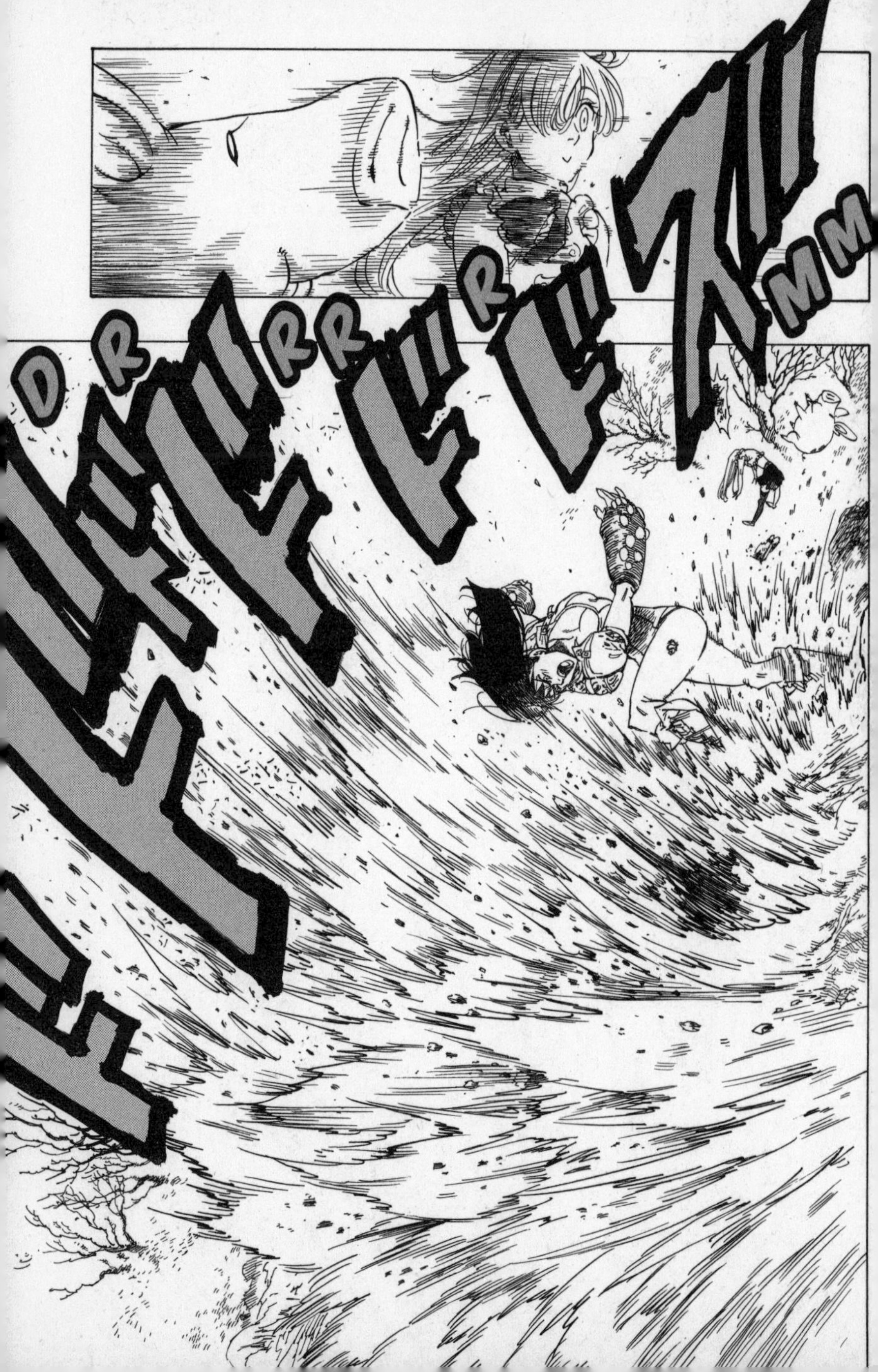
DRRRRMM

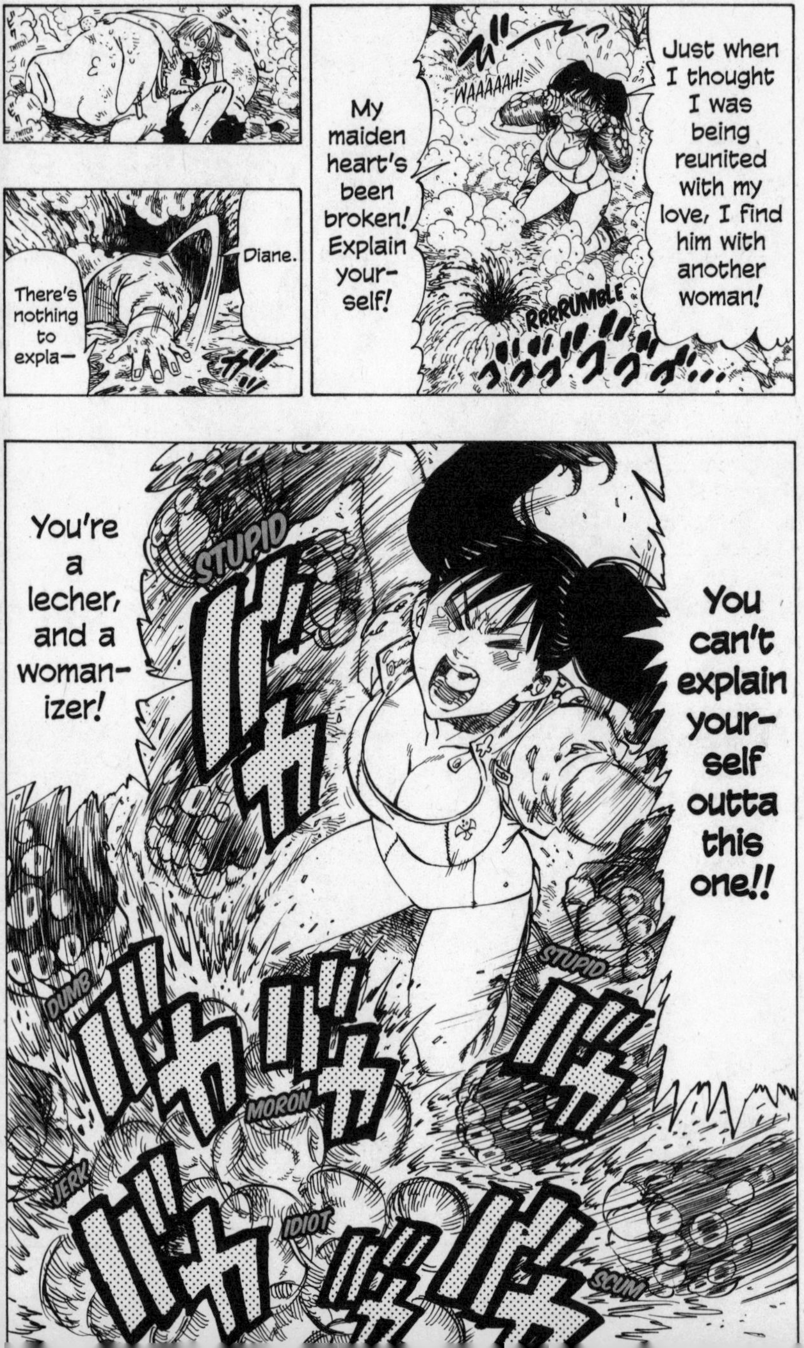
Just when I thought I was being reunited with my love, I find him with another woman!
WAAAAAH!
My maiden heart's been broken! Explain yourself!
RRRRUMBLE
TWITCH
TWITCH
Diane.
There's nothing to expla—
You can't explain yourself outta this one!!
STUPID
You're a lecher, and a womanizer!
STUPID
DUMB
MORON
JERK
IDIOT
SCUM

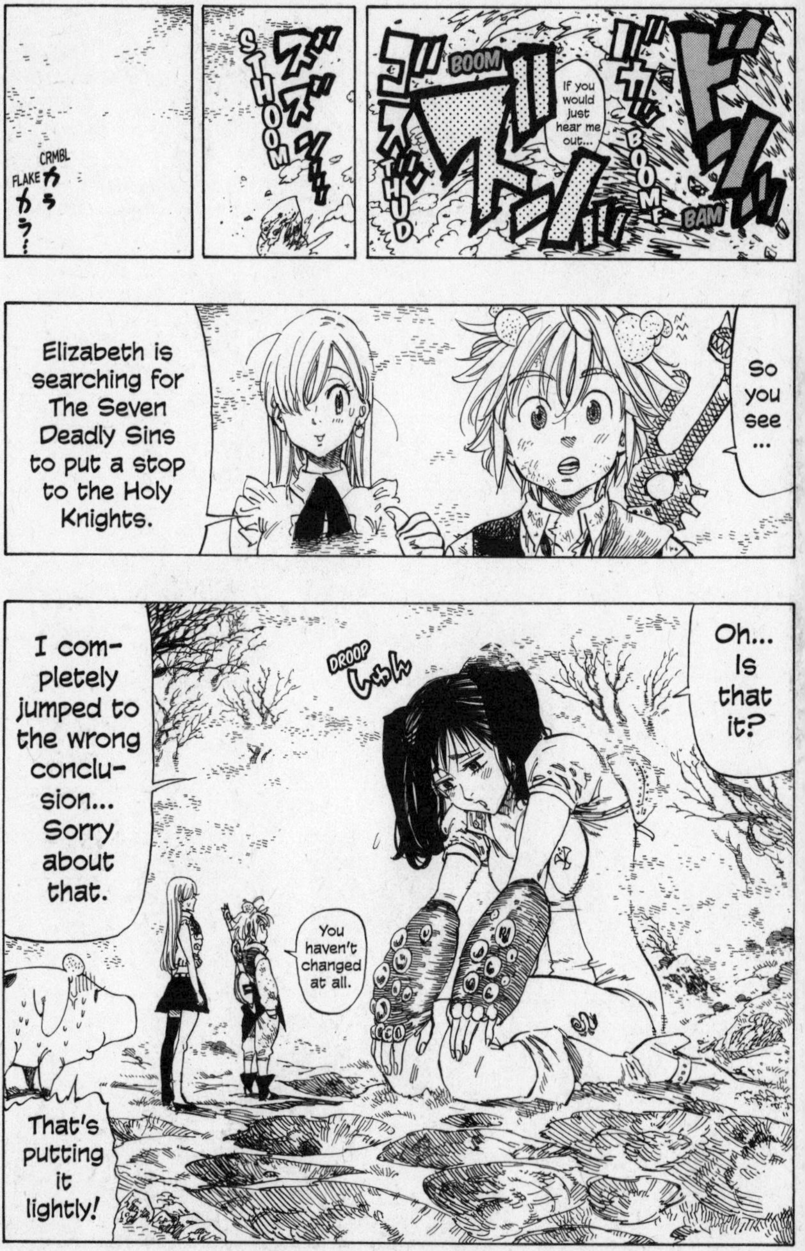
BAM
BOOMF
If you would just hear me out...
BOOM
THUD
STHOOM
CRMBL
FLAKE
カラ
カラ…
So you see...
Elizabeth is searching for The Seven Deadly Sins to put a stop to the Holy Knights.
Oh... Is that it?
DROOP
I com-pletely jumped to the wrong conclu-sion... Sorry about that.
You haven't changed at all.
That's putting it lightly!

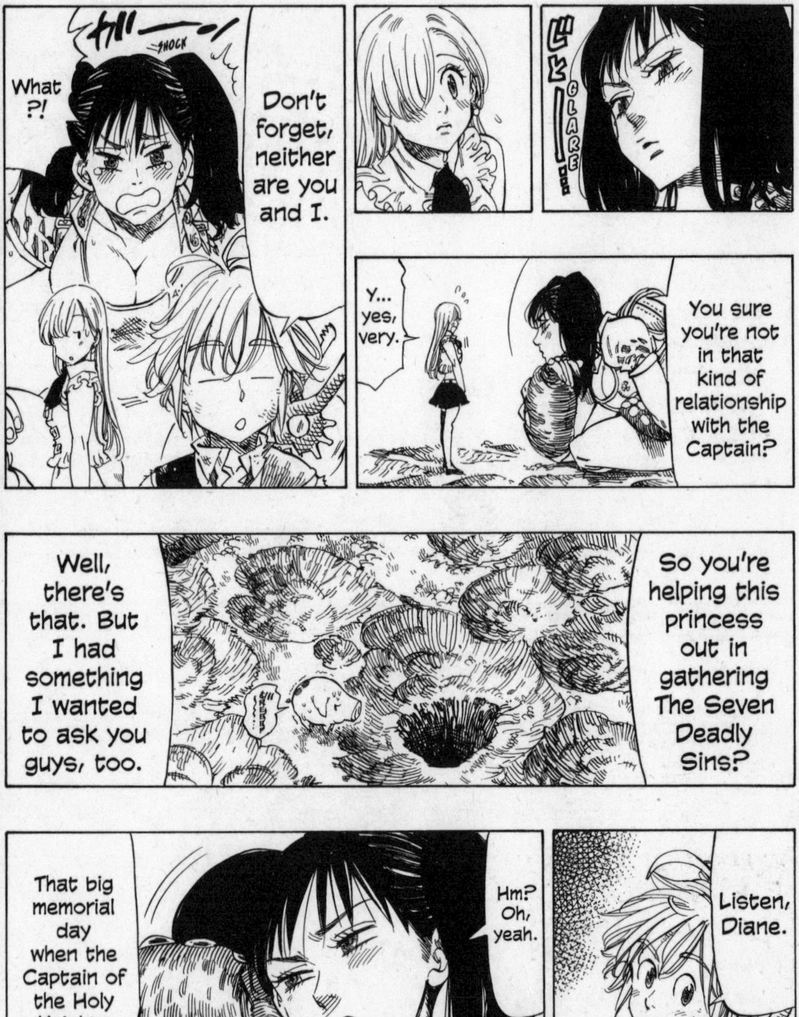
GLARE
You sure you're not in that kind of relationship with the Captain?
Y... yes, very.
Don't forget, neither are you and I.
What?!
SHOCK
So you're helping this princess out in gathering The Seven Deadly Sins?
Well, there's that. But I had something I wanted to ask you guys, too.
Listen, Diane.
It's about what went down ten years ago.
Hm? Oh, yeah.
That big memorial day when the Captain of the Holy Knights called for us?

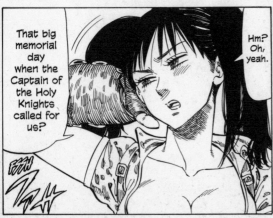

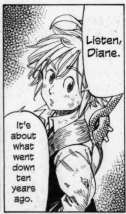

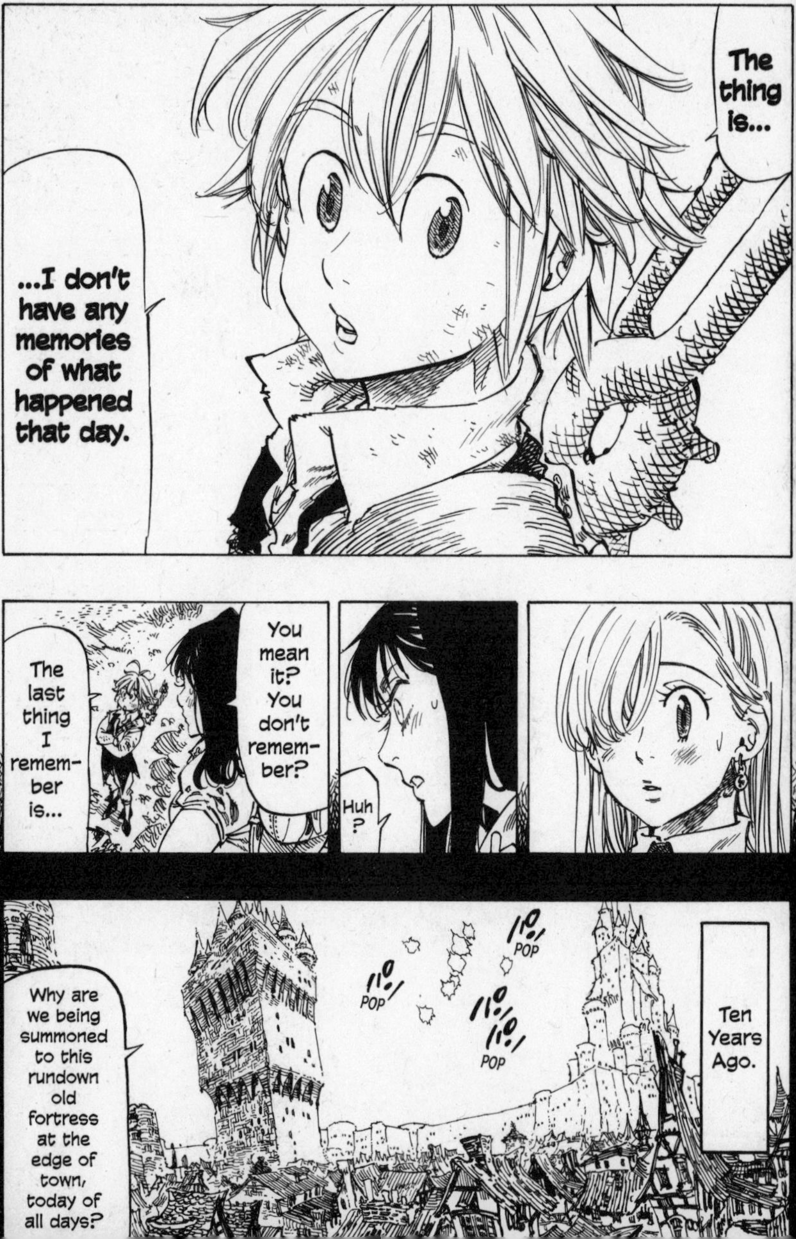
The thing is...
...I don't have any memories of what happened that day.
Huh?
You mean it? You don't remember?
The last thing I remember is...
Ten Years Ago.
POP
POP
POP
Why are we being summoned to this rundown old fortress at the edge of town, today of all days?

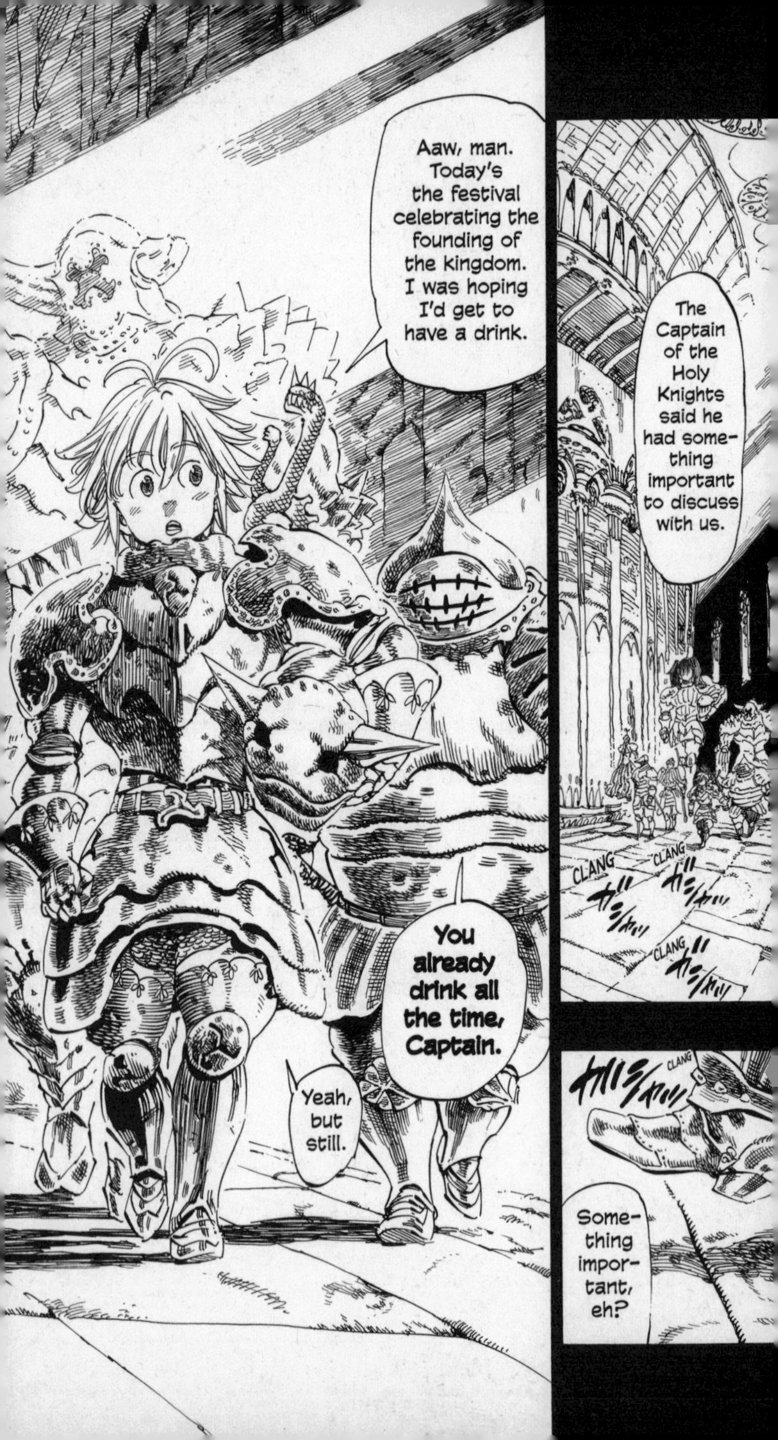
The Captain of the Holy Knights said he had something important to discuss with us.
CLANG
CLANG
CLANG
CLANG
Something important, eh?
Aaw, man. Today's the festival celebrating the founding of the kingdom. I was hoping I'd get to have a drink.
You already drink all the time, Captain.
Yeah, but still.

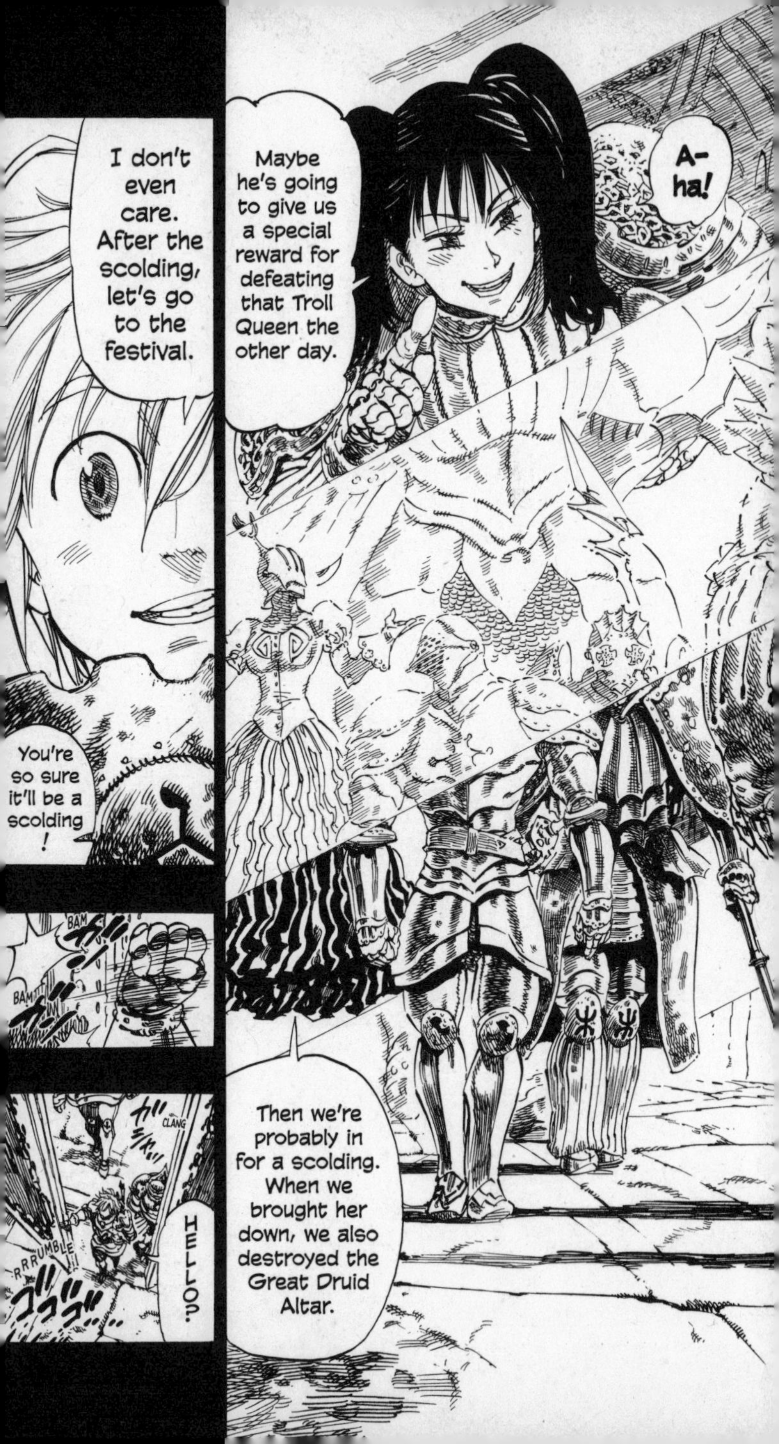

A-ha!
Maybe he's going to give us a special reward for defeating that Troll Queen the other day.
Then we're probably in for a scolding. When we brought her down, we also destroyed the Great Druid Altar.
I don't even care. After the scolding, let's go to the festival.
You're so sure it'll be a scolding!
BAM
BAM
CLANG
HELLO?
RRRUMBLE

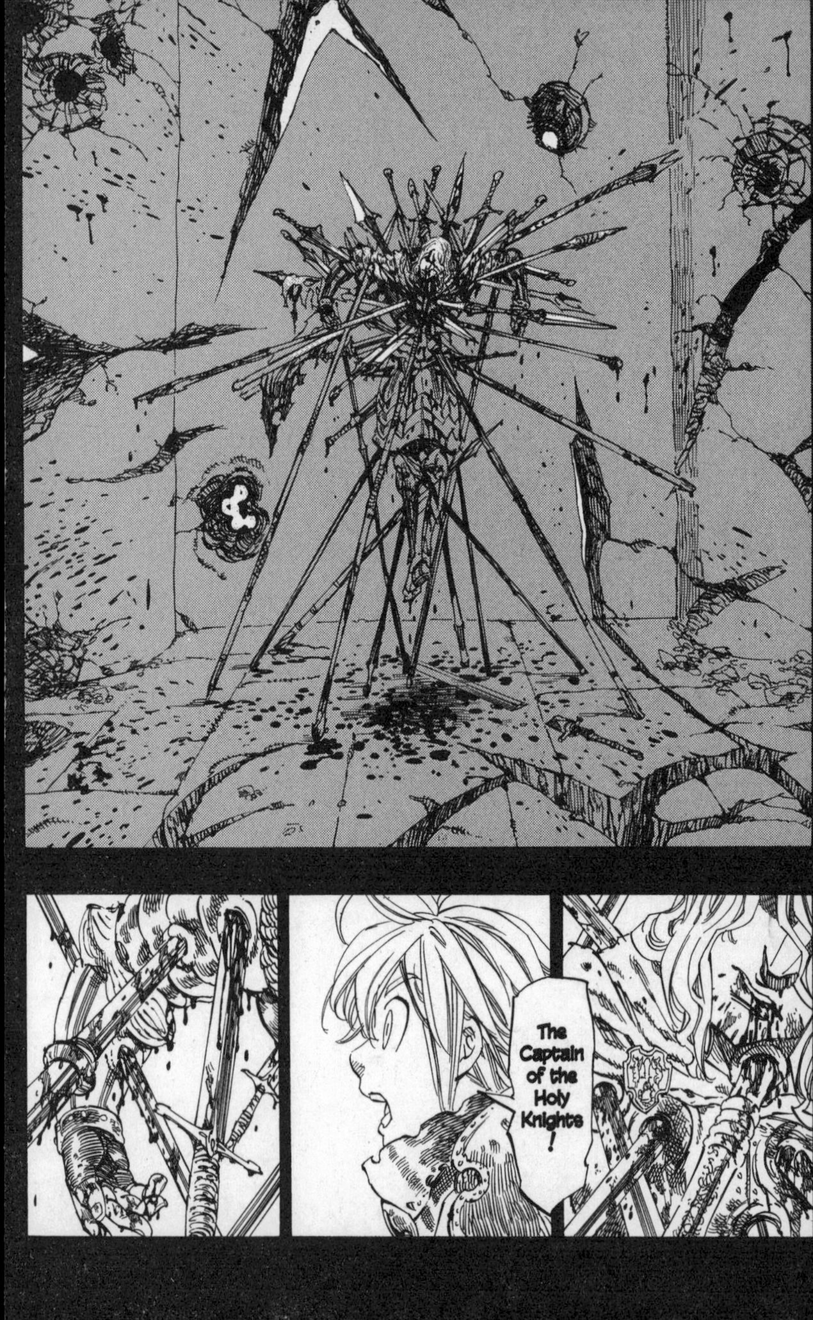
The Captain of the Holy Knights!

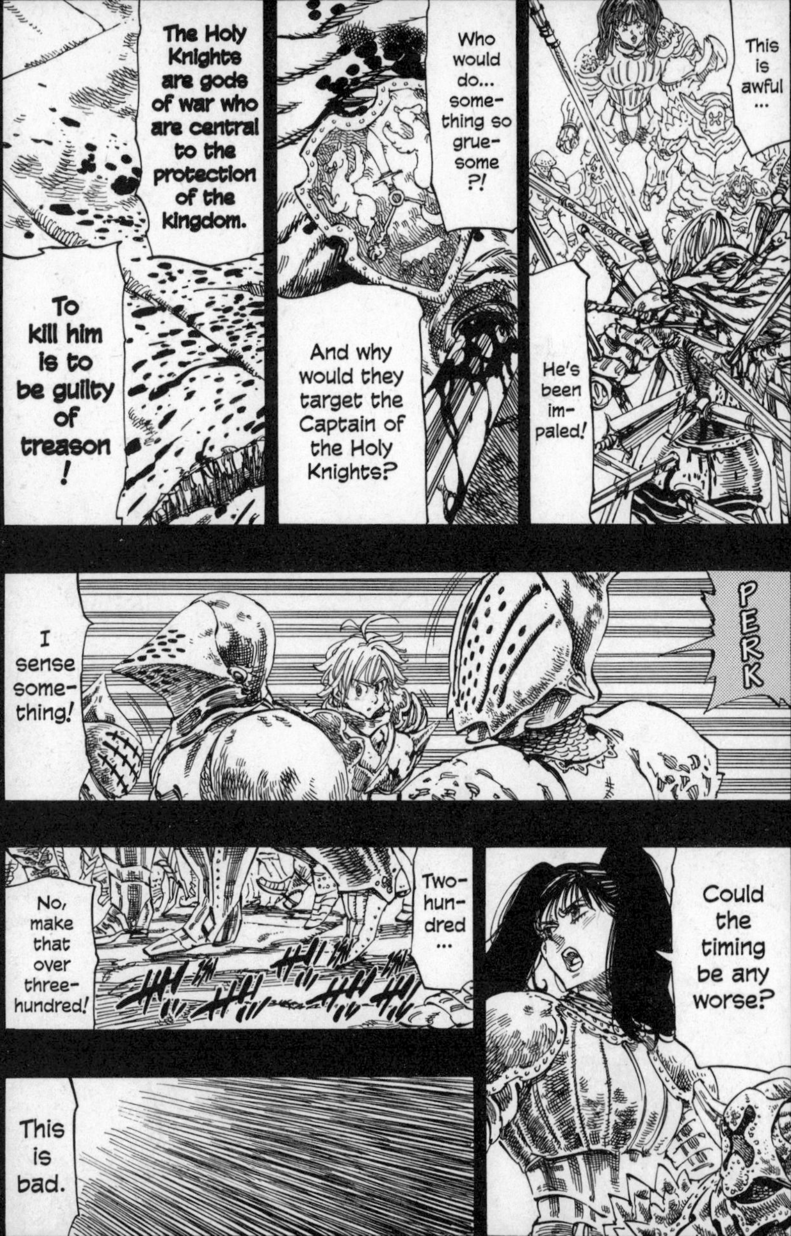
This is awful...
He's been impaled!
Who would do... something so gruesome?!
And why would they target the Captain of the Holy Knights?
The Holy Knights are gods of war who are central to the protection of the kingdom.
To kill him is to be guilty of treason!
PERK
I sense something!
Could the timing be any worse?
Two-hundred...
No, make that over three-hundred!
This is bad.

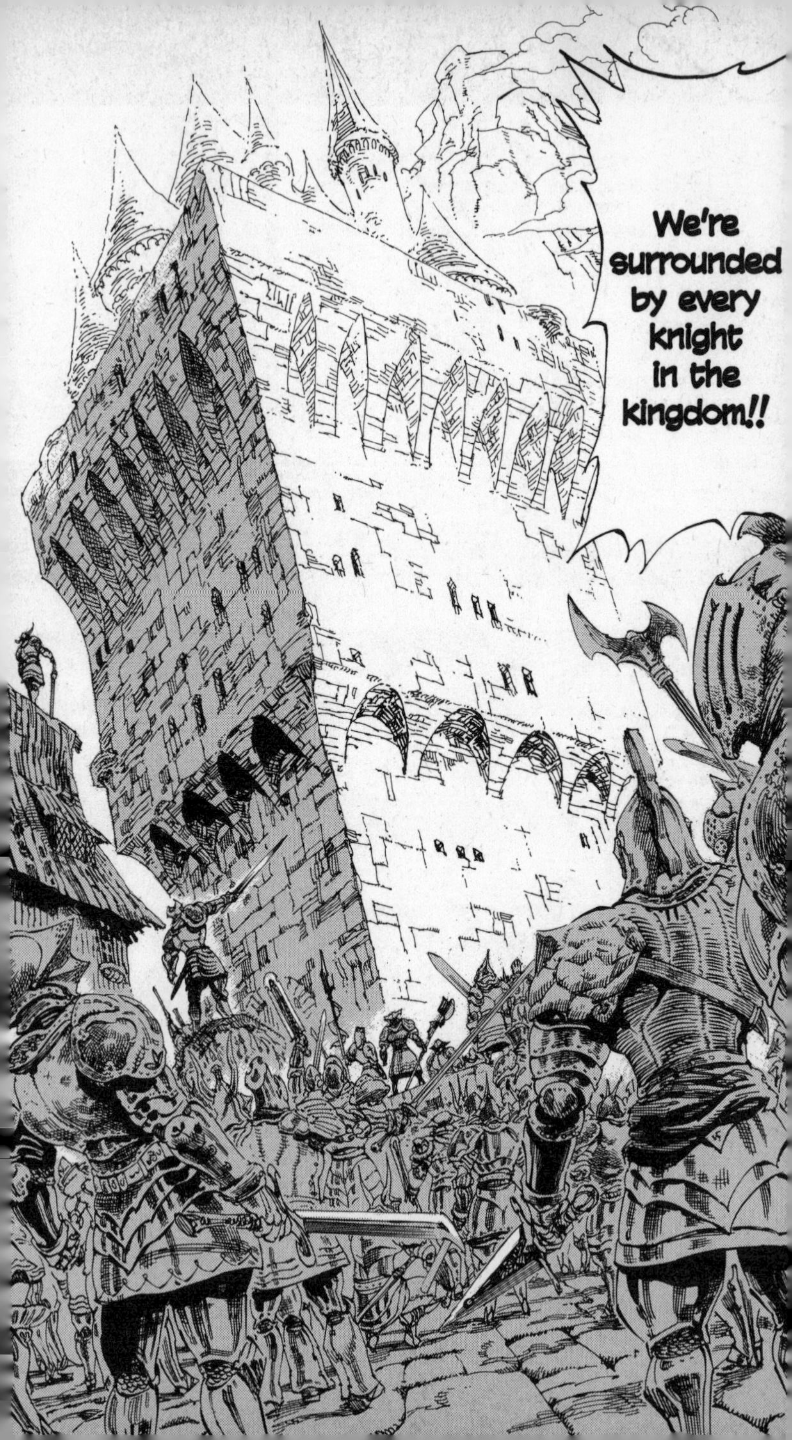
We're surrounded by every knight in the kingdom!!

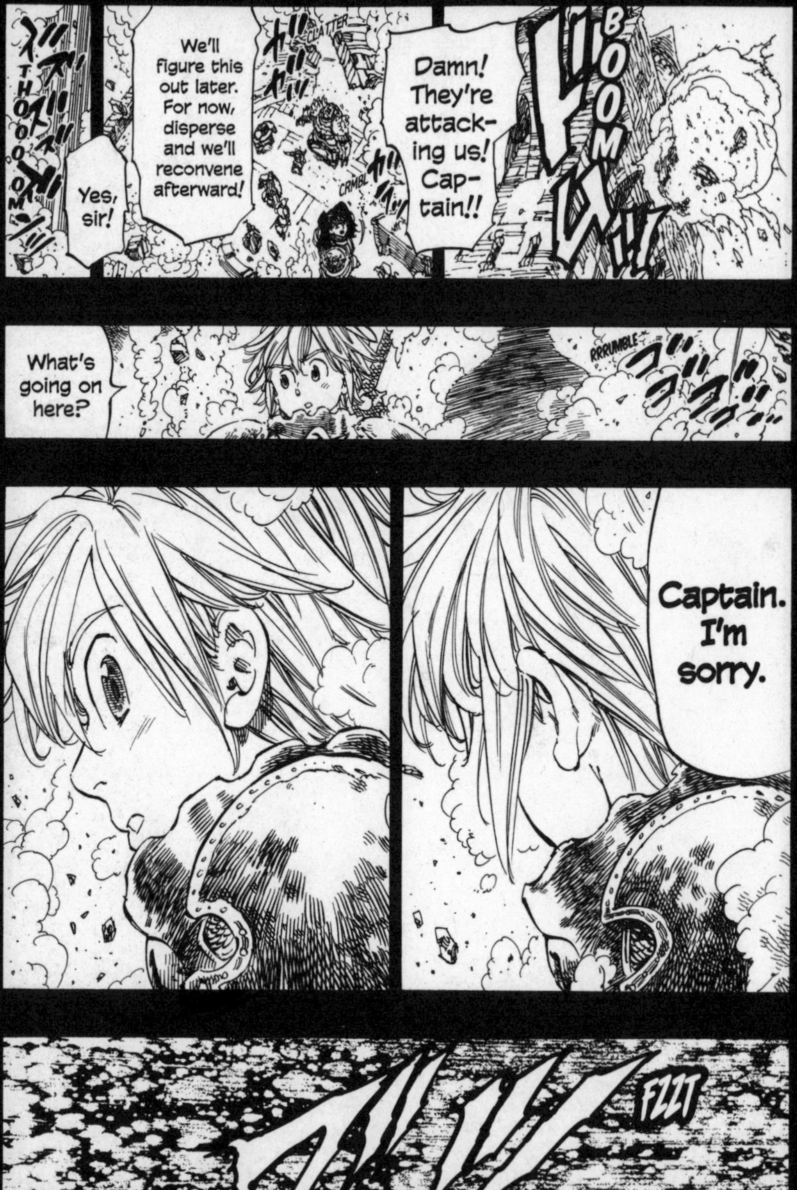
BOOM
Damn! They're attacking us! Captain!!
CLATTER
CRMBL
We'll figure this out later. For now, disperse and we'll reconvene afterward!
Yes, sir!
THOOOOOM
RRRUMBLE
What's going on here?
Captain. I'm sorry.
FZZT

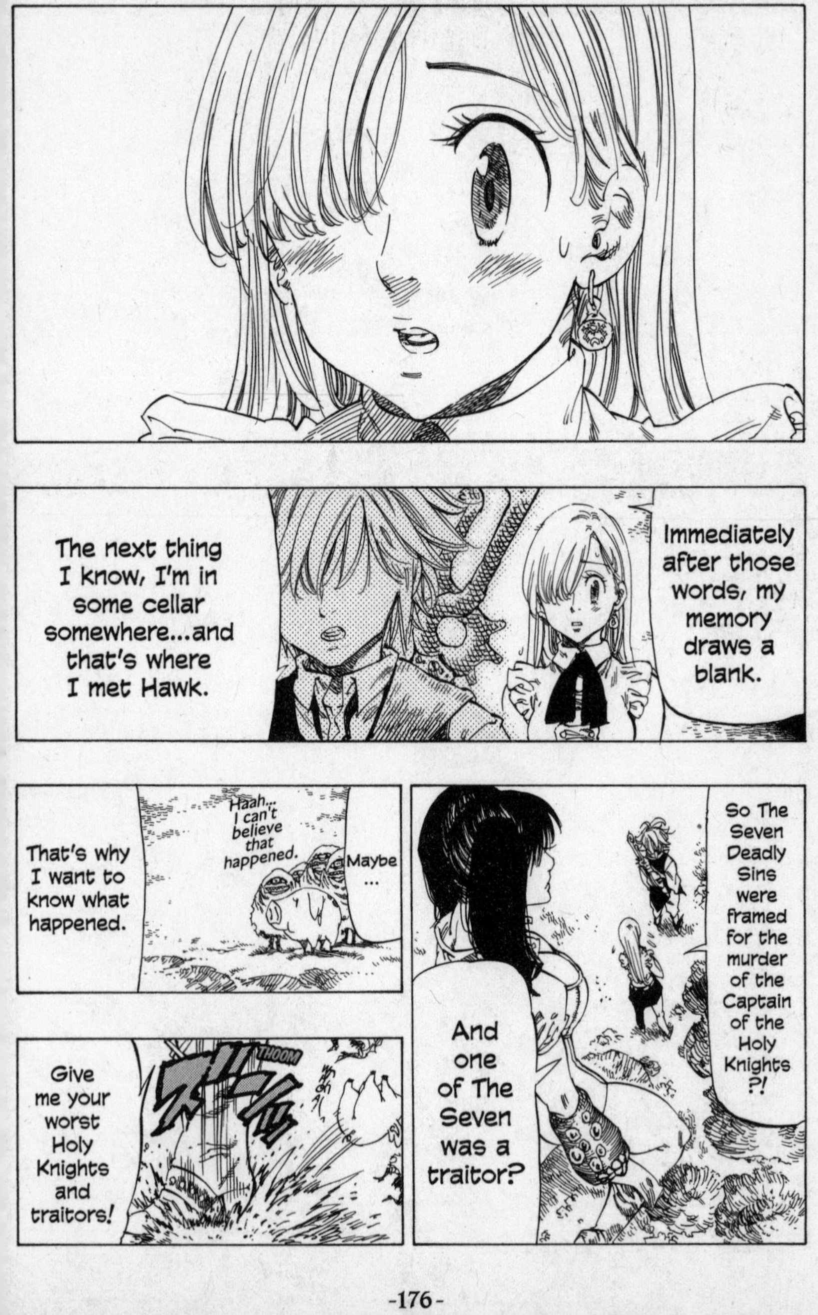
Immediately after those words, my memory draws a blank.
The next thing I know, I'm in some cellar somewhere...and that's where I met Hawk.
So The Seven Deadly Sins were framed for the murder of the Captain of the Holy Knights?!
And one of The Seven was a traitor?
Maybe...
Haah... I can't believe that happened.
That's why I want to know what happened.
THOOM
Give me your worst Holy Knights and traitors!

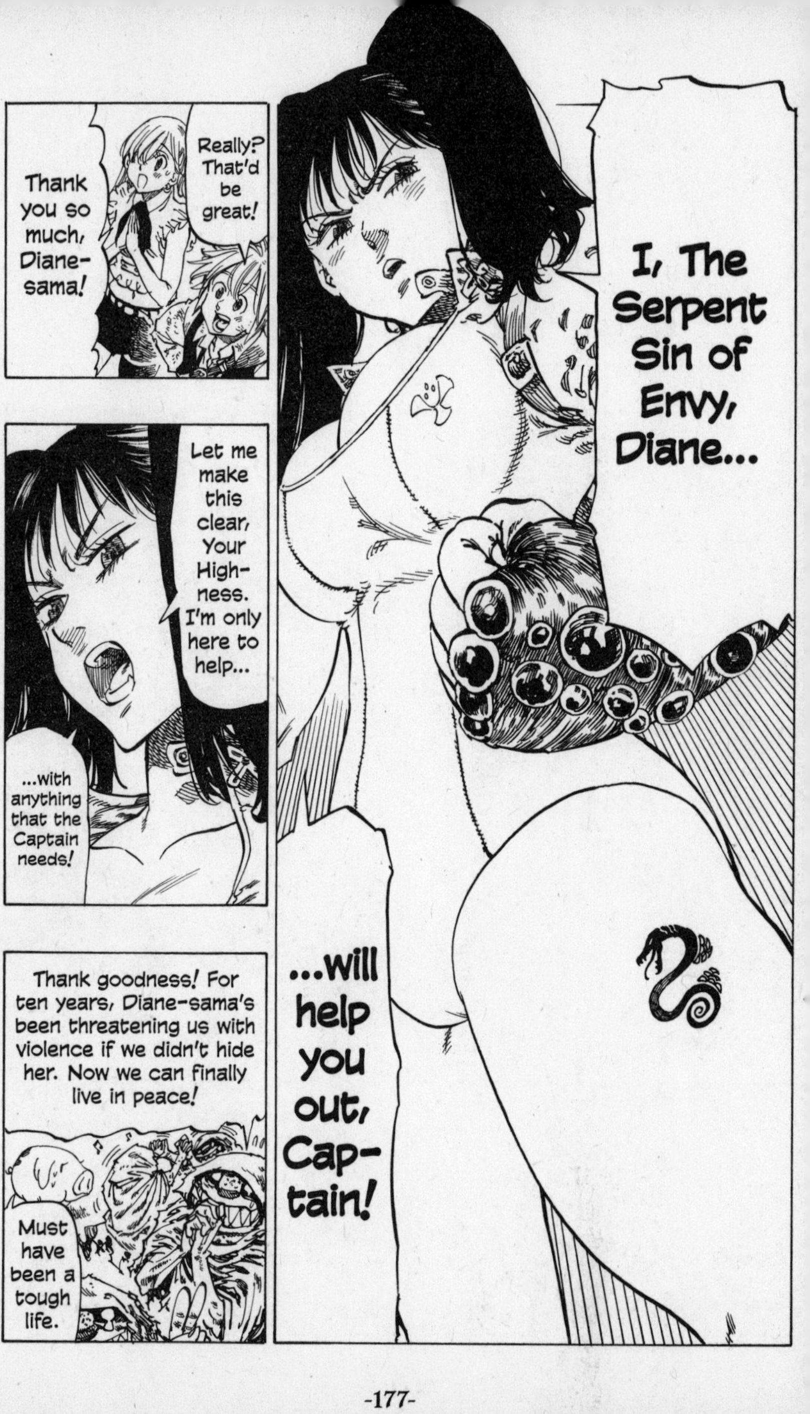
I, The Serpent Sin of Envy, Diane...
...will help you out, Captain!
Really? That'd be great!
Thank you so much, Diane-sama!
Let me make this clear, Your Highness. I'm only here to help...
...with anything that the Captain needs!
Thank goodness! For ten years, Diane-sama's been threatening us with violence if we didn't hide her. Now we can finally live in peace!
Must have been a tough life.

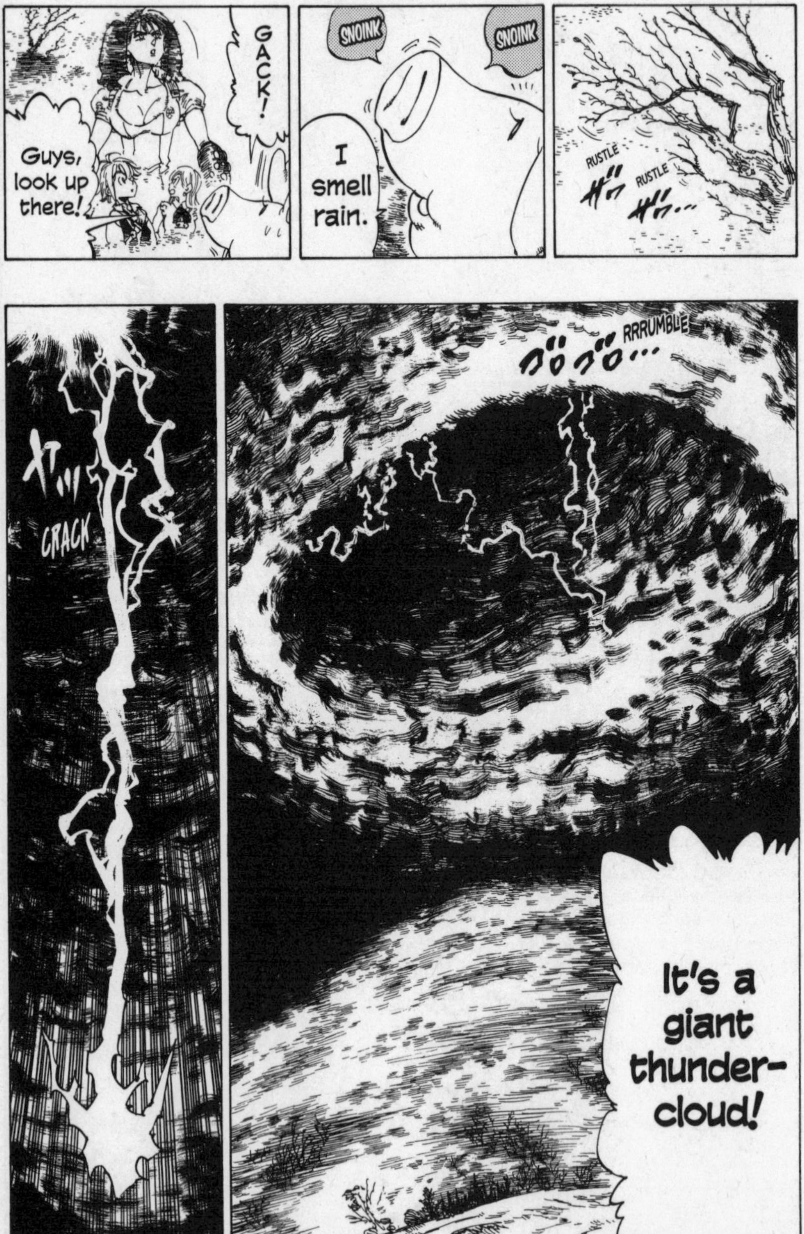

RUSTLE
ザワ
RUSTLE
ザワ…
SNOINK
SNOINK
I smell rain.
GACK!
Guys, look up there!
RRRUMBLE
ゴロゴロ…
It's a giant thunder-cloud!
CRACK

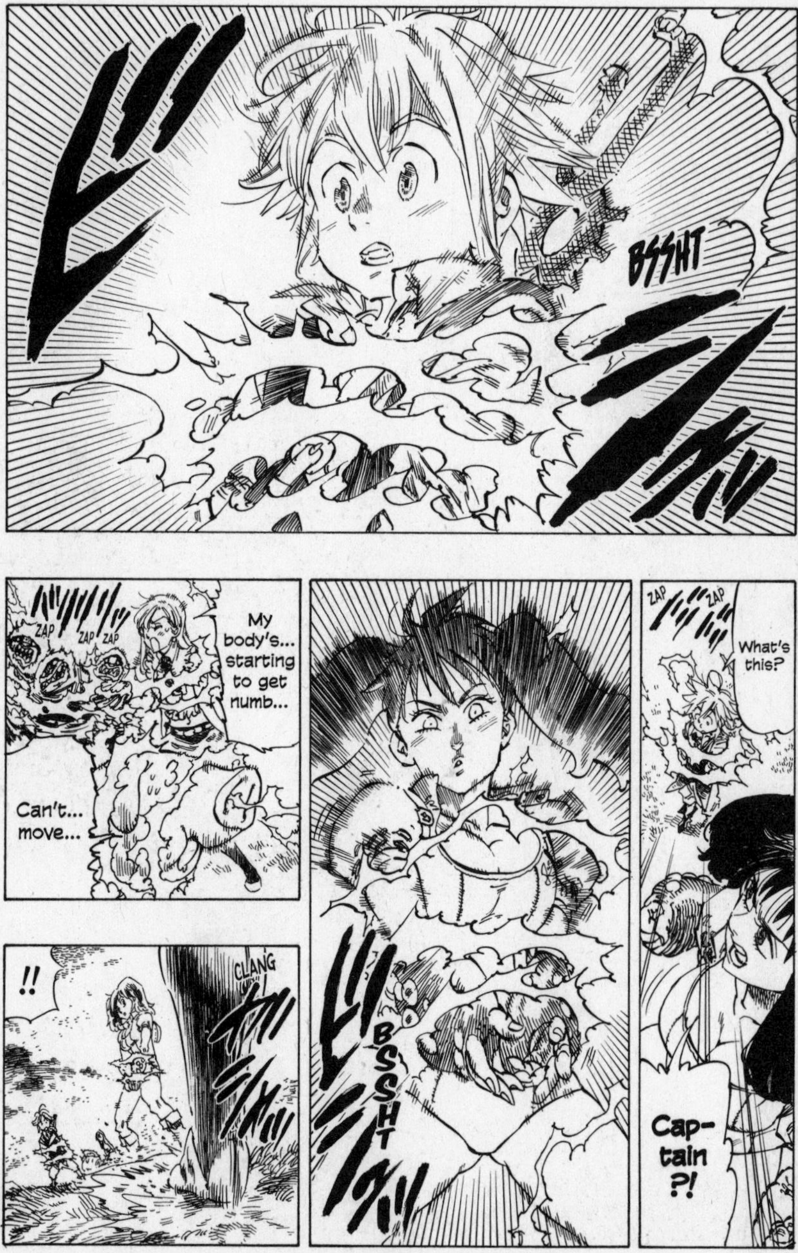
BSSHT
ZAP
ZAP
What's this?
Captain?!
BSSHT
ZAP
ZAP
ZAP
My body's... starting to get numb...
Can't... move...
!!
CLANG

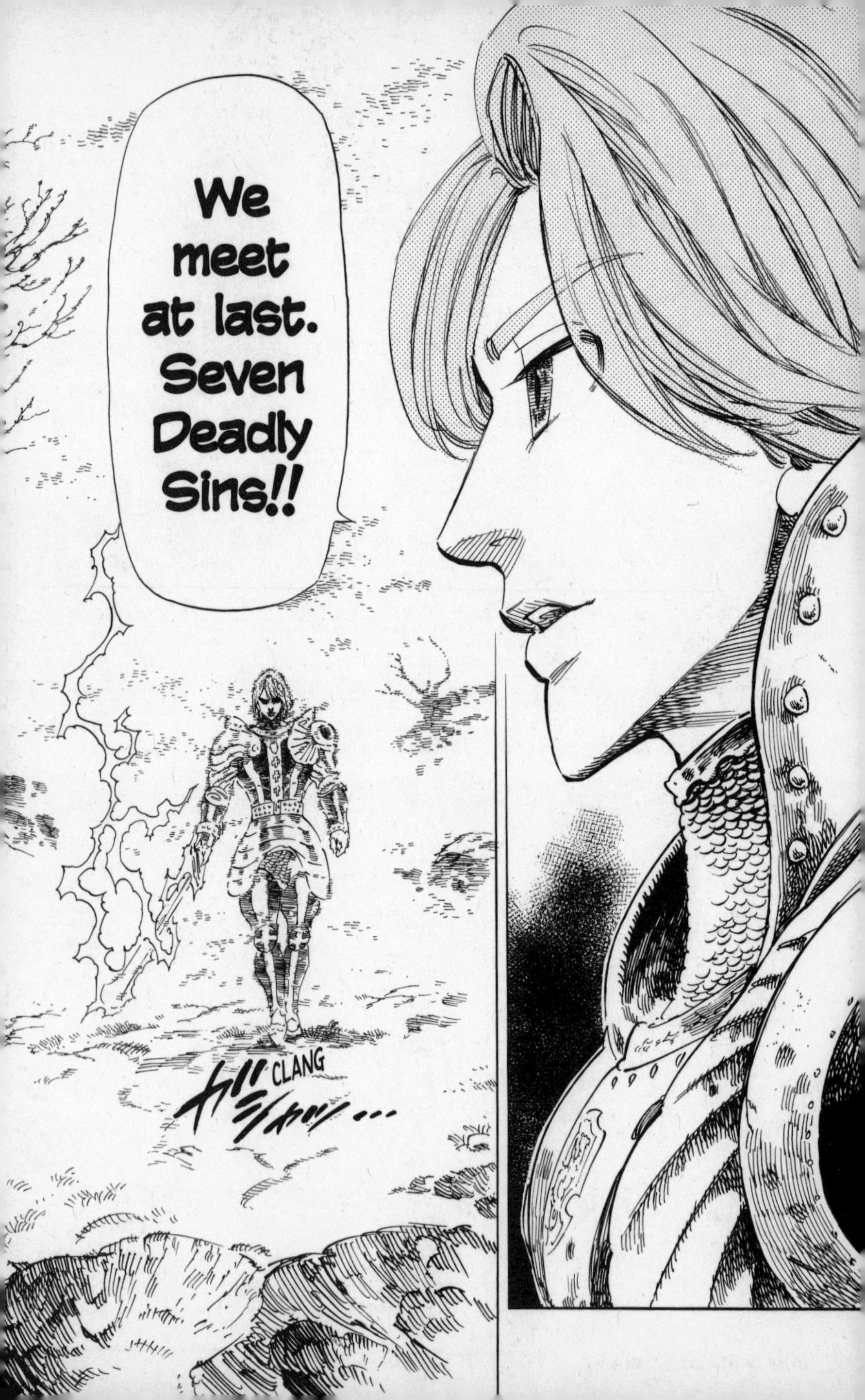
We meet at last. Seven Deadly Sins!!
CLANG

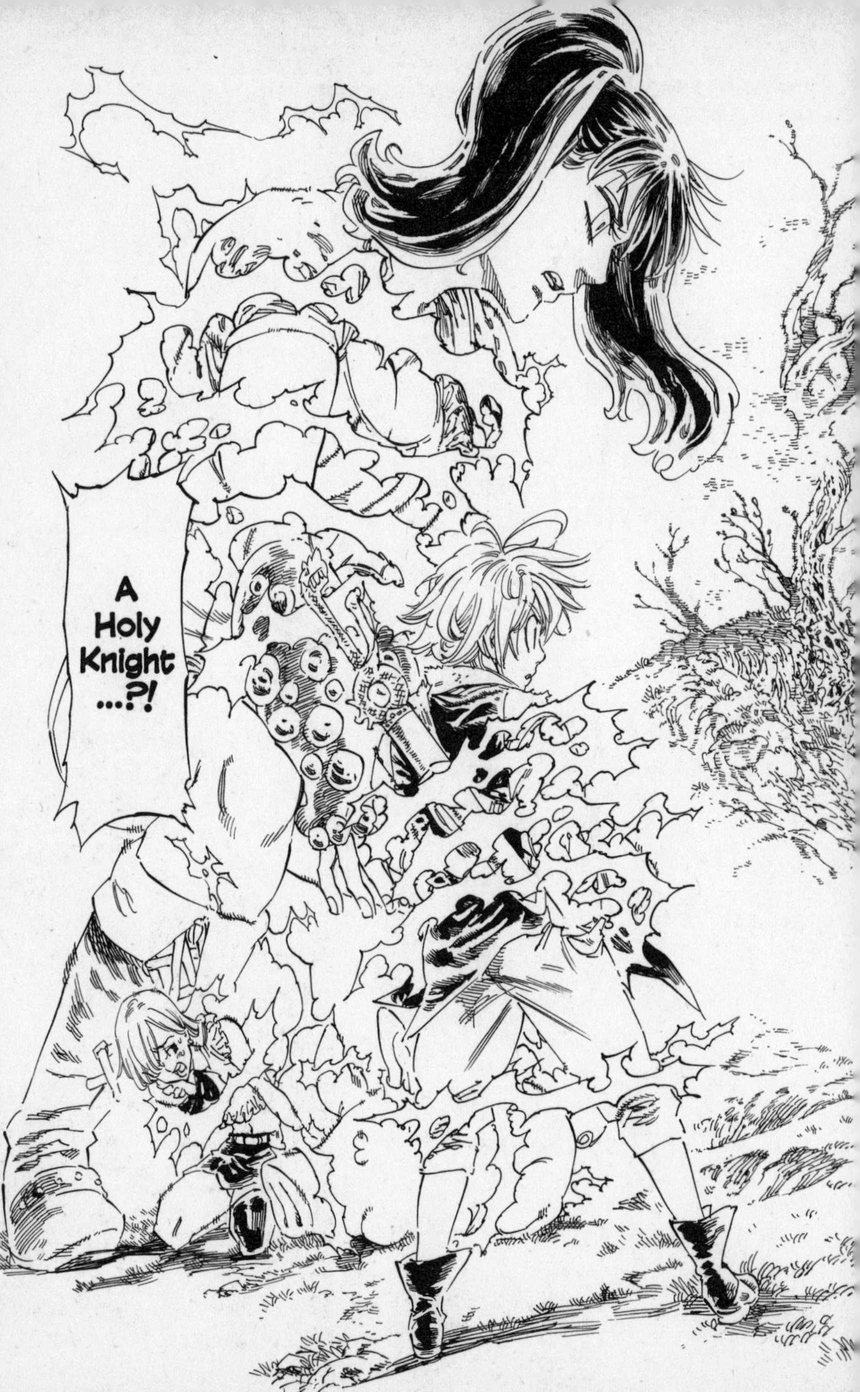
A Holy Knight ...?!

To Be Continued in Volume 2

"The Seven Deadly Sins" Wanted Posters

ESCANOR

MELIODAS

DIANE

GOWTHER

BAN

KING

MERLIN

The chivalric order who used to serve the kingdom but is wanted for conspiring to overthrow the kingdom. It is still unknown why they are called "The Seven Deadly Sins" nor what kinds of sins they are guilty of.

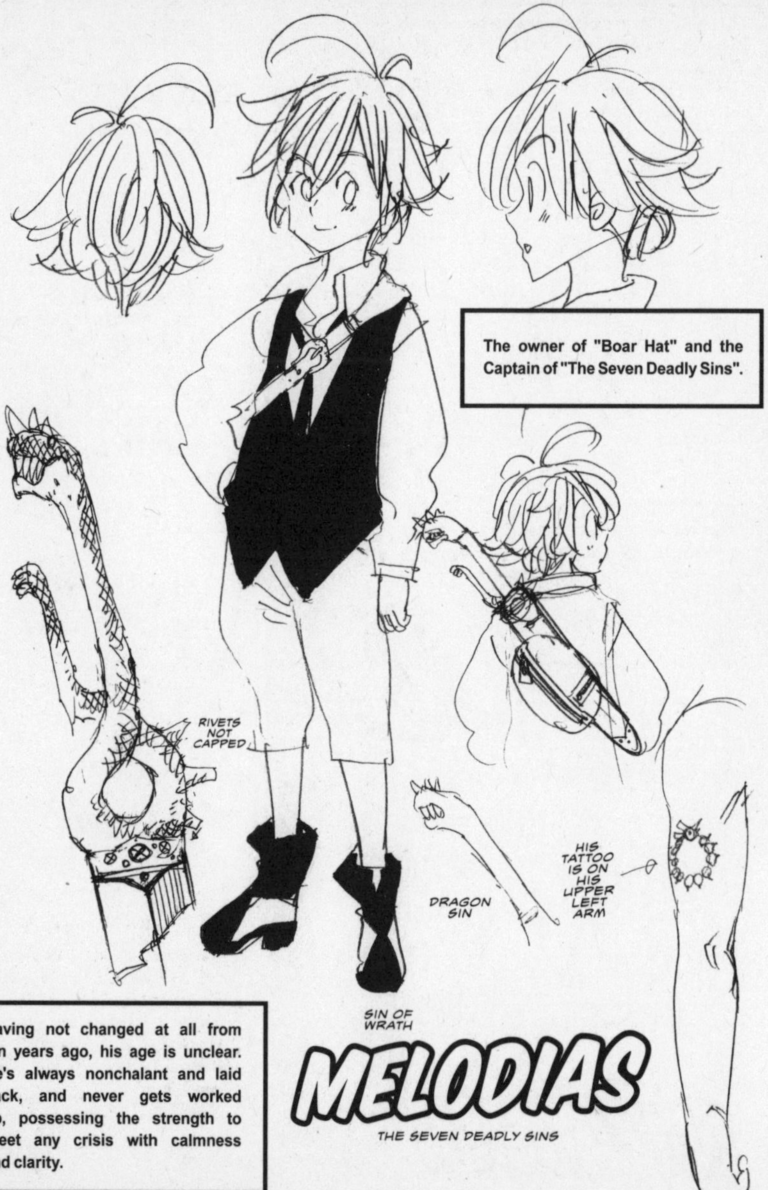
RIVETS NOT CAPPED
DRAGON SIN
HIS TATTOO IS ON HIS UPPER LEFT ARM
SIN OF WRATH
MELODIAS
THE SEVEN DEADLY SINS

The owner of "Boar Hat" and the Captain of "The Seven Deadly Sins".

Having not changed at all from ten years ago, his age is unclear. He's always nonchalant and laid back, and never gets worked up, possessing the strength to greet any crisis with calmness and clarity.

The third princess of the Liones royal family who rules the land of Britannia. She goes on a journey to find "The Seven Deadly Sins" in order to save her country and its people who have been taken over by the Holy Knights.

She may be scatterbrained and clueless about the world, but this sixteen-year-old girl has inner strength that makes her courageous in any situation.

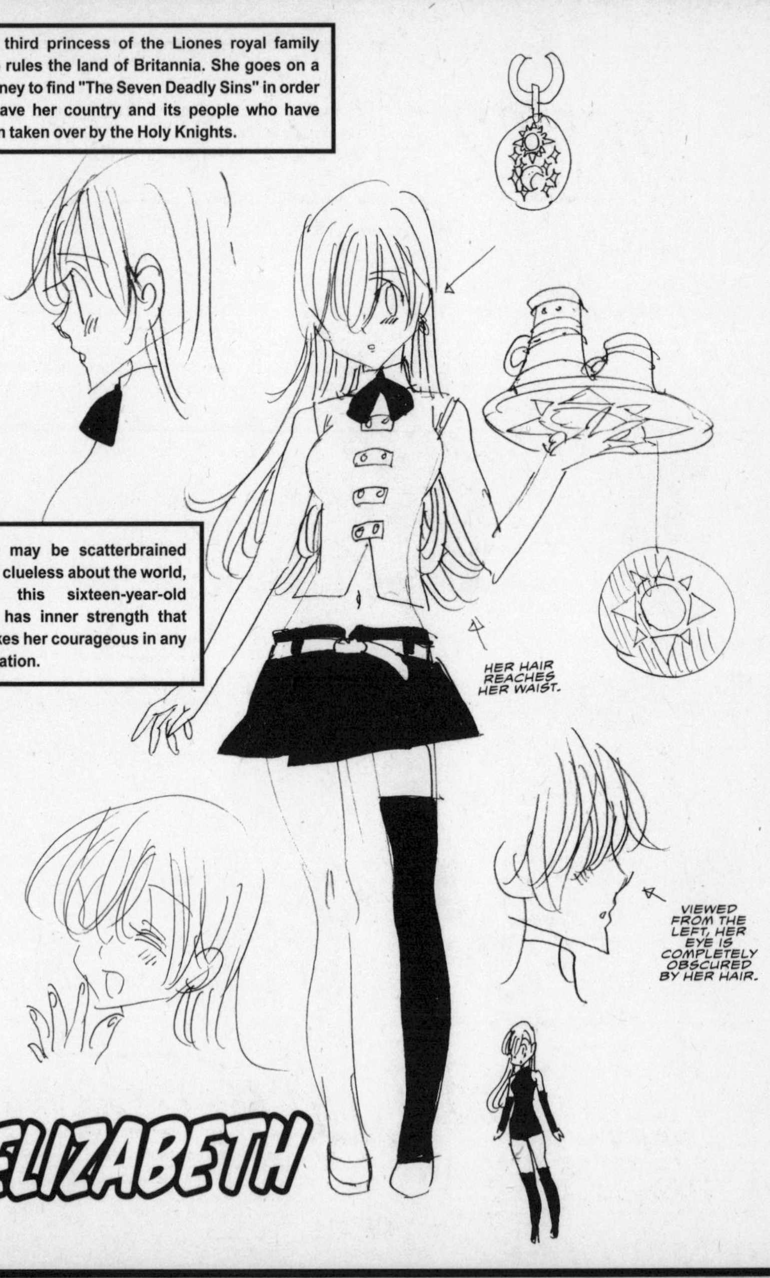
HER HAIR REACHES HER WAIST.
VIEWED FROM THE LEFT, HER EYE IS COMPLETELY OBSCURED BY HER HAIR.

ELIZABETH

HAWK

The main attraction at "Boar Hat". For unexplained reasons, he can speak and understand human speech. His favorite thing to eat is leftovers and his nose can detect food scraps up to one mile away.

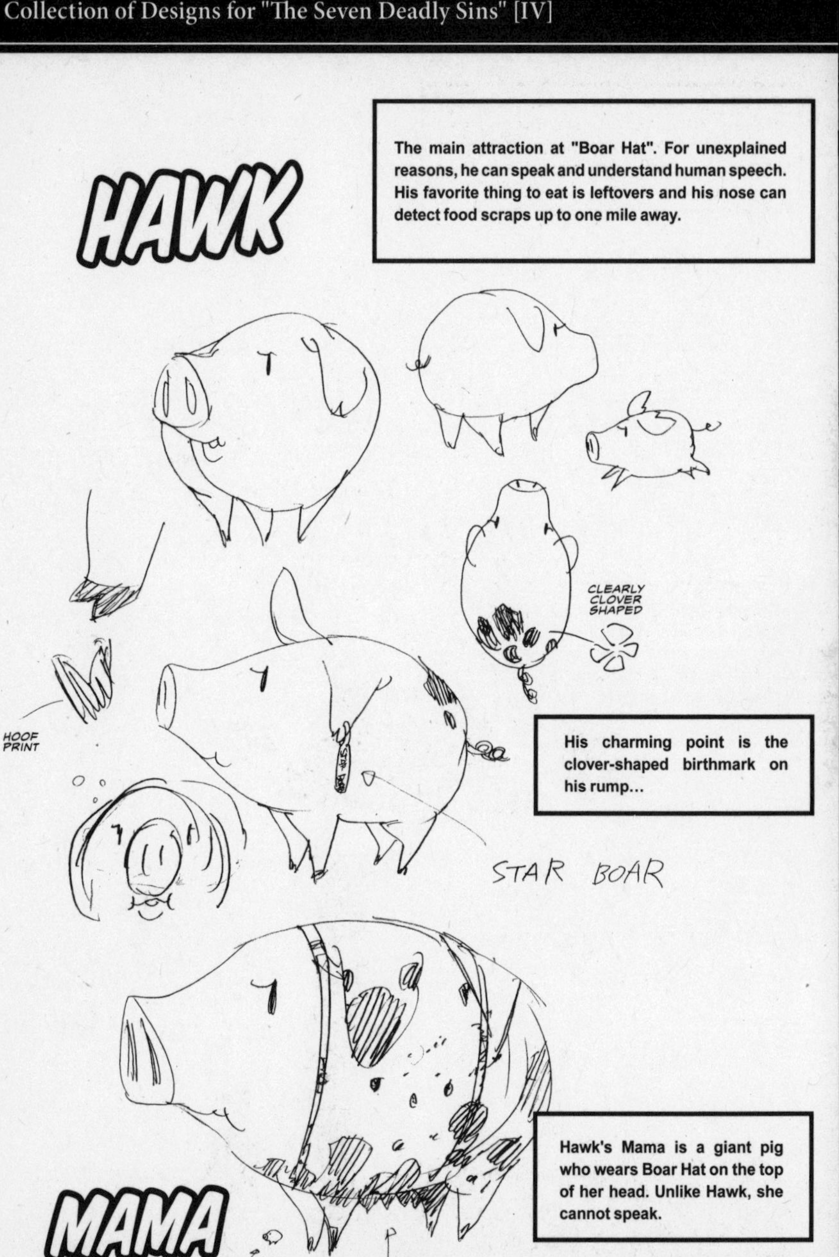
CLEARLY CLOVER SHAPED
HOOF PRINT
STAR BOAR
HAWK
UDDER-LIKE FEATURES (?)

His charming point is the clover-shaped birthmark on his rump...

MAMA

Hawk's Mama is a giant pig who wears Boar Hat on the top of her head. Unlike Hawk, she cannot speak.

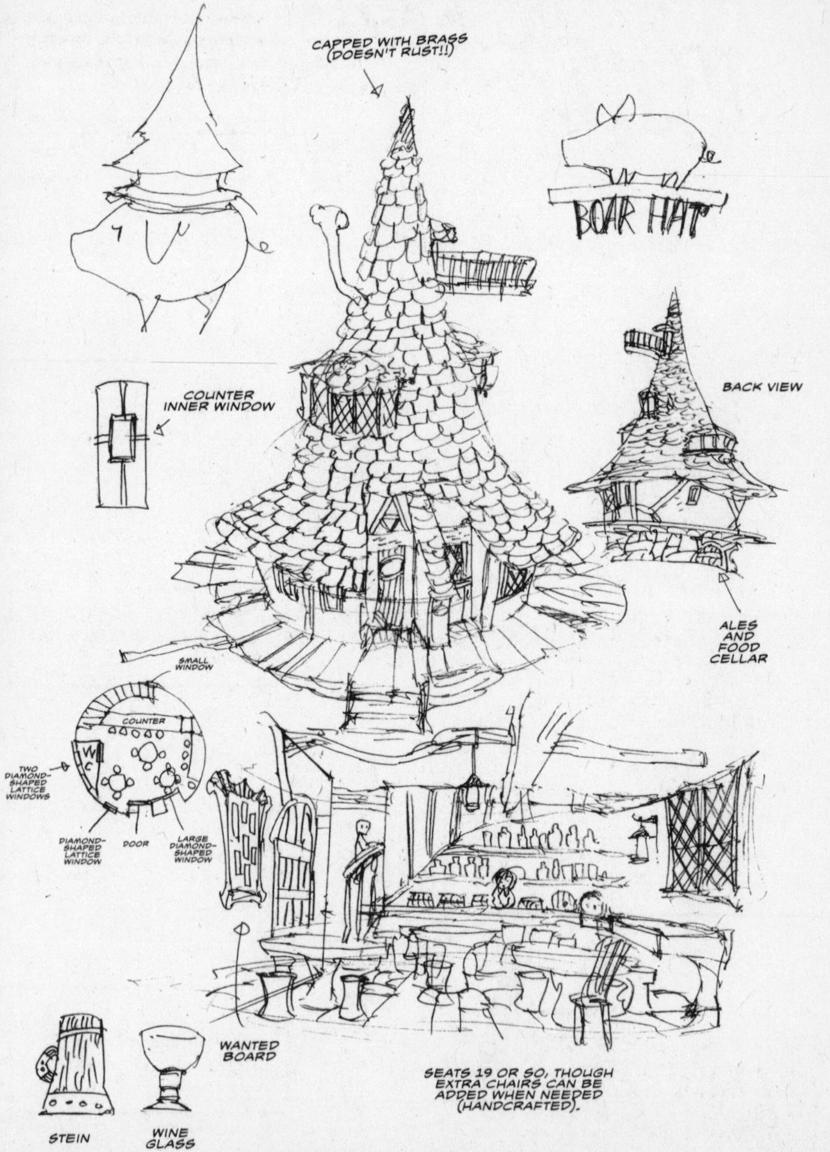
CAPPED WITH BRASS (DOESN'T RUST!!)
BOAR HAT
COUNTER INNER WINDOW
BACK VIEW
ALES AND FOOD CELLAR
SMALL WINDOW
COUNTER
WC
TWO DIAMOND-SHAPED LATTICE WINDOWS
DIAMOND-SHAPED LATTICE WINDOW
DOOR
LARGE DIAMOND-SHAPED WINDOW
WANTED BOARD
SEATS 19 OR SO, THOUGH EXTRA CHAIRS CAN BE ADDED WHEN NEEDED (HANDCRAFTED).
STEIN
WINE GLASS

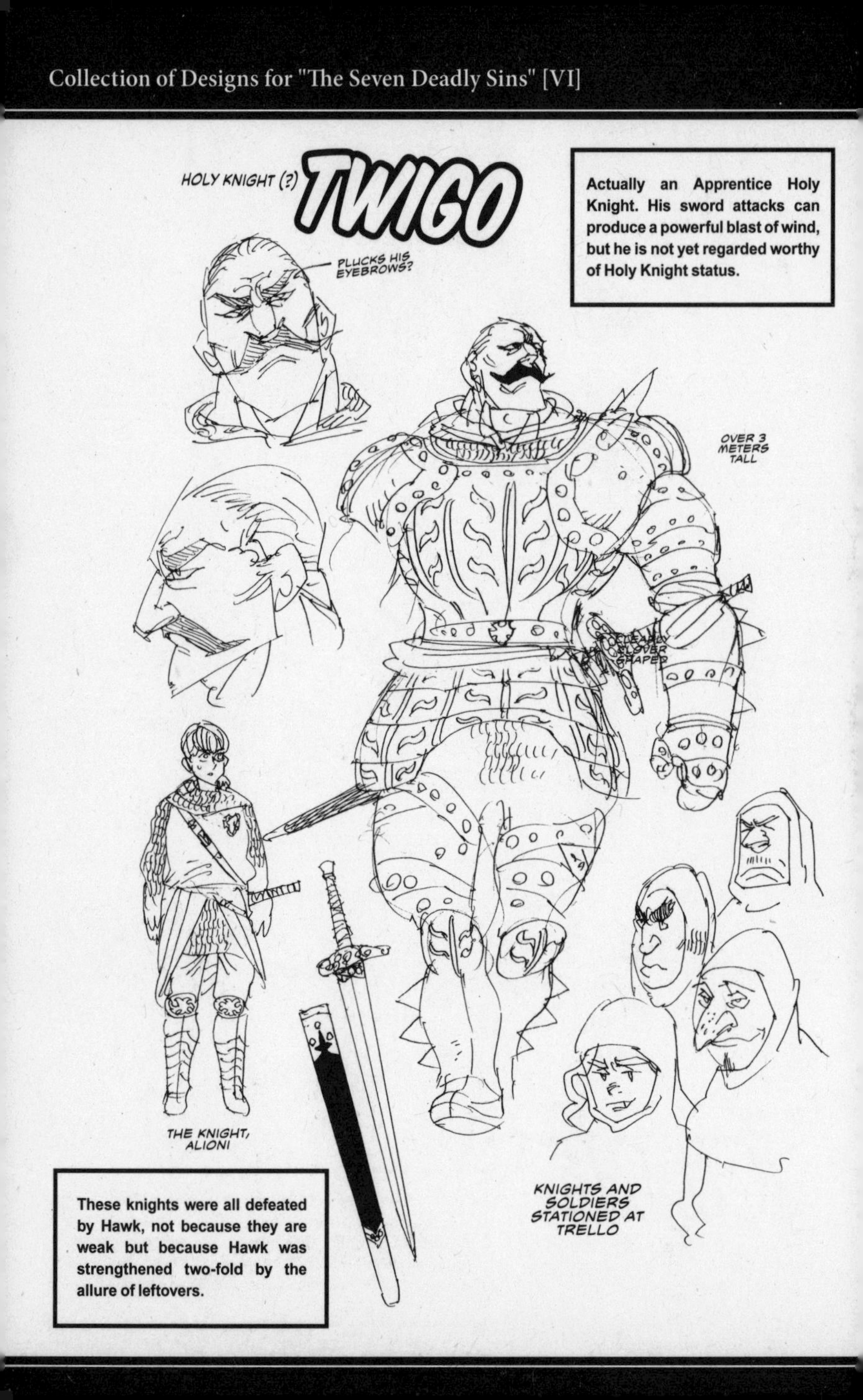
HOLY KNIGHT (?)
TWIGO
PLUCKS HIS EYEBROWS?
OVER 3 METERS TALL
CLEARLY CLOVER SHAPED
THE KNIGHT, ALIONI
KNIGHTS AND SOLDIERS STATIONED AT TRELLO

Actually an Apprentice Holy Knight. His sword attacks can produce a powerful blast of wind, but he is not yet regarded worthy of Holy Knight status.

These knights were all defeated by Hawk, not because they are weak but because Hawk was strengthened two-fold by the allure of leftovers.

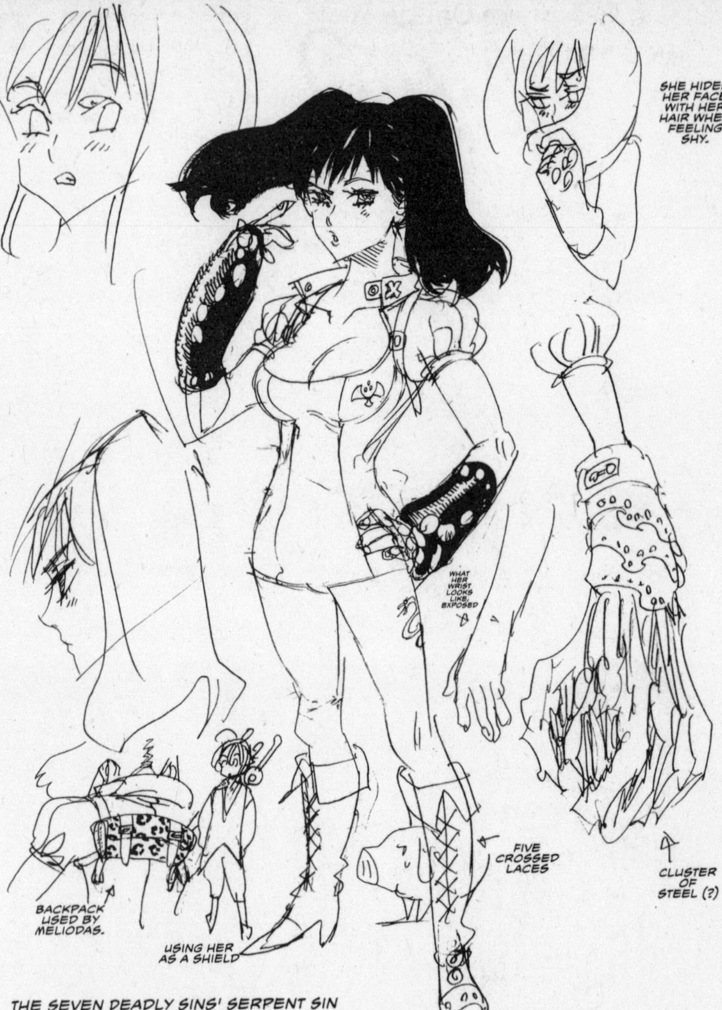
SHE HIDES HER FACE WITH HER HAIR WHEN FEELING SHY.
WHAT HER WRIST LOOKS LIKE, EXPOSED
FIVE CROSSED LACES
CLUSTER OF STEEL (?)
BACKPACK USED BY MELIODAS.
USING HER AS A SHIELD

THE SEVEN DEADLY SINS' SERPENT SIN

DIANE

SIN OF ENVY

A woman from the giant clan and a member of The Seven Deadly Sins. She has a huge crush on Meliodas and can become jealous very quickly. But that's apparently unrelated to her title of "Serpent Sin of Envy". Her future dream is to become little and have children with Meliodas.

Design Sketches for the One-Shot of "The Seven Deadly Sins"

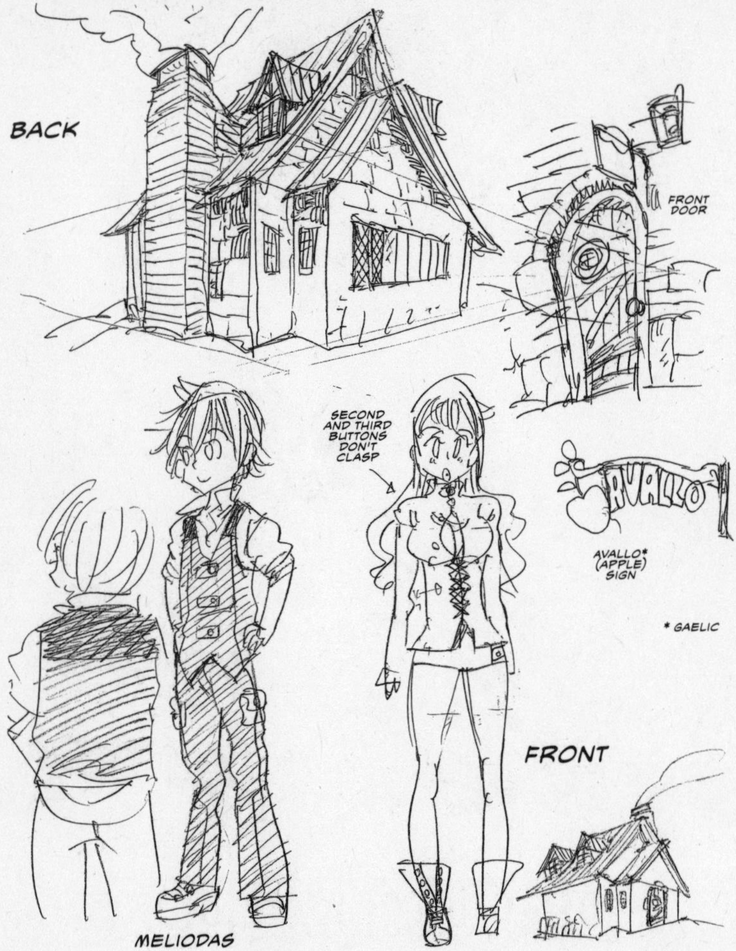
BACK
FRONT DOOR
SECOND AND THIRD BUTTONS DON'T CLASP
AVALLO
AVALLO* (APPLE) SIGN
* GAELIC
FRONT
MELIODAS

The tavern in the one-shot version was called Apple. The appearance is completely different, and only the feature of it being a mobile tavern is a shared point. But what the tavern was riding on was a giant spider-shaped mechanism. Meliodas' and Elizabeth's appearances, clothes and personalities are pretty identical to the serialized version, and the cast was a little simpler in that there was no mascot-like character. Also, the enemy Holy Knight is Alioni who showed up in chapter one of the serialized version.

SHERLOCK BONES

KC KODANSHA COMICS'

DEDUCTIVE DOG DETECTIVE

When Takeru adopts a new pet, he's in for a surprise—the dog is none other than the reincarnation of Sherlock Holmes. With no one else able to communicate with Holmes, Takeru is roped into becoming Sherdog's assistant, John Watson. Using his sleuthing skills, Holmes uncovers clues to solve the trickiest crimes. 🐾

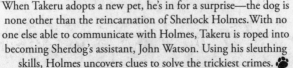

ANIMAL LAND

BY MAKOTO RAIKU

In a world of animals, where the strong eat the weak, Monoko the tanuki stumbles across a strange creature the likes of which has never been seen before–a human baby! While the newborn has no claws or teeth to protect itself, it does have the special ability to speak to and understand all different animals. Can the gift of speech between species change the balance of power in a land where the weak must always fear the strong?

ANIMAL LAND 1

MAKOTO RAIKU

Ages 13+

VISIT KODANSHACOMICS.COM TO:

- View release date calendars for upcoming volumes
- Find out the latest about upcoming Kodansha Comics series

The Seven Deadly Sins volume 1 is a work of fiction. Names, characters, places, and incidents are the products of the author's imagination or are used fictitiously. Any resemblance to actual events, locales, or persons, living or dead, is entirely coincidental.

A Kodansha Comics Trade Paperback Original.

Published in the United States by Kodansha Comics, an imprint of Kodansha USA Publishing, LLC, New York.

Publication rights for this English edition arranged through Kodansha Ltd., Tokyo.

First published in Japan in 2013 by Kodansha Ltd., Tokyo.

ISBN 978-1-61262-921-6

Printed in the United States of America.

www.kodanshacomics.com

9 8 7 6 5 4 3 2 1

Translator: Christine Dashiell
Lettering: James Dashiell